Fearless and forensic, this incendiary indictment from one of Britain's most celebrated political journalists lays bare the full extent of British complicity in the destruction of Gaza.

In a gripping narrative informed by original reporting, Peter Oborne tells how Britain's Conservative and Labour parties converged to back Israel's criminal assault—in the process occupying disturbing common ground with the far right.

Rather than challenge this political cartel, British media colluded in its misrepresentations. The shocking result was that, as British authorities helped Israel set Gaza as well as international law aflame, almost everything the public was told about this momentous conflagration was untrue.

When citizens still turned out in their hundreds of thousands to demand a ceasefire, roiling the nation's politics as they stayed faithful to the ancient British tradition of popular protest in defence of liberty, the political-media machine bared its fangs. The investigative reporting in this book exposes the methods by which peaceful demonstrations were smeared as 'hate marches'.

Formerly chief political commentator at the *Daily Telegraph* and *Spectator*, Oborne knows the British establishment from within. In this book he names names and provides receipts. His demand is accountability—for atrocities, and their accomplices.

ADVANCE PRAISE

'This book shows how British involvement in the Gaza genocide extended beyond passive endorsement into active participation. It is a critical document for understanding not just this war but the workings of Western imperialism'

—Ghassan Abu-Sittah

'This work is both an act of resistance and a testament to the power of truth. Every seeker of justice should not only read it but truly reckon with its message'

—Ahmed Alnaouq

'An utterly damning and devastating indictment of Britain's shameful complicity in genocide. This is a masterclass in truth-telling—and will prove essential in bringing about justice for the Palestinian people. This is what real journalism looks like'

—Jeremy Corbyn

'Peter Oborne is one of the most respected and important writers on the tragedy of the Palestinians and Britain's complicity in their ethnic cleansing'

—William Dalrymple

'An absolutely devastating indictment of Britain's criminal role in Israel's genocide. A must-read, utterly compelling contribution to the coming reckoning'

—Owen Jones

'Gaza is being murdered; Britain is guilty: here's the proof. Savage, merciless Truth from a superb writer. Read it and hold the guilty to account'

—Miriam Margolyes

'Readers will be astonished to learn how significant was the contribution of British journalists and politicians to Israel's impunity during the genocide in Gaza. This is a damning document recording British betrayal of Palestine that began a century ago and continues today'

—Ilan Pappé

'Deeply researched and very readable, this book is both a triumph of investigative journalism and a blistering attack on the government, the opposition, and the mainstream media that coalesced behind Israel's monstrous offensive. Peter Oborne deserves full credit for bearing witness and for exposing the moral depravity of our ruling elite. This is a remarkable book that deserves the widest possible readership among policymakers and the general public'

—Avi Shlaim

'Incisive, detailed, and brutally honest, *Complicit* cuts through the daily noise and propaganda. Peter Oborne holds up a mirror to decision makers and opinion formers as he makes the damning case that some of the most powerful in British politics and media have not just turned a blind eye but have been complicit in the unfolding genocide in Gaza'

—Sayeeda Warsi

COMPLICIT

COMPLICIT

BRITAIN'S ROLE IN THE DESTRUCTION OF GAZA

PETER OBORNE

O/R

OR Books

New York • London

Published by OR Books, New York and London

Visit our website at www.orbooks.com

All rights information: rights@orbooks.com

First printing 2025

The manufacturer's authorized representative in the EU for product safety is Authorized Rep Compliance Ltd, 71 Lower Baggot Street, Dublin D02 P593 Ireland (www.arccompliance.com)

Typeset by Lapiz Digital. Printed by BookMobile, USA, and CPI, UK.

paperback ISBN 978-1-68219-426-3 • ebook ISBN 978-1-68219-452-2

In memory of the heroic and selfless journalists who have given their lives reporting on Israeli atrocities in Gaza.

Dead, your Majesty. Dead, my lords and gentlemen. Dead, right reverends and wrong reverends of every order. Dead, men and women, born with heavenly compassion in your hearts. And dying thus around us every day.

—*Charles Dickens, Bleak House*

CONTENTS

ACKNOWLEDGMENTS

This book is the result of long, intensive collaboration rather than the work of a single author. It has been a privilege to work for David Hearst and the formidable reporting and comment team at *Middle East Eye*; it has also been an education. I am indebted in particular to Lubna Masarwa, Jerusalem bureau chief for *Middle East Eye*, and her magnificent team of journalists across the West Bank and Gaza. The two primary researchers, Irfan Chowdhury and his colleague who wishes to remain unnamed, have been sources of deep insight, expertise, and illumination. Their contribution has been immense. Jamie Stern-Weiner of OR Books has played a far greater role than editor. He has shaped this book and explained to me with lucid brilliance much that I had failed to notice or understand. I am immensely grateful to Mahdi Mustafa and Kirsty Fitzgerald, always ready to come to the rescue at a moment's notice with careful, accurate research. Evan Robins provided a Rolls Royce fact-checking service for key chapters of the book.

Alex Nunns helped me delineate the moral, political, and intellectual journey of Sir Keir Starmer from human rights maestro to war crimes apologist. Forensic work by Al Jazeera producer Richard Sanders enabled me to tell the story of British media coverage of October 7 and beyond, including the misreporting of the so-called 'pogrom' in Amsterdam in early November 2024. Jessica Murray brought her unparalleled expertise to this task. Professor Des Freedman of Goldsmiths, University of London, was a source of original advice. Josiah Mortimer, chief reporter of *Byline Times*, carried out an investigation into the so-called Islamist takeover of parliament in February 2024. At a late stage Peter McNamara came up with extra sleuthing.

Sixteen years ago Dorothy Byrne commissioned me to present a Channel Four *Dispatches* film on the pro-Israel lobby in Britain; it helped me to understand some of the political background to the British role in Gaza. Daryll Billington kept me company during the chilly winter months when much of the book was written or conceived. Lindsay Codsi kept me organised while my wife Martine tolerated long absences and my near permanent state of nervous distraction.

INTRODUCTION

IN JANUARY 2024 the International Court of Justice convened at The Hague to rule on South Africa's grave allegation that Israel was committing genocide against Palestinians in Gaza.

This hearing had its roots deep in the history of post-war liberation struggles. The ICJ, part of the global architecture created by the victorious powers after World War Two, heard its first case in 1947. The following year came the creation of Israel and with it the Palestinian Nakba—Arabic for 'catastrophe'. This saw some 750,000 Palestinians, more than half the population, driven from their homes.

Two weeks after Israel declared independence, a racist coalition government led by the National Party took power in South Africa. It went on to ethnically cleanse black South Africans as part of a programme of formal apartheid, a barbarous experiment in social engineering that systematically discriminated between citizens according to their 'race'.

Each of these developments was in critical respects out of step with the times, as European empires disintegrated into national states and racist ideology was increasingly discredited. The decolonisation period saw the anti-apartheid and Palestinian liberation struggles assimilated into the global movement against colonialism. As Israel and South Africa developed closer ties in the 1970s, the Palestinian cause became more directly associated with the fight against apartheid.[1]

Already in 1961, South African prime minister Hendrik Verwoerd noted with approval that 'Israel, like South Africa, is an apartheid state'.[2] This insight was shared by Archbishop Desmond Tutu, who would later chair post-apartheid South Africa's Truth and Reconciliation Commission. He compared the predicament of Palestinians in Israel's occupied territories with 'what happened to us black people in South Africa'.[3] Nelson Mandela, the first democratically elected president of a post-apartheid South Africa, famously insisted that 'our freedom is incomplete without the freedom of the Palestinians'.[4]

At The Hague these two freedom struggles came together. In the 1960s the independent states of Africa had applied to the Court to effectively determine that apartheid was illegal. The hearings became 'the international *cause célèbre* of the century'.[5] But applicants' faith in an egalitarian liberal order was dashed as the judges decided after years of litigation to throw the case out.[6]

Fast forward a half-century and we find post-apartheid South Africa asking the same ICJ to uphold international law and redress the burning moral injustice of Israel's persecution of the Palestinians. South Africa now spoke for the postcolonial Global South and invested Court proceedings with the moral authority of the anti-apartheid cause. World opinion held its breath as the integrity of the liberal order once more hung in the balance. The South African challenge was stark: in the face of overwhelming pressure from Israel and its Western allies, would the Court vindicate the law's universal promise?

The historical resonances did not end there. In a terrible irony South Africa was charging Israel, whose existential legitimacy is rooted in the Nazi genocide of European Jews, with breaching the 1948 Genocide Convention, which had been drafted and adopted in response to the Holocaust. Revulsion and repentance for that horrendous crime had helped inspire the post-war international legal framework, but had also provided warrant for subordinating Arab to Jewish rights in Palestine.

In these ways The Hague was playing host to an epoch-defining clash between the two conflicting visions that have shaped the world since 1945. On the one hand the idea of a universal order upholding human rights for all. On the other hand a restrictive application long favoured by the United States, Britain, and other former empires; a constricted justice that effectively excludes the global majority. Israel had long been treated as an exception to international rules justified by the exceptional suffering endured by the Jewish people. But decades of Israeli intransigence, aggression, and human rights abuses—culminating per South Africa in genocide—were putting that carve-out to the test.

January 11, The South Africa Case

On the first day the judges heard the case for the prosecution. Lawyers for South Africa told the Court that Israel had killed more than twenty-three thousand Palestinians in barely three months, with a further seven thousand people lost under the rubble. Each passing day saw an average of 247 Palestinians killed and 629 wounded, as well as 3,900 homes damaged or destroyed.[7] The Court was told that Palestinians in Gaza risked death by starvation, thirst or disease because Israel had imposed siege conditions.[8]

One challenge in proving the crime of genocide is that the perpetrators often go to great lengths to hide their intentions. Not so in Gaza, said South Africa. '[T]here is an extraordinary feature in this case: that Israel's political leaders, military commanders and persons holding official positions have systematically and in explicit terms declared their genocidal intent'.[9]

South Africa quoted a 'situation update' from Israeli defence minister Yoav Gallant to the Israel Defence Forces (IDF). He had announced 'a complete siege on Gaza', meaning 'no electricity, no food, no water, no fuel'. Gallant declared that Israel 'is fighting human animals' and instructed troops massed along the Gaza perimeter that he had 'released all the restraints'.[10]

Gallant's language was also employed by Ghassan Alian, the head of Israel's military government in the Occupied Palestinian Territory. In an address to 'Hamas and the residents of Gaza' he had warned that 'human animals are dealt with accordingly'. Alian said that 'Israel has imposed a total blockade on Gaza, no electricity, no water, just damage. You wanted hell, you will get hell'.[11] Crucially Alian was not just condemning Hamas in the above statement; all Palestinians were included in the category of human animals.

Cabinet ministers agreed. Israel Katz, Israel's minister of energy and infrastructure, called for denying water and fuel on the grounds that 'this is what will happen to a people of children killers and slaughterers'.[12] Heritage

Minister Amichai Eliyahu had said that Israel 'must find ways for Gazans that are more painful than death'.[13]

South Africa argued: 'These statements are not open to neutral interpretations, or after-the-fact rationalisations and reinterpretations by Israel. The statements were made by persons in command of the State. They communicated State policy. It is simple. If the statements were not intended, they would not have been made'.[14]

South Africa supplied testimony showing that the genocidal discourse of the Israeli politician class was directing the 'actions and objectives' of serving soldiers in Gaza. It provided horrifying examples of genocidal incitement within Israeli civil society, concluding that 'the intentional failure of the Government of Israel to condemn, prevent and punish such genocidal incitement constitutes in itself a grave violation of the Genocide Convention'.[15]

South Africa ended its evidence by asking the Court to order an immediate suspension of Israel's military operations in and against Gaza, that Israel should stop committing and take all reasonable measures to prevent genocide, and that Israel should take action to halt genocidal incitement.[16]

January 12, Israel Responds

The following day Israel presented her defence. Israel's counsel Tal Becker opened with the powerful statement that Israel is 'singularly aware of why the Genocide Convention, which has been invoked in these proceedings, was adopted. Seared in our collective memory is the systematic murder of six million Jews as part of a pre-meditated and heinous programme for their total annihilation'.[17]

He told the Court that '[f]or some, the promise of "Never Again" for all peoples is a slogan; for Israel, it is the highest moral obligation'.[18]

Becker accused South Africa of cheapening this language by invoking the term genocide 'in the context of Israel's conduct in a war it did not start and did not want. A war in which Israel is defending itself against Hamas, Palestinian Islamic Jihad and other terrorist organizations whose brutality knows no bounds'.[19]

Becker provided a graphic description of the atrocities committed by Hamas-led forces on October 7: 'Openly displaying elation, they tortured children in front of parents, and parents in front of children, burned people, including infants, alive, and systematically raped and mutilated scores of women, men and children.

'All told, some 1,200 people were butchered that day, more than 5,500 maimed, and some 240 hostages abducted, including infants, entire families, persons with disabilities and Holocaust survivors, some of whom have since been executed; many of whom have been tortured, sexually abused and starved in captivity'.[20]

Becker accused South Africa of all but ignoring these terrible events: '[W]e are compelled to share with the Court some fraction of its horror—the largest calculated mass murder of Jews in a single day since the Holocaust'.[21]

He acknowledged that these Hamas atrocities did not release Israel from the obligation to uphold the law. But he insisted that 'it is impossible to understand the armed conflict in Gaza, without appreciating the nature of the threat that Israel is facing, and the brutality and lawlessness of the armed force confronting it'.[22]

The Israeli defence comprised several core elements. The provisional measures sought by South Africa to halt military operations would deprive Israel of the right to defend itself against an enemy that was itself genocidal and which had taken hostages it still held. Israel acknowledged that Palestinian civilians had suffered, but said this was unintentional. Collateral damage was unavoidable when fighting an armed conflict in a densely populated urban area. Civilian deaths were the responsibility of Hamas because it had embedded itself in the civilian population by building tunnels under schools, hospitals, mosques, and United Nations facilities. Israel also contested the casualty figures presented by South Africa.

Malcolm Shaw KC, the author of a standard work on international law, challenged South Africa's claims that Israel had displayed genocidal intent. Shaw produced a minute of a meeting of the Ministerial Committee on National Security Affairs showing that Israel's prime minister Benjamin Netanyahu had 'stated time and again' that 'we must prevent a humanitarian disaster'.[23] Shaw unveiled edicts from the Operations Directorate of the Israeli army stipulating that 'attacks will be solely directed towards military targets' and that collateral damage should be reduced.[24] Shaw also produced a number of other exculpatory statements made by Netanyahu. On January 10, 2024, Netanyahu said:

> Israel has no intention of permanently occupying Gaza or displacing its civilian population.
>
> Israel is fighting Hamas terrorists, not the Palestinian population, and we are doing so in full compliance with international law.
>
> The IDF is doing its utmost to minimize civilian casualties, while Hamas is doing its utmost to maximize them by using Palestinian civilians as human shields.[25]

By contrast, asserted Shaw, the bellicose Israeli quotes provided to the Court by South Africa were 'clearly rhetorical, made in the immediate aftermath of an event which severely traumatized Israel, but which cannot be seen as demanding genocide'.[26]

Israeli counsel concluded: 'The Genocide Convention is too important a foundation in humanity's aspiration to defeat barbarism and evil to be belittled in this way. And the faith that has been placed in international law and its institutions is too cherished an asset to be squandered'. It asked the Court to reject South Africa's case.[27]

Israel has powerful allies in the United States of America, Britain, and across Europe. On the day Israel gave evidence Germany announced that it would intervene as a third party in the ICJ case in Israel's favour. Many observers wondered whether the judges would be prepared to reach a decision that would be inconvenient to the West.

Judgment

Reassembling to make its ruling two weeks later, the Court took note of the widespread destruction in Gaza, quoting at length from a harrowing assessment by Phillippe Lazzarini, head of the United Nations Relief and Works Agency for Palestinian Refugees in the Near East (UNRWA). The judges took seriously the dehumanising language used by Israeli leaders, ignoring the Israeli claim that this was empty rhetoric. In a special humiliation for Israel, the Court highlighted the chilling statement made by the country's head of state, President Isaac Herzog, that '[i]t is an entire nation out there that is responsible' for the crimes of October 7.[28]

The Court paid only passing attention to the central plank of Israel's argument, its right to self-defence. This claimed right has also been the primary justification offered by every Western leader for supporting Israel's actions. The Court also brushed aside Israel's claimed wish to avoid harming civilians and ignored its attempt to cast doubt on the scale of civilian casualties in Gaza. The Court relied instead on the consensus of UN and human rights authorities.

The Court finished by examining the South African contention that Israel was in breach of the Genocide Convention. Here its language became technical. The Court determined that 'at least some of the rights claimed by South Africa and for which it is seeking protection are plausible. This is the case with respect to the right of the Palestinians in Gaza to be protected from acts of genocide and related prohibited acts.'[29] In plain English, the Court had determined that South Africa's charge that Israel was committing genocide was plausible.[30]

On this basis, the Court indicated provisional measures to protect the rights of Palestinians not to be subjected to genocide and related acts pending the final ruling on the case. The Court ordered that Israel must take all measures within its power to prevent genocide in Gaza, prevent and punish genocidal incitement, enable the provision of humanitarian aid in Gaza, and preserve evidence related to allegations of genocide. The Court also instructed Israel to submit a report on the measures taken to implement the order within a month.[31] The Court's historic decision was supported by an overwhelming majority of the seventeen judges. Even the German judge, George Nolte, voted with the majority, while Israel's own appointee, Aharon Barak, rejected most but not all the measures.[32]

Israel reacted with fury. Prime Minister Netanyahu declared that 'the court's willingness to discuss this at all is a mark of disgrace that will not be erased for generations.'[33] President Herzog was 'disgusted by the way they twisted my words' and declared that the case was 'a blood libel that undermines the very values on which this court was established'.[34] Defence Minister Gallant insisted that Israel 'does not need to be lectured on morality in order to distinguish between terrorists and the civilian population in Gaza'.[35] National Security Minister Itamar Ben-Gvir accused the Court of seeking 'the persecution of the Jewish people'.[36] The US position remained unchanged: 'We continue to believe that allegations of genocide are unfounded'.[37] Already before the ruling, over two hundred members of the US Congress, both Democrats and Republicans, had signed a letter denouncing the South African initiative.[38]

The British media for the most part suppressed, played down or castigated the ICJ's momentous decision. The lead item on that evening's BBC *News at Ten* dealt with the latest of innumerable legal setbacks suffered by US President Donald Trump.* There was no mention at all of the ICJ ruling in *The Times*, often referred to as a paper of record, until page 42 (page 3 of the International Section). No report either in the following day's *Sunday Times*, though buried in the paper was a denunciation of antisemitism in South Africa, the country that brought the case.

There was no news report at all in the *Daily Mail*, which did however dedicate its leader column to a scathing attack on the judges for conducting a 'show trial'.[39] The same dismissive epithet was deployed by *The Economist*.[40] The fairest and fullest report could be found in the *Financial Times*.[41]

Political Complicity

Israeli and US outrage at the ruling was to be expected. No less predictably, Britain followed suit. Foreign Secretary David Cameron mocked the case as 'nonsense' even before the Court had reached its judgment. Israel is 'a democracy, a country with the rule of law, a country with armed forces that are committed to obeying the rule of law', Cameron told Sky News on

* The Court decision was the second item. The BBC report ignored the key domestic consequence of the ICJ ruling: British ministers had been put on notice of a plausible risk of genocide in Gaza.

January 14. 'The South African action is wrong, I think it is unhelpful, I think it shouldn't be happening.'[42]

The Foreign Office issued an unusual statement declaring that it was 'wrong and provocative' of South Africa to bring the case. 'Our view is that Israel's actions in Gaza cannot be described as a genocide.'[43]

The Foreign Office did not explain how it reached this opinion, which remained the official British view as this book went to press in the summer of 2025. We can, however, guess why Cameron attacked the judgment of the World Court. Before the ICJ ruling, Cameron and his fellow ministers could rally behind Israel to their hearts' content without fear of legal consequence. Not thereafter. The ruling threatened to place ministers such as Cameron in personal jeopardy because the Genocide Convention can be enforced in British courts. Unusually for an international treaty it is incorporated in British domestic law under the International Criminal Court Act of 2001.

This Act does more than make it an offense to commit genocide. Section 52 makes it an offence to engage in 'conduct ancillary to genocide.' There is now a mountain of evidence showing that Britain has enabled and assisted Israeli military operations inside Gaza. Britain has supplied military equipment to Israel for use against the Palestinian population of Gaza, provided communications intelligence, and carried out aerial surveillance.

Meanwhile the British Foreign Office has consistently given Israel diplomatic support, most significantly by obstructing United Nations ceasefire resolutions.

As matters stand the British ministers responsible are in the clear, legally if not morally. But the ICJ ruling meant they could no longer sleep soundly. If and when the Court decides that Israel has committed a genocide in Gaza, an outcome which becomes more likely with every fresh Israeli massacre or obstruction of humanitarian aid, senior British politicians and officials will find themselves vulnerable to prosecution under British domestic law. In the event that occurs, the ICJ ruling would have another significant consequence: Any prosecutor will be able to show that, from the date of the ICJ order indicating provisional measures on January 26, 2024, ministers had been warned of a clear and indisputable risk that Britain was complicit in genocide, and that such a risk should have been sufficient to terminate our support for Israel's offensive. I will explore this aspect of British complicity in greater detail in the final chapter.

How Complicity Works

This book will draw to public attention the legal penalties that a select group of ministerial accomplices (from both main parties) might in due course pay for their support for Israel while it committed atrocities in Gaza. But British complicity stretches much deeper than that. A full reckoning with Britain's culpability for the destruction of Gaza requires an assessment of the failing institutions that misgovern British public life: the dishonesty of the media, the moral bankruptcy of the foreign policy establishment, growing domestic authoritarianism, the corruption of parliament, and the collapse of a party system increasingly manipulated by special interests and the super-rich.

In the first chapter I will describe how the two main parties overcame their differences and joined forces to hold the line on British support for Israel. They entered into what amounted to an informal pact, especially marked in the early months of the onslaught. During this period only the Scottish National Party (SNP) fulfilled the true role of a parliamentary opposition, asking difficult questions and challenging the belligerent stance of the two main parties by calling for a ceasefire.

In a democracy, even one as flawed as Britain, and even in the relatively insulated sphere of foreign affairs, political projects need to command a degree of popular consent. Mass media collaboration was therefore essential if the British people—generally speaking a kindly lot—were to be persuaded to turn a blind eye to the unimaginable suffering of the Palestinian people.

In Chapter Two I will show how, with a handful of noteworthy exceptions, established media repeated the falsehoods and fabrications spread by Israeli and British politicians. Some produced fresh misrepresentations of their own. Their selective reporting deprived citizens of facts crucial to an understanding of the violence. Media outlets consistently used language that twisted their reports in favour of the Israeli cause. Reports of Israeli atrocities either did not appear or were muted. Hamas atrocities, though gruesome enough already, were still further embellished or invented. Dissident voices were suppressed or sidelined. To demonstrate this I have examined the record of individual newspapers as well as media organisations, including the BBC.

To illustrate the scale of media failings, in Chapter Three I carry out a detailed case study of British media coverage of October 7. Though Hamas carried out many dreadful atrocities that day, I show how British journalists, credulous of Israeli sources, reported atrocities that never happened. These stories of butchered and beheaded babies then became embedded in the rhetoric of Western politicians and were used as justification for the savagery of the Israeli response.

In Chapter Four I demonstrate that the merger of the media and political class left advocates for peace—who polls showed happened to comprise a majority of the British public—without a voice. To be heard those opposed to the war had little choice but to take to the streets. At this point both main parties, amplified by the mainstream press, turned on the marchers. They were cast as sectarians, supporters of terrorism, and antisemites. I will show that the marchers were overwhelmingly peaceful and document some of the smear campaigns against them. So far from being 'hateful' or extreme, demonstrators for a Gaza ceasefire should be understood as a contemporary iteration of an ancient British tradition of popular protest stretching from Tom Paine and William Cobbett through the Chartist movement and the suffragettes up to the Stop the War rallies ahead of the 2003 invasion of Iraq.

At this point I pause the narrative and examine structural reasons for the pro-Israel tendency among the British political/media class. British support for Israeli atrocities did not start on October 7, 2023, any more than the Hamas atrocities themselves should be understood in isolation. British policy has been many years in the making; understanding it requires looking carefully over Britain's long record of assisting Israeli war crimes across the Occupied Palestinian Territory. I will examine the pro-Israel lobby in Britain, showing how, sometimes with the Israeli embassy in London, it has worked effectively to influence British policy towards Israel and shape language in the media. This means telling the history of the Conservative Friends of Israel (CFI), in recent years the most consequential of Britain's pro-Israel advocacy groups. I will give examples of CFI's formidable influence in

British politics, highlighting its triumphs. There is no remotely comparable Palestinian lobby at Westminster.

I scrutinise the pro-Israel forces at work within the Labour Party through an analysis of the political formation of the British prime minister Sir Keir Starmer. The Labour Party, like the Tories, is fundamentally committed to the Atlantic alliance, and Starmer's general approach after October 7 was to follow the US lead. But Starmer's handling of the Gaza onslaught makes no sense without also grasping his deep ties to pro-Israel currents within Labour, some formed against the background of the alleged antisemitism crisis that dogged his predecessor as Labour Party leader, Jeremy Corbyn.

I next turn to Labour's handling of the war. Once in power Foreign Secretary David Lammy reversed some of Cameron's most disreputable decisions: resuming funding for UNRWA, ending the Tory attempt to thwart the International Criminal Court investigation of Hamas' and Israeli war crimes, and halting a handful of arms contracts to Israel. Military collaboration with Israel continued however. This relationship is much deeper and more important than the British public understands because the subject has been almost completely ignored by Britain's respectable press and broadcasting organisations. I have relied heavily on the groundbreaking investigative journalism conducted by *Declassified UK* as well as foreign outlets, especially Al Jazeera.

This brings me back to a further study of the British media, which continued to publish false reports right up to the January 2025 ceasefire and beyond. I provide a long analysis of the anti-Jewish 'pogrom' against supporters of Maccabi Tel Aviv, an Israeli football club, that reportedly unfolded on the streets of Amsterdam. Major international news outlets led their reports with footage or photographs showing a mob of Maccabi fans attacking Dutch citizens. But this footage was almost universally represented as showing the precise opposite, presenting Maccabi hooligans as the victims.

While researching this book, I found myself grappling with an overpowering question: How is it that so many British public figures, both politicians and journalists, have been happy to justify, enable, and in some cases actually to applaud Israeli atrocities and the slaughter of Palestinian civilians? Towards the end of the book I explore the reasons for this insensibility and denial. These are not evil people. For the most part they think of themselves as decent and kind. They believe that the actions of the Israeli armed forces are admirable, morally correct, and justified.

This led them to become part of the same barbaric, immoral, and homicidal universe as Netanyahu and Ben-Gvir, joining them as they waged war on the United Nations, the International Court of Justice, the International Criminal Court, Amnesty International, and the international order that Britain played a significant role in constructing after World War Two. In the process they have enabled the criminal slaughter of countless innocent Palestinians. This is hard to understand, let alone to explain. I will do so in this book.

1

CROSS-PARTY CARTEL

> The President of Israel, President Herzog, has made it clear that his country will abide by international humanitarian law.
>
> —*Andrew Mitchell, then a minister of state in the UK Foreign, Commonwealth, and Development Office, November 14, 2023*[1]

BRITAIN REACTED to the atrocities committed by Hamas on October 7 with horror and repugnance, along with heartfelt sympathy for Israel. The number of dead, reported at first as fourteen hundred, was unimaginable.[2] Adjusted as a percentage of population it was the equivalent of fourteen thousand people in Britain, or more than seventy thousand in the United States. Almost every Israeli knew or was related to someone who had been killed or been taken hostage; some knew scores of the dead. It is impossible to overestimate the scale of the grief.

Sunak in Tel Aviv

Prime Minister Rishi Sunak flew into Tel Aviv twelve days later. His visit recalled the journey made by Tony Blair to Washington in the aftermath of the Al Qaeda attack on the Twin Towers. Indeed, the October 7 attack was more traumatic for most Israelis than 9/11 in all its horror had been for most Americans.

But events were moving at a terrifying pace. Thanks to an authoritative report from Airwars, which documents the human cost of war, we now know that hundreds of Palestinian civilians were being killed daily by Israeli strikes throughout most of this period.[3] On the most lethal day of the bombing, some 420 civilians were slaughtered.[4] By the end of the month, the number of recorded Palestinian civilian deaths would stand at more than five thousand.[5]

Sunak may or may not have known the exact numbers. But as prime minister he would have been briefed by British security experts. Well connected with the Israeli and United States militaries, they would have had a shrewd idea of the magnitude of the bloodletting.

Members of the most senior Israeli political and military echelons made no secret of what lay ahead. They spelt out their view that there were no innocents in Gaza; that everyone was a target. The scale of the Hamas atrocities liberated Israel from any constraints of war. The frankly articulated assumption in Tel Aviv was that Israel now had a free hand to destroy, maim, and slaughter. The torrent of genocidal statements from senior Israeli ministers and commanders, later compiled into voluminous dossiers by the Republic of South Africa in support of its historic submissions to the International Court of Justice, were already on the record and being enacted. In a speech on October 28, 2023, Israeli prime minister Benjamin Netanyahu had invoked a biblical instruction to the Israelites to destroy their Amalekite enemies. As the IDF began its ground invasion of Gaza, Netanyahu urged: 'remember what Amalek has done to you'.* Israel was set on a bloodthirsty mission of revenge that would smash every rule of war.

---

* In Deuteronomy, the followers of Moses are instructed to 'blot out' the 'memory' of the Amalekites, a people that attacked the Israelites as they fled Egypt. In the Book of Samuel, the prophet commands King Saul to 'attack Amalek . . . Spare no one, but kill alike men and women, infants and sucklings, oxen and sheep, camels and asses'. The legal team for South Africa cited Netanyahu's invocation of Amalek as evidence of incitement to genocide in its application to the ICJ. Netanyahu's office said in response that South Africa's 'false and preposterous charge reflects a deep historical ignorance'; the office claimed that the biblical reference had simply described the actions of Hamas on October 7 and communicated the 'need to confront them'. Netanyahu's office also cited the presence of the phrase 'Remember what Amalek did to you' on a banner in Yad Vashem, the Israeli Holocaust museum, and in The Hague, where it adorns a memorial

Any British prime minister would have felt obliged to offer sympathy and aid to an ally mourning its dead. But with Israel unleashing unprecedented murder and mayhem upon an occupied and besieged civilian population, Sunak ought also to have warned Netanyahu not to advance further down a path that would bring death to countless Palestinians as well as disgrace on Israel. Britain claims to be a close ally of Israel. It is the task of a true friend to give candid advice.

Sunak did not rise to the challenge. Even before his arrival, he had sent the message to Netanyahu—by now consolidating his deserved reputation as a butcher—that Israel could rely on Britain's 'unequivocal' support.[6] This amounted to carte blanche for the Israeli authorities to commit, with Britain's blessing, whatever crimes they wanted. Sunak had leverage. Britain had already deployed a Royal Navy task force to the Eastern Mediterranean, including a company of Royal Marines, two ships, and three helicopters. British surveillance aircraft also began to patrol the region.[7]

There has never been any hint that the British prime minister imposed conditions on this military support. Although Sunak did assert that Israel must act 'in line with international humanitarian law' and 'take every possible precaution to avoid harming civilians',[8] these pro forma caveats were not serious demands for restraint. The Conservative government never took the necessary measures to deter or punish Israel's violations, even as the crimes became massive and undeniable.

---

for Dutch Jews murdered in the Holocaust, as evidence that it lacked genocidal meaning. B'Tselem, the Israeli information centre for human rights in the Occupied Territories, described Netanyahu's reference to 'Amalek' as 'a dog whistle that anyone who has gone through Israel's education system will recognise' as an order 'to wipe out Gaza'. ICJ, *South Africa v. Israel*, Application Instituting Proceedings and Request for the Indication of Provisional Measures (29 December 2023), para. 101. Israel Prime Minister's Office, 'Prime Minister's Office Announcement', gov.il (16 January 2024). B'Tselem, *Manufacturing Famine: Israel Is Committing the War Crime of Starvation in the Gaza Strip* (April 2024), p. 11.

Following Netanyahu's use of the passage, other high-ranking Israeli officials referenced Amalek to press for violence against Palestinians in Gaza, as when Finance Minister Bezalel Smotrich urged the 'destruction' of Rafah, Deir al-Balah, and Nuseirat to '[b]lot out the memory of Amalek'. Amnesty International, *'You Feel Like You Are Subhuman': Israel's Genocide Against Palestinians in Gaza* (December 2024), p. 7.

Britain's military support for Israel was never put to a vote in parliament. It always took the form of executive action, which saved MPs from having to take a clear position. The Labour Party seemed content with this: His Majesty's Official Opposition never called for such a vote. Indeed, as the two parties converged, *opposition* seemed to be Labour's smallest concern.

Starmer in London

There comes a moment in many people's lives when we adopt a course of action that defines us. Such a moment came to Labour leader and future prime minister Sir Keir Starmer when he joined LBC presenter Nick Ferrari in the studio a few days after October 7. At this point an unknown future stretched ahead. If Israeli politicians were to be believed it would assuredly include one of the most monstrous crimes of the twenty-first century. Israel's defence minister Yoav Gallant had just issued his grim announcement of a 'complete siege' on Gaza: 'No electricity, no food, no water, no fuel. Everything is closed.'[9]

The Starmer moment can still be witnessed on YouTube. It unfolds when Ferrari asks whether cutting off water and electricity supplies is an appropriate response to the Hamas attacks.

It should have been an easy question. Before entering politics Starmer was an acknowledged expert on international law. He would have known for certain that Israel did not have the right to cut off water and electricity supplies. Collective punishment of a civilian population is a war crime. In that day's reporting, there is no ambiguity.

But when Ferrari pressed: 'A siege is appropriate? Cutting off power? Cutting off water?' Starmer tried to have it both ways by simultaneously standing up for Israel and international law. 'I think Israel does have that right', he affirmed. 'It is an ongoing situation. Obviously, everything should be done within international law but I don't want to step away from the core principles that Israel has a right to defend herself and Hamas bears responsibility.'[10]

Sir Keir's attempt to argue that Israel had the right to deny water and fuel to Palestinians in Gaza while respecting international law made mockery of the law and of his own professional standing. Gallant's openly stated plan amounted to a grave breach of international law as well as domestic

British law. Subject to a pro forma caveat, the leader of the Labour Party was therefore giving the green light to a crime against humanity, as set out in the Rome Statute, and enabling whatever atrocities Israel cared to inflict on Gaza's two million inhabitants, one half of whom were children.

Starmer was not speaking out of turn. This was party policy, as became clear the following day when Shadow Attorney General Emily Thornberry, also a human rights lawyer, joined the Labour leader in refusing to state that cutting off 'food, water and electricity' breached international law.[11] Labour's shadow foreign secretary David Lammy, a graduate of Harvard Law School, followed suit by declining to acknowledge that the 'siege' of Gaza was unlawful. 'I'm hoping one day to be foreign secretary and a chief diplomat', he confided to the BBC's Victoria Derbyshire, 'so it's not a yes or no'.[12]

Starmer later claimed his words had been misconstrued and that he had simply asserted Israel's 'right' to defend itself.[13] This was disingenuous. In the original clip it is crystal clear Starmer was responding affirmatively to the question: 'A siege is appropriate? Cutting off power, cutting off water?' In his clarification Starmer said he was pressing 'for humanitarian aid to come in' to Gaza. He seemed to officially reverse his position on October 23, 2023, when he told the House of Commons that 'basic services, including water, electricity and the fuel needed for it, cannot be denied'.[14]

Remarkably, Labour and the Tories agreed in opposing an immediate ceasefire. Instead, they echoed the White House in calling for 'humanitarian pauses'.* When, on November 15, the Scottish National Party submitted

* On October 24, 2023, Antony Blinken, the US secretary of state, told the UN Security Council that 'the vital need to protect civilians' and get humanitarian aid into Gaza meant that 'humanitarian pauses must be considered'. The next day, Prime Minister Sunak told the House of Commons that his government recognised the need for 'specific pauses' in the fighting, 'as distinct from a ceasefire'. A spokesperson for Sir Keir Starmer confirmed Labour's support for the same measure: 'We saw that Antony Blinken said last night that humanitarian pauses must be considered, that seems to be something that Downing Street is now echoing and we would obviously fully support that position'. Starmer also gave a speech to Chatham House on October 31, in which he said: 'while I understand calls for a ceasefire, at this stage I do not believe that is the correct position now'; by contrast, he argued that calling for 'pauses' was 'right in practice as well as principle . . . it

an amendment to the King's Speech that called for an immediate ceasefire in Gaza, Sir Keir Starmer whipped Labour MPs to abstain while the Tories voted the amendment down. Although fifty-six Labour MPs rebelled, the vote remained a symbol of the concord between government and opposition.[15] Labour would not call for an immediate ceasefire until February 2024.[16]

Meanwhile Sunak's home secretary, Suella Braverman, busied herself inflaming domestic tensions by suggesting that simply waving a Palestinian flag could become a criminal offense.[17] By the end of October 2023, the Conservative prime minister and the leader of the Labour opposition had together established the political foundation that would make Britain complicit in massacres, indiscriminate bombing, torture, ethnic cleansing, and arguably the crime of crimes itself.

Cameron at the Foreign Office

Shortly afterwards Sunak appointed David Cameron as foreign secretary. The move was widely seen as a stroke of good fortune for the discredited former prime minister whose reputation had been ruined by Brexit and then further trashed by his role in the Greensill lobbying scandal.

Here was an opportunity for Cameron to recast himself as a serious international statesman.

And at first sight it seemed as if Cameron's resurrection might help Palestinians, too. As a young politician Cameron had been sympathetic to the by now almost defunct tradition of 'Tory Arabism'. Other members of the Arabist set included Winston Churchill's grandson Nicholas Soames, a minister of state in the John Major government; and Lord Lothian, who, as

---

is also the position shared by our major allies in the US and the EU'. U.S. Department of State Office of the Spokesperson, 'Secretary Antony J. Blinken at the UN Security Council Ministerial Meeting on the Situation in the Middle East', 2021-2025.state.gov (24 October 2023). UK House of Commons, 'Engagements', hansard.parliament.uk (25 October 2023) (Sunak). Nicola Slawson, 'Starmer Holds "Constructive" Meeting with Labour MPs over Party's Position on Israel and Gaza—As It Happened', *The Guardian* (25 October 2023). 'Keir Starmer's Speech on the International Situation in the Middle East', labour.org.uk (31 October 2023).

a Conservative minister in the 1990s, had played an important and sometimes personally brave role in the early negotiations with the IRA that ultimately led to the Good Friday Agreement. Lothian later engaged with Hamas in an attempt to apply the lessons of Northern Ireland to the Middle East. In the aftermath of Hamas' victory in the 2006 Palestinian legislative election, Lothian and I drove across the Bekaa Valley to meet the group's political chief Khaled Meshaal in Damascus. After a ninety-minute meeting in a secret location—Israel had previously tried to assassinate Meshaal by poisoning, and has a record of killing Hamas negotiators—Lothian turned to me and said: 'He is the kind of man we could do business with.'

Two other Tory Arabists had tutored Cameron. One was Douglas Hurd, regarded by some as the finest British foreign secretary of modern times. Cameron inherited Hurd's Witney constituency. Chris Patten had been Tory chairman when Cameron was rising up the party ranks. It may have been a harrowing conversation with Lord Patten, by then president of Medical Aid for Palestine, that led Prime Minister Cameron to remark in 2010 that conditions in Gaza resembled a 'prison camp.'[18]

In the very early days of his new role Lord Cameron brought a sense of purpose and a swagger that had eluded his mediocre predecessor James Cleverly. But Cameron's dream job soon turned into a nightmare. He is still remembered as the incompetent prime minister who set in motion the Brexit debacle and after leaving office was dragged into the gutter by Lex Greensill. But now something darker, less easy to overlook, and impossible to forgive is on his record, too.

In his first three months in office Lord Cameron made a handful of decisions that defined Britain's role in the destruction of Gaza. They were politically convenient, drew applause among Conservative supporters, went down well in Tel Aviv, and were welcome in Sunak's Downing Street. They sent Netanyahu the message that Britain was fully behind the Gaza slaughter.

On December 8, 2023, Britain abstained on a UN Security Council resolution calling for an immediate humanitarian ceasefire.[19] Then came Cameron's flabbergasting claim, made to Sky News' Trevor Phillips on January 14, that there was no evidence of Israeli genocidal intent.[20] As Cameron ought to have known (and Phillips failed to point out), the eighty-four-page document presented by South Africa to the International Court of Justice in late December had provided abundant evidence of exactly that.

Phillips' failure to challenge Cameron on this point was disappointing. The government had already undertaken one review of arms sales to Israel in December 2023 and would conduct two more before it was voted out of office in the July 2024 general election. Any decision to permit an export license includes a judgment about how the arms will be used. Cameron was effectively parroting the Israeli defence, made at The Hague two days earlier, that the genocidal language employed by senior Israeli politicians was just empty rhetoric. We have already seen that the ICJ rejected this claim with contempt. Phillips had the chance to learn from Cameron whether and why he had been convinced by the Israeli argument. He did not take it.

We have already examined Cameron's third intervention: his mockery of South Africa's genocide case. Cameron's fourth fateful decision was his refusal to fully accept the ICJ's provisional ruling when it was made at the end of January. This was confirmation that Cameron as foreign secretary was ready to tear up even the pretence of an international legal order in defence of Israel. Britain was a founder signatory of the ICJ, still claimed to celebrate its values, and had a duty to pay the Court respect.

The day after the ICJ judgment, Cameron made his fifth error—to put it generously. He ordered the suspension of British funding for the United Nations Relief and Works Agency.

Defunding Refugees

UNRWA was set up by the United Nations in the aftermath of the mass displacement of Palestinians during the 1948 Arab-Israeli war.

Without UNRWA conditions of life for these exiled Palestinians would have been unsustainable. This was the case for many decades even before the Israeli assault that followed October 7. Thereafter UNRWA became still more essential to survival. There were and are other humanitarian organisations serving Gaza, but UNRWA is by far the most important.[21]

Its existence has long been detested by Israel, in part because UNRWA is an institutional reminder of the refugee status of many Palestinians and by implication a statement that they have a right to return.[22] As the Israeli attacks mounted, UNRWA infrastructure was targeted, many of its buildings were destroyed, and large numbers of its employees were killed.[23]

This forms the backdrop to the diplomatic assault on UNRWA launched by Israel within hours of the ICJ's provisional ruling. Israel issued a confidential document to certain media organisations asserting that more than ten UNRWA staffers had taken part in the October 7 assault. UNRWA employs thirteen thousand people.[24] Even if true, the Israeli allegation should not have led donors to suspend funding for an organisation that was keeping displaced civilians alive amidst a murderous onslaught. All the more so since it quickly emerged that the Israeli document was based on negligible evidence.[25]

Israel's UNRWA offensive worked on two levels. Substantively, if Israel was bent on emptying out Gaza, and if UNRWA served as a lifeline for Gaza's population, then destroying UNRWA would expedite the Israeli mission. At the propaganda level, the timing of the UNRWA attacks gave away the game: within hours of the ICJ order, Israel had changed the subject. A pliant western media no longer focussed on the devastating ICJ finding that Israel was plausibly committing genocide. Editors and reporters could shift the conversation to Israel's new allegations about links between UNRWA and Hamas.

This behaviour would be repeated time and again as Israel manipulated and managed international consent for the massacre of Palestinians. Although superficially effective, it seems unlikely that such crude tactics could have worked except on co-conspirators or else willing dupes.

Britain duly announced a pause in future payments to UNRWA. Given the existence of Israel's clear-cut and long-standing anti-UNRWA agenda, it appals that Britain (and other donor countries) should have swallowed Israeli claims so uncritically and acted so rashly. It's not as if Israel deserved to be automatically believed. The Israeli military had repeatedly been caught out lying and making fabricated statements about events in Gaza and elsewhere.[26] At the very least Cameron should have conducted his own investigation before suspending funding. But this was part of a pattern.

Just compare the British government's dismissive response to the ICJ's January ruling with Britain's instant readiness to act on Israeli charges against UNRWA. The ICJ produced an evidence-based document to support its ruling that there was a plausible risk that Israel was committing genocide in Gaza. This was informed by a lengthy and exhaustively referenced application submitted by South Africa. Yet Sunak and Cameron trashed the case even before the Court had issued its judgment and did so again right afterward. They treated Israel's flimsy document, by contrast, with deference and respect.

A source told me that Cameron paused funds to UNRWA 'only on the basis of information in the public domain'. On February 6, I asked the Foreign Office if this was true—no answer. If my source is right, Cameron made a decision with potentially appalling consequences for the lives of starving Palestinians on the basis of allegations he had no way of judging were true—and good reason to suspect may have been fabricated.

This deprivation of donor aid was a hammer blow aimed at Gaza's population. Christopher Gunness, a former UNRWA spokesperson, argued that the decision was arguably a violation of the Genocide Convention, because 'it will devastate the lives of 1.2 million people who are on UNRWA's food lines'.[27]

It must be accepted that Israel made a serious allegation. But Britain did not have to act immediately. The government could have waited for the results of the independent review of UNRWA then being carried out by Catherine Colonna, the former French foreign minister, whose interim report was due in March.* Or Britain could have made up her own mind.

---

* The UN secretary-general appointed an Independent Review Group headed by Colonna to 'assess whether the Agency is doing everything within its power to ensure neutrality and to respond to allegations of serious breaches when they are made'. He also ordered the UN's Office of Internal Oversight Services (OIOS) to investigate the specific allegations. The Colonna Review found that 'UNRWA has established a significant number of mechanisms and procedures to ensure compliance with the humanitarian principles, with emphasis on the principle of neutrality, and that it possesses a more developed approach to neutrality than other similar UN or NGO entities'. It noted that UNRWA regularly shared staff lists with Israel and that 'the Israeli Government has not informed UNRWA of any concerns relating to any UNRWA staff based

Instead Cameron jumped to attention on the basis of a threadbare, unevidenced dossier produced by a government with a strong interest in discrediting UNRWA and distracting from growing international criticism of its onslaught. As the one million children of Gaza endured saturation bombing and teetered on the brink of starvation, the British foreign secretary put their lifeline in jeopardy.[28]

Whereas several donor states resumed their funding for UNRWA in March and April—including Norway, Finland, Sweden, Iceland, Germany, Australia, and Japan—Britain did not.[29] As so often, we adhered to the US position.

---

on these staff lists since 2011'. (*Final Report for the United Nations Secretary-General: Independent Review of Mechanisms and Procedures to Ensure Adherence by UNRWA to the Humanitarian Principle of Neutrality* (20 April 2024), pp. 4–5, 21–22, 47)

The Review also said: 'The Israeli Ministry of Foreign Affairs informed [*sic*] that until March 2024, they had received staff lists without identification (ID) numbers. On the basis of the March 2024 list, which contained staff ID numbers, Israel made public claims that a significant number of UNRWA employees are members of terrorist organizations. However, Israel has yet to provide supporting evidence of this'. (Ibid., p. 22)

The Israeli government has stated that it shared information with OIOS and with 'close intelligence partners' rather than UNRWA. ('The UNRWA-Hamas Linkage', gov.il (n.d.)) The OIOS investigation was concluded in August 2024. It covered nineteen UNRWA staff members. One case was closed because there was no evidence to support the allegation. In nine other cases, it was found that there was insufficient evidence of UNRWA staff members' involvement. As to the remaining nine cases, evidence indicated that they *may* have been involved in the attacks, and their employment was terminated. (UNRWA, 'Note to Correspondents—on the OIOS Investigation of UNRWA', unrwa.org (5 August 2024))

UNRWA has reported that only 0.66 percent of its thirty thousand staff were implicated in breaches of neutrality from January 2022 to November 2024. (UNRWA, 'UNRWA: Claims versus Facts', unrwa.org (February 2025))

Announcing the decision to reinstate British support for UNRWA, the UK Foreign Office said: 'Following an independent review by Catherine Colonna and the subsequent action plan UNRWA has provided setting out detailed management reforms, the government is confident that UNRWA is taking action to ensure it meets the highest standards of neutrality'. (UK FCDO, 'UK to Restart Funding to UNRWA', gov.uk (19 July 2024))

I now turn to Cameron's most deadly judgment: As evidence of Israeli war crimes in Gaza mounted, Britain continued to supply weapons to Israel.

Arms Sales to Israel

Britain's military relationship with Israel long precedes the present hostilities in Gaza. The export of military equipment requires an official licence from the government.

According to analysis of official figures by the Campaign Against the Arms Trade (CAAT), the UK licensed arms sales to Israel worth £488 million between April 2015 and September 2023.[30] This sum includes 'technology for military radars', components for targeting equipment, and components for military aircraft.[31]

But this is an underestimate. The £488 million excludes exports using (rather opaque) open licences, under which components for the F-35—the stealth fighter aircraft that has played a major role in pummelling Gaza—are sold.

Israel has used F-35s in Gaza since October 8, 2023. In July 2024, an F-35 dropped three two-thousand-pound bombs on al-Mawasi in Khan Younis. Israel had designated this area a 'safe zone' and instructed civilians to move there. Ninety people were killed.[32]

The UK supplies spare parts for the F-35, enabling them to continue being used in Gaza. According to CAAT, the F-35 is 'almost certainly the single largest and most important part of the UK arms trade with Israel'.[33]

By law the British government is obliged to assess licences according to the Strategic Export Licensing Criteria. Under criterion 2(c), the government will '[n]ot grant a licence if it determines there is a clear risk that the items might be used to commit or facilitate a serious violation of international humanitarian law'.[34]

The Tory government undertook several such reviews of arms exports to Israel. Each time the Foreign Office concluded that arms sales should continue—an affirmation that Israel's use of the weapons was within the law.[35] As this judgment looked less and less plausible, the new Tory foreign secretary benefited from a significant piece of luck.

David Cameron had resigned as prime minister following the Brexit referendum and stood down as MP the year after. Convention insists that ministers must be members of parliament. This created a problem for Prime Minister Sunak when he decided to appoint Cameron as foreign secretary in November 2023. Sunak got round the difficulty by arranging for Cameron to join the House of Lords. Since peers as members of the House of Lords do count as members of parliament the constitutional proprieties were observed.

As a peer, however, Lord Cameron was not permitted to answer questions from the Commons dispatch box. This meant he was spared the need to defend government policy. That task fell to a middle-ranking minister, Andrew Mitchell. In this way Mitchell, a politician of the second rank whose career dated back to the Thatcher years in the 1980s, inscribed his footnote in history as the most consistent and reliable British apologist for Israel's destruction of Gaza.

Mitchell's reports to parliament were bereft of insight, integrity, and humanity. But they did shed light on official thinking.

Echoing Netanyahu's own talking points,[36] Mitchell brushed aside the idea that Israel would commit genocide:

> It is hard to overestimate the offence caused by the extraordinary rhetoric of accusing Israel of being guilty of genocide, given the antecedents and events that took place in the holocaust during the war and the fact that more Jewish people were murdered on that one day of 7 October than at any time since the end of the second world war.[37]

It appears that for Mitchell it was even harder to estimate the 'offence caused' by Israel's deliberate starvation of civilians in Gaza—to mention just one aspect of the horror British arms were fuelling.

Mitchell—as spokesman for the UK government—also defended Israel against accusations that it had breached international humanitarian law (a genteel phrase employed by officials and politicians to describe war crimes and atrocities).

In November 2023 Mitchell reassured MPs that the Israeli president Isaac Herzog 'has made it clear that his country will abide by international humanitarian law'.[38] The following month, with the slaughter of Palestinians and razing of entire neighbourhoods on open display, he set out the British government position: 'The Government have heard the words of President Herzog that Israel will respect international humanitarian law, and the Government expect Israel to abide by the words of the President'.[39]

Speaking at the end of January, in the wake of the ICJ's provisional order, Mitchell informed parliament that 'Israel plans to act in accordance with international humanitarian law and has the ability to do so'.[40]

As we have seen, President Herzog's bloodthirsty rhetoric was explicitly cited by the ICJ in its provisional order on genocide, while South Africa had compiled a voluminous dossier of genocidal statements by Israeli officials, politicians, combatants, and commentators.

Asked in parliament what steps the UK was taking to hold people to account for human rights violations in Gaza, Mitchell said that 'the UK Government would expect the Israeli domestic legal system to investigate and, where appropriate, take action against those accused of human rights violations and abuses'.[41]

In fact, Israeli and international human rights bodies have uniformly concluded that Israel does not fairly investigate or punish war crimes against Palestinians. The leading Israeli human rights group B'Tselem refuses even to cooperate with what it calls Israel's 'whitewash mechanism'.[42]

Rejecting South Africa's ICJ case against Israel, Mitchell said: 'Israel is a state party to the Geneva convention of 1949, so it is obliged to take action against those accused of grave breaches of international humanitarian law. Because of the nature of Israeli society, that is something that we would expect it to do, were those circumstances to arise'.[43]

Mitchell's remarks to parliament may have lacked integrity, but they did not want for cunning.

As a minister he never quite denied that Israel had breached international law. Such a statement could have risked opening him up to charges that he had lied to parliament. On the other hand, he stopped short of acknowledging that Israel had committed atrocities. Such an admission would have created a different problem: Israel and more importantly Israel's US patron would have been furious while pressure within Britain to suspend arms sales might have become impossible to resist.

Mitchell found a compromise. He hid behind empty assurances that Israel would conduct itself within the rules of war. He even praised 'the work of the Israel Defence Forces, and indeed the training they undergo, which respects international humanitarian law and understands the obligations a military force owes to civilians.'[44]

Mark in this context the repeated and ambiguous verb 'expect': articulated in the tone of a scolding schoolmaster it conveyed that Israel was being put on notice, while at the same time putting on record the absurd proposition that the government predicted Israel would abide by the law. Like a good deal of British rhetoric since October 2023, the word superficially appeased Israel's critics while giving the government cover for continued participation in Israel's offensive.

Questioned about the deployment of drones against civilians in Gaza, Mitchell claimed: 'Just as in the UK military, targeting in Israel is subject to lawyers being present in the room and legal advice.'[45]* In November 2024, a retired British surgeon who volunteered at a hospital in Gaza offered MPs a different perspective: 'The drones would come down and pick off civilians—children.... [I]t was a persistent act—persistent targeting of civilians day after day.'[46] Human Rights Watch documented Israel's use of drones to target civilians in Gaza as far back as 2009.[47] In December 2023, it was reported that the Ministry of Defence has conducted exercises with Israeli drones first deployed in Gaza.[48]

In May 2024, the chief prosecutor of the International Criminal Court (ICC), Karim Khan KC, applied for arrest warrants to be issued for Israeli prime minister Netanyahu and defence minister Gallant as well as three

* *Haaretz* revealed in December 2024 that the IDF has a 'flash procedure' by which an airstrike can be called in an 'emergency' situation. Under this procedure, an airstrike is 'guaranteed' within thirty minutes—'with no approvals needed.' Yaniv Kubovich, '"No Civilians. Everyone's a Terrorist": IDF Soldiers Expose Arbitrary Killings and Rampant Lawlessness in Gaza's Netzarim Corridor', *Haaretz* (18 December 2024).

Hamas leaders.[49] Mitchell opposed this request as 'we do not think that the ICC has jurisdiction in this case', then denied that he had taken this position, then reaffirmed it, all in the space of a single parliamentary debate.[50]

The Silence of Sir Keir Starmer

Serviceable a tool though he was, Mitchell could not completely shield the foreign secretary from public scrutiny. On January 9, 2024, parliament's Foreign Affairs Committee summoned Cameron to give evidence. Three months into Israel's assault, the foreign secretary would at last have to deal with forensic questioning from well-informed MPs.

The rank-and-file Tories on the committee, as was to be expected, gave Cameron a soft time. Labour MPs also caused him little trouble. Cameron might have got away with it but for Brendan O'Hara of the Scottish National Party. Emerging as the foreign secretary's biggest tormentor, O'Hara asked whether Cameron had received advice from Foreign Office lawyers that Israel was in breach of international humanitarian law.[51]

The resulting exchange makes for painful viewing.[52] Cameron ducked and dived, dodged the question, and answered other questions he had not been asked. Responding to Alicia Kearns, a dissident Tory who was making a reputation as a formidable Foreign Affairs Committee chair, Cameron implausibly claimed that he could not remember what advice he'd received from officials.[53]

At one point he said: 'one issue we would like the Israelis to look at is switching the water back on into northern Gaza, because that would make a difference'.[54] This was an admission that Israel had turned the water off—collective punishment of a civilian population and a war crime. Cameron was at first unable to tell the committee whether Gaza was occupied, an unexpected confession of ignorance about one of the salient facts.[55] O'Hara was stoutly supported by Kearns. Eventually Cameron stated that he had not been advised that Israel's actions were illegal, but still left the matter ambiguous.[56]

Cameron survived this debacle—and for one reason: Sir Keir Starmer, leader of the opposition, wasn't doing his job. Cameron's Commons humiliation ought to have been meat and drink to an opposition leader. Starmer could have mocked the foreign secretary's forgetfulness, asked why he could not remember what papers he'd read, and made fun of his evasive answers. Labour could have demanded the urgent publication of the Foreign Office legal advice but they were slow to do so, waiting until March 2024.[57] When Labour took power after the June 2024 election, it also declined to publish the legal advice.

Starmer could have exploited Cameron's admission that Israel had turned the water off. He could have mocked Cameron's claim that he did not know whether Gaza was occupied, given that thousands of Israeli troops were physically present on the ground. He could have asked why Britain was providing arms to a country committing war crimes in plain sight. He would have been justified in asking whether the British government would back Israel under *any* circumstances.

Starmer asked none of these questions. Silence too from David Lammy, Labour's shadow foreign secretary.[58] The last thing Starmer appears to have wanted was a Labour foreign affairs spokesman asking tricky questions about British tolerance of Israeli atrocities.

The Labour leadership's position reflected its embrace of a US-led foreign policy. Labour branches had reportedly been discouraged from discussing the conflict and the party's elected representatives 'strongly advised' not to attend pro-Palestine demonstrations.[59] This had been the Labour leader's pattern of behaviour ever since Hamas' October 7 attack. Indeed, even Joe Biden's White House expressed surprise that the British prime minister stuck his neck out so far in sending unequivocal backing to Netanyahu. Israeli diplomats in London likewise expressed private amazement (and relief) at the absence of pushback from Conservative ministers.[60]

I will examine the logic behind Starmer's decision not to challenge the Sunak government over its unequivocal support for Israel in Chapter Seven below. Its consequences were stark. Starmer's support for the Tories meant that, when it came to Gaza, government and opposition merged. This cross-party cartel came together in defiance of majority British opinion, in denial about Israeli atrocities, and oblivious to the genocidal incitement frothing forth from the most senior Israeli politicians.

An embarrassing and unruly intruder was soon knocking on the door and demanding to join this cross-party consensus.

Gaza and the Far Right

As a general rule the far right has defined itself as an insurgent force against British mainstream political parties. Israel's assault on Gaza was an exception. The far right threw itself behind the Sunak/Starmer policy of uncritical support for Netanyahu, differing from the British government only to accuse it of not being supportive enough.

Reform UK is the polished representative of the modern British far right. On October 19, 2023, Reform leader Nigel Farage wrote: 'Egypt and other Arab states won't take any refugees from Gaza because they don't want to import terrorism. If their neighbours aren't prepared to take any, I don't see why we should either'.[61]

Farage did not accurately express the concerns of the Arab States. They were not merely being asked to take in Palestinian refugees, but to participate in the ethnic cleansing of Gaza. When Palestinians had been displaced previously they were never allowed to return to their homes; this is why some 80 percent of Gaza's population consists of refugees and their descendants. Israeli leaders indicated from the outset their desire to force out the Gazan population—a policy that Prime Minister Netanyahu and US president Donald Trump later made explicit.[62]

Farage's incendiary claim that taking in Palestinian refugees was tantamount to importing terrorism migrated into conventional opinion. His views were soon being repeated in yet more invidious form in the mainstream media[63] and probably helped to frame policy for the Sunak and then Starmer governments.*

In December 2023, Nigel Farage again intervened in the politics of the Middle East. He complained that it was 'an insult to the Israelis' to suggest

* In February 2025 Starmer told parliament that his government was working to close what he called a 'loophole' allowing Palestinians from Gaza to enter the UK. He made the pledge after Conservative leader Kemi Badenoch raised the case of a family of six whose home in Gaza had been destroyed by an air strike and who then applied to join their relatives in the UK under the Ukraine Family Scheme. The family had originally been refused entry under the Sunak government. Becky Morton, 'PM Pledges to Close Loophole That Let Gazans Settle in UK', bbc.co.uk (12 February 2025).

that 'civilians had been targeted' in Gaza.[64] Israeli officials had repeatedly made clear their intention to target civilians and had already unleashed one of the most devastating bombing campaigns in the twenty-first century, in the course of which they had killed over 1,900 children in just twenty-five days.[65] I can find no evidence that this unprecedented killing disturbed Farage as much as the notion that somebody might censure Israel for its war crimes.

Meanwhile, Farage's lieutenant Richard Tice (then still formally the leader of Reform) fulminated against any and all expression of solidarity with the Palestinian people. He branded the Green Party as the 'Gaza Party' and Mayor of London Sadiq Khan as the 'Mayor of Gaza'.[66] The hundreds of thousands of British citizens demonstrating against Israeli atrocities were a 'vile pro Hamas mob' whose demonstrations were 'dominated' by 'antisemitic hate'.[67] Tice condemned the ICC as a 'total joke' and a 'laughing stock' in view of its issuance of arrest warrants for Israeli leaders.[68] 'Those calling for arms sales to Israel to be stopped', Tice declared for good measure, 'are Hamas' useful idiots'.[69]

English Defence League co-founder Tommy Robinson is the dominant figure at the thuggish end of Britain's far-right milieu. 'I stand with Israel', Robinson proclaimed. 'I stand against Jihad'.[70] 'Incase [*sic*] anyone was confused', he clarified, 'I wholeheartedly stand with Israel' and 'give zero fucks how many jihadist/Jew haters that upsets'.[71] Robinson explained that Palestinians 'just hate the Jews' because of 'their scriptures' and agreed with Tice's description of the pro-Palestine movement: 'islamists roam our streets every weekend, screaming for the destruction of Israel, harassing rabbis, waving isis flags, defacing monuments, even running campaigns for election over their combined hatred'.[72] Rishi Sunak's government and its supporters in the mainstream media concurred with Tommy Robinson's analysis, as I will demonstrate in Chapter Four.

This far-right support for Israel was the culmination of long-term trends. The US-led 'Global War on Terror' had accustomed large numbers of people to think of Muslims as security threats: terrorists, infiltrators, or rapists. British Muslims became the enemy within; a dangerous social element that had to be subjected to special forms of surveillance and control. The far right exploited these fears to its advantage as demonising Islam and Muslims became its primary venture. Again and again the dominant political parties failed to challenge such ideas. At the same time, antisemitism was gradually redefined to mean criticism of Israel rather than animus or discrimination against Jews. This conceptual hijacking allowed the far right to posture as an opponent of antisemitism. And if the far right opposed antisemitism—well, perhaps it wasn't racist after all.

In this way an unholy alliance of convenience congealed after October 7. It stretched from the centre left to the extremist right. It was an alliance that today leaves the leadership of both main British political parties open to the charge that they have aided and abetted what many respected experts have come to view as a genocide. The identical charge can be directed at British media, as I explore in the next chapter.

2

THERE ARE NO JOURNALISTS IN GAZA

> The thief holds a Gavel; the liar holds a journalism degree; and the butchers' knives are publicly funded.
>
> —*Mohammed El-Kurd*

IN THEORY a good reporter should tell the truth and hold power to account. British broadcasters and newspapers did not fulfil this function after October 7. Their failure to do so made it much easier for the Tory government and the Labour opposition to give their unconditional support for Israeli war crimes in Gaza.

Large sections of the media repeated the lies promoted by Israeli and British politicians. Some produced fresh lies of their own. They twisted their reports in favour of the Israeli cause. For a long time, reports of Israeli atrocities appeared either in muted form or not at all. Hamas atrocities were exaggerated or fabricated. Dissident voices were suppressed. Across much of the media spectrum a general implicit consensus emerged: Israelis count and Palestinians don't.

Deference to the Israeli Narrative

Israeli voices were rarely challenged, especially in the early months of the war, however disturbing their language or troubling their record. For example, the former Israeli diplomat Dan Gillerman told Sky News' Mark Austin: 'I am very puzzled by the constant concern which the world—and also Britain, I must say, Mark—is showing for the Palestinian people, and is actually showing for these horrible, inhuman animals who have done the worst atrocities that this century has seen'.[1] Austin did not challenge this language. It would be invidious to single out Austin, a decent reporter: few if any British journalists did so during the period after October 7.

Interviewers withheld vital information. Israel's ambassador to the UK Tzipi Hotovely was interviewed and cited many times in the month after October 7. As the representative of a close British ally at such a desperate time, this was as it should be. Ms. Hotovely does, however, have a well-documented history of supremacist views and naked anti-Palestinian racism. In the influential Israeli newspaper *Haaretz*, she has been described as 'an unabashed Islamophobe and religious fundamentalist who denies the existence of the Palestinian people and supports annexation of the entire West Bank and Jewish control of the Temple Mount', as well as 'the proud spokeswoman of the ideological hardcore pro-settler community in Israel'.[2]

Not once during these many interviews, according to a study by the Centre for Media Monitoring (an offshoot of the Muslim Council of Britain), was Hotovely confronted with or asked to explain her racist statements.[3] When she made false or fabricated claims, they were almost never corrected.[4] During an interview with Sky News' Kay Burley on October 16, 2023, Hotovely alleged that Hamas 'fired on babies and beheaded them' on October 7, and that 'everyone saw the horrific footages of those beheaded babies'. Burley did not challenge this.[5] These assertions were false, as the next chapter sets out. In defence of Burley, who is often a robust interviewer, Hotovely's claims were widely treated as fact at the time: to engage them with even a modicum of scepticism was to invite charges of atrocity denial.

During an interview with BBC News on October 29, 2023, Hotovely stated: 'We're not targeting civilians in the south [of Gaza]. The only thing that has been targeted in the south is military targets, so it's very clear that Israel is not targeting civilians. Israel is just targeting the military machine of Hamas'.[6] This was nonsense as Chapter Eight will show. There was no pushback.

The *Daily Express* featured a ninety-five-year-old Israeli reservist called Ezra Yachin, telling readers that 'his mission goes beyond the traditional duties of a soldier—he has been enlisted to boost morale among the troops by sharing his incredible life story, filled with resilience, hope, and the indomitable spirit that helped shape Israel'.[7]

It neglected to tell readers that Yachin had been a member of the Lehi, a Zionist terrorist group,[8] or that he was present at Deir Yassin, a notorious massacre of Palestinians during the Nakba.[9] The Lehi, also known as the Stern Gang, claimed the lives of many British soldiers as well as the assassination of the British minister to the Middle East, Lord Moyne.* Lehi assaulted the British police station in Haifa, killing four and wounding 140 in what has been called 'the world's first true truck bomb.'[10] It tried to blow up Whitehall, leaving twenty-four sticks of explosives at the Colonial Office, and would have succeeded but for a technical fault.[11] Such was its enmity for Britain that during World War Two Lehi contemplated an alliance with Nazi Germany.[12] Regardless, the *Daily Express* declared that 'Ezra Yachin's life experiences serve as a testament to the strength of the human spirit'. We wrote to *Express* editor Tom Hunt asking why the paper had omitted any reference to Yachin's gruesome record as a member of a terrorist organisation responsible for the killing of British soldiers and police officers as well as Arab civilians. We received no reply.

It is astonishing that one of the great titles in British newspaper history could have described a former member of a terror gang that killed so many British soldiers in these glowing terms. There was, moreover, a real story here rather than the motivational homily presented in Israeli and British papers. In order to boost morale as its troops entered Gaza, Israel had disinterred a former participant in one of the most notorious Nakba massacres. This was a portent of Israel's genocidal intent. The British media ignored the warning.

* Lord Moyne's two killers were apprehended by the British and hanged. After their bodies were returned by Egypt to Israel in 1975 as part of a prisoner exchange, they were awarded a state funeral with full military honours. See Ray Esten, 'The Assassination of Walter Edward Guinness -Lord Moyne – 1944', theirishstory.com (3 June 2021).

Double Standards

Twenty-four Israeli soldiers were killed in Hamas attacks in Gaza on January 22, 2024. This date was instantly christened the 'deadliest day' for Israel since October 7. As Professor Des Freedman has shown, the same phrase was employed by the BBC and ITV News and by Reuters and the AFP.[13] The *Daily Telegraph*,[14] *Sun*,[15] *Guardian*,[16] *Evening Standard*,[17] *Financial Times*,[18] and *Independent*[19] followed suit. Several published names and prominent photographs of the dead soldiers as well as words from Prime Minister Netanyahu.

On the same day, almost two hundred Palestinians were killed in Gaza. There were no headlines for these deaths. At most they were noted in passing as part of daily round-ups of events. Freedman found that media outlets used the phrase 'deadliest day' 856 times between October 7, 2023, and January 25, 2024. Not one of these usages referred directly to evidence of Palestinian deaths.[20]

There was a 'media consensus that only Israelis are the victims of the "deadliest days" in the region and not Palestinians', Freedman showed, 'despite the latter accounting for 95% of deaths since 7 October'. Freedman speculated that this illustrative example of 'the unequal and profoundly distorted coverage of this war' reflected 'a deep-rooted idea in the western media that the lives of Israelis and Palestinians are not of equal value'.

Media Bigotry

Some British journalists displayed open contempt for Palestinian life. *Mail on Sunday* columnist Dan Hodges said that he did not want a 'single penny' of British taxpayers' money to be spent on reconstructing Gaza 'until every Hamas terrorist is either dead or in jail'. When he was asked on the social media platform X (formerly Twitter) whether he agreed that '[i]n the meantime the civilian population—including hundreds of thousands of children—can just go to hell', Hodges replied: 'Yes. Basically'.[21]

'We need to face reality: much of Muslim culture is in the grip of a death cult that sacralises bloodshed. Not all, but many Muslims are brainwashed by it. That is a big part of the problem', tweeted *Jewish Chronicle* editor

Jake Wallis Simons in the aftermath of October 7.[22] Untroubled by these remarks, the BBC invited him as a panellist onto its flagship political show *Question Time*.

The tweet has since been deleted, but Wallis Simons remains greatly in demand on many British media outlets. It is reasonable to surmise that had any British journalist made the same remark about Jews or Jewish culture it would have marked the end of their media career, and rightly so.

'Admitting Gazan Refugees Would Be Proof That Britain Has a Death Wish', ran one *Telegraph* headline. The sub-head informed readers: 'We have no idea how many Palestinians support their murdering, raping masters'.[23] In the *Daily Express* Richard Ferrer described the Hamas attack as 'plain and simple historic Islamic bloodlust, passed down through the generations from birth. An ever-present cancer, lurking in the shadows, now stands fully exposed, its medieval ambition shocking to the core—the genocide of the Jewish people'. Ferrer, editor of *Jewish News*, went on: 'The Gaza Strip will never be the same again. A regime-change invasion is surely hours away and, with it, a surely futile attempt to separate Hamas from its citizens. The cancer is too deeply entwined within the body'.[24] This last remark echoed Israeli president Herzog's notorious comment, already quoted, that 'it is an entire nation out there that is responsible'. Following criticism, Ferrer's term 'Islamic bloodlust' was changed to 'Islamist bloodlust'.[25]

Fathom, house journal of the Israel lobby group BICOM (Britain Israel Communications and Research Centre), published an article in October 2023 urging the imposition of 'a dramatic, continuous, and strict siege over Gaza'. This would involve cutting 'the supply of energy, water and diesel to the Strip'. The author explained: 'The people should be told that they have two choices; to stay and to starve, or to leave'.[26]

I note this article from a little-known magazine because of its author: a retired Israeli major general named Giora Eiland. His thoughts foreshadowed the so-called 'Generals' Plan', published in late September 2024.[27] That plan, which the Israeli military put into effect, involved ethnically cleansing Gaza's northern half and then starving out anyone who remained, who would be assumed to be Palestinian fighters. Though the suggestion came from a group of senior reservists, it was presented by Eiland and many credited the idea to him.[28]

At least the editors of *Fathom* made it clear they disagreed with the article, stating that Eiland's starvation policy was 'wrong in principle, wrong for building international alliances, and wrong in terms of the battle for global public opinion'.[29] But the fact that a version of what became the Generals' Plan was first floated by its architect in a British outlet as far back as October 2023 is, nevertheless, significant. Eiland's remarks in *Fathom* were subsequently cited by the South African legal team in their application charging Israel with genocide.[30]

The pro-Israeli writer Douglas Murray toyed with the idea of ethnic cleansing in *The Spectator* magazine shortly after October 7: 'Maybe they will finally put an end to this insoluble nightmare, raze Hamas to the ground, or clear all the Palestinians from that benighted strip', he mused, adding that '[i]t could be a good time to do it'.[31] Mass forcible population transfer is a war crime under the Fourth Geneva Convention.[32] Unlike the editors of *Fathom* with respect to the Eiland proposition, I can find no evidence that *The Spectator* clarified that they considered ethnic cleansing to be wrong.*

Ahead of publication of this book I wrote to Douglas Murray to give him a chance to reply to criticism, but received a dismissive response. I also wrote to Michael Gove (who was *not* responsible for the decision to publish the Douglas Murray comments: he was appointed editor of *The Spectator* after the fall of the Conservative government in July 2024). Gove wrote back: 'Douglas Murray is a brave and brilliant writer. *The Spectator* is proud to publish him. We do not censor or censure our writers. Upholding free speech is a good in itself and needs no defence. But, as it happens, Douglas has always made clear he believes humanity is better served by supporting democracies against death cults'.

* In a January 2025 article for the *New York Post*, Murray doubled down on his advocacy for transferring the Palestinian population out of Gaza, writing: 'the reason why the war shouldn't be over is because it cannot be over until the people who started the war have lost. And are forced to realize that they have lost. That is why I was so encouraged this past week by comments from President Trump where he talked about clearing people from the Gaza Strip'. Murray denied that this proposal constituted 'ethnic cleansing', saying: 'it is no such thing. Recommending that a population might move from where it is living is not the same thing as killing it'. Douglas Murray, 'Douglas Murray: Gaza Must Reject Terror of Hamas for War to End', *New York Post* (31 January 2025).

Media Ignorance

Many problems in British reporting were the result of ignorance. Once Israel's destruction of Gaza was underway, Sky News gave air time to the defence analyst Philip Ingram, who explained to viewers that the West Bank is 'occupied by the Palestinians inside the area we have as Israel'.

On another occasion Ingram produced a map which presented the Golan Heights as part of Israel, with no explanation that the area was internationally recognised as being part of Syria.* When Labour's shadow chancellor Rachel Reeves told BBC *Today* that 'Gaza is not occupied by Israel', presenter Nick Robinson allowed the error to pass without demurral.[33]

Most Western journalists are liberal-minded people who consider themselves humane and decent. They would be angered and upset by any suggestion that they are apologising for, enabling or making life easy for war criminals. But many are open to this charge. Part of the explanation is that many British reporters know little of what they are writing about when they leave central London. Their foreign travel tends to be confined to the pack of political journalists who accompany the prime minister on overseas visits, or European or American holidays.

As we will see, in so far as they travelled to Israel it was often on trips as guests of lobby groups. Such reporters tend to be ignorant of the history of Israel, the structure of the occupation, and the wider Middle East. The Jerusalem correspondent for a famous title told me that it takes about a year to get enough of an idea of the bureaucracy of occupation to take on Israeli spokespeople on equal terms.

Six weeks after October 7, I visited the shop of Mahmoud Muna, a Palestinian bookseller in occupied East Jerusalem.** He told me that he'd

---

* The UN Security Council considers Israel's 1981 annexation of the Golan 'null and void'. See: UN Security Council Resolution 497 (17 December 1981).

** Mahmoud's bookstore was raided by undercover Israeli forces at the beginning of February 2025. He and his nephew Ahmed were taken into custody and charged with 'violating public order'. All books with Palestinian flags on them were reportedly seized; among the volumes taken and later returned were Banksy's *Wall and Piece* and *Gaza in Crisis* by Noam Chomsky and Ilan Pappé. Mahmoud's brother said that police examined an English-language copy of *Haaretz*, with images of released hostages on the front, and just been visited by a reporter from a well-known TV channel whose trip had ended and who wanted something about the region to read for the flight home. Mahmood offered recent scholarly works but the journalist rejected them in favour of a basic primer on Israel and Palestine. This was at the end, not the start, of her trip. There's no way this correspondent could have possessed the knowledge or understanding to report accurately and fairly. However well-meaning, the reporter was doomed to be a plaything of the Israeli authorities. Her employer, who takes a pro-Israeli line, is unlikely to have been worried, and might even have preferred it that way.

While the journalists and politicians cited above are more likely to be guilty of ignorance or naivety than of deliberate misrepresentation, it's notable that the resulting misunderstandings almost always favour Israel. This isn't surprising: lack of independent knowledge encourages conformity to the established line and makes a reporter more open to persuasion by special interests. In Britain, elite wisdom on the Palestine question and the balance of lobbying influence both skew towards Israel.

Indeed it has been painfully clear since October 2023 that those dominating the national conversation on Gaza lack the knowledge to scrutinise Israeli claims. British TV and radio studios are chock full of loudmouth presenters with big salaries but negligible understanding. Experts who have mastered the history of the Israel-Palestine dispute tend to be excluded from public discussion. The most telling example is Avi Shlaim, by common consent one of the finest historians of our time. He is an emeritus professor and fellow of St Anthony's College at the University of Oxford, and a fellow of the British Academy. His books on the Israel-Palestine conflict are standard scholarly works.

---

told the owners that it constituted incitement. Israeli human rights group B'Tselem stated: 'The attempt to crush the Palestinian people includes the harassment and arrest of intellectuals. . . . Israel must immediately release [Mahmoud and Ahmed] from detention and stop persecuting Palestinian intellectuals.' Emma Graham-Harrison and Quique Kierszenbaum, 'Israeli Police Raid Jerusalem Bookshops and Arrest Palestinian Owners', *The Guardian* (10 February 2025). See also David Issacharoff, 'In Israel, Selling Books About Palestinians Is Now "Incitement to Terrorism"', *Haaretz* (10 February 2025).

Shlaim, who defines himself as an 'Arab Jew', was born in Baghdad.[34] His family emigrated to Israel shortly after its establishment and as a young man he served in the Israel Defence Forces. He then came to Britain, where he made his reputation as one of a group of scholars (the so-called 'new historians') who have put forward a critical interpretation of the history of Zionism and Israel. I wrote to Professor Shlaim as follows: 'I would have thought the BBC and other media outlets would have wanted to interview you on a regular basis to give your interpretation of events. Am I right in thinking you have never been on the BBC since October 7?'

The answer came back: 'The BBC have not asked to interview me even once since the start of the Gaza war. I cannot remember when was the last time but it was many years ago. Al Jazeera English and Arabic have interviewed me often about the war'. One can only speculate why the BBC and other British broadcasters will not invite Professor Shlaim into their studios. Professor Ilan Pappé at Exeter University, a fellow Israeli 'new historian', is another eminent scholar who is apparently not allowed on the BBC. I wrote to the BBC asking why it hadn't invited Shlaim and Pappé. It ignored my question.

The expertise of Shlaim and Pappé is beyond question. My guess is that their reputations as critics of Israel make them uncomfortable prospects as guests, because they can be expected to challenge the prevailing orthodoxy and as a consequence to draw criticism from the pro-Israel lobby. But it is surely the duty of national broadcasters to present all points of view, all the more so from those who bring the authority of high scholarship. BBC impartiality rules indeed insist on this.

British Media and the Pro-Israel Lobby

Reporters know that, when it comes to Israel, any mistake or wrong word will trigger complaints to their bosses and might cost them their job. Reporters or presenters who cast Israel in a poor light get targeted. The popular LBC presenter Sangita Myska abruptly left the channel after she challenged an Israeli government spokesman, Avi Hyman. There's been speculation that she was sacked as a result of that exchange, although that has been denied by LBC; Myska herself is bound by a non-disclosure agreement.[35]

Whatever lies behind the Myska mystery, there's a long history of journalists who have been targeted by Israel and its allies. In 2001, *Times* correspondent Sam Kiley took the brave, principled, and highly unusual step of resigning from the paper because of interference with his work on the Middle East. Writing during the Second Intifada, Kiley recorded that

> the *Times'* foreign editor and other middle managers flew into hysterical terror every time a pro-Israel lobbying group wrote in with a quibble or complaint, and then usually took their side against their own correspondent—deleting words and phrases from the lexicon to rob its reporters of the ability to make sense of what was going on. So, I was told, I should not refer to 'assassinations' of Israel's opponents, nor to 'extrajudicial killings or executions'. The professional Israeli hits in which at least four entirely innocent civilians have been killed were, if I had to write about them at all, just 'killings', or best of all—'targeted killings'. The fact that the Jewish colonies on the West Bank and in Gaza were illegal under international law because they violated the Geneva Convention was not disputed by my editors—but any reference to this fact was 'gratuitous'. The leader writers, meanwhile, were happy to repeat the canard that Palestinian gunmen were using children as human shields.

Kiley noted that *The Times* was owned by Rupert Murdoch's News International and that Murdoch was a close friend of Ariel Sharon, Israel's prime minister. He wrote:

> No pro-Israel lobbyist ever dreamed of having such power over a great national newspaper. They didn't need to. Murdoch's executives were so scared of irritating him that, when I pulled off a little scoop by tracking, interviewing and photographing the unit in the Israeli army which killed Mohammed al-Durrah, the 12-year-old boy whose death was captured on film and became the iconic image of the conflict, I was asked to file the piece 'without mentioning the dead kid'. After that conversation, I was left wordless, so I quit.[36]

Judging by the *Times'* coverage of the obliteration of Gaza, nothing much has changed.* Today Kiley recalls one consequence of his article:

> I was happy to make new enemies among some of the British upper classes when, after my resignation, some would mistake my criticisms of Israeli policy for me being a fellow antisemite. I loudly left a shire dinner party when one vile bigot launched into an antisemitic tirade under the pretence of support for Palestinian human rights. That there are bigots and morons in the world does not mean we should censor ourselves for fear of encouraging their stupidity. We can't cure that, but we can help to fix ignorance. It's a pity that journalists lose sight of this. The fourth estate should be made up of trouble makers who use the truth as the pin to pop pomposity and enlighten us all. Making editorial judgments is nuanced, there's no obvious set of rules so when lobbyists set the rules to suit their own agenda—many journalists cling to those rules like life rafts.[37]

Sixteen years ago I documented an attempt to bully *The Guardian*, organised with the aid of the Israeli embassy, after it published an article by its correspondent Chris McGreal comparing Israel to South African apartheid.[38] Then *Guardian* editor Alan Rusbridger told me how Community Security Trust chairman Gerald Ronson sat down on his sofa without taking off his coat and announced: 'I'm in favour of free speech but there is a line which can't be crossed and, as far as I'm concerned, you've crossed it, and you must stop this'.

He went on to accuse *The Guardian* of being responsible for antisemitic attacks in Britain. *The Guardian* was not the only newspaper to come under pressure. Rusbridger told me: 'There are a lot of newspaper and broadcasting editors who have told me that they just don't think it's worth the hassle to challenge the Israeli line. They've had enough'. Another newspaper editor

---

* There is one remarkable exception. In June 2024, Catherine Philp and Gabrielle Weiniger unpacked Israeli claims about Hamas sexual violence on October 7. Their investigation is in such sharp contrast to the rest of the paper's reporting that one wonders how they got it published. I salute them. Catherine Philp and Gabrielle Weiniger, 'Israel Says Hamas Weaponised Rape. Does the Evidence Add Up?' *The Times* (7 June 2024).

confirmed to me this was true: 'I have taken on every vested interest in this country, but not this one. They come at you from above and from below. Through the proprietor and through the advertisers.'[39]

In 2002, the Israeli government press officer Danny Seaman boasted that he had forced *The Guardian* to move correspondent Suzanne Goldenberg after she had been transferred from Israel to Washington. 'We simply boycotted them', said Seaman; 'the editorial boards got the message and replaced their people'.[40] Seaman compared one BBC documentary about Israeli nuclear weapons, entitled *Israel's Secret Weapon*, to 'the worst of Nazi propaganda'.

One journalist who carries the scars of battling the pro-Israel lobby is the BBC's senior international correspondent Orla Guerin. When she was based in the Middle East two decades ago the Israeli government complained to the BBC that Guerin had a 'deep-seated bias against Israel' and showed 'total identification with the goals and methods of Palestinian terror groups'.[41] On one occasion, in an appalling, unsubstantiated charge, they linked her reporting from the Middle East to the rise of antisemitic incidents in Britain. The BBC stood up for her, as did the British government. It may be significant that a year after the worst of the attacks Guerin was awarded an MBE.

Israeli cabinet minister Natan Sharansky, one of the most determined of Guerin's persecutors, took the award especially badly: 'It is very sad that something as important as antisemitism is not taken into consideration when issuing this award, especially in Britain where the incidents of antisemitism are on the rise'. Officially sanctioned smears like Sharansky's help explain why so many journalists back away from confronting the influence of the pro-Israel lobby. All the more so because pressure from the pro-Israel lobby is even greater today while the BBC has shown itself less resistant, in large part because supporters of Israel have the ear of both main political parties as well as powerful advocates in the press.

Jeremy Bowen, international editor of BBC News, is another reporter who has been savaged by Israel's advocates. The campaign against Bowen had its origins in an essay he wrote for the BBC website to mark the fortieth anniversary of the 1967 Arab-Israel War. Though many people viewed Bowen's essay as a fair and balanced account, erring if anything on the side of conventional wisdom, this was not how Israel partisans saw it. The Zionist Federation and the American pro-Israel media watchdog CAMERA subjected Bowen's article to line-by-line scrutiny. They identified twenty-four instances of alleged bias in his online article and a further four in a subsequent report he filed from the Israeli settlement Har Homa. These complaints were rejected by the BBC's Editorial Complaints Unit, so the complainants appealed to the BBC Trust.[42]

The BBC Trust found that Bowen had breached three accuracy guidelines and one impartiality guideline in his online report, as well as one accuracy guideline in his radio piece. The Zionist Federation called at once for Bowen to be sacked, branding his position 'untenable', while adding the same charge made against Guerin: that what they called Bowen's 'biased coverage of Israel' had been a 'significant contributor to the recent rise in antisemitic incidents in the UK to record levels'.[43] Meanwhile, CAMERA claimed that the BBC Trust had exposed Bowen's 'unethical' approach to his work and insisted that the BBC must now take 'concrete steps' to rectify its 'chronically biased reporting'[44] of the Middle East.

These denunciations might have been justified if the BBC Trust had found Bowen guilty of egregious bias. In fact he was criticised for what were at best matters of opinion. Most of the complaints were found to have no merit, and where changes were made they altered the meaning very little.* Bowen had written an article the previous week for *The Jewish Chronicle* containing most of the sentences that had led the BBC Trust to conclude there had been a breach of accuracy and impartiality. They could still be found on the *Jewish Chronicle*'s website when the BBC Trust condemned

---

* On the grounds of 'accuracy', Bowen's reference to the 1967 Arab-Israel War as a chance to 'finish the unfinished business of Israel's independence war of 1948' was amended to define 'the unfinished business' as 'the capture of East Jerusalem'. On the same grounds, a reference to Zionism's 'innate instinct to push out the frontier' was amended to 'the tendency with Zionism to push out the frontier'. Israel's expansion of its settlements being 'in defiance of everyone's interpretation of international law except its own' was amended to 'in defiance of almost all countries' interpretation of international law except its own'. BBC Trust, 'Editorial Standards Findings: Appeals and Other Editorial Issues to the Trust Considered by the Editorial Standards Committee', *ESC 3 March Bulletin* (3 March 2009), pp. 103–5, 107–8. See also Dimbleby, 'Fearful'.

Bowen.[45] Since October 2023, Bowen and Guerin have been mainstays of BBC reporting on Gaza. They and their colleague Lyse Doucet are hardened, knowledgeable, and hugely experienced war correspondents.

In an article for *Index on Censorship* the veteran BBC broadcaster Jonathan Dimbleby came to Bowen's defence: 'You don't have to search far on the web to find Zionist publications, lobby groups and bloggers all over the world using distorted versions of the report to justify their ill-founded prejudice that the BBC has a deep-seated and long-standing bias against the state of Israel'.[46]

This saga demonstrated the cowardice of the BBC Trust as well as the energy and opportunism of the pro-Israel lobby. It foreshadowed much that would come later. Dimbleby then became a third senior BBC figure to face criticism. His article for *Index on Censorship* itself brought a complaint from the Zionist Federation, which argued that Dimbleby's comments made him unfit to host the BBC's *Any Questions*. Experiences like this, and there are many of them, serve as a cautionary tale for anyone approaching the subject of Israel and may help explain the reporting failures that have long been a structural feature of the BBC when it comes to Israel.

Analysis by media scholars Greg Philo and Mike Berry around that time established that BBC reporting favoured Israel. Israeli narratives featured more prominently in TV news than Palestinian ones. Israel was painted as responding to violence, rather than instigating it. Philo and Berry highlighted the lack of context and erasure of Palestinian perspectives, showing that the kind of language used to describe violence against Israelis was rarely used to describe violence against Palestinians. 'While the broadcast media give a clear account of the Israeli perspective on this conflict', the researchers concluded, 'many journalists and especially in the BBC still find great difficulty in doing the same for the Palestinians'.[47] Philo and Berry's analysis two decades ago applies just as well to recent BBC reporting from Gaza. If anything, BBC structural bias has got worse.

BBC Reporting of Gaza

In June 2025 the Centre for Media Monitoring (CfMM) published a detailed study of the BBC's Gaza coverage during the first twelve months of the violence.[48] Its analysis showed that the corporation operated two sets of rules: one for Palestinians and another for Israelis. The BBC employed the word 'massacre' almost eighteen times more often in relation to Israeli than to Palestinian victims—and never used the term in headlines about Israeli atrocities. BBC correspondents or presenters applied the term 'butcher' 220 times for actions against Israelis but just once for actions against Palestinians. The report showed that the BBC routinely used passive language that obscured Israeli responsibility ('Airstrike on Gaza School Kills At Least 15 People'). The corporation was more than twice as likely to interview an Israeli than a Palestinian. The average Israeli death received thirty-three times more coverage across BBC articles, and nineteen times more across TV and radio, than the average Palestinian death. Israeli deaths were reported in more emotive terms, with victims far more likely to be humanised by details about their names, family background, jobs, and lives. One especially telling example of the BBC's two-tier system of reporting concerns Palestinian journalists. At the time the CfMM report was written the Committee to Protect Journalists listed 167 journalists killed in Gaza by Israel. Just eleven of these deaths (6 percent) had been reported by the BBC's English news service. In telling contrast, the BBC's English-language articles had reported on the deaths of seven out of the sixteen journalists (42 percent) killed in Ukraine since the Russian invasion in 2022.

Above all the BBC failed to provide the context that would have enabled its audience to interpret Israel's campaign of destruction in Gaza. Across tens of thousands of news items, the occupation was mentioned just fourteen times as providing background to the violence. Israel's settlements were hardly referenced at all as an explanatory factor; nor was the blockade Israel had imposed on Gaza for seventeen years leading up to October 7. History was erased. Even as a majority of Gaza's inhabitants are refugees from the 1948 expulsion or their descendants, the Nakba was barely mentioned.[49] The BBC also barely covered the Israeli military's 'Hannibal Directive'. This is a shocking omission because, as I will explain in the next chapter, it is essential to a full understanding of the events of October 7. The directive licenced the killing of Israeli citizens and soldiers, often by Apache helicopter fire, rather than allowing them to be captured. Its application has been documented by the United Nations and well reported in the Israeli press, including a major investigation by the Israeli newspaper *Haaretz*, but ignored by the BBC.

Equally striking is that, barring one passing mention, the BBC did not report on Israel's notorious 'Dahiya doctrine'. I give that dark subject close attention in Chapter Four. This BBC failure is negligent because Israel's destruction of Gaza cannot be understood without knowing that Israel's established military doctrine licenses the indiscriminate obliteration of civilian infrastructure such as schools, hospitals, and universities. As with the Hannibal Directive, the subject has been covered seriously in the Israeli press. That the BBC did not explain the Dahiya doctrine to its audience was a consequential reporting failure. It is hard to believe that it was not deliberate.

The CfMM report also shows that the BBC has failed to adequately report evidence of Israel's genocidal intent. Incredibly the BBC seems *never* to have reported Israeli prime minister Benjamin Netanyahu's references to 'Amalek', seen by many as the invocation of a divine command to annihilate an enemy nation, until Jeremy Bowen briefly mentioned it in an article in June 2025.[50] This failure is especially baffling in view of the fact that two of these references were cited by South Africa in its application to The Hague. This omission forms part of a pattern of missing evidence or credible charges of genocide. On more than a hundred occasions BBC presenters shut down genocide claims made by BBC guests.* It is also significant

---

* At the end of October 2023 presenter Kirsty Wark slapped down UN special rapporteur Francesca Albanese after she spoke of potential genocide on BBC *Newsnight*, stating: 'Can we just be quite clear that genocide is not what's happening here'—before turning this statement into a supposed question. More recently, interviewer Matthew Amroliwala responded, 'I don't want to go down the avenue around genocide' when a Palestinian interviewee spoke of '15 months of genocidal assault'. (CfMM, *BBC on Gaza-Israel*, pp. 73–75). See: BBC *Newsnight* (30 October 2023), viewable at the Internet Archive, https://archive.org/details/BBCNEWS_20231030_223000_Newsnight/start/1320/end/1380; post by @I_amMukhtar on X (15 January 2025), https://x.com/I_amMukhtar/status/1879588775766216816. There are many other examples. We wrote to the BBC giving the organisation an opportunity to respond. Charlotte Morgan, senior head of communications at BBC News, replied: 'Interviewees have consistently raised the issue of genocide on the BBC. The job of interviewers is to question, and sometimes challenge, their interviewees. We do this consistently and impartially. Thus your commentary is neither fair nor accurate'.

that genocide scholars have not been invited on the BBC. 'I'm invited to comment by news organisations across the world', the University of Sussex emeritus professor Martin Shaw reflected, 'but not British'.[51]

The report documenting BBC bias was launched in parliament in June this year. Not a single journalist from Britain's mainstream media reported the event. To his credit Richard Burgess, director of news content at the BBC, was present to defend the corporation's coverage. I asked him why the BBC had ignored references to the Hannibal Directive, the Dahiya doctrine, and genocidal statements by Israeli leaders, especially Netanyahu's invocation of Amalek. I also took the opportunity to ask why the BBC had only covered the deaths of 6 percent of Palestinian journalists. Finally, I asked Burgess why the BBC had never asked University of Oxford professor Avi Shlaim onto one of its programmes. I suggested to Burgess that these failures of reporting made him and the BBC complicit.

Burgess didn't account for why the BBC had ignored the Hannibal Directive, Dahiya doctrine, and the slaughter of so many Palestinian journalists, appearing to excuse himself on the basis that he was not an expert on the Middle East. I told him that if he was not qualified to answer questions, the BBC should have sent along someone who was. The journalist Hamza Yusuf of *Declassified UK*, which has reported extensively on British military assistance to Israel, later asked Burgess why the BBC had not given attention to British spy planes operating over Gaza from RAF base Akrotiri on Cyprus. Burgess' answer was even more troubling: 'I don't think we should overplay the UK's contribution to what's happening in Israel'.[52]

Since the BBC's coverage of Britain's role in providing military assistance to Israel during the destruction of Gaza can most generously be described as patchy,[53] it is impossible to know on what basis Burgess made this assessment. Burgess is the executive answerable for the BBC's Gaza coverage, on a salary of £200,000 a year. His responses were embarrassing. It became plain that the BBC's news director was too ignorant of even basic facts to properly make even elementary decisions about the corporation's coverage. It is therefore impossible to avoid the judgment that the BBC's coverage of Gaza has been a reporting disaster and a moral calamity. Out of fairness to Burgess and the BBC it should be noted that much of the mainstream newspaper coverage was even worse.

The Myth of Impartiality

Defenders of British media like Richard Burgess will often point out that they receive criticism from both sides in the Israel/Palestine conflict as evidence they are achieving balance.[54] This claim ignores the existence of a powerful, well-funded lobby in Europe and the US that exists largely to bring pressure on media organisations from the Israeli side. While attempts to bring pressure from the Palestinian side may sometimes be coordinated, pro-Palestinian groups have nothing like the resources of their pro-Israel counterparts.

This defence also wrongly implies that balance is achieved by picking a spot half-way between two positions. Journalism should be guided by the facts. Reporting of Gaza abounded with examples of bogus 'two sides-ism'. Jane Corbin's in many ways admirable hour-long *Panorama* documentary, *October 7th: One Year On*, was a case in point.[55]

'This is the story of two families in Israel and two in Gaza, living through a year of war', Corbin tells us at the start. Just under four minutes is taken up with history and political analysis. The remainder of the film divides roughly equally between the Israeli families and general descriptions of Palestinian aggression/Israeli suffering on the one hand, and the Palestinian families and general descriptions of Israeli aggression/Palestinian suffering on the other.

On a superficial level we have balance. But around 1,200 Israelis and foreign nationals were killed on October 7. At the time the film was made, as Corbin points out, more than forty thousand Palestinians had already been killed in Gaza—a ratio of at least thirty-three to one. In November it was reported that more than 40 percent of the Palestinian dead verified by the UN's Human Rights Office were children,[56] compared to 3 percent of those killed on October 7.[57] The ratio of reported Palestinian to Israeli child deaths was about 315 to 1.[58]

Panorama, as is always the case with the BBC, insists on qualifying the Palestinian figures with the caveat, 'according to the Hamas-run Health Ministry'. The Gazan Health Ministry's figures in previous conflicts have been subject to rigorous analysis by multiple international bodies and found to be reliable.[59] 'Our assessments are very close to theirs, and in some cases, we even had higher figures', a spokesperson for the Office of the United

Nations High Commissioner for Human Rights told *Le Monde* in October 2024.[60] An Israeli intelligence official told *VICE News* in January 2024 that the Israeli intelligence services consider the numbers produced by the Gaza Health Ministry to be 'generally credible'.[61]

The destruction of large parts of the Gazan health system by Israel made the collection of statistics increasingly difficult. A peer-reviewed study by researchers from the London School of Hygiene and Tropical Medicine, published in *The Lancet*, concluded that the Health Ministry was underreporting 'traumatic injury deaths' by approximately 41 percent.[62] Once deaths resulting from lack of access to medicines and healthcare are included, it's possible the final Palestinian toll of dead and injured will far exceed the figures published so far.

In the face of these statistics, the BBC policy of suggesting equivalence of suffering and brutality between the two sides engages in what some might interpret as a fundamentally racist arithmetic.

Israeli Denials

A recurring problem for the BBC—and many other news outlets—is how it deals with Israeli claims and denials. Even when it doesn't lead with the Israeli version of events, the BBC almost always gives them considerable prominence.

Perhaps the most notorious example of the Israeli authorities successfully seeding doubt in the face of overwhelming evidence is the killing of Al Jazeera journalist, Shireen Abu Akleh. Abu Akleh was shot in the head while reporting from Jenin on May 11, 2022. She was wearing a press vest and there was no fighting in the area at that moment.

Within hours the Israeli prime minister Naftali Bennett said: 'It appears likely that armed Palestinians—who were firing indiscriminately at the time—were responsible for the unfortunate death of the journalist'.[63] A later study of initial media coverage in the West said that it 'essentially minimized the facts and testimonies that were provided by eyewitnesses, creating a false sense of equivalence and probability between the story presented by Al Jazeera and the story presented by Israel'.[64]

The New York Times was an egregious example. Its headline carefully avoided pointing the finger of blame: 'Shireen Abu Akleh, Trailblazing Palestinian Journalist, Dies at 51'.[65] The accompanying article said that 'Al Jazeera and the Palestinian Health Ministry' were 'blaming Israeli forces for her death', adding: 'The Israeli military said on Twitter that "Palestinian armed gunfire" might have been responsible'.[66]

There were rational grounds at this point for doubting the Israeli claim. The circumstances of Abu Akleh's killing belied the Israeli explanation, for which Israel supplied no evidence. More broadly, Israeli authorities had a long history of making exculpatory claims that turned out to be untrue. This track record of propaganda dated all the way back to the 1950s when Israeli officials falsely attributed Palestinian displacement in 1947–48 to Arab radio broadcasts that had supposedly instructed the population to evacuate,[67] through the 1967 Arab-Israel War when Israeli foreign minister Abba Eban falsely claimed that Egypt had struck first,[68] to Israel's 2008 assault on Gaza when the Israeli military falsely denied having deployed white phosphorus, and the 2018 March of Return protests in Gaza when the Israeli military published 'deceptively edited' video footage to discredit Razan al-Najjar, a Palestinian paramedic killed by Israeli fire.[69]

But the *New York Times* article did not mention any of this. Readers were thus presented with two contradictory accounts and no basis for choosing between them. Had the *Times* provided a full and accurate picture of events, the article may have provoked public alarm at the prima facie murder of a journalist by a US ally. Instead, the article's uncritical amplification of Israeli denials muddied the waters, neutralising the story's potential to galvanise public concern.

As Palestinian mourners processed through Jerusalem, some of them holding Abu Akleh's coffin aloft, others waving Palestinian flags, the Israeli police attacked. They savagely beat unarmed mourners and pallbearers with batons, so that at one point Abu Akleh's coffin nearly fell to the ground.[70] The BBC reported that the coffin had been 'jostled as Israeli police and Palestinians clashed'.[71] Abu Akleh was later buried at a Christian cemetery on Mount Zion.

Israeli authorities eventually acknowledged there was a 'high probability' an Israeli soldier had shot Abu Akleh 'by mistake'.[72] A UN report concluded the Al Jazeera journalist was the victim of 'lethal force' deployed 'without justification' by Israel.[73] Again and again the Israeli authorities distort, obfuscate, and straightforwardly lie. Their deceitful statements are given prominence by Western media. By the time Israel's denials and distortions have unravelled, the news agenda has moved on and the potential for Israeli misconduct to arouse public indignation abroad has dissipated.

I attended the memorial service for Abu Akleh at St Bride's church in London. Najwan Simri, an Al Jazeera colleague, spoke in Arabic of the irreparable loss she felt upon Shireen's death: 'She was a mother to me. She was a sister to me'. The British Palestinian singer Reem Kelani brought tears to the eyes of many in the congregation with a rendition of *The Singer Said*, which features lyrics by the Palestinian national poet Mahmoud Darwish. Some of the words could have been written specifically to describe Abu Akleh's final moments on Earth: 'This is how I died / standing, standing / I died like the trees'.

I looked around. The BBC, Sky News, *The New York Times*, the Associated Press, the AFP—none of these media organisations had an official presence at the service.[74] This indifference to the killing of one of their colleagues foreshadowed British media indifference to Israel's slaughter of media workers operating in Gaza.

Killing Palestinian Journalists

By September 2024, eleven months into its offensive, Israeli forces had killed more than 130 journalists in Gaza.[75] The toll rose to at least 167 by the following April.[76] Reporters Without Borders characterised it as '[t]he Israeli army's elimination of journalists in Gaza'.[77] This was a killing spree without precedent or parallel. For comparison, sixty-three journalists were killed during the entire twenty-year Vietnam War.[78] Aid workers in Gaza have been picked off in even greater numbers.[79] This lent compelling force to claims that Israel was not conducting a 'war' in Gaza but something far more sinister.

Israeli authorities often defined the journalists they killed as 'terrorists'. The killing of Al Jazeera correspondent Ismail al-Ghoul and his cameraman Rami al-Rifi in a strike on their clearly marked press vehicle in the al-Shati refugee camp on July 31, 2024, is an example. The Israelis produced a document 'found on Hamas computers seized in the Gaza Strip' that they said contained a list of names showing that 'Mr. al-Ghoul was an engineer in the Hamas Gaza brigade'.[80] They refused to provide any more details about the origin of this document. It stated that al-Ghoul received military rank in 2007, when he would have been ten years old.[81]

Al Jazeera firmly denied that al-Ghoul was a Hamas operative.[82] By December 2024 it had been reported that a total of five journalists, including cameramen, had been killed while working for Al Jazeera in Gaza.[83] A sixth was paralysed after being shot in the neck.[84] In addition, the wife, son, daughter, and grandson of Al Jazeera bureau chief Wael Dahdouh were killed in a strike on the Nuseirat refugee camp on October 25, 2023.[85]

On October 24, 2024, Israeli authorities accused six other Al Jazeera journalists of being terrorists. The allegation was again denied by Al Jazeera and the documentation provided by Israel was unverifiable.[86] This was a sinister development that could be interpreted as preparing the ground for the murder of these men. Had this been the Russian authorities making similar allegations against Ukrainian journalists, in the same context, there would have been international outrage and a campaign of solidarity by news organisations around the world.

So widespread is Israel's targeting of journalists in Gaza that when local reporters seek to rent property there, they are obliged to pay a premium.[87] Like everyone else in the enclave they are now required to spend a fair proportion of their day searching for food and clean water. Filing copy to head office is frequently impossible because of the lack of electricity to charge mobile phones. It is often difficult to find somewhere to sleep, especially because families sometimes shun journalists for fear they will be targeted. The cruel truth is that when Palestinians in Gaza see a journalist, many do not want to go near them. If a journalist's phone rings, others move away in the knowledge that an Israeli missile could be on its way.[88]

Yet Palestinian journalists have carried on filing the reports and sending the pictures that enable us to understand something of what is going on in Gaza. Their testimony is of incalculable value given that Israel refuses to allow in foreign journalists. Life for these reporters in Gaza, some of whom are colleagues of mine at *Middle East Eye*, is hard beyond the imagination of British newspaper columnists working in well-appointed London offices and television studios.* Many of the latter earn a six-figure salary for their opinions. They take no risks and have little or no interest in the truth, especially not when it comes to Israel and Palestine.

'The press vests we are wearing mark us as a target. They do not protect us', twenty-two-year old Palestinian freelance reporter Abubaker Abed said in a moving appeal posted on X in January 2025.[89] 'We have been let down by . . . the international media organisations. We haven't seen . . . a single word of support . . . Maybe if we were Ukrainians or of any other citizenship with blonde hair and blue eyes the world would rage and rant for us. But because we are Palestinians we have only one right, which is to die and be maimed'.

All this makes British foreign secretary David Lammy's statement, made in the House of Commons in November 2024, that '[t]here are no journalists in Gaza' difficult to stomach.[90] Lammy's comments would have been welcomed in Tel Aviv because they could be construed as validating the official Israeli narrative that reporters in Gaza are just terrorists in disguise. Lammy's comments arguably reflected the prejudice, all too common among British journalists and politicians, that Palestinian journalists are unreliable

---

* On August 25, 2025, Israel killed two of my *Middle East Eye* colleagues, Ahmed Abu Aziz and Mohamed Salama, in a double-tap strike on Nasser Hospital in southern Gaza. 'I never imagined my journalism career would be like this', Aziz had written in April 2025. 'People can't begin to imagine what we're going through, daily bombing and loss. I'm not made of steel. I am internally shattered'. He added: 'I work every day just to avoid staying at home, because that would destroy me. I'd rather be martyred on the field . . . Although I'm wounded, I can't stop working. For my colleagues and for their memory'. See: MEE Staff, 'Israel Kills Middle East Eye Journalists in Double-Tap Strike on Gaza's Nasser Hospital', *Middle East Eye* (25 August 2025). Daniel Hilton, 'Ahmed Abu Aziz: MEE's Gaza Correspondent Who Reported Through Pain and Loss', *Middle East Eye* (25 August 2025).

or incapable of doing a professional job. As Chris Doyle of the Council for Arab-British Understanding has written, '[t]his attitude is contemptuous and disrespectful of those journalists and their families who have been killed, in some cases assassinated'.[91] Perhaps Lammy did not intend all this by his remark. But even as his comment drew immediate public criticism, Lammy has yet to withdraw or even clarify it, let alone apologise to the courageous men and women who have risked and all too often sacrificed their lives to bring the truth to the world.

British War Reporting Inside Gaza: Douglas Murray

After October 2023 the world relied on Palestinian journalists for information about events in Gaza. During this time a small number of Britons were given permission by Israel to report from the enclave. The far-right commentator Douglas Murray was one of them, invited on a visit arranged by the Israeli military on November 14, 2023.

In his report for *The Sun* the following day, Murray wrote this about the besieged al-Shifa hospital:

> They [the Israeli military and 'others'] say that Hamas does not only use the hospital as an HQ and weapons depot but as a place to keep Palestinians as human shields. This is a long-time tactic of Hamas, which regularly places its leadership and weapons depots beneath hospitals, schools and other 'soft' targets in the knowledge that if Israel strikes them it will reap international condemnation.[92]

Murray does not question the IDF claim that Hamas is using al-Shifa as 'an HQ and weapons depot' and 'as a place to keep Palestinians as human shields'.[93] Murray provides no evidence for his assertion that Hamas 'regularly places its leadership and weapons depots beneath hospitals, schools and other "soft" targets'.*

---

* To reinforce the allegation that Hamas uses al-Shifa as a base, Murray paraphrases a report by Amnesty International released in the aftermath of Israel's Operation Protective Edge in 2014. He tells *Sun* readers that according to Amnesty, 'Hamas used the hospital as a place to imprison, torture and execute Palestinians'. These are serious

Murray witnessed the mass forced displacement of Palestinians from the north to the south. This is what he wrote:

> At Salahadin Street we got the first glimpse of the tide of Palestinians leaving their homes and moving south. Men, women and children were standing in line as the IDF stood guard. This is the 'humanitarian corridor' that the Israelis have set up to allow Palestinians to leave the zone of the most intense fighting and get to safety. The process is an incredibly delicate one and every movement has to be carefully watched. The Israelis have three objectives. The first is to allow safe passage to innocent Palestinians who do not want to get caught up in the war. The second is to prevent Hamas terrorists – let alone their leaders – spiriting themselves away among the local population. The third is to avoid any of the 240 Israeli hostages being taken deeper into Gaza along this route. As a result the messages broadcast out at the crowds by megaphone were in Arabic and Hebrew. The messages in Arabic advised the people to raise their hands if they understood the messages and to move slowly forward past the checkpoint. Some of the Palestinians waved white flags.

Note that Murray does not say 'The Israelis *claim* they have three objectives'—he says 'The Israelis *have* three objectives' (my italics). He is therefore asking his readers to accept at face value Israel's account of its goals, i.e., safe passage for Palestinian civilians, stopping Hamas, and

---

crimes but do not amount to evidence of human shielding. Amnesty specified that Hamas committed the abuses in 'abandoned areas'. (Amnesty International, *'Strangling Necks': Abductions, Torture and Summary Killings of Palestinians by Hamas Forces During the 2014 Gaza/Israel Conflict* (May 2015), p. 6) Murray also fails to tell readers that, in a separate report from 2015, Amnesty could not verify claims that Hamas used human shields. (Amnesty International, *Unlawful and Deadly: Rocket and Mortar Attacks by Palestinian Armed Groups during the 2014 Gaza/Israel Conflict* (March 2015), pp. 47–49) For a sceptical analysis of Amnesty's findings, see Norman G. Finkelstein, *Gaza: An Inquest into Its Martyrdom* (University of California Press, 2018), pp. 248–49.

rescuing the hostages.* He does not subject these claims to scrutiny or scepticism. Murray is here acting as a mouthpiece for the IDF.

This is especially troubling because in his report he addresses two prima facie war crimes: the siege of a hospital and the forced displacement of Palestinians.

It is important to bear in mind that by the time Murray went on his tour two premature babies had died in al-Shifa as a result of Israel cutting off electricity to the hospital, with thirty-seven more premature babies at risk of death.[94] Murray does not mention these fatalities.

Physicians for Human Rights–Israel had already stated: 'The hospital is besieged, with no option to bring in the corpses and injured people sprawled outside. There is no movement in or out of the hospital . . . The picture we are now seeing at Shifa is no longer of a humanitarian catastrophe—it is a collective death sentence'.[95]

Despite this, a caption under a photo accompanying Murray's article, showing Israeli soldiers in the hospital, states: 'IDF troops are continuing the precise and targeted operation against Hamas in the al Shifa Hospital'. To be fair Murray did not write this cynical example of unvarnished Israeli propaganda. We are dealing here with atrocity denial from *The Sun* itself.**

---

* South Africa recorded in its application to the ICJ that senior Israeli government and military officials had called to 'take down Gaza' (Finance Minister Bezalel Smotrich), resettle Gaza (Heritage Minister Amichai Eliyahu), 'eliminate everything' (Defence Minister Yoav Gallant), inflict another 'Nakba' (Agriculture Minister Avi Dichter), cause 'the civilian population' in Gaza to 'leave immediately' (Energy and Infrastructure Minister Israel Katz), and exact 'vengeance' by making Gaza a 'fallow land' (Colonel Yogev Bar Sheshet, deputy comptroller in the Ministry of Defence). Murray does not mention these stated objectives, all of which were articulated before his article appeared. ICJ, *South Africa v. Israel*, Application Instituting Proceedings and Request for the Indication of Provisional Measures (29 December 2023), paras. 101, 103.

** Douglas Murray, 'I've Seen Hamas' Brutality First Hand', on *The Sun* website. We wrote to Douglas Murray to give him a chance to respond to criticisms of his reporting, receiving an acknowledgment but no reply. We also wrote to *The Sun* to give the newspaper the chance to answer the charge of atrocity denial. Our letter was acknowledged but we had received no reply by the time we went to press.

The Al Jazeera film *Gaza*, broadcast one year after October 7, illustrated the undiluted terror of the flight south through contemporaneous filmed testimony from reporters Youmna ElSayed (a mother of four pre-teen children fleeing south) and Mohammed ElHelou. They documented dead bodies lying in the streets, Israeli tanks and snipers lining the route, and children being forced to walk with their hands in the air.

In *Gaza*, we see young men taken from the line at random, stripped to their underwear, and then marched away, many in danger of ending up in Israel's notorious detention centres. Douglas Murray, watching people moving south down Salahadin Street at roughly the same time (with a difference of perhaps some weeks) as the Al Jazeera film,[96] describes this process as follows: 'A number of young men were pulled out of the crowd and put aside for a secondary check. Young men of fighting age are clearly of interest to the Israelis and need more checks than most'.

In June the following year, during an interview with Peter Robinson of the Hoover Institution,[97] Murray explained his reporting as follows:

> There's only two ways to be in Gaza. One is to be embedded with the IDF, as I've been. And, the other is to have permission of Hamas. Hamas are not very good hosts. And, they're untrustworthy hosts. And so most of the Western media rely on journalists who are Gazans. All of whom are operating under Hamas restrictions at best, and most of whom are going to be Hamas supporters.

The allegation that 'most' Gazan journalists are supporters of Hamas was not substantiated.

Many foreign journalists were in Gaza during Israel's 2014 onslaught, dubbed 'Operation Protective Edge'. The *Columbia Journalism Review* found that 'journalists who reported in Gaza dismissed the allegations of pressure from Hamas as baseless'.[98] A journalist for *VICE News*, Danny Gold, said: 'Were we threatened? Were we warned? No'[99]—although he added that Hamas did not give access to its fighters for the purpose of interviews. With regard to the claim that Hamas are 'untrustworthy hosts', Hamas almost certainly would like to shape the media narrative in a particular direction. But so does Israel, as Murray's own dispatch demonstrates.

Lucy Williamson in Al-Shifa Hospital

The day after Murray's propagandistic account appeared, the BBC aired a report from its Middle East correspondent Lucy Williamson, who embedded with the IDF on a visit to al-Shifa hospital.[100] Williamson reports:

> We had to go in darkness through a hole in one of the perimeter walls, and we were taken to one specific department, the MRI department in the hospital. We weren't allowed to talk to other people—not to doctors, not to patients. We were shown the items that the IDF said they had found there hidden amongst the medical equipment.

Williamson is talking here as if accompanying an invading army into a hospital in occupied territory is the most natural thing in the world for a British reporter to do. It is hard to imagine that a BBC journalist would feel so relaxed about embedding with the Russians in such circumstances, or that she would be so compliant with her chaperone's instructions.

Williamson rightly informs viewers that she has not been allowed to talk to doctors and patients, but it's surprising that she makes nothing more of this. Refusal to allow Williamson such access is censorship. In my view she should have refused the embed on such terms. Certainly warning lights should have flashed. Williamson's failure to question why the IDF did not want her to talk to doctors and patients is a serious omission.

Williamson then enters the MRI department. She shows that the Israelis have destroyed the door to the department and then points the camera at military supplies allegedly 'found' by the IDF in the hospital:

> The Israeli army has been really searching through this hospital, you can see they've had to force the door of the MRI room here to get inside. They've been looking for evidence of this being a Hamas base, a place where Hamas planned attacks, and they say that among the things they've uncovered are more than a dozen Kalashnikovs, grenades, personal protective equipment, some of it

> with the Hamas military brigade insignia on it. You can see some of them here hidden under these bags of medical supplies. We're also told that there have been laptops found with some information about the hostages. They also found some recent files that suggest this may have been a Hamas operating base as recently as a few days ago.

There's no way that Williamson can have known for certain that the Israelis have been 'searching' for anything. That's what they say they've been doing. Based on the destroyed door to the MRI department it might have been more accurate to observe, 'The Israeli Army has been *rampaging through* this hospital'.

Nowhere does Williamson express scepticism towards IDF claims, let alone acknowledge that the guns and equipment mixed up with medical equipment might have been planted or manipulated by Israeli forces. Perhaps the IDF has told her the truth about the machine guns. But maybe it hasn't—as we have seen, the Israeli army has a track record of fabrication.

Williamson tells viewers: 'They also found some recent files that suggest this may have been a Hamas operating base as recently as a few days ago'. There's no way she can possibly know that Israeli troops 'found' those files. I have done a few 'embeds' myself and know from experience that this type of journalism does involve sensitive and complicated judgments and that sometimes there is no right or wrong decision. There is often a price to be paid for obtaining the rare access both Williamson and Murray were granted by the Israeli military. To be fair to Williamson her dispatch was more sceptical and detached than Murray's. I nevertheless wonder whether she came close to framing her story in terms of what the Israelis wanted the world to see.*

---

* I put this criticism of Lucy Williamson to the BBC, which pointed to an earlier statement: 'We were invited along with one other crew to go with the IDF to look at the hospital and what the IDF says it has found. We reported our position and the conditions with absolute transparency at the top of our stories. Subsequently, we have published several pieces further analysing what we saw in context of what else we know'.

Al-Shifa Hospital or Hamas Base?

By the time of Williamson's visit to the hospital the Israeli government had repeatedly asserted that al-Shifa hospital was effectively a Hamas base—a command and control centre, replete with extensive catacombs, masquerading as a medical facility. Israel said al-Shifa was Hamas' 'main headquarters' and published infographics and animations alleging a large Hamas infrastructure beneath the hospital.[101] In the words of Palestinian analyst Mouin Rabbani, al-Shifa was depicted as a 'Palestinian Pentagon'.[102]

Israel's bold claims of an expansive military infrastructure in or beneath al-Shifa have not been verified by independent observers, and some of them have been contradicted.[103]

For instance: Israel alleged that there were five hospital buildings within the al-Shifa complex that were directly involved in Hamas operations. It also alleged that these buildings sat on top of tunnel networks that could be accessed from inside hospital wards.[104] Analysis by *The Washington Post* found that none of the five buildings identified by Israeli forces seemed to connect to tunnels while no evidence of access to tunnels from hospital wards was produced.[105]

The UN's Independent International Commission of Inquiry on the Occupied Palestinian Territory and Israel said that it was 'unable to independently verify' Israel's claims about the military use of al-Shifa hospital. The Commission confirmed that there was a tunnel and a shaft on the hospital grounds but it could not confirm that these were used for military purposes. Further, the Commission 'did not find any evidence of a military presence in the specific hospital departments that Israeli security forces shelled in November, including the maternity ward and the intensive care unit'.[106] For these reasons, the Commission concluded that when Israeli forces attacked al-Shifa, the hospital had special protection under international law and should not have been targeted.[107]

The Commission also found that Israel's attacks on al-Shifa and other hospitals, 'in view of the excessive number of civilian deaths and injuries, as well as the damage caused to and the destruction of the hospitals' facilities', amounted to 'the war crimes of wilful killing and attacks against protected objects'.[108] Moreover, despite the Commission making several requests to Israel for access and information, Israel ignored them all.[109]

It is important to keep in mind the precise nature of Israel's claims. The IDF did not merely charge that some militants were in the vicinity of al-Shifa hospital at some point. It claimed that al-Shifa hospital was Hamas' *main military base*. It is clear that no remotely satisfactory evidence of this has been produced: a few guns, even if they really were found in the hospital and not planted, do not a command and control centre make.

The above concerns did little to curb the enthusiasm of the British press. *The Sun* published an article entitled, 'Israeli Troops Bring Baby Incubators & Supplies to Gaza's Al-Shifa Hospital After "Targeted Operation" to Hunt Hamas'. The first paragraph read: 'ISRAEL said Gaza's largest hospital is the "beating heart" of Hamas as it launched a raid to hunt down evil terrorists using it as cover'.[110] This framing might have been appropriate for a trashy spy novel, but it was a far cry from responsible reporting.

Former British Army officer Richard Kemp, an old hand at putting a generous gloss on Israel's conduct, complained in *The Telegraph* that people were far too apt to believe Hamas and unduly sceptical of Israeli claims. Despite the absence of independent verification before or after the Israeli raid, he boldly asserted that 'Hamas uses hospitals and other protected places like schools and mosques for terrorist purposes'.[111]

The Spectator admitted that 'so far there is no concrete proof that there was a large command centre present in the hospital'. However, its writer went on to plead that new evidence produced by Israel showed that 'the site has indeed been used by terrorists' because, for example, weapons appeared to have been stored there and tunnels 'may', according to the IDF, 'lead to a command-and-control centre'.[112]

The author also suggested on the basis of weak evidence that there was 'prolific terrorist activity within and directly underneath the hospital'. In response to concerns about the lack of independent verification, the article cited unspecified 'American intelligence'[113]—intelligence agencies are known, of course, for their unimpeachable integrity—to prove that Israel was not alone in its assessment, as though the US did not have a direct interest in validating the innocence of one of its closest allies, in the midst of a military campaign being conducted with massive American support.

These reporters failed to ask the obvious question: If Israel had compelling evidence proving there was a Hamas base in or under al-Shifa, *why didn't it invite independent journalists and UN investigators to confirm this?* Had such a base existed, a transparent approach by Israel would have removed any doubts. In fact, Israel systematically prevented independent scrutiny. The rational conclusion from Israel's failure to provide evidence and obstruction of third-party observation is that its claim that al-Shifa was Hamas' headquarters was a fabrication.

In retrospect the attack on al-Shifa in November 2023 feels like a test case for what became a systematic assault on Gaza's health system. In July 2025, a report by Physicians for Human Rights–Israel found that 'Gaza's health system has been systematically dismantled' as Israel attacked almost every hospital and killed or detained more than 1,800 medical staff. The report concluded that this was an act of genocide intended to destroy the Palestinian people in Gaza.[114]

Clarissa Ward in Rafah

A month after Lucy Williamson's al-Shifa excursion CNN's Clarissa Ward reported from Rafah in southern Gaza—*without* an Israeli escort.[115] Driving through the wrecked streets she tells viewers: 'Up until now, Israel and Egypt have made access for international journalists next to impossible, and you can see why'.

Ward makes clear that Israel has banned journalists because it does not want the world to see the destruction it has inflicted: 'Since October 7, the Israeli military says it has hit Gaza with more than twenty-two thousand strikes—that by far surpasses anything we've seen in modern warfare in terms of intensity and ferocity, and we really honestly are just getting a glimpse of it here'.

She then describes how, despite 'Israel's heavy bombardment, there are people out on the streets. A crowd outside a bakery, where else can they go? Nowhere is safe in Gaza'. We have already gotten a more accurate picture of life on the ground in Gaza than in the whole of Murray or Williamson's reporting.

Ward visits an Emirati field hospital in Rafah, from where she narrates: 'One thing none of the doctors here have got used to, is the number of children they are treating. The UN estimates that some two thirds of those killed in this round of the conflict have been women and children.' More crucial information.

In the hospital, she speaks to an eight-year-old girl, Jinan, whom she describes as having survived an airstrike on her family home that crushed her femur. Ward communicates with the child in Arabic, asking her if she is in pain. Jinan speaks in a soft and croaky voice about how Israel first bombed the house next door and then their own house. She tells Ward that she was sitting next to her grandfather when the bomb struck.

Jinan cries as she tells her story. Ward cries herself as she comforts Jinan in Arabic. As Ward leaves Jinan's bedside, Jinan's doctor Abdullah al-Naqbi approaches and informs her about the outcome of an Israeli airstrike just ten minutes earlier (Ward heard the blast when she walked in).

Ward does not shrink from the human costs of the Israeli assault: 'A man and a thirteen-year-old boy are wheeled in, both missing limbs, both in a perilous state.' She shows the difficult working conditions of the doctors and describes how they apply a 'tourniquet improvised with a bandage' to the man's leg. The boy is shown screaming in pain with an oxygen mask attached to his mouth, bloodied and bruised.

Dr. al-Naqbi is shown telling Ward that this is one of the only hospitals that still has free beds; the neighbouring facility was handling four hundred to five hundred patients with only two hundred beds. 'We've been here fifteen minutes,' Ward comments, 'and this is already what we're seeing.'

Ward speaks to an injured twenty-year-old woman, Lama:

> Ten weeks ago, she was studying engineering at university and helping to plan her sister's wedding. Today, she is recovering from the amputation of her right leg. Her family followed Israeli military orders and fled from the north to the south, but the house where they were seeking shelter was hit in a strike.

The conversation powerfully amplifies Ward's earlier remark that 'nowhere is safe in Gaza'. Lama and her family followed the IDF's orders and evacuated from the north to the south, and when they got to the south, Israel bombed the house in which they had sought shelter.

Ward concludes: 'Like Grozny, Aleppo, and Mariupol, Gaza will go down as one of the great horrors of modern warfare. It's getting dark, time for us to leave—a privilege the vast majority of Gazans do not have'.

This downplayed the scale of the devastation in Gaza, where it was revealed a week later that the destruction wreaked by Israel had already surpassed that inflicted on both Aleppo and Mariupol.[116] It was a powerful analogy nevertheless.

Most striking of all was Ward's empathy. This contrasted with both Murray's posturing and Williamson's rather mechanical detachment. Ward did not mention 'human shields' or any other unevidenced excuse that the IDF employed to explain away its atrocities. She anchored herself in the observable suffering of the civilians in Gaza at the hands of the Israeli military. While unusual in Western reporting, this was reasonable framing because Israeli leaders have been remarkably candid about their deliberate targeting of Gaza's civilian population.*

* On October 7, 2023, Israeli prime minister Benjamin Netanyahu referred to Gaza as a 'wicked city'. On October 10, 2023, Major General Ghassan Allian, the head of Israel's military administration in the occupied territories, referred to 'the citizens of Gaza' as 'human beasts' who 'will not have electricity or water, just destruction'. On November 11, 2023, Israel's then national security minister Itamar Ben-Gvir stated: 'To be clear, when they say that Hamas needs to be eliminated, it also means those who sing, those who support and those who distribute sweets, all of these are terrorists. And they should be eliminated!' In early December 2023, the then deputy mayor of Jerusalem said that Palestinian detainees are 'not human beings and not even human animals, they are subhuman and that is how they should be treated. Erase the memory of Amalek, we will not forget'. See Amnesty International, *'You Feel Like You Are Subhuman': Israel's Genocide Against Palestinians in Gaza* (2024), pp. 239–40, 241, 242, 244–45, 255, 257–62.

3

OCTOBER 7 IN THE BRITISH MEDIA

> We saw a little baby in an oven. These bastards put these babies in an oven and put on the oven. We found the kid a few hours later.
>
> —*Eli Beer, president of United Hatzala, which helped collect bodies on October 7*

ISRAEL'S ASSAULT on the Gaza Strip was a response to the Hamas attack on Israel on October 7. More than a thousand gunmen from Hamas' Nukhba, or 'elite', unit poured through the fence separating Gaza from Israel in what Hamas called Operation Al Aqsa Flood. Over the next few hours close to 1,200 Israeli and other nationals were killed. More than eight hundred of them were civilians.[1]

Some 250 soldiers and civilians were taken hostage.[2]

A music festival was underway close to Kibbutz Re'im. Dozens of young people took refuge in the small bomb shelters that dot the main 232 highway that runs north to south along the edge of the Gaza Strip.

The shelters had no doors. Within minutes Hamas gunmen arrived. They found a ready-made trove of hostages. But instead of taking them prisoner, at each of the shelters the gunmen stood outside, threw in hand grenades, and sprayed automatic fire at those hiding within.

Dozens were killed. Many of the survivors were transported back to Gaza, already hideously maimed.

The carnage at the bomb shelters was among a number of grave war crimes committed by Hamas and others who followed them through the fence that day.[3]

British Reporting of October 7

But in the days and weeks that followed the focus of Israeli and Western commentators was not on the crimes Hamas had committed, but on crimes it had not. This reporting of the events of October 7 served to justify Israel's response, and the West's reaction to that response.

On October 10, Nicole Zedeck, a journalist for Israel's i24News, broadcast two reports from Kibbutz Kfar Aza claiming Hamas had killed forty babies, some of whom were beheaded.[4]

The following day the majority of British papers led with variations of this story. 'Hamas Massacres Babies and Children' read the headline in the *Daily Telegraph*.[5] *The Independent* used a quote from an 'Israeli major' as its headline: 'They Decapitated Women and Children. We Saw Dead Babies'.[6]

'Hamas "Cut the Throats of Babies" in Massacre', announced *The Times*.[7] The *Daily Express* ran with 'Horror at "Pure Evil Beheading of Babies"',[8] while the *Daily Mail* declared: '"This Was a Holocaust Pure and Simple"'. The sub-heading claimed: 'Babies beheaded. 40 children shot in a single settlement'.*

* Sam Greenhill, '"This Was a Holocaust Pure and Simple', *Daily Mail* (11 October 2023). We wrote to Sam Greenhill asking how he had verified his information and whether the *Daily Mail* had issued a correction. Greenhill wrote back: 'All I would say is that you would surely acknowledge that conducting a historical appraisal, with the benefit of nearly two years' of time, is not the same exercise as reporting a live and fast-moving event for a daily newspaper. If I reported things that people (including people in positions of authority) said on the day—and October 7 was horrific too—then of course it is right that their claims may

Numerous other horror stories concerning babies quickly emerged. On October 28 Eli Beer, the president of an organization called United Hatzala which had helped collect bodies on October 7, told the US Republican Jewish Coalition: 'We saw a little baby in an oven. These bastards put these babies in an oven and put on the oven. We found the kid a few hours later'.[9]

The murder and mutilation of babies quickly became a standard reference point for politicians.

'When you are taking babies, cutting them and tying them together and burning them to death you are treating them less than an animal', the Israeli ambassador in London Tzipi Hotovely told Sky News on October 16, 2023—unchallenged by her interviewer Kay Burley.[10]

On November 16, 2023, at the White House, President Joe Biden referred to Hamas 'cutting babies' heads off'.[11] A year on from October 7, the British prime minister Keir Starmer was still referring to 'children and babies killed, mutilated, and tortured by the terrorists of Hamas'.[12]

None of these stories were true. The Israeli newspaper *Haaretz* has confirmed that in total, two babies were killed on October 7.[13] One was killed when a bullet was fired through a safe room door in Kibbutz Be'eri; the other was a Bedouin child, born by emergency Caesarean after her mother was shot; the baby died a few hours later.[14]

Neither was burned or mutilated.

The readiness of Western media to uncritically accept accounts by Israeli media, politicians, and military officials was remarkable given Israel's track record of flagrant dishonesty in its public statements over the years.

---

later be tested with the benefit of many months of research, and I wish you well in your endeavours'. We also received a reply from Katrina Bell, joint head of editorial compliance. She told us that 'IPSO fully investigated the matter and found that our reporting did not breach the Editors' Code'. She referred us to the case brought against the *Daily Mail* by Daniel Vulliamy: IPSO, *21812-23 Vulliamy v Daily Mail*, ipso.co.uk (30 May 2024). She told us that: 'In particular the Committee concluded that it was satisfied our article had "adequately distinguished the statements ... as claims ... as opposed to statements of fact"'.

It also suggested that few lessons had been learned from media susceptibility to propaganda hoaxes in the Gulf wars, such as the false allegation that Iraqi soldiers had thrown Kuwaiti newborns out of incubators in 1990 or unevidenced claims of Iraqi nuclear weapons and collusion with Al Qaeda ahead of the US-led invasion in 2003.

At a time when Israel's political and military leaders were making explicitly genocidal statements, the media's presentation of Israeli politicians, officials, and military personnel as unbiased sources was profoundly reckless.

Turning Palestinians into Savages

Atrocity stories served to dehumanise Palestinians by portraying Hamas as psychotic sadists, guilty of behaviour so depraved as to place them and anyone who supports them outside of the family of humanity.

Palestinians became savages who had relinquished the right to humane treatment. Any analysis of the wars against Native Americans in the nineteenth century, the repression of the Indian mutiny in 1857, and indeed any military campaign against indigenous, colonised or enslaved peoples throughout history shows it is a strategy of dehumanisation that has been deployed again and again.*

One incident sums up the inadequacies of Western journalism on the events of October 7.

* Frantz Fanon wrote in *The Wretched of the Earth* that the French viewed the Algerians as 'born slackers, born liars, born robbers, and born criminals', and subscribed to such beliefs as: 'The Algerian frequently kills other men', 'The Algerian kills savagely', and 'The Algerian kills for no reason'. Fanon wrote that European colonisers viewed the whole of Africa as 'the haunt of savages, a country riddled with superstitions and fanaticism, destined for contempt, weighed down by the curse of God, a country of cannibals—in short, the Negro's country'. Fanon further described how Europeans justified colonialism in the Arab world by referring to 'the inherent barbarity of the Arabs'. Frantz Fanon, *The Wretched of the Earth* (Grove Press, 1963), pp. 211, 217, 296, 297.

Kibbutz Be'eri

Kibbutz Be'eri, the largest in the region, was the epicentre of the Hamas-led assault on October 7. Over a hundred residents were killed, more than in any other community.[15]

Journalists were shown around the kibbutz just a few days later. Many homed in on one particular building: a house belonging to a resident named Pessi Cohen, where Hamas fighters had made a last stand as the kibbutz was retaken by police and army units in the late afternoon and early evening. The Hamas gunmen had taken several people hostage.

'Of all the massacres in this kibbutz settlement this one is the worst I've heard', said Sam Greenhill, chief reporter for the *Daily Mail*, in a video report for *MailOnline*.[16] 'A military commander's just told me that he saw nineteen bodies at this house, including eight babies'.

The military commander Greenhill quoted was Colonel Golan Vach of the National Rescue Unit. Vach also claimed he'd seen a beheaded baby at a separate house nearby.

'I call it the example of what we are facing right now in Gaza. And this is exactly the reason that we need to clear . . . all this region . . . from this kind of threat', Vach told journalists.[17]

Yossi Landau, the regional head of ZAKA, gave an equally horrifying but entirely different account of what he had encountered in Pessi Cohen's home.

'You are talking children, two piles of ten children each, were tied to the back, burned to death', he said.*

This account was later repeated and embellished by Israeli prime minister Benjamin Netanyahu in a phone conversation with President Biden. 'They took dozens of children, bound them up, burned them, and executed them', Netanyahu said.[18]

In fact thirteen hostages died in Pessi Cohen's house. There were no babies among them.[19] There were two twelve-year-old twins, but no other children.

---

* Al Jazeera Investigations, *October 7* (2024), 36m54s.

Yossi Landau was later confronted with these facts on camera for the documentary *October 7* by Al Jazeera's Investigative Unit.[20]

'Well, not children, but it's an eighteen year-old. They were all together when you look at them and they're burned. So we're talking about eighteen year-old, twenty year-old, you can't, you just don't look on the spot, for identification to see the ages or something like that', he said.

Landau, like all ZAKA volunteers, has no forensic training. 'Our volunteers were confronted with traumatic scenes and sometimes misinterpreted what they saw', a ZAKA spokesman has conceded.[21]

Soldiers and first responders certainly encountered horrific sights on October 7. Traumatised and overwhelmed, it's understandable if sometimes their accounts were confused.

But in the case of the house at Be'eri it is very hard to escape the conclusion that Vach and Landau were not telling the truth.

Some clue as to why they might have done so was provided by Netanyahu in an address to ZAKA volunteers in December 2023.

'We need to buy time, which we gain by turning to world leaders and to public opinion', he told them. 'You have an important role in influencing public opinion, which also influences leaders.'[22]

In other words the accounts given to the world's press were seen by the Israeli government as part of its propaganda war.

The disinformation regarding the deaths at Pessi Cohen's house in Be'eri is all the more remarkable because we know that twelve of those who died were almost certainly killed not by the Hamas gunmen but by Israeli forces as they stormed the building.

We know this because there were two survivors who later gave detailed interviews to Israeli media.[23]

'They were killed from shrapnel. They weren't killed because they were murdered', an eyewitness named Yasmin Porat told Israel's Channel 12. 'There was crazy shooting there at the house. Insane. A tank came and shot shells at it. Unbelievable. If all the hostages died it was only from the shooting'.

The Hamas gunmen 'didn't harm us,' Porat said in a separate interview. 'They treated us very humanely . . . They give us something to drink now and then. When they see we were anxious they calmed us down. It was very frightening but no one behaved toward us violently.'[24]

An investigation by the Israeli military concluded that 'most of the hostages were likely murdered by the terrorists,'[25] a verdict that flatly contradicts the evidence of the two surviving civilian witnesses.

Haaretz and other Israeli newspapers have since produced compelling evidence that the Israeli military issued what is known as the 'Hannibal Directive' at a number of locations on October 7.[26] This is an order to prevent the taking of hostages even if it means killing the hostages.

On that evidence, it would seem that this massacre in the worst affected community, which was held up repeatedly as an example of Hamas' readiness to cold-bloodedly murder and mutilate large numbers of babies and children, in fact involved no babies and may have been carried out not by Hamas but by Israeli forces.

The twins who died at Be'eri were among fifteen children aged twelve or under who were killed on October 7.

Complicity of Western Media

On September 16, 2024, the Gazan Health Ministry published a list of the names of 34,344 Palestinians killed in Gaza since October 7. This did not include more than seven thousand people confirmed dead but whose identity remained unknown. It did not include an estimated ten thousand bodies believed to be buried under rubble. And it did not include the thousands of people believed to have died for lack of access to medication and healthcare.

Among the 34,344 were 710 babies under the age of one.[27] The first 115 of the list's 649 pages were taken up with children under the age of ten.[28]

The atrocity stories emerging after October 7 created the emotional, psychological, and political space for this horror to occur. There is now abundant evidence that the most sensational of these were untrue.

Western media has still to confront its own complicity.

4

MORAL PANIC AT WESTMINSTER

> That this House calls for an immediate ceasefire in Gaza and Israel; notes with shock and distress that the death toll has now risen beyond 28,000, the vast majority of whom were women and children; further notes that there are currently 1.5 million Palestinians sheltering in Rafah, 610,000 of whom are children; also notes that they have nowhere else to go; condemns any military assault on what is now the largest refugee camp in the world; further calls for the immediate release of all hostages taken by Hamas and an end to the collective punishment of the Palestinian people; and recognises that the only way to stop the slaughter of innocent civilians is to press for a ceasefire now.
>
> —*Scottish National Party Opposition Day Motion, February 21, 2024. Sabotaged by Speaker Lindsay Hoyle after private conversation with Labour Party leader Sir Keir Starmer*

THUS FAR I have shown how a triple alliance coalesced in support of the Israeli offensive which followed October 7. It incorporated the government, the official opposition, and the mainstream media. Though impromptu and lacking formal agreements, discipline was tight and for several crucial months close to unbreakable. Britain's resurgent extreme right also supported Israel as an unruly fourth participant on the alliance's fringe.

This arrangement would not have been possible but for Sir Keir Starmer's decision that Labour should not play the usual role of an opposition. That would have involved probing, questioning, and where appropriate challenging government policy, while praising where appropriate. Instead Sir Keir downed tools, quietly accepting the role of junior partner alongside the Sunak government. This strategy condemned the Labour Party to joining the Tories in an echo chamber for Benjamin Netanyahu's far-right coalition.

Starmer and Sunak opposed a ceasefire. Britain refused to support any of the early United Nations Security Council ceasefire resolutions (and failed to do so until March 2024, when a US-sponsored resolution proposed a ceasefire for Ramadan).* Policy was led by Sunak's Tories but Labour generally went along with it.** All the nationalist parties—Plaid Cymru, Sinn Féin, and the Scottish National Party—were urging an immediate end to hostilities as early as November 2023. It was hard for them to make an impact, even though the Liberal Democrats also called for an immediate ceasefire from November 2023.[1] Those who wanted to raise their voice against British government support for Israeli atrocities in Gaza, lacking mainstream representation in parliament, had little choice but to take to the streets.

This situation recalled early 2003, when the Conservative opposition led by Iain Duncan-Smith had thrown its weight behind the Blair government's illegal invasion of Iraq. Back then the Stop the War Coalition (STWC) organised momentous marches in opposition to British involvement in

---

* The US-supported resolution demanded 'an immediate ceasefire for the month of Ramadan respected by all parties leading to a lasting sustainable ceasefire' rather than expressly calling for a permanent ceasefire. (UN Security Council Resolution 2728 (2024), S/RES/2728)

** Sunak called for 'pauses for aid but not a ceasefire' in October 2023, which Starmer echoed nine days later. By December 2023, both Sunak and Starmer called for a 'sustainable ceasefire' rather than an immediate end to Israel's assault on Gaza. See Guardian News, 'Rishi Sunak Calls for "Pauses" for Aid but Not a Ceasefire in Gaza' (25 October 2023), https://www.youtube.com/watch?v=W3jmIYDMbuc; 'Keir Starmer Defends Call for Humanitarian Pause in Gaza' (3 November 2023), https://www.youtube.com/watch?v=Euhs4pe8Lm8. See also Peter Walker, 'Keir Starmer Joins Rishi Sunak in Calling for Sustainable Ceasefire in Gaza', *The Guardian* (18 December 2023).

the war. After October 7, 2023, Stop the War re-emerged alongside the Palestine Solidarity Campaign (PSC) as a primary organiser of anti-war activity throughout Britain.*

It was here that the third element of the coalition—the media—came into its own. Their objective was to discredit the ceasefire movement. In this way the British media, already a powerful auxiliary voice for the Netanyahu government, became an essential weapon for Sunak and Starmer as they set about shaping and policing public opinion.

The media faced a difficulty: the marches were remarkably peaceful. This should surprise nobody. With few exceptions, the protestors were defending the law-based international order. They were on the same side as human rights groups like Amnesty International and global bodies like the United Nations and the International Criminal Court. By contrast the Sunak government, supported by Starmer and the established media, was throwing its weight behind a lawless state daily committing war crimes whose leading politicians were unabashed about their genocidal intentions and openly contemptuous of human rights groups and the UN.

British journalists solved this conundrum by resorting to fantasy. They had no choice. While laughably false, their claims were believed by many and endorsed by the most senior members of the government. Radical Islamists were taking over the streets of London, using their muscle to intimidate politicians and destroying the authority of parliament. 'For the first time in my life I'm beginning to fear for the future of Britain',[2] fretted Camilla Tominey in the *Daily Telegraph* on November 3, 2023. 'A country that prided itself on tolerance has now shown itself to be home to many thousands of people who are not only happy to be useful idiots for Hamas but who revel in their anti-Semitic ideology'. The columnist focussed her attention on the pro-Palestinian march scheduled to coincide with Remembrance Day:

---

* Alongside the STWC and PSC, the demonstrations were organised by the Campaign for Nuclear Disarmament, Muslim Association of Britain, Friends of Al-Aqsa, and Palestinian Forum in Britain.

> And now, we are facing a threat to disrupt the Remembrance commemorations at the Cenotaph, one of the most sacred state occasions in this proud nation's calendar. It is tempting to ask how on earth did it come to this? But deep down, we already know the answer. We know that it has come to this because our politicians and our police have allowed it to happen. In the same way they initially turned a blind eye to the Rochdale grooming scandal, they have sat back and watched anti-Semitism and Islamist extremism flourish.

The far-right polemicist Douglas Murray picked up the same theme in an interview with John Anderson on November 8:

> Muslim groups, Palestinian groups, pro-Hamas groups in the UK have announced what they call the Million Man March in this city on Remembrance Day, on Armistice Day, when they will again defile the Cenotaph and the statues of our dead and our war leaders, and I believe that the British people will not take this lying down. I think that the police in the UK have failed by allowing people to march through our streets, past our monuments and holy places, past Westminster Abbey and much more, chanting 'Allahu Akbar' and 'Jihad Jihad'. The police have protected the people doing that, and have tried to arrest anyone who dislikes that.[3]

He said that the police had 'lost control of the streets', then went on:

> Now, is it time to send in the army? At some point, probably yes. But *if the army will not be sent in, then the public will have to go in, and the public will have to sort this out themselves.* (my italics) And it will be very very brutal. It will be very brutal because the soul of England, the soul of Britain, is about to be trampled on very very visibly—by people who are gleeful in their trampling. And they have defaced and defiled all of our holy places. And I think, I know, that the British soul is awakening and stirring with rage at what these people are doing. These people came into our house—many of them broke into our house illegally.

A few days earlier Murray had posted on X (formerly Twitter) to his approximately one million followers: 'This is the tipping point. If such a march goes ahead then the people of Britain must come out and stop these barbarians'.[4] We met (see Chapter Two above) Murray acting as a self-appointed publicist for the IDF when writing for *The Sun* after his embed in Gaza on November 14. We now find him, six days earlier, calling for the British Army to be deployed against pro-Palestine protestors or, failing that, for 'very brutal' action against those who 'have defaced and defiled all of our holy places'.

Murray and Tommy Robinson were in their contrasting ways manifestations of an increasingly familiar phenomenon in Europe as well as Britain: the far right acting as apologists for Israeli aggression and war crimes abroad while turning on the ceasefire marchers at home.

There was indeed trouble at the Cenotaph—but not from the ceasefire marchers. The extreme right came out in significant numbers* and engaged in violent confrontations with police as well as demonstrators. The Metropolitan Police condemned the 'extreme violence from right-wing protesters'[5] that led to scores of arrests. Some of the hooligans were carrying

---

* *The Independent* reported that social media posts urging people to defend the Cenotaph came from the English Defence League, the Democratic Football Lad's Alliance, Turning Point UK, and Active Patriot. Tommy Robinson was also present and called on his supporters to go to London. Anger was additionally stirred up by an AI-generated video of London mayor Sadiq Khan threatening to move Armistice Day back a week to accommodate pro-Palestinian protests. The PSC-led march did not go within a mile of the Cenotaph and no pro-Palestinian protestors were arrested at the Cenotaph before, during or after the march. The Metropolitan police did report arrests of pro-Palestinian demonstrators in Grosvenor Place following the march when fireworks struck officers in the face, but stated that 'the vast majority' of the 145 total arrests on the day were of counterdemonstrators. See: Kit Heren, 'Route Revealed for London Palestine Protest on Armistice Day, as March to Go Ahead Despite Concerns', lbc.co.uk (8 November 2023). Amy-Clare Martin, 'Who Are the Far-Right Groups Caught in Violent Clashes at Remembrance Day Rallies?' *The Independent* (11 November 2023). Post by @metpoliceuk on X (11 November 2023), https://x.com/metpoliceuk/status/1723420872403296605. Thomas Mackintosh and Emily Atkinson, 'London Protests: Seven Charged and 145 Arrested as Police Appeals Continue', bbc.co.uk (12 November 2023).

weapons, others had illegal drugs, and yet others were intoxicated. If a real example of a mob were wanted, this was it.

Had this mob violence emanated from pro-Palestinian marchers it would have generated massive headline coverage and a political storm, with future marches surely banned. Coming from the far right the media coverage, as well as the political response, was muted.

The *Mail on Sunday* dedicated its front-page splash to cabinet minister Michael Gove being 'jostled and abused' by a 'pro-Palestinian hate mob'. The newspaper paid less attention to the arrests of scores of far-right extremists; it preferred to say that 'extremists from ALL sides' had tarnished Armistice Day. The *Sunday Express* front page reported that, 'as the nation remembers our war dead, extremists of left and right march for hate'. Other papers engaged in similar false equivalencies.[6] Far-right violence was not the story editors appeared to want.

In reality, the Gaza ceasefire demonstration had embraced both Muslims and non-Muslims, including many Jews.* The organisers at this point enjoyed a relatively good working relationship with the police.[7] Chris Nineham, vice chair of the STWC, later told parliament's Home Affairs Committee: 'We have just been analysing all the stats coming from the police on arrests. On the demonstrations themselves, there have been almost no examples of any kind of disorder, which is something the police themselves have said'.[8]

These remarks were endorsed by Matt Twist, then assistant commissioner for Met Operations, who added: 'I am very clear in saying that the overwhelming majority of people on these marches are there to do so lawfully and peacefully'.[9] Only a tiny fraction of marchers were arrested, and some of those arrests have felt political.[10] One such was the so-called 'coconut trial'. Marieha Hussein, a schoolteacher, was charged with committing a racially aggravated public order offence while on the November 11 ceasefire demonstration.

* For a lively and warm account of the growing presence of the Jewish bloc in support of Palestinians in Gaza, see Julia Bard and David Rosenberg, 'For Your Freedom and Ours', *The Morning Star* (22 December 2023).

I was present through both days of Hussein's subsequent trial at Westminster Magistrates' Court as an expert witness. The court heard how Hussein had held a placard with pictures of Prime Minister Sunak and Home Secretary Suella Braverman depicted as coconuts. The prosecution sought to prove that this was a racial slur. It became apparent during the course of the trial that the Crown had failed to find an expert on race to give evidence in its favour. By contrast the defence had mustered two of the most distinguished authorities in the field,[11] both of whom made a mockery of the Crown argument.

I cannot say for certain, but my own sense having sat through the trial was that the prosecution was aware that the case was politically motivated and only went ahead reluctantly after pressure from above. The defence established that there had not been a single complaint on the march about the poster. Significantly, the police revealed under cross-examination that they had been alerted to the poster in the afternoon and therefore late on in proceedings by *Harry's Place*, an anonymous, pro-Israeli blog based in the United States.*

My role was to speak to the political context. I told the court that the primary role of a British home secretary was to show responsibility, exercise good judgment, and above all not to inflame grievances. I highlighted that Braverman had made a series of statements that were liable to have provoked hatred and disorder.[12] For instance, at the end of October she had told reporters: 'To my mind there is only one way to describe those marches: they are hate marches.'[13] Ben Reiff, a Jewish writer who attended the marches, responded: 'if you ask any of the hundreds of thousands of people who have actually attended the protests, they'll wonder what on earth these politicians

* Counsel for the defence asked the police: 'Are you aware that Harry's Place is a secretive political blog headquartered in Washington DC that has a particular interest in opposing any criticism of the Israeli state?' (Areeb Ullah, '"Coconuts' Trial: London Protest Arrest Prompted by Tweet by "Secretive" Pro-Israel Blog', *Middle East Eye* (12 September 2024)) *Harry's Place* has since upped its conspiratorial rhetoric, writing that *Telegraph* columnist 'Allison Pearson even goes so far as to ask if the massacre and march were co-ordinated—and given the UK's shining record in producing jihadis, who is to say that this is too far-fetched a conspiracy?' (Harry's Place, 'UK's Shameful Hate Marches', hurryupharry.net (7 February 2025))

are talking about. For one thing, the arrest rate at the demonstrations is lower than at a typical football match or the annual Glastonbury music festival'.[14]

Reiff further observed that 'the crowds are probably the closest thing you will find to a representative cross-section of British society: from toddlers to pensioners, and comprising virtually all ethnic, religious, and social backgrounds'. He also explained that in some weeks the Jewish bloc at the London marches numbered more than a thousand people, thus 'roughly tracking with Jews' proportion in the British population as a whole'.[15]

In early November Sunak sacked Braverman, though not for her remarks about hate marches. She wrote an article for *The Times* attacking the police for applying a 'double standard', claiming they were taking a tougher stance with right-wing demonstrators than with pro-Palestinian marchers.[16] Downing Street requested that she tone down her comments, and sacked her after she refused.[17] This political drama released tension, but allegations against the marchers would soon reemerge, and this time even more angry and virulent—though just as unfounded.

Enter the Scottish National Party

In Gaza the death toll, already horrifying, was rising. By mid-to-late February, 2024, according to figures from the Gaza health authority,[18] more than twenty-nine thousand Palestinians were dead. Thousands more bodies lay uncounted, presumed to be under the rubble. The International Court of Justice had launched its hearing on South Africa's charge of genocide, while the International Criminal Court was investigating Hamas and Israeli leaders for war crimes.[19] Details were beginning to emerge of British military collaboration with Israel in Gaza thanks to investigative reporting by *Declassified UK*.[20] Arms sales to Israel continued unabated while Britain protected Israel on the international stage and continued negotiations on a new trade deal.[21]

The Sunak/Starmer coalition held, but it was easier for Sunak. Every Tory newspaper group—Murdoch, Associated Newspapers, Telegraph, and Express—thunderously supported Israel. Most Conservative MPs were relaxed. There was no risk of a serious revolt on the Conservative benches.

Sir Keir Starmer on the other hand had a problem. Discontent was growing in Labour over his blind support for Sunak and by extension Netanyahu. Constituents as well as councillors and MPs were asking questions and causing trouble. Many could not understand why Labour was backing arms sales and were incredulous that it opposed a ceasefire.* To make matters more delicate, the general election was expected within months. Starmer faced the prospect of going to the polls with his party at odds over Gaza. There was no obvious way out. Concessions to Labour's anti-war faction might help to unite the party, but the Tory media would then accuse him of bowing to the supposedly antisemitic mob. Standing firm would lead to party rebellion.

It was at this point that the Scottish National Party made its move. As the third-largest party in parliament, it had the right to a rare and valued 'opposition day motion' when it was allowed to set the agenda for debate. February 21 was awarded to the SNP. It tabled a motion calling for an immediate ceasefire in Gaza and framed this demand in strong and vivid language. The motion accused Israel of 'collective punishment' and demanded an end to 'the slaughter of innocent civilians'. This went too far for Starmer, not least because the accusation of 'collective punishment'—a war crime—could have had legal implications for continued arms sales to Israel. On the eve of the vote the well-connected ITV political editor, Robert Peston, explained that Sir Keir 'hates the SNP's charge that Israel is engaging in the collective punishment of Palestinians'. Peston added that Starmer was therefore 'implacably opposed' to the SNP motion.[22] By this point the United Nations Satellite Centre had reported that over 30 percent of all buildings in Gaza were damaged or destroyed.[23]

But Starmer was in trouble. Up to a hundred Labour MPs—more than a third of the parliamentary party—were threatening to vote with the SNP.[24] Two shadow cabinet ministers reportedly pondered resignation. The Labour leader faced a hideous choice. If he went along with the brutal but

* Labour took over four months to call for an immediate ceasefire. When it did, in February 2024, it appended the caveat that a ceasefire should be 'humanitarian'. See Kiran Stacey, 'What Is Labour's New Position on Gaza Ceasefire – and Will It Unite the Party?' *The Guardian* (20 February 2024).

accurate SNP language he would offend the establishment press and the White House. If he refused to do so, the Labour Party would split. In this desperate predicament Starmer resolved to submit Labour's own watered-down ceasefire amendment, even though this smashed the parliamentary convention that other opposition parties do not amend opposition day motions.[25] In this way, Labour MPs would be able to vote for a ceasefire without taking a firm stance against Israel's crimes.*

With the debate about to start there came a surprise announcement from Speaker Hoyle: Labour would be allowed to table an amendment. Hoyle overruled the advice of his own Commons clerks to breach long-standing parliamentary convention on opposition day debates. Starmer was off the hook. The SNP chief whip complained that the 'convention and the Standing Orders of this House were overruled'.** The Conservatives agreed. The row deepened after it emerged that, in an irregular initiative, Sir Keir Starmer had personally visited the Speaker early that day.[26]

There were calls for Hoyle to quit amid accusations that he had compromised his office in order to curry favour with the likely next prime minister.[27] Emotions ran high. Chastened and visibly upset, Speaker Hoyle returned to the Commons later that day to apologise: 'It is clear that today has not shown the House at its best. I will reflect on my part in that, and of course I recommit myself to ensuring that all Members of this House are treated fairly'. He also introduced a factor, the security of MPs, which had *not* been mentioned when he had announced his intention to breach Commons procedure earlier in the day. 'I was very concerned', the Speaker now told MPs. 'I am still concerned, and that is why the meetings I have had today were about the security of Members, their families and the people involved'.[28]

---

* The Labour amendment contained no mention of 'collective punishment' and did not condemn Israel's conduct even as it unambiguously denounced Hamas. UK House of Commons, 'Order Paper for Wednesday 21 February 2024', commonsbusiness.parliament.uk (21 February 2024).

** It's doubtful that Hoyle did breach Standing Orders. See: Tom Fleming, 'The House of Commons Row over Opposition Day Amendments: Procedural Background and Implications', constitution-unit.com (29 February 2024).

Tory cabinet minister Michael Gove was quick to spot the political significance of the Speaker's comments. In an interview with *The Sun* he theatrically came out in support of Hoyle, insisting that MPs should 'respect the ref'. This meant tearing up the official Tory line, as set out by Leader of the Commons Penny Mordaunt, that the Speaker was to blame for breaking with 'long-standing and established processes and procedures'.[29] Gove told the newspaper that accusations of bias against the Speaker weren't the 'real issue'.

This, Gove explained to *Sun* readers, was 'being able to say to extremists outside the House of Commons: get back. You are not going to force elected representatives to vote in a particular way because of your tactics, and because of your commitment to extremist causes'.[30]

Neither Gove nor Speaker Hoyle named the extremists. Nigel Farage stepped in. He was in Washington that evening, attending the Conservative Political Action Conference (CPAC). Speakers would include Steve Bannon, Donald Trump, and Liz Truss, amidst a cattle call of far-right and authoritarian agitators.*

Speaking at an eve-of-conference event, Farage told his audience that Britain faced 'a huge internal problem, the scenes that we witness today in London, in Parliament Square, and indeed within the House of Commons'. This, he claimed, was 'a new phenomenon, religious sectarianism now beginning to dominate British politics'. As evidence he pointed to the protestors outside the Commons: 'Parliament Square, as we speak, is full of thousands of people waving Palestinian flags'.[31] He complained about 'religious hatred' that 'exists against Israel, against the Jewish people'. For this he blamed 'completely irresponsible immigration policies' and the failure to integrate Muslim immigrants. 'Radical Islam is becoming mainstream in British politics', said Farage. He predicted:

* Far-right influencer and conspiracy theorist Jack Posobiec addressed CPAC attendees (perhaps in an attempt at humour): 'Welcome to the end of democracy—we're here to overthrow it completely. We didn't get all the way there on January 6, but we will endeavour to get rid of it and replace it with this right here'—alluding to a crucifix he held in his clenched fist. Post by @AccountableGOP on X (22 February 2024), https://x.com/AccountableGOP/status/1760761957437599856.

'By the 2029 general election, we will have a radical Islamic party represented in Westminster'. He also said: 'You can't be a proper country unless you control your borders'.[32] Douglas Murray was also quick to ring alarm bells: 'it seems that British MPs are finally waking up. Now that the Islamist threat is coming at them'.[33]

The media, which at first presented Hoyle as a quiescent Starmer sycophant,[34] then flipped the narrative.[35] The story was no longer about a feeble Speaker bowing to intimidation from the Labour Party leader, but instead about an Islamist threat to parliamentary democracy. The British press has a long, well-documented record of bigotry towards minorities.[36] The Starmer/Hoyle stitch-up was forgotten. Muslims were the juicier target. Much more vulnerable. And ever so convenient.

Moral Panic at Westminster

The Speaker's comments, amplified by Gove, Farage, Murray, and others, unleashed a moral panic. 'These are extremists', Melanie Phillips informed readers of *The Times*, 'bent upon forcing conformity to Islamic theological dogma and who are driven by theological Jew-hatred'.[37] The *Daily Telegraph* gave space to Suella Braverman to develop her favourite theme that 'the Islamists, the extremists and the anti-semites are in charge now'.[38] Robert Jenrick, shortly to run for the Tory leadership, told *Mail* readers that 'the age of careless and naive mass immigration to the UK must be consigned to the history books. Delaying this necessary action only allows the cancer of Islamist extremism to grow'.[39]

Jacob Rees-Mogg, then a Conservative MP, told GB News that 'British democracy last week prostrated itself to an Islamist mob'. He added: 'Uncontrolled mass migration with a lack of integration, coupled with extremism and anti-British, anti-Western, antisemitic ideology, has led to this point'. He claimed this was 'a critical moment in the history of Parliament' and 'a moment that defines our civilisation'.[40]

Others criticised the London mayor Sadiq Khan for losing control of London's streets. The police, traditionally valorised on the right for their role in maintaining law and order, became villains. The phrase 'two-tier policing', expressing a belief that pro-Palestinian protestors were being given preferential treatment, was entering political language. It was not true, but articulated frustration on the right that police were arresting the wrong type of people. Commentator Isabel Oakeshott complained: 'This gutless government and London Mayor Sadiq Khan have lost control of our streets. Give extremists an inch, and they take a mile'.[41]

Rupert Lowe, a politically ambitious businessman making a short-lived reputation with the Reform Party, expressed his 'worry that Islamism is now deep-rooted into communities all across the UK. Our pathetic establishment has deliberately ignored the threat, right up until it comes knocking at the door—they enabled its growth, against all warnings. Zero-tolerance is urgently required'.[42] Tommy Robinson was more succinct: 'Stop cowering to Muslim mob rule!'[43]

Prime Minister Sunak amplified Farage and Robinson's street oratory with an emergency statement:

> Legitimate protests hijacked by extremists to promote and glorify terrorism, elected representatives verbally threatened and physically, violently targeted, and antisemitic tropes beamed onto our own Parliament building. And in Parliament this week a very dangerous signal was sent that this sort of intimidation works. It is toxic for our society and our politics and is an affront to the liberties and values we hold dear here in Britain.[44]

These were reckless and inflammatory comments; it is the responsibility of a British prime minister to show statesmanship and calm sectarian division.

Allegations of Antisemitism

I now examine the charge made by Prime Minister Sunak, and reiterated in the media and by Tory MPs, that the protestors had beamed 'antisemitic tropes' onto parliament. This was an especially powerful allegation because it linked the pro-Palestinian marchers directly with the noxious antisemitism that had been a feature of English society from the Middle Ages up to Oswald Mosley's British Union of Fascists ('Blackshirts') and beyond.

On the day of the SNP motion the protestors did project the phrase 'From the river to the sea / Palestine will be free' onto Elizabeth Tower, which houses Big Ben.[45] Rishi Sunak, as we have seen, denounced this slogan as antisemitic while Tory backbencher Andrew Percy labelled it a 'genocidal call'.[46] James Cleverly, by now the home secretary, said: 'They are deeply, deeply offensive words. They cause huge amounts of distress to the Jewish community. The implication is the eradication of the state of Israel. Both personally and as a government I completely reject that'.[47]

The Tory government was operating a double standard. The charter of Israel's governing Likud party declares that 'between the Mediterranean and the Jordan River there will be only Israeli sovereignty'.[48] This is the official policy of the Israeli government, implemented over decades of occupation. Israeli prime minister Benjamin Netanyahu drove the point home during a speech at the UN in September 2023, when he brandished a map that showed only Israel and no Palestine.[49] Israel's ambassador to the UK, Tzipi Hotovely, has repeatedly asserted that Israel has sole title to the land 'between the sea and the Jordan River'.[50] Israel's leading human rights organisation, B'Tselem, concluded already in 2021 that 'from the Jordan River to the Mediterranean Sea: This is apartheid'.[51]

Those who argue that 'from the river to the sea' is antisemitic or genocidal therefore have an obligation to explain why they are more outraged by street protestors expressing aspirations for justice than by the policy currently being put into practice through settler violence and ethnic cleansing by the Israeli government, in flagrant defiance of international law.

Many Palestinians say that their slogan is consistent with a just political settlement, which acknowledges that the only long-term answer to the Israel/Palestine conflict must involve a solution where all those living between the Jordan River and the Mediterranean Sea have equal rights. It is disturbing that the British government insisted on delegitimising the slogan as antisemitic when leaders of the Palestine solidarity movement have repeatedly described it as a call for equality.*

---

* Ben Jamal of the PSC told the Home Affairs Committee: 'I speak as a Palestinian. That chant is used by the vast majority of Palestinians. It describes how they are deprived of their rights across all of historic Palestine, whether they are citizens in the state of

What Really Happened on February 21?

The prime minister, Tommy Robinson, Nigel Farage's Reform, the *Daily Telegraph*, and the bulk of the mainstream media had concocted between them a shared version of reality: a Muslim mob had taken over London, intimidated MPs with threats of violence, and upended parliamentary democracy.

Before we examine the evidence for these claims, it is important to remember that threats to the safety of MPs are real and deadly serious. On the eve of the historic Brexit referendum the Labour MP Jo Cox was murdered in the street by a far-right fanatic shouting 'Britain first'.[52] Five years later the Conservative MP Sir David Amess was stabbed to death by a supporter of the Islamic State while carrying out a constituency surgery.[53] Many MPs receive death threats and some need regular protection.

Tensions had grown since October 7. Recorded levels of antisemitism and Islamophobia spiked, prompting London mayor Sadiq Khan to warn in November 2023: 'There's this thing called heightened fear. People are now scared to leave their homes'.[54] Speaker Hoyle himself was forced to contact the police after being targeted by a constituent with threatening messages over Gaza. The constituent, who sent an 'aggressive email with disturbing images', was arrested approximately a month before the vote and later punished with a six-week suspended prison sentence.[55] According to *The Sun*, one of the messages 'is believed to have included a picture of dead babies'.[56]

An even more frightening case involved the Labour MP Jess Phillips, who received abusive emails from a man called Nabil Arif over a four-month period starting shortly after October 7. The final one, threatening that she would 'burn until her skin is no more', arrived on the eve of the SNP vote. Arif was jailed for three months in July 2024. In her victim impact statement, Phillips set out how the threats had changed her life as she feared physical harm.[57]

Israel or living under military occupation. It in no shape or form seeks the abrogation of anybody else's rights, and to suggest that it does is a way of saying, "Let's not listen to Palestinians when they say what they mean and when they choose the words they say"'. UK House of Commons Home Affairs Committee, *Oral Evidence: Policing of Protests*, HC 369, committees.parliament.uk (6 December 2023), Q23.

Dreadful though these threats were, they had nothing to do with the SNP motion or with pro-Palestinian supporters outside parliament. Pro-Palestine MPs also received threats[58] while Jess Phillips was among those who, in the wake of the vote, argued that fears of intimidation should not be used to shut down protest and that pro-Palestine protesters should not be depicted as a mob. She testified that '[n]o one bullied me (any more than on any issue)'.* She did however call for 'rules and boundaries' on protest and distinguished between legitimate demonstrations at her place of work and potentially dangerous protests outside MPs' homes. Diane Abbott, who has been on the receiving end of more threats and abuse than almost any living British politician, said: 'the suggestion that police could close down peaceful demonstrations outside MPs' offices, town halls, and parliament is appalling'.[59]

I now turn to the widespread media claims that an Islamist mob threatened MPs outside parliament on February 21. Alicia Fitzgerald, a political reporter, said on TalkTV that she'd been talking to Labour MPs, particularly women, who were 'absolutely terrified' of leaving the Commons in the face of what Julia Hartley-Brewer termed 'a very angry, very threatening mob' outside.[60] These remarks were contradicted by another political reporter, Hugo Gye of *The i Paper*, who left parliament at 7:30 p.m. that same evening 'and didn't see a single protestor. So any fears that MPs may understandably have had were unfounded'.[61] The Metropolitan Police confirmed that no arrests were made outside parliament on February 21.[62]

The Tory MP Rachel Maclean went on BBC *Politics Live* to complain about 'extremely aggressive and violent protests from Islamist extremists' outside parliament. She also insisted that 'we are concerned about what we are seeing in our capital city week after week after week'. These claims were not challenged by presenter Jo Coburn, who instead asked another studio guest, Labour MP Luke Pollard, if Maclean was expressing legitimate concerns.

* She wrote on social media: 'Level of Islamophobia people are displaying currently is sickening. My constituents, family and friends are not Islamists, they do not hate any of these things. They are not a mob, they are just people. No one bullied me (any more than on any issue)'. Quoted in Eleni Courea and Josh Halliday, 'British MPs Fearful of Violent Attacks as Tensions over Gaza War Increase Threats' *The Guardian* (23 February 2024). See also: Jess Phillips, 'Political Pressure Is Great. Bullying MPs Like Me at Home Is Utterly Wrong', *The Guardian* (25 February 2024).

Pollard affirmed that 'there's been some really violent threats and some utterly unacceptable behaviours from a small group of people'.[63] This studio discussion shows that the narrative about aggressive and violent protests, though without foundation, had become established fact—so much so that it was accepted without question by a respected TV presenter and MPs from Britain's two largest political parties.[64]

We examined video evidence of protestors outside the Labour Party headquarters and later that day in Parliament Square. There was at times a lively atmosphere, with Palestinian flags being waved and chants of 'free Palestine'. But the scenes depicted in footage we have unearthed are peaceful.* For ease of reference I have provided links to the video footage in a footnote at the bottom of this page; readers are invited to watch it and see for themselves.

Despite long and earnest searching my researchers and I have discovered no evidence to support the proposition that a mob, Islamist or otherwise, threatened parliament on February 21, as has been widely and vividly alleged across British media. Scottish Labour MSP Paul Sweeney did say that his Glasgow office had been 'stormed' by Gaza protestors. They were 'terrifying and threatening our staff', he added. But *The National*, which supports Scottish independence, investigated this and found no evidence of 'threatening' behaviour: 'Police Scotland has now confirmed it was not aware of anyone storming in or threatening Labour staff'.[65] *The National* added that 'Police Scotland also said it was made aware of a "peaceful protest" that officers attended with no issues because the protesters involved left of their own accord'.

This episode may help explain the basis of the idea that 'Islamists' were intimidating Labour MPs. There's no reason to think politicians like

---

* *Morning protest outside Labour HQ*: https://news.sky.com/video/pro-palestinian-protests-outside-labour-hq-before-ceasefire-vote-13076988. *Outside parliament (daytime)*: https://www.youtube.com/watch?v=QADiumNFhno. *Outside parliament (evening)*: https://www.youtube.com/watch?v=C7J_edSFJpI. *Outside parliament (evening)*: https://www.newsflare.com/video/627292/london-uk-21-feb-2024-projections-on-big-ben-demand-a-gaza-ceasefire-at-rally-to-demand-mps-vote-for-a-cease-fire-in-palestine-organised-by-swp-psc-and-stop-the-war-coalition. *Bell Ribeiro-Addy MP's speech outside parliament during the debate*: https://www.youtube.com/watch?v=wqBcoHi40ug.

Sweeney were being dishonest. Some did feel threatened and harassed. But in the judgement of others—including the police—they had endured no more than peaceful protest. A demonstration outside their office for sure. Possibly chanting and verbal abuse. But all this lies within the limits of what the law regards as legitimate democratic activity when passions rise high over an issue as grave as a call for an end to the mass slaughter of civilians.*

My researchers and I have gone to great lengths to proactively seek out and document threats to MPs. This was not an easy task since few concrete examples were specified and we met with little cooperation. We sent a freedom of information request to Speaker Hoyle's office requesting details of threats, abuse, and hate speech directed at MPs since October 2023. The request was turned down on grounds of cost, as was a similar request to the Metropolitan Police.**

A *Guardian* investigation published two days after the abortive SNP vote cited Tan Dhesi, Labour MP for Slough, who said he had been subjected to death threats that forced him to maintain a police presence at his constituency surgeries. He said that Thames Valley police had contacted and charged the person behind one death threat.[66]

The Crown Prosecution Service told us it was unaware that anyone had been charged. We approached Thames Valley police. They stressed that they took all threats against MPs seriously and confirmed that Tan Dhesi had been threatened in a case that had led to a conviction. However, the police told us that the case in question took place in 2019 and 'clearly, would not have been related to the conflict in Gaza'. We asked *The Guardian* whether it had corroborated Mr. Dhesi's claim but received no reply. A spokesman for Mr. Dhesi told us that 'whilst Tan is unable to recall the exact words used when he spoke to *The Guardian*, if he did state an individual had been

* For a helpful guide to the legal limits of protest, see: William Downs, *Police Powers: Protests*, House of Commons Library (13 December 2024). See also: 'Protest Rights and Laws in the UK', thompsons.law (21 April 2023).

** A similar request to the House of Commons Information Compliance Service was turned down on grounds of cost. We also asked for records of the meeting between Sir Keir Starmer and Speaker Hoyle. This was rejected on grounds of 'parliamentary privilege'.

"charged" we think this is likely to have been inaccurate at that time, and what Tan would have likely meant to say was "arrested"'.

The police eventually told us that a twenty-eight-year-old man was issued with a conditional caution after being arrested following a 'malicious communications report' on October 17, 2023. So Tan Dhesi had real and serious grounds to feel alarmed, but the claim—ventilated in a *Guardian* report shortly after the SNP vote—that the police had charged an individual in connection with a death threat seems to have been false.

The Speaker's Account Unravels

When the Speaker set out his decision to breach Commons procedure at the start of the debate, at 1:30 p.m. on February 21, he made no mention of threats to MPs; Hoyle confined himself to saying that Gaza was 'a highly sensitive subject, on which feelings are running high, in the House, in the nation, and throughout the world'. He explained: 'I think it is important on this occasion that the House is able to consider the widest possible range of options'.[67] He then involved himself in an elaborate explanation of why his decision was consistent with Commons procedures. It was only when he made his second statement, more than five hours later and following outrage from both government and opposition MPs, that he raised the subject of MPs' safety.[68]

The belated claim that convention was breached to keep MPs safe makes little sense. If Hoyle believed that MPs were subject to intimidation and threats of violence sufficiently serious to warrant breaching parliamentary convention, why didn't he explain to parliament right at the start that he had ignored the advice of Commons clerks and broken the rules of procedure because of threats to the safety of MPs? Had he done so he would not have been forced to come back and explain himself five hours later.

Better still, why didn't he and Starmer issue a joint statement and order an investigation into this apparently terrifying new threat to parliament? Who had made these threats? How serious were they? Did they come from Islamists? From the far right? Were they coordinated? Could foreign influence be detected? How many MPs had been threatened? This is what serious politicians would have done—assuming Hoyle's scenario was real. On the other hand, it is hard to see how the sinking of the SNP's motion and the scenes of parliamentary disorder that predictably ensued contributed to the safety of any MP.

The Speaker's decision to leave these questions unanswered, especially after raising the subject himself, was negligent. It left a vacuum for unfounded but inflammatory speculation by newspaper columnists and far-right troublemakers. Even if the Speaker had chosen not to order his own investigation, a Commons Committee could have called witnesses, demanded answers, and reached conclusions.

The allegation made by senior politicians, and amplified by the media, is exceptionally serious: a howling mob intimidated MPs who, fearful for their personal safety, voted against their conscience. If true, it would be a unique event in the modern history of the House of Commons. This makes it inexplicable that, in the eighteen months that have passed since, parliament has never sought to establish the truth. More than inexplicable, this is in my view suspicious.

Stephen Flynn, the SNP leader at Westminster, told MPs in the Commons in the wake of the fiasco:

> This should have been the chance for the UK Parliament to do the right thing and vote for an immediate ceasefire in Gaza and Israel—instead it turned into a Westminster circus. It is a disgrace that Sir Keir Starmer and the Speaker colluded to block Parliament voting on the SNP motion for an immediate ceasefire and against the collective punishment of the Palestinian people. More than 29,000 Palestinian children, women and men have been killed—and huge swathes of Gaza have been obliterated while Westminster equivocates.[69]

Many Labour MPs agree, though have not dared to speak out for fear of being punished. One Labour insider told us that 'games were definitely being played that day. Keir and the Speaker were in the room behind the chamber for a long time while this was playing out. Essentially, I think a deal was struck that if he [Lindsay Hoyle] didn't allow it [the SNP motion] he would have Keir's support in being the Speaker, because by forming a government and having the majority you have de facto support to ensure that person's position in the next parliament. I believe that is what happened in that room'.

This interpretation has been supported by a new book from two of Britain's most highly regarded and best-connected political reporters.[70] Patrick Maguire and Gabriel Pogrund unequivocally state that Starmer told Hoyle that if he did not select Labour's amendment, 'the first act of a Labour government would be to whip its MPs to elect a new Speaker after the election they were expected to win'. The authors also report that Starmer told the Speaker that voting against the SNP motion could expose Labour MPs to 'violence and intimidation outside their own homes'.

The political editor of BBC *Newsnight*, Nicholas Watt, gave a similar description, taken from 'senior Labour sources':

> Senior Labour figures tell me [the Speaker] was left in no doubt that Labour would bring him down after the general election unless he called Labour's Gaza amendment. The message was: you will need our votes to be re-elected as Speaker after [the] election with strong indications that this would not be forthcoming if he failed to call the Labour amendment. The Speaker's office have been in touch to say: 'This is not true'. For clarity, senior Labour sources briefed me on the messages: you will need our support after the election and this may not be forthcoming.[71]

The Times reported that, before the ceasefire debate, Labour MPs and whips had 'gathered behind the Speaker's chair, near the reasons room, talking loudly of how "Keir is going to fix the Speaker"'.[72]

Sir Keir Starmer has denied threatening the Speaker, and Hoyle has denied being threatened. If these accounts are true, however, both Starmer and Hoyle behaved disgracefully. Erskine May, often called the 'bible of parliamentary procedure', states that the 'chief characteristics attaching to the office of Speaker in the House of Commons are authority and impartiality'.*

---

* Erskine May, para. 4.23. Erskine May also says: 'Confidence in the impartiality of the Speaker is an indispensable condition of the successful working of procedure, and many

This is the reason why, at general elections, rival parties never run candidates against an incumbent Speaker. At all events, Hoyle's ruling was a massive political favour to the opposition leader. For Labour MPs the Speaker's decision amounted to a get out of jail free card. They were spared an agonising choice between offending their constituents by voting against the SNP ceasefire motion or wrecking their prospects of ministerial office by voting with it.[73]

It is impossible to make a certain judgment about the events on February 21. We do not know exactly what was said during the long conversation between Starmer and Hoyle. We do know that both Sir Keir and the Speaker found that real or imagined threats of violence against MPs provided a heaven-sent excuse. As far as Starmer is concerned, they got him out of the deepest hole of his time as opposition leader. For the Speaker, they rescued him from the wounding allegation that he had given into threats from the future prime minister.

The Speaker's innuendo about unspecified threats to MPs convulsed the media and was exploited by the extreme right. As media hysteria developed over the course of the week, pro-Palestinian protestors were integrated into the roster of far-right hate figures. There was a general failure at any point to engage with the serious moral, humanitarian, and legal arguments made by protestors and critics of Israeli conduct towards Palestinians in Gaza. Instead the British political and media class concentrated on smears, character assassination, and ad hominem public attacks. Prime Minister Sunak, as we have seen, participated vigorously in this irrational, hate-filled discourse—a British prime minister abusing the power of his office and descending into gutter politics in order to malign protestors who demanded an end to killing. Sir Keir Starmer was more restrained. But he did not challenge the explosion of bigotry, which suited him well because it got him off the hook. On the contrary, the frenzy was wittingly or unwittingly fuelled by his machinations with the Speaker.

In the year ahead, pro-Palestinian demonstrators would increasingly become targets themselves as politicians and journalists continued to

---

conventions exist which have as their object not only to ensure the impartiality of the Speaker but also to ensure that that impartiality is generally recognised'.

denounce them as terrorist sympathisers while the British state addressed them as criminals. The campaign of demonisation was only getting started. There is a mystery about all this. From the start of the war public opinion has been on the side of the peace marchers. Overwhelmingly so. An opinion poll in October 2023 showed that fully 76 percent of the British public supported a ceasefire, and just 8 percent were opposed.[74] This majority for peace increased as the war continued. It is the politicians from the two main parties, along with their supporters in conventional media, who have been isolated.

There is a regular pattern with many popular movements. William Wilberforce, the anti-slavery campaigner, was excoriated in newspapers while suffragette campaigners for women's voting rights were denounced as extremists. Marchers against the Iraq war were condemned as supporters of Saddam Hussein. Almost everybody now accepts they were right.

The great twentieth-century British historian A.J.P. Taylor noted that radicals and fighters for justice tend to be ostracised and despised in their own era. 'If you want to know what the foreign policy of this country will be in twenty or thirty years' time', observed Taylor, 'find out what the Dissenting minority are saying now'.[75] What once sounded heretical becomes the orthodoxy. History will salute the bravery and the stamina of the Gaza protestors, who turned out month after month to demand an end to mass killing. Across the country, in student encampments, street marches, and through direct action, they mobilised in vast numbers and in defiance of persistent attempts to demonise, marginalise, and criminalise their movement. They have been an essential voice of decency and compassion during a shameful period in British public life. By the same token, history will condemn the politicians and their lackey journalists who have made Britain complicit in some of the most terrible crimes of the twenty-first century.

5

BRITISH COMPLICITY BEFORE OCTOBER 7

Oh rascal children of Gaza,
You who constantly disturbed me with your screams
under my window,
You who filled every morning with rush and chaos,
You who broke my vase and stole the lonely flower on my balcony,
Come back

—*Excerpt from a poem by Khaled Juma, written during Israel's 2014 assault on Gaza*

ON NOVEMBER 2, 1917, Arthur James Balfour, the foreign secretary, dispatched a letter to Lord Rothschild, a leading figure in Britain's Jewish community. The Balfour Declaration, as it came to be known, expressed support for 'the establishment in Palestine of a national home for the Jewish people'. Balfour did not sign his letter because he loved Jews or because he felt any special enmity towards the Arabs whose land he was giving away. Balfour was acting out of what he perceived to be the self-interest of the world's greatest imperial power.

During the 1920s and '30s, the British administration in Palestine provided the crucial political and military shield behind which the Jewish community there developed into a state. British mandatory authorities blocked democratic self-government and overruled consistent Arab majority opposition to Jewish immigration and settlement. When the Arab inhabitants of Palestine erupted in nationalist revolt, in 1936, Britain deployed overwhelming and often brutal force to crush the uprising.[1] This left the Zionists in a position to dominate when Britain left. Zionist leaders declared independence in May 1948; the new State of Israel won the resulting war for Palestine, expelling most of the Arab inhabitants and expanding Israel's boundaries to encompass four-fifths of the land.

Israel conquered the remaining 20 percent of Palestine in the June 1967 Arab-Israel War. In the aftermath the UN Security Council adopted Resolution 242, which called for Israel to return the captured territories in exchange for peace and mutual recognition. In 1973, Arab states led by Egypt resorted to military action and an oil embargo to overcome Israeli intransigence. By this point the Palestine Liberation Organisation (PLO) had revived the Palestinian self-determination struggle and begun to push for an independent Palestinian state alongside Israel. The diplomatic package of Israeli withdrawal from the territory occupied in 1967, Palestinian statehood on the West Bank and Gaza, and mutual recognition became known as the 'two-state solution'. Over the 1970s and '80s this two-state framework for resolving the conflict gained widespread international support, including from the mainstream Palestinian leadership and the frontline Arab states.

The collapse of the British Empire after World War Two had relegated Britain to a minor role on the world stage. Once the US effectively adopted Israel as a regional client in the 1970s, Britain sought to balance between the US and the Arab states and avoid being outflanked on the issue by more pro-Arab European powers. The record of Sir Alec Douglas-Home, the short-lived Tory prime minister who later became foreign secretary in the Heath government in the early 1970s, illustrates how this worked.

His policy might today bring a nod of approbation (if hardly a cheer) from the Palestine Solidarity Campaign. Sir Alec discussed the right of return for Palestinian refugees expelled by Israel in 1948.[2] In 1970 he took the first step towards recognising Palestinian 'political aspirations'.[3] Ignoring Israeli protests, he allowed the PLO to set up a London office. Douglas-Home, like his Labour counterpart George Brown, interpreted

UNSC Resolution 242 as a demand for unconditional Israeli withdrawal from all Arab territories captured in the June 1967 War. During the 1973 War he refused to deliver arms to Israel. On the other hand, Britain opposed a Palestinian state throughout the 1970s and '80s and connived behind the scenes to thwart PLO initiatives for a two-state solution at the UN.[4]

The Soviets had been a significant presence across the Middle East, supported a two-state solution, and bolstered the Palestinians. When the Soviet empire collapsed in 1991, the United States—by now a near-unconditional protector of Israel—assumed unchallenged hegemony in the region. Britain was reluctant to offend its superpower ally, especially after Tony Blair became prime minister in 1997. The view from the European Union was that Britain's position on the Israel-Palestine conflict transited in this period 'from the middle ground in Europe to a position closer to Washington than most others'.[5]

Supplication to the United States, along with an ever-stronger domestic pro-Israel lobby, condemned Britain to running parallel policies. Rhetorically Britain supported some form of Palestinian self-determination and was alert to Palestinian rights under international law. The Blair government held out Palestinian statehood as a possible outcome of negotiations and then officially endorsed a two-state solution in 2003 along with the EU and United States. In practice, Britain played along as Israel entrenched its domination over the Occupied Palestinian Territory and suppressed independent Palestinian organisation.

The Oslo Accords signed by Israel and the PLO in the mid-1990s were sold as a step towards Palestinian self-rule and a negotiated end to the conflict. In reality they did not prohibit Israel from settling Palestinian land, did not commit Israel to accepting a Palestinian state, and set up a subordinate 'Palestinian Authority' to administer and police Palestinians on Israel's behalf. Throughout the 1990s Israel intensified its settlement of the West Bank, increasingly known to Israeli politicians by the biblical names of Judea and Samaria. Including East Jerusalem, the number of Israeli settlers nearly trebled from 250,000 to over 700,000 in the three decades from the first Oslo agreement in 1993.

British governments have recognised that these settlements are illegal and acknowledged that each new Israeli settlement makes a two-state solution less viable. They know that Palestinians are being driven off their land by terrifying settler violence. But Britain will not confront Israel.

In short, British diplomacy towards the Israel-Palestine conflict has been a story of protracted, multi-layered, and systematic deception. After Israel captured the West Bank and Gaza Strip along with other Arab lands in 1967 it pursued the de facto annexation of the Occupied Palestinian Territory, all the while pretending its military administration was temporary pending a diplomatic settlement. Britain fitted in snugly with Israel. We enabled this illegal annexation in practice all the while pretending to oppose it. From approximately 2015 onward, Israel dropped even the pretence of respecting the international law prohibition on conquest.* This left Britain in an increasingly embarrassing position. In general our politicians sought to brazen their way through, ever more contemptible but also confident that the domestic media would never turn this pitiful spectacle into a crisis. That policy of smoke and mirrors was critically enabled by the fact that the US still kept up its own pretence of supporting a negotiated settlement to the

---

* In 2009 the Israeli prime minister Benjamin Netanyahu acquiesced in principle to a Palestinian 'state' albeit one subject to vague and onerous conditions not sanctioned by international law. In 2014 Netanyahu said Israel would have permanent 'security control of the territory west of the River Jordan'. During the 2015 Israeli election campaign Netanyahu vowed he would not allow a Palestinian state to be established on his watch. He repudiated his 2009 commitment as 'null and void' and a leaflet published by his party asserted that 'Netanyahu's entire political biography is a fight against the creation of a Palestinian state'. After winning the election Netanyahu rhetorically backtracked under pressure from the Barack Obama administration. Once Donald Trump entered the White House in 2017 all remaining pretence was dropped. In February 2024, Netanyahu declared openly that he 'flat out reject[s]' a two-state solution and boasted that 'everyone knows that I am the one who for decades blocked the establishment of a Palestinian state'. Israel Ministry of Foreign Affairs, 'Address by PM Netanyahu at Bar-Ilan University', gov.il (14 June 2009) (acquiesced). David Horovitz, 'Netanyahu Finally Speaks His Mind', *The Times of Israel* (13 July 2014) ('security'). Barak Ravid, 'Netanyahu: Bar-Ilan 2-State Speech No Longer Relevant in Today's Reality', *Haaretz* (8 March 2015) ('null', 'biography'). TOI Staff, 'Netanyahu Boasts of Thwarting the Establishment of a Palestinian State "for Decades"', *The Times of Israel* (20 February 2024) ('reject[s]', 'decades').

conflict. As we shall see in Chapter Seven, when the second Trump administration followed Netanyahu in openly rejecting this prospect, Britain's charade was left completely exposed.

Israel's commitment to military occupation required repeated resort to violence, normally in violation of international law. Britain's dishonest policy towards Israel's occupation accordingly required further deceptions in respect of Israel's international law violations. Britain consistently claimed to respect the law yet acquiesced or participated in Israeli crimes.

Press Release Diplomacy

A pattern developed. The British consulate in East Jerusalem would respond to especially serious settler outrages with an expression of 'concern'. In very rare cases it would call for an inquiry. All the while British officials knew perfectly well that Israel would take no notice of the concern and treat any call for an inquiry with contempt. In the exceptionally rare cases when an inquiry did take place, there were no meaningful consequences. These statements from British officials were performative.[6]

Three months before October 7, then British ambassador to Israel Neil Wigan gave an interview to the *Jerusalem Post,* Israel's oldest English-speaking newspaper dating back to the days of the British Mandate in the 1930s.

Mr. Wigan told the *Post* that Palestinian issues counted far less in British-Israeli relations than when he had been a junior diplomat serving in Tel Aviv twenty years earlier. He said that Britain was 'very concerned' about settlement construction in the West Bank: the same empty expression of disapproval issued by every British diplomat or politician for decades. There was no mention of the wave of Israeli settler attacks on Palestinians and their property that had displaced hundreds of Palestinians and forced three entire communities to flee in the first six months of 2023.[7] Settler attacks were often supported by the Israeli army and incited by senior members of the Netanyahu government.[8] Mr. Wigan made no comment on this.

The wretched Wigan was also silent on the first guiding principle of the coalition agreement formed by Netanyahu's Likud party with new far-right allies.[9] This asserted that 'the Jewish people have an exclusive and unquestionable right to all areas of the land of Israel', writing off any prospect of a two-state solution. The programme also pledged to 'advance and develop' Israeli settlements on the West Bank—a flagrant war crime under international law. Wigan should have been furious about this, given that the two-state solution is official British policy and Britain claims to oppose settlement building.

Wigan did not refer to the fact that Amnesty and Human Rights Watch, along with the Israeli human rights group B'Tselem and its Palestinian counterpart Al Haq, had recently found that Israel was perpetrating the international crime of apartheid. Wigan expressed no hint of alarm that Israel was governed by the most overtly racist and extreme right government in the country's seventy-five-year history. The *Jerusalem Post* headline read: 'UK Ambassador: Ties with Israel "Strongest They've Ever Been"'.

Wigan's interview was published the same day as scores of settlers rampaged through the West Bank village of Turmusaya burning thirty houses and destroying sixty cars. One local man, Omar Jibra, had been shot dead. Since I was living in nearby Nablus I travelled to Turmusaya to inspect the damage.

When I reached the village I found Wigan's senior colleague, Consul-General Diane Corner, already there with a delegation of European diplomats. Her meaningless condemnation read as follows: 'This cycle of violence must end. Perpetrators of crimes must be held to account'.

Maybe I shouldn't have turned towards Ms. Corner as I spotted her walking away from a burnt-out house and suggested that she resign. But I'd just had a long conversation with the dead man's uncle, Raja Jibra, who was with Omar when he was shot, and then carried his dying nephew five hundred yards to an ambulance. And another conversation with a villager who had braved settler assault and jumped an eight-foot wall to rescue his family from their burning house. A third conversation with two terrified young women who had been stranded in the basement while settlers outside tried to break in.

Moreover that morning, on the way to Turmusaya, I'd passed through another village where settlers had a few months before gone on the rampage. Once prosperous Huwara was now desolate. Armed settlers prowled the streets. Snipers surveyed the main road through the town from concealed vantage points. Homes had been burned down. Hundreds of vehicles incinerated. Local businesses destroyed. Windows shattered. Dozens of olive trees set alight. Palestinians who attempted to protect their community were tear gassed by Israeli soldiers. 'This was no loss of control', B'Tselem explained. 'In fact, it is exactly what Israel's control looks like: settlers launch an attack, soldiers guard them, and politicians back them up.'[10]

The violence at Huwara was intense enough that Israel's top commander in the West Bank labelled it a 'pogrom carried out by outlaws'.[11] Bezalel Smotrich, however—the finance minister, who also had administrative responsibility in much of the West Bank—was less disturbed. 'I think the village of Huwara needs to be wiped out', he remarked. 'I think the state of Israel should do it'.[12]

The British Consulate in Jerusalem had issued a typical condemnation of the 'abhorrent settler attack' in Huwara.[13] The IDF chief of staff, Herzi Halevi, promised an internal investigation. The probe concluded that the army's response failed—but the soldiers weren't punished.[14] According to Israeli journalist Amira Hass:

> They do not intend to force IDF soldiers who protected the rioters to testify. They do not wish to question hundreds of youths, if not more, and those who sent them, and they do not wish to deal with the well-oiled propaganda machine of the right if they were to indict most of the assailants. Everyone knows, after all, that the so-called rogue attacks are another tool in executing Israeli policy.[15]

I suggested to Ms. Corner that her press releases and Twitter statements were no substitute for taking real measures to ensure that the UK is not complicit in human rights violations. 'You know who you have to speak to', replied the consul-general. Her point was reasonable. She was an official doing nothing more culpable than carrying out instructions, though maybe diplomats should ask themselves more often whether resignation might not be better than joining in such a cynical charade. Only one British diplomat has resigned over British policy towards Gaza since October 7.*

The ultimate responsibility for British complicity in Israeli settler attacks lies with ministers. They are gutless at best. The month before the Turmusaya pogrom, violent settlers drove Palestinians out of a nearby village called Ein Samiya. This was the state-sponsored forcible removal of a population: a war crime. British foreign secretary James Cleverly visited Israel in September 2023. He made plans to visit Ein Samiya but the Israelis would not let him, citing security issues as a flimsy pretext. Cleverly had the option of causing a storm. He remained silent, in public at least.[16] His indifferent posture did not distinguish him from any other recent British foreign secretary.

Four days after October 7, Cleverly endured another inglorious moment when his Israeli counterpart Eli Cohen cut across the stuttering British foreign secretary and answered a question for him.[17] When Cohen used what felt close to genocidal language—'we are living next to monsters, to inhuman people'—Cleverly did not object. Typical of British politicians and officials over many decades, this is exactly the sort of behaviour that has sent Israel the message that Britain will allow it to get away with mass murder.

Israel has been the occupying power in Gaza since 1967. Britain has recognised this along with Israel's corresponding obligations under the Fourth Geneva Convention and other international agreements.[18] Israel has systematically breached its obligations to the extent that in July 2024 the International Court of Justice found that its occupation is illegal.[19] This means that the violence of the first two decades of the twenty-first century

* In August 2024 Mark Smith, a counterterrorism official based at the British embassy in Dublin, resigned in protest against continued arms sales to Israel by the UK, saying he could no longer 'in good conscience continue to work with a government which is complicit in war crimes'. He explained: 'To export arms to any nation, the UK must be satisfied that the recipient nation has in place robust procedures to avoid civilian casualties and to minimise harm to civilian life. It is impossible to argue that Israel is doing that'. Bel Trew and Holly Bancroft, 'British Diplomat Resigns Saying UK May Be Complicit in War Crimes over Arms Sales to Israel', *The Independent* (19 August 2024).

(especially the 2006 Lebanon War, assaults on Gaza in 2008 and 2014, and massacre of Gaza protestors in 2018) can in part be understood as a dry run for what happened after October 7. If Israel was testing the waters, it learnt a vital lesson: the international community, of which Britain was a leading member, would allow Israel to slaughter civilians without consequence. This was especially relevant because senior Israeli officials have long advocated for punishing civilian populations in the Middle East to increase Israel's deterrence.

The Dahiya Doctrine

The 'Dahiya doctrine', named for the Dahiya suburb of Beirut, was developed during the 2006 Lebanon War. That broke out when Hezbollah killed three Israeli soldiers in a cross-border raid and abducted two more for use in prisoner swaps. Israel responded with a massive bombing campaign concentrated in the Lebanese south. Over 850 Lebanese civilians and more than 40 Israeli civilians were killed.[20]

The reason for the high civilian death toll was simple: Israel chose not to distinguish between civilian and military targets. In the course of the bombardment, tens of thousands of homes in Lebanon were damaged or destroyed.[21] As usual, Israel produced the excuse of collateral damage: Hezbollah was embedded in the Lebanese population and using civilians as human shields. And as usual, the allegation was weakly supported while there was other evidence to contradict it.* According to Human Rights

* According to Human Rights Watch, although Hezbollah sometimes fired rockets from, and stored weapons in, populated areas, the practice was not widespread: 'Hezbollah stored most of its rockets in bunkers and weapon storage facilities located in uninhabited fields and valleys . . . in the vast majority of cases Hezbollah fighters left populated civilian areas as soon as the fighting started and . . . Hezbollah fired the vast majority of its rockets from pre-prepared positions outside villages'. Although some civilian deaths in Lebanon were the result of attacks on military targets, 'during the vast majority of the deadly air strikes we investigated, we found no evidence of Hezbollah military presence, weaponry or any other military objective that would have justified the strike'. Human Rights Watch, *Why They Died: Civilian Casualties in Lebanon during the 2006 War* (September 2007), pp. 5, 6. See also pp. 14–17; HRW did accuse Hezbollah of regularly firing rockets from positions near UN outposts.

Watch, the principal cause of the slaughter was that Israel's 'widespread bombardment . . . did not discriminate between military objectives and civilians'.*

This account of events was supported by the declarations of senior Israeli military personnel. Gadi Eizenkot, who headed the IDF's Operations Directorate during the 2006 war, issued the following warning afterwards: 'What happened in the al-Dahiya district', he said, 'will happen in every village from which Israel is shot at. We will subject it to disproportionate force and cause enormous damage and destruction. We don't consider them to be civilian villages but military bases . . . This is not a recommendation, this is the plan. And it has already been approved'.[22]

In 2014, an Israeli national security expert, Eitan Shamir, noted tersely that Eizenkot had 'supported the destruction of Beirut's Dahiya suburb and called for attacking Lebanese infrastructure as an act of deterrence'.[23] That year Eizenkot was promoted to the post of IDF chief of staff—proof that the brutal destruction of civilian infrastructure is considered an acceptable, even laudable, military strategy in Israel. Other research has validated this general picture of Israel's conduct. Zeev Maoz, the author of an exhaustive military history of Israel, observed that Israel pursued in Lebanon a 'strategy of compellence through deliberate destruction of civilian targets during the war'.[24]

Israel has a record of attacking civilians—not as collateral damage, or as the result of unscrupulous enemies hiding behind innocent populations, but as a deliberate strategy. This vital point must be kept in mind in relation to Israel's onslaught against Gaza after October 2023.

---

* Ibid., p. 6. Israel also made massive use of cluster munitions, especially in the final few days of the conflict; it is estimated that four million submunitions were dropped on south Lebanon. Human Rights Watch, *Flooding South Lebanon: Israel's Use of Cluster Munitions in Lebanon in July and August 2006* (February 2008), p. 1. The Convention on Cluster Munitions, first signed in 2008, seeks to ban the use of these weapons, noting their propensity to kill and maim civilians and to persist in causing damage long after conflicts have ended.

Destroying Palestinian Democracy

In January 2006 Hamas won a majority of seats in Palestinian legislative elections. The vote was held in part at US prompting and was certified as fair by international observers. Hamas had traditionally adhered to a maximalist programme that offered no basis for peace with Israel. But the elected Hamas leadership indicated that it was prepared to moderate its positions to achieve a negotiated agreement.[25] 'Hamas has been carefully and consciously adjusting its political program for years', a US government agency study reported in 2009, 'and has sent repeated signals that it is ready to begin a process of coexisting with Israel'.[26]

Alvaro de Soto, the UN's special coordinator for the Middle East Peace process from 2005 to 2007, believed that international engagement could have encouraged Hamas to further 'evolve in a pragmatic direction that would allow for a two-state solution'.[27] The House of Commons Foreign Affairs Select Committee recommended in 2007 that the British government 'urgently consider ways of engaging politically with moderate elements within Hamas' to fully explore the potential for diplomatic progress.[28] This advice was rejected.

Israel responded to the Palestinian election by refusing to engage with the Hamas government, escalating its military repression, and stealing Palestinian tax revenues crucial for the government to function. Despite having pushed for Palestinian elections, the US and European Union, including Britain, cooperated with this punitive policy. The UN special rapporteur for human rights in the Occupied Territories observed that 'the Palestinian people have been subjected to possibly the most rigorous form of international sanctions imposed in modern times'—the 'first time', he added, 'that an occupied people have been so treated'.*

---

* This UN rapporteur was John Dugard, a towering figure in South African human rights law who, after October 2023, led the South African legal team at The Hague. UN Special Rapporteur on the Situation of Human Rights in the Occupied Palestinian Territory Professor John Dugard, 'Human Rights in Palestine' (Geneva: UN Human Rights Council, 21 June 2006).

As Palestinian poverty soared and the government collapsed, Hamas and its factional rival Fatah formed a government of national unity in a bid for economic relief. But Western and Israeli pressure did not relent while the US—and reportedly Britain, too—cultivated a Palestinian militia to topple the elected Hamas administration.[29] When internal Palestinian conflict escalated, a US envoy privately declared 'I like this violence' because 'it means that other Palestinians are resisting Hamas'.[30] In the civil war that resulted, Hamas seized Gaza while Fatah held the West Bank.

Instead of respecting democratic elections and exploring diplomatic openings, Western policy helped entrench a division that has paralysed Palestinian politics and facilitated Israel's domination ever since. By sabotaging the unity government, channelling financial assistance outside official channels, and funding Fatah-aligned security forces accused of widespread torture,[31] Britain arguably contributed as well to increased Palestinian authoritarianism in the West Bank.

Once Hamas assumed control of Gaza in June 2007, Israel and its Western allies tightened the economic siege they had imposed on the Strip after Hamas' electoral victory. The siege caused what Amnesty International and humanitarian NGOs called a 'humanitarian implosion',[32] devastating Gaza's economy and raising unemployment levels to among the highest in the world.[33] 'It's like a meeting with a dietician', a senior Israeli advisor had explained. 'We have to make them much thinner, but not enough to die'.[34] In November 2008, just weeks before Israel launched a major attack on Gaza, former UN high commissioner for human rights Mary Robinson visited the besieged enclave. 'Their whole civilisation has been destroyed', she said. 'I'm not exaggerating'.[35]

Human rights authorities agreed that the Gaza siege was 'a collective punishment imposed in clear violation' of international law.[36] But the British government refused to categorise it in these terms, confining itself to empty expressions of humanitarian concern.* We discussed the political back-

* According to Tom Porteous of Human Rights Watch, a Foreign Office official 'privately agreed that it was collective punishment, but said that for political reasons it was impossible for the British Government to say'. Tom Porteous, 'Oral Evidence to House of Commons Foreign Affairs Select Committee', publications.parliament.uk (30 April

ground to this shameful silence above. Britain increased its humanitarian funding and urged Israel to allow humanitarian aid in, but did not pressure Israel to lift the closure regime.

Britain's own House of Commons International Development Committee argued that the government 'should not only have more assertively condemned the blockade of Gaza but should have exerted much greater diplomatic pressure on the Government of Israel to lift the blockade in practice'.[37] Human Rights Watch went further as it charged that Britain had 'tacitly or openly supported' the unlawful blockade and 'itself participated in an economic embargo' of the elected Hamas government, which had 'exacerbated' the blockade's devastating effects.[38] 'The international community appears to have accepted the blockade', a coalition of human rights groups concluded in 2009.[39]

Israel's unlawful and devastating siege of Gaza has been maintained with varying intensity ever since, guaranteeing repeated rounds of bloodshed and foreshadowing the starvation policy employed by Israel after October 7.

Cast Lead

In late 2008 Israel breached a ceasefire with Hamas and launched an assault on the occupied and besieged Gaza Strip. Operation Cast Lead embraced many features that would recur in Operation Swords of Iron, the name given by the Israeli army to its flattening of the enclave after October 7, 2023.

A UN inquiry chaired by Richard Goldstone, a retired South African judge who was Jewish and who identified as a Zionist, concluded that Cast Lead was 'a deliberately disproportionate attack designed to punish, humiliate and terrorize a civilian population'.[40]* Israel struck residential areas with

---

2008), Q42. See also Amnesty International, 'Memorandum to the House of Commons Select Committee on Foreign Affairs', publications.parliament.uk (April 2008).

* Norman Finkelstein has shown that Goldstone's subsequent retraction of his eponymous report was not justified by any novel evidence that exonerated Israel. Norman G. Finkelstein, *Gaza: An Inquest into Its Martyrdom* (University of California Press, 2018), pp. 117–32.

white phosphorus, which 'causes deep burns through muscle and down to the bone'. One Palestinian woman reported witnessing her family members burn alive after white phosphorus shells smashed through the roof of her home.[41] The deployment of white phosphorus has been confirmed by Human Rights Watch in both Gaza and Lebanon after October 7.[42]

Amnesty International later found that there was no credible evidence for Israel's allegations that Hamas employed human shields during the hostilities. It did, however, find that Israel used Palestinians as human shields.[43]

More than a thousand Palestinian civilians were killed in three weeks. Three Israeli civilians and ten Israeli soldiers were killed—four from friendly fire.[44] The final casualty toll from the three-week assault is shown in Table I.

TABLE I. Casualties from Operation Cast Lead, 2008–9

	Gaza	Israel	Ratio
People killed	1,400	13	140:1
Civilians killed	1,170	3	390:1

Some 6,300 homes in Gaza were destroyed or severely damaged during Cast Lead.[45] Amnesty International concluded from '[t]he patterns and scale of the attacks, statements by Israeli officials', and other evidence that 'the wholesale destruction was to a large extent deliberate and an integral part of a strategy at different levels of the command chain, from high-ranking officials to soldiers in the field'.[46]

Israeli forces destroyed the two top floors of al-Quds hospital as well as its warehouse and administrative building. Al-Wafa hospital was hit with two missiles, eight tank shells, and thousands of bullets. The European hospital of Khan Yunis suffered damage to its electricity, water mains, and its walls. Al-Dorah hospital and al-Awda hospital were also damaged.[47]

Israel claimed that Hamas used hospitals extensively for military purposes, but investigations by Amnesty International, Physicians for Human Rights–Israel, and the Goldstone inquiry found no evidence to support this claim.[48]

Israel destroyed thirty mosques and damaged fifteen more during its assault. In relation to one missile attack that killed at least fifteen people, Goldstone found 'no evidence that this mosque was used for the storage of weapons or any military activity by Palestinian armed groups'. There was also no credible evidence of mosques being used to store weapons in general.[49]

One soldier who took part in the Israeli invasion later testified: 'The amount of destruction there was incredible. You drive around those neighborhoods, and can't identify a thing. Not one stone left standing over another. You see plenty of fields, hothouses, orchards, everything devastated. Totally ruined. It's terrible. It's surreal'.[50]

Major General Herzi Halevi, who would lead the IDF in its 2023 Gaza offensive, later observed: 'there are streets [in Gaza] that look like [cities] after the Second World War. Destruction and devastation that even the pictures shown on TV don't adequately capture. Still, the proportionality of our operation, given the location and traps set by the enemy, was very appropriate . . . The Iranians, the Syrians, and Hezbollah looked at what happened here, and got the message'.[51]

Israel's military advocate general had to deal with over five hundred criminal complaints filed by civil society organisations on behalf of victims of the hostilities in Gaza. Fifty-two investigations were opened; four cases resulted in indictment and conviction. The highest sentence was seven-and-a-half-months imprisonment for a soldier who stole a credit card.[52]

British Government Reaction

David Miliband, the British foreign secretary, set out the government position in a speech delivered on January 12, 2009, shortly before the end of hostilities.[53] He spoke of Israel's onslaught in terms that have since become all too familiar. On the one hand, he said that Hamas' rocket attacks manifested 'a cruel choice . . . to target Israeli civilians'. On the other hand, Palestinians were victims of 'the horror of war'. In other words, he acknowledged that Palestinians were suffering on a large scale, but did not impute cruelty to Israel or accuse Israel of having deliberately targeted civilians. All this despite the fact that the Palestinian civilian death toll was magnitudes greater than the Israeli one.

Miliband praised Israel as 'a thriving, democratic state with an independent judiciary'—credit-card thieves, beware—that was 'a beacon of democracy in the Middle East'.

Although Miliband called for investigations of the 'extremely serious allegations' made against both Israel and Palestinian militants, Britain abstained on a UN resolution demanding further action to uphold international law after the devastating Goldstone Report accused Israel of having deliberately terrorised Palestinian civilians.[54] According to Miliband, Britain had earlier pushed for the General Assembly 'to agree a resolution which does not endorse the Goldstone report'.[55]

In December 2009 the Westminster Magistrates' Court issued an arrest warrant for Tzipi Livni, Israel's foreign minister during Cast Lead, following a request from lawyers representing Palestinian victims. Livni had boasted that Israel went 'wild' in Gaza, which she said was 'a good thing'.[56] Livni was scheduled to address a meeting of the Jewish National Fund in London but she cancelled her trip. The warrant was therefore withdrawn.[57]

The prospect that international law might be enforced against Israeli officials or politicians embarrassed British ministers. Gordon Brown, the prime minister, declared that he was 'completely opposed' to the arrest warrant, while Miliband expressed his 'shock' and said the 'government is looking urgently at ways in which the UK system might be changed in order to avoid this sort of situation arising again'.[58] After all, noted Miliband, Israel was 'a strategic partner and a close friend of the UK'.[59] The implication was that Britain would only enforce the law against countries that are not strategic partners or close friends. In 2011 the Cameron government changed the law to make it harder to issue arrest warrants involving universal jurisdiction[60]—more evidence that British complicity with Israeli atrocities dates back long before October 7.

Protective Edge

Operation Protective Edge, launched in the summer of 2014, was Israel's most devastating assault on Gaza before the slaughter that unfolded after October 2023. A reminder of the disproportionate scale of the Israeli killings is presented in Table 2.[61]

TABLE 2. Casualties in Operation Protective Edge, July–August 2014

	Gaza	Israel	Ratio
Civilians killed	1,600	6[62]	270:1
Children killed	550	1	550:1
Homes severely damaged or destroyed	18,000	1	18,000:1

Seventy percent of Gazan fatalities were civilians as compared to 8 percent of Israeli fatalities.[63]

British Government Reaction

This gross imbalance attested to a massacre not a war. But it did not trouble the Cameron government: By the time of Protective Edge the pattern of British complicity had been firmly established. It has become a template for British defence of Israeli atrocities and has been employed consistently since October 2023:

1. **Remind everybody that Israel has a right to defend itself.** 'I have been clear throughout this crisis that Israel has the right to defend itself. Those criticising Israel's response must ask themselves how they would expect their own Government to react if hundreds of rockets were raining down on British cities today'. (Prime Minister David Cameron)[64]
2. **Unambiguously condemn and blame the official enemy.** 'The crisis was triggered by Hamas raining hundreds of rockets on Israeli cities, indiscriminately targeting civilians in contravention of all humanitarian law and norms'. (Prime Minister Cameron)[65]
3. **Limit discussion of Palestinian victims to nonspecific lamentations over the tragedy of man. Do not impute any bad intent or criminal responsibility to Israel.** 'It is tragic that so many innocent civilians, including women and children, have been killed and injured'. (Foreign Secretary Philip Hammond)[66]

4. **Express 'concern' about civilian casualties and issue pro forma declarations about the general need to comply with international law.** 'I share the grave concern of many in the international community about the heavy toll of civilian casualties. The figures are very disturbing'. (Prime Minister Cameron)[67]

5. **Issue futile calls for investigations that will lead nowhere.** 'We do not yet have the full details of the recent attack near the UN school . . . We must look at the evidence and all the parties must cooperate with the inquiries, the reviews that there will now be, seeking to establish exactly what happened around these terrible incidents and how they came about, whether proper rules of engagement, proper international laws have been followed or not'. (Foreign Secretary Hammond)[68]

6. **Refuse to support international investigations despite previous calls for investigations.** On July 23, 2014, the UN Human Rights Council voted on a resolution entitled 'Ensuring respect for international law in the Occupied Palestinian Territory, including East Jerusalem'. The resolution deplored Israel's massive military operations in Gaza, condemned Israel's occupation, condemned the killing of Israeli civilians by rocket fire, demanded an end to the blockade that was suffocating Gaza, and supported the formation of 'an independent, international commission of inquiry . . . to investigate all violations of international humanitarian law and international human rights law' during the violence.[69] Britain abstained. Philip Hammond, the foreign secretary, said that the resolution was 'fundamentally unbalanced', would not help to achieve a ceasefire, and would 'complicate the process by introducing unnecessary new mechanisms'.[70]

7. **Keep sending arms to Israel, no matter what.** Between 2010 and 2014, Britain licensed £42 million of military equipment to Israel, including targeting equipment and drone components.[71] The government identified twelve arms export licences that it considered 'could be part of equipment used by the Israel Defence Forces in Gaza'. These included 'components for military

radar systems, combat aircraft and tanks'. After the conclusion of a ceasefire, the government stated that, in the event of *future* hostilities in Gaza, it would suspend these twelve licences as a precaution. Business Secretary Vince Cable explained that the government had 'not been able to clarify if the export licence criteria are being met'.[72] In 2015 even this minimal precautionary measure was abandoned. The government asserted that it was 'confident that all export licences in circulation for Israel' met the arms export licensing criteria and therefore no additional measures were necessary.[73]

8. **Send humanitarian aid to Gaza in order to affect balance and moderation.** 'The UK is providing £349 million for humanitarian relief, state-building and economic development for Palestinians up to 2015, and providing about £30 million a year to help the people of Gaza'. (First Secretary of State William Hague)[74]

9. **Reflexively blame the official enemy whenever ceasefire negotiations fail.** On July 14, 2014, former prime minister Tony Blair and the Egyptian dictator Abdel Fattah el-Sisi put forward a truce plan that did not commit Israel to ending the illegal blockade that was suffocating Gaza. Hamas predictably rejected these terms.[75] This rejection was then used to justify an Israeli ground invasion. The British government reinforced the misleading narrative: 'This unprecedented [rocket] barrage continues to this moment, with Hamas rejecting all proposals for a ceasefire'. (Prime Minister Cameron)[76]

10. **Gravely reiterate support for a two-state solution, back Israel while it blocks a two-state solution, and act mystified when a two-state solution continually fails to appear.** 'A negotiated two-state solution remains the only way to resolve the conflict once and for all and to achieve a sustainable peace'. (First Secretary Hague)[77]

11. **OPTIONAL: Confide later what was really going on to Israel lobby groups.** Philip Hammond gave an idea of what was happening behind the scenes during Protective Edge in an address to the Conservative Friends of Israel in 2015: 'During the Gaza

> conflict last summer, the Prime Minister, I, and the Chancellor made a clear decision that we would stand behind Israel and defend what Israel was doing. We took a bit of flack for it and we are proud of that, and we will stand behind Israel again when it is defending its right to exist and its right to defend itself against attacks.'[78]

There was one ministerial resignation during this period: Sayeeda Warsi resigned from the cabinet on August 5, 2014. She had been senior minister of state in the Foreign Office. She observed in her resignation letter that the 'approach and language during the current crisis in Gaza is morally indefensible, is not in Britain's national interest and will have a long term detrimental impact on our reputation internationally and domestically'.[79] George Osborne, chancellor of the exchequer, called her decision 'disappointing and unnecessary'.[80] She was never forgiven. Her political career was over.

Gaza's Sharpeville That Wasn't

In 2018 Palestinians undertook a campaign of overwhelmingly nonviolent protest near Gaza's border fence.* They demanded their rights as refugees and an end to Israel's unlawful blockade. They called it the Great March of Return.

Israel reacted with extraordinary violence (see Table 3) while Western media outlets spread a series of myths about the demonstrations that made it hard for them to gain broad public support.[81] These included the fictions that the protests were themselves characterised by violence and that Hamas had either initiated or taken over the movement.

---

* UNRWA reported one year into the Great March of Return that 'the protests have continued to be largely non-violent and the vast majority of those in attendance are unarmed', although noted that 'there are often reported incidents of stone throwing, as well as tire burning, attempts to damage the fence and, since April, some demonstrators flew kites or balloons towards Israel that carried burning rags and damaged Israeli property, including agricultural land'. UNRWA, *Gaza's 'Great March of Return', One Year On* (2019), p. 6.

TABLE 3. Casualties in the Great March of Return, March–December 2018[82]

	Gaza	Israel	Ratio
People killed	183 Palestinians killed by live ammunition, including 32 children	0	183:0
People injured[83]	9,204—including more than six thousand injured by live ammunition	4	2301:1

A UN Commission of Inquiry found that Israeli snipers systematically targeted civilians:

> The Commission found that demonstrators who were hundreds of metres away from the Israeli forces and visibly engaged in civilian activities were intentionally shot. Journalists and health workers who were clearly marked as such were shot, as were children, women and persons with disabilities.[84]

Israel refused to cooperate with the Commission.[85] It prevented the Commission from accessing the Occupied Palestinian Territory or Israel and it ignored repeated requests for information.[86]

Other human rights authorities condemned Israel's repression. During the protests, Amnesty International said that 'Israel is carrying out a murderous assault against protesting Palestinians, with its armed forces killing and maiming demonstrators who pose no imminent threat to them'.[87]

The British reaction hewed to the pusillanimous playbook itemised above. Alistair Burt, the minister for the Middle East, confined himself to saying that the violence was 'shocking' and 'tragic' without condemning Israel. He also borrowed from the propaganda line that 'extremist elements have exploited the protests for their own violent purposes'—even as not a single Israeli had been killed by the protesters from March to December and only four Israeli soldiers had been injured.[88] Meanwhile, there were 183 dead Palestinians and thousands of injured. Wouldn't it have been more accurate to say that Israel's leaders were behaving like violent extremists?

As this book was going into production I rang up Mr. Burt and told him I was planning to lacerate him for his reaction to the March of Return. His response was more open, interesting, and thoughtful than I expected. 'I know exactly what I did', he replied. 'I know why I did it. And it's grim'. Burt went on:

> I have thought about this a lot. The strongest memory I have was the shooting of the young paramedic Razan al-Najjar. She was clearly targeted and murdered by the Israelis. The government relied on the Israeli response that they know all about every shot that was fired by the IDF. I am pretty sure that in the Commons I called for an inquiry. My suspicion then—since confirmed—is that these investigations were effectively useless and used as a cover by the Israelis for the killing and covering up such as this. I and the UK should have been more bold in calling this out.

Burt, who has always been viewed with a degree of respect by supporters of Palestinians, cited another IDF killing in the village of Nabi Salih in the occupied West Bank. In 2011 an Israeli soldier shot a tear gas canister directly in the face of Mustafa al-Tamimi while he was protesting against the theft of water by settlers. Burt told me: 'We called for an investigation. I was promised there would be a response. Nothing. I do not recall that there was any answer at all'.

Burt also said about the March of Return: 'I was also angry about the organisers of the march, who must have known [about] Israeli orders to shoot those they deemed too close to the fence, no matter how wrong such shootings might be. They appeared deliberately reckless to me in putting people at risk in that way'.

When the massacre was debated in the Commons, most Tory backbenchers rallied to Israel's cause, reiterating Netanyahu's assertion that Hamas, not Israel, was to blame.[89] An exception was Sir Nicholas Soames, who condemned the 'wholly unacceptable' conduct of the Israeli army. Two ambitious young Labour backbenchers agreed with him. Shabana Mahmood told the Commons: 'The fate of the people of Gaza is to be condemned to live in an open-air prison camp and to be shot dead when they protest and remind the world of their despair. The actions of the

Israeli military yesterday are indefensible on any measure'. Wes Streeting warned Israel that 'defending the border is not a licence to kill'.[90] Today Mahmood (lord chancellor) and Streeting (health secretary) are senior members of the Starmer cabinet.

The 2018 March of Return bears a tragic comparison with the Sharpeville massacre in March 1960, when an unarmed crowd protesting apartheid's notorious Pass Laws was mown down by South African police.[91] Officially sixty-nine people were killed (the real count was probably higher) and many others injured as police suddenly opened fire.

The killings were condemned in a United Nations resolution, became a catalyst in the African National Congress' shift from nonviolence to armed resistance, and led swiftly to South Africa's international isolation. It was a milestone towards the fall of apartheid.

Mirroring Sharpeville, the March of Return was a historic gamble by Palestinians from all walks of life in Gaza on the sincerity of the international community's claimed commitments to law and humanity. As the Palestinian writer Yousef Munayyer had previously argued, Palestinian non-violence requires global non-silence.[92]

For week after week, ordinary Palestinians gathered along that perimeter fence and marched unarmed towards the rows of Israeli snipers stationed behind it. Their only armour, their only protection, was the willingness of the international community to restrain Israel's hand. What happened? Israel shot thousands with live ammunition, as Britain along with other Israeli allies did nothing.

Commentators sympathetic to Israel often ask of Israel's critics: after October 7, what was Israel supposed to do? The question is legitimate. It is also one-sided because it avoids a much bigger issue: the history and context of how we got here in the first place.

This chapter has shown that for decades countless available off-ramps and alternative routes were spurned, overlooked, and sabotaged—with the active connivance of successive British governments. We have consistently rewarded Israel's refusal to make peace. We have helped Israel neutralise not just violent but also all forms of nonviolent Palestinian struggle for internationally recognised rights.

We have done this by refusing to recognise a Palestinian state; by undermining the campaign for Boycott, Divestment, and Sanctions against Israel; by obstructing Palestinian diplomatic initiatives at the UN; by hindering Palestinian appeals to the courts; by deceiving British and world opinion about the balance of responsibility for the failure to reach a peace deal; and by maintaining military and economic ties with Israel notwithstanding its repeated resort to criminal violence and imposition of a criminal siege against the civilian population of Gaza.

We have fragmented and degraded the Palestinian national movement by empowering an authoritarian and undemocratic Palestinian Authority to police the occupied West Bank on Israel's behalf while thwarting Palestinian democracy. We bear a heavy responsibility for trashing Hamas peace overtures after the Palestinian legislative elections in 2006. Britain, in short, has enabled Israel's criminal repression over decades while sabotaging each and every Palestinian attempt to resolve the conflict. In this way we are not just complicit in the destruction of Gaza over the last two years; we also helped pave the way for the horrors of October 7 itself.

6

THE PRO-ISRAEL LOBBY IN BRITAIN

> The largest organization in Western Europe dedicated to the cause of the people of Israel.
>
> —*Robert Rhodes James on the Conservative Friends of Israel*

ONE HUNDRED days into the destruction of Gaza, the Conservative Friends of Israel (CFI) threw its customary annual lunch—never a modest affair—at the Intercontinental hotel in central London. Among more than 650 guests were 200 Tory MPs or peers. Twenty out of twenty-three cabinet ministers were in attendance. The principal speaker was Prime Minister Rishi Sunak.[1]

By now more than twenty-five thousand Palestinians were dead.[2] Oxfam noted that the daily death rate in Gaza was higher than any major twenty-first-century conflict,[3] amidst a mountain of evidence that Israel was committing grave war crimes. Although Sunak did stress that 'the human suffering is immense', he offered not a single word of reproach aimed at Israel.[4] He came up with the usual pro-forma praise for the two-state solution. In reality Sunak's Tory government, in common with its predecessors, had been conniving with Israel to undermine any possibility of a Palestinian state.

From an Israeli point of view the prime minister's speech contained two especially welcome points. The first concerned Boycott, Divestment, and Sanctions (BDS), the nonviolent civil society movement that advocates a consumer boycott, economic sanctions, and disinvestment against Israel so long as it continues to break international law. Sunak promised to press through legislation to stop public bodies from adopting BDS policies: 'In this party we won't let tin pot, town hall Jeremy Corbyns run their own anti-Israel foreign policy'. I will examine Sunak's handling of this BDS initiative at the end of this chapter.

Sunak's second intervention dealt with the then imminent International Court of Justice provisional ruling in the Gaza genocide case. Sunak called the legal proceedings 'completely unjustified', adding: 'There is a horrific irony in Israel, of all countries, being accused of genocide'. Sunak was in effect telling his audience that his government would reject the ICJ decision if the judges reached a decision that upset Israel. Israeli president Isaac Herzog, one of the speakers at the lunch over a video link from Jerusalem, praised Sunak and his Conservative Party for their 'indispensable' support and 'moral clarity'. Herzog said: 'I have seen how your strong and unified voice for Israel has rung clearly. I have seen it cut through the dishonesty, cowardice, intimidation and hypocrisy of so many quarters of the world'.[5]

As already noted, when the ICJ issued its provisional order the following week, the judges highlighted language used by President Herzog as evidence that Palestinians in Gaza faced a plausible risk of genocide. Palestinians are entitled to feel bewildered and frightened that a British prime minister was happy to speak alongside the most senior perpetrator of the genocidal discourse that set in motion the carnage in Gaza.

The Forgotten Legacy of Margaret Thatcher

Margaret Thatcher is Sunak's personal hero. Thatcher was a fierce enemy of antisemitism, strongly pro-Israel, and an opponent of a Palestinian state. But she was also willing to introduce substantive differences between British and Israeli policy. Thatcher's foreign secretary, Lord Carrington, was the driving force behind the 1980 Venice Declaration by which the European Economic Community recognised the 'right to self-determination' of the 'Palestinian people'.[6] And when Palestinians organised a mass popular rebellion against Israeli occupation in 1987—the First Intifada—Britain voted with an overwhelming consensus at the UN General Assembly for a 'comprehensive peace' based on a full Israeli withdrawal from 'the Palestinian territory occupied since 1967' and the 'legitimate national rights of the Palestinian people'. Only the United States and Israel stood opposed.[7]

Thatcher was also prepared to call out Israeli war crimes. When the Israel Defence Forces enabled the slaughter by Christian Phalangists of Palestinians and Lebanese Shia in the Sabra and Shatila refugee camps, Thatcher condemned the massacre as 'an act of sheer barbarism'.[8] She wrote to US president Ronald Reagan of 'an urgent need for a balanced policy', adding that 'unlimited support for Israel can only lead to growing polarisation and despair in the Arab world'.

The previous year she had been equally outspoken after Operation Babylon, the Israeli attack on an unfinished Iraqi nuclear reactor near Baghdad, stating that Israel was guilty of a 'grave breach of international law'. In the wake of this intervention Thatcher spoke to *The Jewish Chronicle*. The interviewer, Monty Modlyn, accused Britain of being 'the leading advocate of the Arab case against Israel'. Thatcher stood her ground: 'I uphold international law. Once we go away from that, we shall not know where we are'.[9]

In 1988, when Israeli troops crushed Palestinian anti-occupation protests with 'force, might, and beatings'[10] as well as the routine use of torture,[11] Britain's deputy permanent representative to the United Nations forthrightly condemned the repression. Addressing the Security Council, Sir John Birch deplored Israel's 'brutal and often indiscriminate actions against civilians' that he said had rightly 'shocked and disgusted' world opinion. Denouncing Israeli abuses as 'immoral, illegal and politically self-defeating', Britain's representative condemned Israel's policy in resonant terms now unimaginable from high office:

> In the first half of this century the Jewish people suffered from arbitrary rule, violence, discrimination and attempted genocide. They were denied the status of equals in their own lands. They were persecuted and hounded, millions to their death. Israel was

> founded as a place where such dreadful events could not and would not happen. For many of us, it is painful that echoes of that old intolerance, that harsh belief in the right of might, should be heard there today.[12]

After Operation Babylon, Thatcher herself had delivered a moral lecture for the ages: 'If we are not going to live by a system of international law, we are going to live by international anarchy. Then no people anywhere in the world are safe.'[13] It is impossible to imagine any of Thatcher's recent successors as prime minister uttering this sort of principled criticism of Israel, and it is important to understand why.

Like many of her generation Maggie Thatcher had memories of the sustained campaign of violence and assassination against British Mandatory troops and officials carried out by the men who went on to lead Israel. Menachem Begin, Israeli prime minister at the time of the Sabra and Shatila massacres, had been the head of the Irgun terror gang that conducted multiple attacks on British targets during the 1940s, most notably the 1946 bombing of British headquarters in Jerusalem, the King David Hotel, which claimed ninety-one lives. In all her extensive international travels Queen Elizabeth II never visited Israel, and was even reluctant to allow Israeli officials into Buckingham Palace. 'She believed that every one of us was either a terrorist or a son of a terrorist', explained former Israeli president Reuven Rivlin after she died, adding that King Charles was much easier to deal with.[14]

Thatcher, who grew up during World War Two, also knew the consequences that flow from ignoring international law, a lesson her recent successors have apparently forgotten. I will return to this serious theme, which has relevance far beyond the Middle East, in the final chapter.

The primary reason for the loss of even a semblance of balance in Britain's Middle East policy is Britain's subordination in foreign affairs to the United States, which has maintained more-or-less unqualified support for Israel even as Israeli governments refused peace with the Palestinians and pursued the permanent annexation of Palestinian land. I will examine the importance of this cross-party Atlanticism more closely when I discuss the Labour Party in the next chapter. In this chapter, I pay attention to one significant factor that has played out distinctively within the Conservative Party and helps explain their slide from a pro-Israeli position to one of fanatical support for the Israeli right. This is the growing power of Britain's pro-Israel lobby.

Journalists have generally avoided this field of inquiry,* fearing with good reason that merely to broach the subject might open them up to accusations of antisemitism. Ahead of the 2024 general election, Faiza Shaheen was dropped as Labour candidate for Chingford and Woodford Green after complaints about her social media output, such as when she 'liked' a tweet that referred to the 'Israel lobby'.[15] The *New Statesman* political editor Rachel Cunliffe explained that this term is 'widely considered an anti-Semitic trope'.[16]

It is not easy to reconcile Cunliffe's claim with the fact that the *New Statesman* has itself repeatedly published articles referencing the 'Israel lobby'.[17] But even if many do consider discussion of the pro-Israel lobby as antisemitic, this doesn't make it true. The pro-Israel lobby exists and has been a powerful force in British public life for many years. In a recent study of BBC reporting of the Gaza conflict for *Declassified UK*, the historian Mark Curtis noted that a quarter of all MPs—including one third of the Starmer cabinet—have been funded by pro-Israel groups. 'In no article has the BBC flagged the possible influence of these groups over parliament or government policy-making', notes Curtis. He adds that 'in the BBC's written news outputs, the Israel lobby appears not to exist at all: the term "Israel lobby" has been used just once in quote marks'.[18] *Declassified UK* journalists Matt Kennard and Phil Miller have also done important work uncovering the role of the pro-Israel lobby in securing the proscription of Hezbollah in 2019, quoting

* As part of my study of the pro-Israel lobby in Britain (2009) I commissioned a search of the newspaper database Lexis Nexis. It showed there were 154 mentions of the Conservative Friends of Israel in the British press between 1985 and 2009. The Tobacco Manufacturers Association, another lobby group, enjoyed 1,083 citations during the same period and the Scotch Whisky Association 2,895. There were over two thousand citations for a single Tory donor, Michael Ashcroft. In my view, political journalists regarded the influence of the tobacco manufacturers and other domestic lobbies as a safer subject to cover than the pro-Israel lobby. Peter Oborne and James Jones, 'The Pro-Israel Lobby in Britain: Full Text', *openDemocracy* (13 November 2009).

CFI Honorary President Lord Stuart Polak's giveaway boast: 'It took us ages with Hezbollah'.[19]

A telling example of the omertà surrounding the pro-Israel lobby concerned the publication in spring 2024 of Ilan Pappé's *Lobbying for Zionism on Both Sides of the Atlantic*.[20] Pappé, one of the most eminent of the 'new historians' who rewrote Israel's foundation story, felt obliged to flee Israel after the publication in 2006 of his pathbreaking work *The Ethnic Cleansing of Palestine*.* Published only six months after October 7, Pappé's detailed study of the pro-Israeli lobby bore directly on a story that still dominated media headlines. No mainstream British newspaper reviewed his book. To add insult to injury the BBC and other major media outlets have consistently ignored the existence of Professor Pappé himself, even though he is today a professor at Exeter University and an internationally renowned expert on Israel and Palestine. Pappé is Jewish, one of the most well-respected historians of Israel, and remains an Israeli citizen. It is hard not to reach the conclusion that Pappé, like Professor Shlaim at Oxford, has been excluded from the public square because he is a critic of Israel.

There are nevertheless serious grounds for taking care when discussing the pro-Israeli lobby. As Hil Aked noted in a rare and scrupulous study of the subject, it is important to acknowledge that there are 'very real racist fantasies about "Jewish power"'.[21] The *Report of the All-Party Parliamentary Inquiry into Antisemitism* (2006) cautioned that '[n]o-one would seek to deny that there is well-organised support for Israel in Britain, but in some quarters

* Professor Pappé was denounced in the Knesset. Israel's minister of education called on the University of Haifa to sack him and one of Israel's best-selling papers pictured him in the centre of a target, next to which a columnist had written: 'I am not telling you to kill this person, but I shouldn't be surprised if someone did'. After death threats he left Israel and was lucky to be able to find a billet at Exeter University. French publisher Fayard recently halted distribution of his *The Ethnic Cleansing of Palestine*. Pappé was interrogated for two hours by federal agents upon arrival in the United States. He was eventually let in but only after they copied the contents of his phone. This kind of harassment, Pappé later said, is nothing compared to what Palestinians routinely face. Peter Oborne, 'Why Ilan Pappé's New Book on the Israel Lobby Is a Must-Read', *Middle East Eye* (24 June 2024).

this becomes inflated to the point where discourse about the "lobby" resembles discourse about a world Jewish conspiracy'.[22]

Conservative Friends of Israel

There are many Israel advocacy networks in Britain, with diverse politics and modes of operation. Over the past two or three decades, the most active and influential pro-Israel organisation has been the Conservative Friends of Israel. The Conservative historian and politician Robert Rhodes James described CFI as 'the largest organization in Western Europe dedicated to the cause of the people of Israel'.[23] That was thirty years ago; the group's salience has since grown substantially while the influence of the countervailing Tory Arabist tradition has collapsed.[24] Some of the most eloquent Arabist representatives, such as Ian Gilmour or Nicholas Soames, have died or retired. The primary reason for the collapse of Tory Arabism, however, has been the decision by Arab states themselves, especially Saudi Arabia and other Gulf despotisms, to turn their backs on the Palestinian cause. By 2014, CFI boasted that its membership included 80 percent of Tory MPs.[25] With the Conservatives in power from 2010 to 2024, CFI was uniquely well-positioned to shape British policies towards Israel.

The group could whistle up cabinet ministers for its lunches and dinners, and had superlative access to Downing Street, Westminster, and Whitehall. There were queues around the block for its celebrated annual party at every Tory conference. It became part of the Conservative Party family. In early 2024 I asked CFI whether it had criticised Benjamin Netanyahu or any member of his government since the Israeli onslaught had begun. No reply.[26] The organisation seems never to have uttered a peep about what Sir Richard Evans, historian of Nazi Germany, has labelled the 'murderous criminality' of Israeli settlers in the West Bank.[27]

As far as I can establish CFI didn't criticise Israel's 2018 nation state law, which effectively established separate categories of Israeli citizenship: one for Jews and one for Arabs. Nor have I found evidence that CFI has rebuked the extreme genocidal incitement emanating from Netanyahu, his ministers, and other Israeli politicians. Indeed, so far as I have been able to ascertain,

CFI has never once criticised any policy or action carried out by the State of Israel, neither before October 2023 nor since.

CFI has, in contrast, been ready to criticise Britain. In March 2023, Lord Polak accused the Sunak government of 'effectively boycotting' an Israeli minister after then foreign secretary James Cleverly said he had no plans to work with Itamar Ben-Gvir.[28] 'It is not about whether one agrees with minister Ben-Gvir', said Polak. 'We work with all elected Israeli politicians, and we must be very careful not to go down a route of suggesting that our support for Israel is somehow conditional on any individual politician.' Polak asked: 'Could we be holding Israel to a different standard from other countries?' This was a pointed question, as CFI had defined 'applying double standards' to Israel as antisemitic.[29]

Ben-Gvir, then Netanyahu's national security minister, had been convicted in Israel of incitement to racism and supporting a terrorist organisation. He heads the political party Otzma Yehudit (translation: Jewish Power), which champions annexation of the Occupied Palestinian Territory as well as 'transfer of the enemy, an exchange of populations' to 'ensure a Jewish majority'.[30] Ben-Gvir admires the late Meir Kahane, a race supremacist whose Kach party was banned by the Israeli government and classified a terrorist organisation by the US. Until Ben-Gvir's election to the Knesset a picture of Baruch Goldstein hung on his wall at home. In 1994, Goldstein murdered twenty-nine Palestinians in a terror attack in Hebron.

Otzma Yehudit has been part of Israel's governing coalition for most of the period since October 2023, with Ben-Gvir serving as Israel's minister for national security. In this capacity he pushed for denying 'even a gram of food or aid'[31] to Gaza's civilian population, called for expelling Palestinians from Gaza and establishing Jewish settlements in their place,[32] and reportedly oversaw the 'systematic abuse' and 'torture' of Palestinian detainees.[33] Ben-Gvir's conduct and statements were so extreme that in February 2025 several governments allied to Israel, including Britain, imposed sanctions on him for having 'incited extremist violence and serious abuses of Palestinian rights'.[34] This is who the CFI insisted that the British government 'work with'. Over the last few years the CFI has come to look less like a friend of Israel and more like the London outpost for Netanyahu's coalition of far-right, racist extremists.

Assessing the Influence of CFI

There is an insoluble problem when it comes to estimating the influence of any lobby group: the 'preaching to the choir' factor. If CFI advocates sanctions on Iran, for example, and then Britain adopts this policy, this might reflect CFI's influence. It might alternatively reflect the fact that other powerful forces in British politics were already inclined to a hawkish position on Iran so that CFI was pushing on an open door. Had CFI instead advocated for sanctions on the US, the limits of its influence would have quickly become apparent. In the section below I will set out some of the ways in which CFI has directly influenced Conservative policy towards Israel, but it is important to remember that the underlying trend in British politics has often been on their side.

Fundamentally, Britain's pro-Israel posture during the years of Tory rule was determined in large part by the cross-party commitment to Atlanticism. But on top of this underlying political position were political dynamics that reinforced and radicalised the right's pro-Israel orientation. Over the last decade Israel itself has shifted ever further to the extreme right. All things being equal one would have expected Conservative support to have diminished in consequence. Instead it became ever more fervent. It is fair to speculate that the Tories' own lurch towards extremism created an environment in which Israel's supporters could make their case with greater ease than ever before.

For one thing, many Conservatives began to mobilise support for Israel as part of a broader domestic culture war. Even a casual reading of the Tory press shows how right-wing commentators have come to link support for the pro-Palestinian movement with an alleged lack of British patriotism, an embrace of multiculturalism, and support for mass immigration in general or Islam in particular. Conversely the British right presents support for Israel as part and parcel of a pro-American, hawkish, anti-immigrant battle for 'Western civilisation' against Islamic barbarism. This is at the softer end of a wider trend that has seen Israel increasingly championed by the global far right, which lauds that state's unabashed racist supremacism as a validation and vanguard of its own ethnonationalist project.[35]

When Labour was led by the pro-Palestinian left-winger Jeremy Corbyn between 2015 and 2019, the Tories monstered Corbyn and his supporters as far-left, terrorist-loving extremists. In this context they used conspicuous support for Israel to differentiate themselves and deployed politicised accusations of antisemitism to delegitimise the left. We will return to this controversy in the next chapter.

These political developments presented opportunities for Israel advocacy groups like the CFI, which did not hesitate to exploit them. Enthusiastic support for Netanyahu's Likud coalition, a grouping with overtly fascist elements, would have been unthinkable in the premierships of Thatcher or John Major. By 2023 it predominated in the Tory mainstream.

CFI Hosts Leadership Hustings

Sixteen years ago I made a documentary for Channel Four called *Inside Britain's Israel Lobby*. It is hard to imagine a comparable documentary being made today.[36] The research process was hard. We found that the financial structure of the CFI was obscure; it did not declare its funding, the identity of its donors or its annual turnover. Despite being composed almost entirely of MPs and Conservative Party members it was registered not as a members association, lobby, company, or charity, but as an unincorporated association. This meant it did not formally exist as an organisation but merely as a collection of individuals.

This allowed its donors to give money without being identified. Some of these donors could have been foreign nationals, who under British electoral rules should not be allowed to fund political parties or members of parliament.[37] I even found it impossible to establish exactly how much money CFI and its supporters had donated to the Conservative Party. According to Aked's admirable study, five influential donors and CFI supporters have served as Tory treasurer so far this century: Howard Leigh, Stanley Kalms, Richard Harrington, Mick Davies, and Stanley Fink.[38] Beyond this, Aked found the organisation's finances as impenetrable as I did.

I revealed that the CFI went into action in 2006 after William Hague, then shadow foreign secretary, called that year's bloody Israeli assault on South Lebanon 'disproportionate' on the floor of the Commons.[39] Mr. Hague's criticism recalled (though it did not match in eloquence or moral grandeur) Maggie Thatcher's denunciation of the Sabra and Shatila massacres as 'sheer barbarism'. Lord Kalms, by then a former party treasurer who had reportedly given more than £500,000 to the Tories, condemned Hague's language.[40] CFI secured a meeting with David Cameron in which the Tory leader gave what was understood as an undertaking not to use the word 'disproportionate'—a term fraught with legal significance for conflicts in urban environments with heavy civilian casualties—again.[41] In retrospect this commitment can be seen as especially significant given that the 2006 war saw Israel's first explicit deployment of the 'Dahiya doctrine'. As we showed in the last chapter, Gadi Eizenkot, head of the IDF Operations Directorate during the war, defined it in terms as the use of 'disproportionate force'.

As far as I can discover Cameron has never again used the word in connection with any Israeli conflict, not even the summer 2014 assault on Gaza which saw 1,600 Palestinian civilian deaths against just 6 civilian deaths in Israel (a proportion of 270:1).[42] Nor did he do so after he returned as foreign secretary for eight months during Israel's destruction of Gaza, even though the term was by this point a gross understatement of the Israeli reaction to October 7. In preparation for this book I wrote to Lord Cameron asking for an example of his use of the word: no answer.

During the Conservative leadership contest of summer 2022 the CFI hosted a hustings, one of the first times that any lobby group supporting a foreign country has played such a role.[43] Ahead of the event Liz Truss wrote to the CFI pledging to consider following the example of US President Donald Trump by moving the British embassy in Israel from Tel Aviv to Jerusalem.[44] This opened up a bidding war between Truss and Rishi Sunak for the support of CFI. Sunak felt compelled to match the offer.*

It has been settled British doctrine since 1967 to keep our embassy in Tel Aviv. This reflected a broad international consensus, notoriously shattered by Trump during his first presidency, that embassies should not be

* This incident reveals again the difficulty in appraising the influence of a lobby like CFI. On the one hand, the group had sufficient clout to host a Conservative leadership hustings in which the rival candidates competed for the approval of its constituency. On the other hand, CFI seemingly didn't have the sway to ensure that Sunak stuck to his promised policy once in office.

established in Jerusalem until a peace settlement is agreed. Moving the embassy would have compromised Britain's support for the two-state solution by legitimising Israel's unlawful annexation of East Jerusalem, which is internationally recognised as occupied Palestinian territory. At no point were the Palestinians consulted about the embassy move. Political reporters averted their eyes from this undignified scramble between rival leadership candidates for the support of the Israel lobby. By this stage, prospective British policy towards Israel was being set in direct dealings between the Conservative Party leadership and the CFI. It should be noted that Liz Truss was following a precedent established by the outgoing Tory leader and prime minister Boris Johnson.

In March 2021 the International Criminal Court's chief prosecutor Fatou Bensouda had infuriated Israel by opening an investigation into alleged war crimes committed in the occupied Palestinian territories. She had dragged her heels for years while also refusing to investigate Israel's murderous 2010 assault on a humanitarian flotilla bound for Gaza, but finally progressed the case just before she left office.[45] A month later Johnson responded: 'We do not accept that the ICC has jurisdiction in this instance', explaining that 'Israel is not a party to the Statute of Rome and Palestine is not a sovereign state'. Had due process been followed an announcement of this nature should have come from the foreign secretary and been made through parliament. Johnson made his statement in a letter from Downing Street to the three senior officers of the CFI.[46] As ever Palestinians were cut out of the process. I can find no complaints from either Sir Keir Starmer or the shadow foreign secretary Lisa Nandy.

Taking Down Alan Duncan

The journal of former Tory minister Alan Duncan, *In the Thick of It*, contains a rare, candid, and colourful account of the CFI's engagement in British high politics. A sense of grievance emerges from these diaries. Duncan believes he was targeted by CFI, which he accuses of 'actively lobbying' against him because of his support for Palestinian rights and the two-state solution. Though the diaries in places feel overwrought and self-serving, there is reason to accept, supposing his account is true, that Duncan was right to feel vulnerable.

According to Duncan, Prime Minister Theresa May offered him the post of Middle East minister in the July 2016 government reshuffle that followed the Brexit referendum. Duncan records that later the same day, the new foreign secretary Boris Johnson told him that CFI had gotten wind of the appointment, was 'going ballistic',[47] and had called him 'incessantly saying I must not be appointed'.[48]

Duncan writes that pro-Israel groups were also lobbying Mrs. May. 'Now Number 10 are telling Boris I cannot have the Middle East', recorded Duncan, adding that in any other country this 'would in my view be seen as entrenched espionage'.[49] In fairness, there were other potential problems that Duncan does not cite, notably his former business connections in the region.[50] In the end he was stripped of responsibility for the Middle East, barring Oman.

This Duncan episode has a sequel, involving the Israeli embassy in London rather than CFI. The following year an official at the embassy was secretly filmed as part of an undercover Al Jazeera investigation.[51] Shai Masot, supposedly serving as a senior political officer at the London embassy, talked about a plot to 'take down' British politicians considered hostile to Israel.[52] One of the MPs cited was Duncan. 'Masot is a First or Second secretary, a member of military intelligence, employed specifically as a parliamentary and undercover propagandist', Duncan recorded in his diaries.[53] It is impossible to judge the accuracy of these claims because within hours of the Masot revelation he was recalled to Tel Aviv, while Johnson's Foreign Office issued a statement saying that the UK has 'a strong relationship with Israel and we consider the matter closed'.[54]

This was bizarre. The Al Jazeera tapes, the result of months of undercover filming, appeared to show Masot meddling deeply in both main British political parties. In another section of the documentary Al Jazeera filmed Masot in conversation with Joan Ryan, who was at that time a Labour MP and head of Labour Friends of Israel (LFI), Labour's counterpart to the CFI. 'Just now we've got the money, it's more than £1m, it's a lot of money', Masot told Ryan, adding 'it's not physical, it's an approval'.[55]

The context of the conversation left viewers under the impression that the cash would be used to send activists and politicians on paid trips to Israel.

The LFI said that this was not the case, telling Al Jazeera that 'the conversation between Masot and Ryan had nothing whatsoever to do with LFI delegations'.[56] Al Jazeera additionally stated that 'the LFI added that no payment of £1m was offered, given or received by them and the names of individuals supplied by Ryan were for a visit arranged, advertised by and paid for by the Israeli embassy. The group said Masot was claiming influence he did not have and that any young LFI grouping would be organised by the LFI and not the embassy'.[57] The Israeli embassy produced a similar story, describing Masot as a junior official who had spoken out of turn.

Whatever the truth, Masot's activities are consistent with the kind of covert influence campaign of which Russia and China have been accused in the United States and Britain. Sir Nicholas Soames, a former minister of state for the armed forces and Winston Churchill's grandson, told me as much the following day. He compared the activities of the Israelis to the KGB: 'This ranks as the equivalent of Soviet intelligence in what they are doing to suborn democracy and interfere in due process'.[58] The decision by Boris Johnson not to hold an inquiry means that we shall never know exactly who Shai Masot really was, which other British MPs had been targeted, whether the then Israeli ambassador Mark Regev knew about Masot's activities, if not why not, the truth about Masot's £1m for Labour Friends of Israel, what happened to it, what other sums had been dispensed to British political organisations, and whether individual payments have been made to MPs and others.

If any other country had been caught red-handed in this kind of influence operation—and that includes allies—a British foreign secretary would have demanded answers. Boris Johnson's lack of curiosity highlighted the Tory role as a facilitator rather than passive victim of Israeli interference in British politics. After leaving Downing Street Johnson published an autobiography, *Unleashed*. In it he revealed that during his time as foreign secretary Benjamin Netanyahu came to his office and asked to use his private toilet. 'Thither Bibi repaired for a while, and it may or may not be a coincidence but I am told that later, when they were doing a regular sweep for bugs, they found a listening device in the thunderbox'.[59] Johnson told the story as if it was all a bit of a joke that the prime minister of a foreign country may have planted a bug in the bathroom.

How the Tories Redefined Antisemitism

Since the 1970s, Israel and many of its supporters have argued that much international criticism of the Jewish state should be understood as a new form of antisemitism.[60] From 2004 pro-Israel advocacy groups in Britain, the US, and elsewhere pushed for this expanded conception of antisemitism to be codified in a regulatory or even legal definition. Their efforts bore fruit in 2016 when the International Holocaust Remembrance Alliance (IHRA)—an intergovernmental body of mainly European countries set up to promote Holocaust education—adopted a version of their text.[61]

IHRA defined antisemitism vaguely as 'a certain perception of Jews, which may be expressed as hatred toward Jews'. It also gave eleven 'examples' of antisemitism which included '[a]pplying double standards' to Israel 'by requiring of it a behavior not expected or demanded of any other democratic nation' and 'claiming that the existence of a State of Israel is a racist endeavor'.[62] Some IHRA member countries objected to these examples, fearing they would be weaponised against Israel's legitimate critics. As a result IHRA did not incorporate them in its official antisemitism definition but endorsed them separately to 'guide' IHRA's own work.[63]

The Israel-related examples were widely criticised by scholars, jurists, and civil liberties campaigners who argued that they could easily be used to stigmatise or silence valid criticism of Israel.[64] Indeed Israel and its supporters frequently accuse international bodies and human rights organisations of antisemitism on these grounds while the IHRA definition has been mobilised in Britain to shut down civil society events in support of Palestinian rights.[65]

CFI credits its then parliamentary chairman Sir Eric Pickles—the former Conservative Party chairman who was appointed Britain's special envoy for post-Holocaust issues in 2015—as having played 'an instrumental role' in IHRA's endorsement of the definition and examples.[66] In December 2016, the Conservative government 'supported by' Pickles became one of the world's first to endorse the IHRA text at a national level.[67] Prime Minister May announced the measure at CFI's Annual Business Lunch, where she also stated that 'Israel guarantees the rights of people of all religions, races and sexualities, and it wants to enable everyone to flourish'.[68]

In November 2020, prominent Palestinian and Arab intellectuals argued that by conflating 'Judaism with Zionism', the IHRA examples counter-productively pitted Jewish rights against Palestinian rights. They warned that adopting the IHRA text would make it difficult to freely criticise Israel or discuss alternative constitutional structures that might safeguard Palestinian as well as Israeli rights.[69] I have found no evidence that Pickles considered this perspective.

On the contrary, whereas Pickles positioned the British government 'at the forefront of establishing' the IHRA definition and 'promot[ing] its adoption across the world',[70] he showed no comparable sense of urgency when the All-Party Parliamentary Group on British Muslims put forward an analogous definition of Islamophobia. 'A definition of anti-Muslim hatred or Islamophobia is a very good idea', he said.[71] But 'there's nothing out there that is really satisfactory . . . don't rush it'.*

Obliteration of Palestinian Voices

The pro-Israel lobby is one of the most formidable lobbies ever to make headway in British life.** Operating inside and outside parliament it has

---

* In response to these criticisms Eric Pickles wrote: 'I would respectfully suggest that the critique from Palestinian and Arab intellectuals reflects a selective reading of the IHRA Working Definition of Antisemitism. The definition does not mention Zionism, and it explicitly states that criticism of Israel, similar to that levelled against any other country, is not antisemitic. Suggesting that the definition equates Judaism with Zionism overlooks this clarity and risks misrepresenting its intent'. He also said that: 'I have long supported efforts to define and combat anti-Muslim hatred. During my period in office as Communities Secretary, the UK Government funded the first monitoring of Islamophobia and established the first cross-government working group on anti-Muslim hatred, composed of respected voices from the Muslim community. In office I funded the memory of the Muslim Genocide at Srebrenica'. He said that: 'While the APPG's proposed definition was a welcome initiative, it did not undergo the same level of international scrutiny and consensus-building as the IHRA definition'.

** For another view see the veteran columnist David Aaronovitch: 'I've been in this business for nearly 35 years, working in news and current affairs. I've come across all the lobbies and received invitations from many, including travel-paid trips to visit this or that place. I've lunched with the food lobby, applauded with the theatre lobby, dinnered with Museumocrats, breakfasted at the Swedish embassy—and turned down many, many played a major role in shaping policy. Meanwhile Palestinian voices have been obliterated almost as comprehensively in London as in Tel Aviv. If heard they are misrepresented. This balance of forces helps explain why Prime Minister Sunak suffered negligible party political damage from his declared policy of 'unequivocal' support for Netanyahu after October 7.

Britain likes to claim to be an even-handed and tolerant country. Over recent decades, especially fourteen years of Conservative government, decency and tolerance has been systematically withheld from Palestinians. Until little more than two years ago, there was no such thing as the Conservative Friends of Palestine. Even now it is a tiny organisation that can claim the support of a just handful of councillors, a few MPs, and no press. It exerts zero influence.

Michael Gove's Economic Activity of Public Bodies (Overseas Matters) Bill is a devastating case study in the elimination of Palestinian voices. It promised to deliver on a central objective of Netanyahu's foreign policy: protecting Israel against the threat of international isolation by blocking public bodies from supporting boycott, sanctions, and divestment campaigns against Israel. As we have seen, Sunak boasted about this legislation when he spoke to the Conservative Friends of Israel annual lunch at the start of 2024.

Most unusually, the bill explicitly singled out Israel, the Occupied Palestinian Territory, and the Israeli-occupied Golan Heights for special protection. It thus put not just Israel but also territories Israel unlawfully occupied or annexed out of reach of the BDS movement.

When the bill entered committee stage in the Commons no Palestinian was invited to give evidence.[72] Yet a raft of pro-Israeli voices were heard.

---

more such approaches. So this idea of the uniquely powerful Israel lobby is bunkum. It really is. The various organisations that support Israel do what everyone else does—they seek to persuade you of their view. They'll send you their bumf, plead with you to meet the ambassador, or take part in a seminar or go on a fact-finding trip. Some are pushy, some take no for an answer right away. And that's it. There is nothing else. You can take notice of it, or not. If you're so much a fool as to be swayed by the simple fact of such attention, then you're in the wrong job'. David Aaronovitch, 'A Lobby Is a Lobby Is a Lobby', *The Jewish Chronicle* (16 January 2017).

CFI gave evidence. But no balancing invitation for Conservative Friends of Palestine. UK Lawyers for Israel gave evidence. There was no balancing invitation for Lawyers for Palestinian Human Rights. The Jewish Leadership Council gave evidence. But not the British Palestinian Committee. The *Times* columnist Melanie Phillips, well known for her hostility to the Palestinian cause, was invited. But no balancing pro-Palestinian columnist.[73] And so on.*

One final omission stands out: No Foreign Office official was invited to give evidence about the effect of the bill on Britain's international standing. By conflating Israel with the territories it has occupied by military force, the bill flatly contradicted existing British foreign policy commitments. Prime Minister Sunak had pressed ahead in the face of warnings from his own Foreign Office officials that the bill contradicted British foreign policy and represented a propaganda gift for Russian president Vladimir Putin.[74] A Foreign Office letter to 10 Downing Street warned that 'Moscow would use it [the bill] to show the UK did not uphold the international rules-based system and was therefore "being hypocritical in our treatment of 'annexed territory'" in relation to Britain's condemnation of Russia's invasion of Ukraine'. Foreign Office lawyers also advised that a clause in the bill 'would significantly increase the risk of the UK being in breach of our commitments' under UN Security Council Resolution 2334. This stipulated that 'Israel's establishment of settlements' in Occupied Palestinian Territory is 'a flagrant violation under international law' and a 'major obstacle' to a two-state solution.

Six of the ten Conservative MPs on the nineteen-member committee had visited Israel on trips organised by CFI. They also formally disclosed that they personally knew or were personal friends of James Gurd, one of the witnesses at the committee hearings in his capacity as CFI executive

* When I put to Michael Gove my criticism that his bill excluded Palestinian voices, he replied: 'The decision over which witnesses to invite at committee stage rests with the Commons, not the Government. The legislation we put forward was supported by civil society organisations who had suffered direct harm in the UK as a result of the activities of the BDS movement. Its leader is opposed to a two-state solution. The UK Government believed and believes that a two-state solution is the best and fairest path to peace'.

director.[75] One MP, Labour's Kim Leadbeater, said she had been on a trip organised by the Council for Arab-British Understanding, which stands up for Palestinian rights. The British government is supposed to be guided by the Nolan Principles of selflessness, integrity, objectivity, accountability, openness, honesty, and leadership. The choice of witnesses, as well as the membership of the committee, proves that the Nolan Principles have ceased to apply when it comes to Israel and Palestine. The failure to seek testimony from the Foreign Office highlights the problems arising from the pro-Israel policy of the last Conservative government. In its eagerness to stretch out a helping hand to an ally, it was happy to disregard Britain's commitment to international law and in the process hand a propaganda weapon to bloodstained President Putin in Moscow.*

The bill was on the verge of becoming law when Sunak called a general election for July 2024. This was a setback for the pro-Israel lobby, but it had already secured almost everything else it wanted.

2030 Roadmap

At the end of March 2023 James Cleverly, then British foreign secretary, signed a 'roadmap' with his Israeli counterpart Eli Cohen. It was hailed by *Jewish News* as 'an ambitious agreement that will ensure the partnership remains modern and continues to innovate to address shared challenges'.[76] Israel's ambassador to the UK Tzipi Hotovely greeted it as 'historic'.[77] Labour Friends of Israel said the roadmap 'should be a basis for enhanced cooperation in bilateral defence, counter-terrorism, and the combatting of Iranian nuclear ambitions and destabilising regional activity'.[78]

It was certainly a noteworthy document. Britain promised to become an apologist for Israel's illegal oppression of Palestinians: 'The UK and Israel will work together to tackle the singling out of Israel in the Human Rights Council as well as in other international bodies'.[79]

---

* Richard Hermer KC wrote a cogent criticism of the bill, commissioned by David Lammy and Lisa Nandy. He was not then the attorney general. Richard Hermer, 'Economic Activity of Public Bodies (Overseas Matters) Bill—Opinion', matrixlaw.co.uk (26 June 2023).

The roadmap went on: 'In this context, the UK and Israel disagree with the use of the term "apartheid" with regard to Israel'.[80] These statements undermined the resolution reached two years earlier by the UN Human Rights Council to investigate breaches of international humanitarian law in Israel, the West Bank, and Gaza.[81] The promise to challenge the term 'apartheid' brought unhappy memories of British support for South Africa.[82] The crime of apartheid is defined under the Rome Statute (which established the ICC) as inhumane acts committed in the framework of an 'institutionalised regime of systematic oppression and domination by one racial group over any other . . . and committed with the intention of maintaining that regime'.[83] By the time Foreign Secretary James Cleverly pledged that Britain would 'disagree with the use of the term', the most prominent international and Israeli human rights organisations had determined that Israel was practicing apartheid.[84] In June 2021 two former Israeli ambassadors to South Africa, Ilan Baruch and Alon Liel, wrote: 'It is time for the world to recognize that what we saw in South Africa decades ago is happening in the occupied Palestinian territories too'.[85]

Cleverly's roadmap committed Britain 'to confront antisemitism, delegitimisation and anti-Israel bias'. This translated into an agreement that Britain would side with Israel against those who criticised its record on human rights. This would mean 'tackling the disproportionate focus on Israel in the UN and other international bodies'. The document also agreed that Israel and the UK would sign a free trade agreement.[86] As usual Palestinians were ignored. In fact the 2030 roadmap avoided any mention of Palestinians, beyond a vague pledge to improve Palestinian 'livelihoods' and 'economic development'.[87]

The agreement did not mention a two-state solution, Israel's illegal settlements or Palestinian human rights. Roadmap 2030 therefore ignored international law while obliging the United Kingdom to shield Israeli abuses by condemning their critics. The timing was beyond belief. Barely three months before the roadmap was signed, Benjamin Netanyahu had formed a coalition with the Religious Zionism Party and Jewish Power to create the most far right, anti-Arab government in Israeli history, with powerful fascist elements.[88] It planned to annex the West Bank and attack democracy within Israel itself. Settler violence was escalating along with a vast expansion of settlement building: part of a programme to make a Palestinian state impossible. Sir Keir Starmer, the human rights lawyer who led the Labour opposition, raised no objections to Roadmap 2030.* In the next chapter I explain his silence.

* In December 2024, over sixty MPs signed a letter calling on Starmer's government to (among other things) revoke the 2030 Roadmap. I have found no evidence that either Lammy or Starmer responded to the letter, and a Labour source told *The Jewish Chronicle*: 'it's shocking but sadly not surprising that the Corbynite rump would write such a letter without even mentioning Hamas or the hostages. The British public resoundingly rejected this far-left approach in 2019 and there's a reason many of the signatories are no longer Labour MPs'. (Lorin Bell-Cross, 'Over 60 Parliamentarians Call for Sanctions against Israel', *The Jewish Chronicle* (1 December 2024)) Starmer did not say anything in parliament—neither for nor against—in response to the 2030 Roadmap being signed. UK House of Commons, 'Sir Keir Starmer—Spoken Contributions', members.parliament.uk (n.d.).

7

THE POLITICAL FORMATION OF SIR KEIR STARMER

I'm well aware of the definition of genocide.

—*Sir Keir Starmer, House of Commons*

THREE WEEKS into Israel's assault on Gaza, on October 31, 2023, several huge explosions tore through the Jabalia refugee camp, transforming the dense jumble of tightly packed homes and narrow streets into an apocalyptic wasteland of craters and concrete dust. Amid the rubble, at least 126 Palestinians—among them 68 children—were dead after what became known as the Jabalia camp massacre.[1] Israel readily confirmed that its bombs had caused the carnage, justifying the mass killing on the grounds that a Hamas commander and other 'terrorists' were targeted.[2] But the UN Human Rights Office said the slaughter 'could amount to war crimes'.[3] Entire families were wiped out in the blasts, which left 'body parts all over the place', according to one survivor, who said 'it felt like the end of the world'.[4]

On the same day, in the refined surroundings of Chatham House on St James' Square in Central London, Sir Keir Starmer, then leader of the opposition, took to a rostrum to explain why the bloodletting must continue. Already more than eight thousand Palestinians had been killed.[5]

Already Israel's political leadership and officials had issued bloodcurdling statements dripping with genocidal intent, declaring: 'We are fighting human animals and we act accordingly'.[6] Already the secretary general of the UN had called for a ceasefire and the overwhelming majority of countries on the planet had voted at the General Assembly for the violence to stop.[7] But Starmer disagreed.

To his surprise, the Labour leader found himself under serious political pressure over Gaza. His determination to outdo the rest of the British political and media class in his fervour for Israel's cause after October 7 had provoked a backlash. The party was haemorrhaging support among Muslim voters.[8] The Labour mayors of London and Manchester, together with Labour's leader in Scotland, had called for a ceasefire. There were rumours of shadow ministers on the verge of resignation.[9] They were not out of step with public opinion. An overwhelming 76 percent of the British public thought there should be 'an immediate ceasefire' in Israel and Palestine as of mid-October, with just 8 percent disagreeing.[10]

Yet when Starmer took the stage in a room full of journalists and foreign policy professionals in Chatham House, he nailed his colours to the mast. '[W]hile I understand calls for a ceasefire', he said, 'at this stage I do not believe that is the correct position'.[11] It would have been to Starmer's political advantage to back the calls. Instead, he chose to expend significant political capital on publicly slapping down other members of his party for doing so. The question is: why?

The answer illuminates what drove the Labour leader's policy not only over the timing of a ceasefire but throughout Israel's assault on Gaza. The Labour leader had dual motivations for backing Israel to the hilt, one of which concerned the state, and the other the party. First and foremost, he was aligning himself with the conventional understanding of British geopolitical interests. This usually meant tucking in behind the US, playing the role of junior partner, and closely following Washington's lead for when to change position. It was no coincidence that the rationale he offered at Chatham House for rejecting a ceasefire—that humanitarian 'pauses' were the only 'credible' way to alleviate Palestinian suffering because the conflict could not be 'frozen' with Hamas undefeated—was precisely in line with

US and, consequently, British government policy at the time. ITV News reported that Labour MPs were told bluntly by the leadership that 'party policy on Gaza will simply follow the White House'.*

So far, so conventional. But Starmer identified himself with Israel's actions to an unusual degree—even initially endorsing its right to lay siege to the Gaza Strip, to his lasting political cost. This is where the second of his dual motivations came to the fore. The explanation for his determination, verging on desperation, to prove his pro-Israel credentials can be found in the circumstances of his rise to power. Starmer and his advisors had crudely exploited the issue of antisemitism in the Labour Party to aid their factional battle against the left. Expressing reverential support for Israel, in contrast to the pro-Palestinian Labour left, thereby became an integral part of their political project.

Together, these dual motivations—external state and internal party—propelled Starmer into the moral abyss of aiding and abetting a genocidal onslaught against the Palestinians of Gaza. For a purported human rights lawyer this was an unworthy path.

---

* One frustrated MP snapped: 'There's no point Starmer trying to convince people that humanitarian pauses are the answer when he will literally be arguing for a new position as soon as [President] Biden and [Prime Minister] Sunak announce one'. Sure enough, just a month and a half later, in line with changing rhetoric from the US, first Prime Minister Sunak and then Starmer began to advocate a 'sustainable ceasefire' (although not an immediate one). In late February 2024 Starmer moved again, calling for an 'immediate humanitarian ceasefire' (with numerous caveats). The timing of this last shift may have been brought forward by the threat of a parliamentary rebellion in Labour ranks but synchronicity was soon restored when, on March 4, US vice president Kamala Harris called for 'an immediate ceasefire for at least the next six weeks'. Israel was not put under pressure to heed these calls and therefore ignored them. Post by @ShehabKhan on X (3 November 2023), https://x.com/ShehabKhan/status/1720464647948468686 ('follow'). Post by @ShehabKhan on X (3 November 2023), https://x.com/ShehabKhan/status/1720469056023597419 ('no point'). Peter Walker, 'Keir Starmer Joins Rishi Sunak in Calling for Sustainable Ceasefire in Gaza', *The Guardian* (18 December 2023) ('sustainable'). Andrew McDonald, 'UK Labour Is Backing an "Immediate" Gaza Cease-fire. But the Devil's in the Details', politico.eu (20 February 2024) ('immediate'). 'US VP Harris Calls for "Immediate" Gaza Truce in Rare Rebuke of Israel', aljazeera.com (4 March 2024) (Harris).

Starmer and Genocide

A year after his Chatham House speech, Starmer, now UK prime minister, was asked in parliament why he would not use the word 'genocide' to describe Israel's actions in Gaza. 'I'm well aware of the definition of genocide', he responded, 'and that is why I've never described this as, and referred to it as, genocide'.[12] In brandishing his knowledge of the topic, Starmer was alluding to his work as a lawyer on behalf of Croatia in 2014, when he argued at the International Court of Justice that Serbian forces had committed genocide against Croats in 1991.[13] It is worth taking a closer look at the Croatia case, to judge whether Starmer was being consistent.

Starmer seized the opportunity to test his legal skills before the highest court in the world after his period as the chief prosecutor in England and Wales came to an end and a year before he shifted careers from law to politics. He joined a distinguished team of lawyers acting for Croatia on a long-running case with its origins in the breakup of Yugoslavia, when Serbian forces had sought to create a 'Greater Serbia' in areas with a significant Croat population.

Starmer's argument at the ICJ bears directly on his later stance over Gaza. The arguments he presented were not merely about the particular circumstances of the crimes committed by Serbian forces. He advanced an interpretation of the legal principles governing the crime of genocide, principles by which Israel's actions in Gaza can also be judged.

The most difficult part of any genocide case is establishing intent, since those contemplating genocide rarely announce the fact. It was Starmer who took on this crucial task for Croatia. Standing before the panel of judges in the Peace Palace in The Hague, he emphasised four factors, each of which, he argued, was enough on its own to 'provide the overwhelming inference that there was a genocidal intent' on the part of the Serb forces, and each of which happens to also be directly applicable to Israel's actions in Gaza. Here are the four factors cited by Starmer in 2014[14] set against comparable Israeli conduct:

1. *The political doctrine of Serbian expansionism which created the climate for genocidal policies aimed at destroying the Croatian population living in areas earmarked to become part of 'Greater*

Serbia'.—Israel has spent decades expropriating, settling, and de facto annexing the Occupied Palestinian Territory, which the Israeli government considers the 'historical homeland' of the 'Jewish people'.[15] Consistent with this longstanding policy, the Netanyahu government has committed to conquering Gaza and expelling its inhabitants.[16]

2. *The statements of public officials, including demonization of Croats and systematic incitement on the part of State-controlled media.*—Israeli officials and public figures have regularly dehumanized the Palestinian people in Gaza as 'evil', 'terrorists', 'animals', 'sons of Satan', and 'Amalek'—an enemy nation that Jews are commanded in the Bible to exterminate. Israeli politicians have publicly affirmed that 'the children of Gaza have brought it upon themselves', urged that 'children should be killed . . . they serve as a human shield', and lamented that even as Israeli soldiers had killed '150 terrorists' in the orthopaedic ward of Gaza's al-Shifa hospital, '300 terrorists were born' in the maternity ward. When an Israeli doctor addressing Knesset members mentioned that a suffering child in Gaza should be able to receive painkillers and basic medical care, multiple lawmakers from the governing coalition objected. 'You are the sickest doctor I've ever seen', one MP exclaimed.[17] Israel's state prosecutor recommended that no criminal investigations be opened against senior public figures who have called to harm civilians in Gaza.[18]

3. *The fact that the pattern of attacks on groups of Croats far exceeded any legitimate military objective necessary to secure control of the regions concerned.*—In March 2025, the UN's Independent International Commission of Inquiry concluded that Israel had 'intentionally' attacked 'the civilian population' of Gaza, including 'children' as well as displaced persons in 'designated safe zones'; caused 'the near total destruction of civilian objects across the densely populated Gaza Strip'; 'destroyed . . . key infrastructures . . . indispensable to the survival of the civilian population there'; and employed 'starvation of civilians as a method of warfare'. The inquiry found that Israel's 'victims were overwhelmingly civilians' as Israel committed against part

of Gaza's civilian population 'the crime against humanity of extermination'.[19]

4. *Contemporaneous video footage evidencing the genocidal intent of those carrying out the attacks.*—Israeli soldiers effectively broadcast their destruction of Gaza live on social media, in what journalists who tracked such posts have dubbed an 'Insta-Genocide'.[20] Much of this footage documented genocidal intent. Amnesty International examined dozens of videos posted online and identified a 'recurrent theme': 'the desire to leave Gaza uninhabitable'.[21] The Israeli military itself ran a social media channel entitled '72 Virgins—Uncensored' which published images of Palestinian detainees and corpses captioned 'exterminating the roaches'.[22]

Starmer argued that 'the destruction of a group, or part of a group, does not require extermination of all the members of the group, or even . . . a substantial part of it'. It is 'not a numbers game', he insisted, unwittingly anticipating a common riposte from those who today deny that Israel has committed genocide in Gaza. These apologists for Israeli crimes have included Starmer's own sometime foreign secretary, David Lammy. Lammy said in October 2024 that the term genocide was 'largely used when millions of people lost their lives in crises such as Rwanda and the Holocaust of the second world war. The way that people are now using those terms undermines their seriousness'.[23] On the contrary, Starmer argued in 2014, '[w]hat must be shown is an intention to destroy a group or part of a group as a functioning entity'.[24]

At another point in the proceedings, Starmer focused on the city of Vukovar, which suffered 'a radically disproportionate attack deliberately intended to devastate the town and its civilian population'.[25] In words that could easily be used to describe the horrors of Jabalia refugee camp—once home to more than a hundred thousand Palestinians but utterly destroyed by the end of 2024—Starmer recounted how 'Serbian forces carried out a sustained campaign of shelling; systematic expulsion; denial of food, water, electricity, sanitation and medical treatment; bombing; burning; brutal killings and torture which reduced the city to rubble and destroyed its Croat population'.[26] It is striking that the same man, less than ten years later, would agree that 'Israel does have that right' to deny water and electricity to Palestinians in Gaza.[27]

The Serbian forces even attacked Vukovar hospital, Starmer continued, in a tone of appropriate moral disgust. The hospital, which had become a place of sanctuary for fleeing civilians, was 'subject to attacks on virtually a daily basis—again, attacks only consistent with an intent to destroy vulnerable citizens rather than military objectives'.[28] Similar crimes have been committed on a much larger, indeed systematic scale by Israel, resulting in 'the destruction of most hospitals in Gaza, pushing the healthcare system to the point of almost complete collapse', according to a report by the UN.[29]

In contending that the treatment of Vukovar was genocidal, Starmer also drew attention to the '"dramatic differences" between the military capabilities of the opposing forces', with the 'extensively equipped and trained' Serbs deploying 'military might . . . far in excess of what was required to overpower the Croat forces'.[30] This 'colossal mismatch',[31] he said, revealed the true purpose: to destroy the Croat population. The comparative military superiority of the Israel Defence Forces over Hamas and other Palestinian resistance fighters is far greater.

The ICJ ultimately rejected Croatia's claim of genocide. Starmer and his colleagues failed to convince the judges that the 'only reasonable inference' to be drawn from the behaviour of Serbian forces was their intent to destroy the Croats in the areas they were attacking, rather than force them to flee to other parts of Croatia.[32] But that does not diminish the relevance of Starmer's contribution. While it may be argued that, as a lawyer, he was paid to advocate for Croatia, the legal principles he enunciated around genocidal intent, which he presumably believed had merit, can equally be applied to Palestine.

When the judgement was delivered in February 2015, Starmer greeted it with a hint of defiance. He took to Twitter to question whether the ICJ would 'develop the law to extend protection from genocide'.[33] Starmer was here expressing his own opinion under his own name, before he was a politician. An interpretation frequently advanced to explain Starmer's political career, with all the zigzags and broken pledges it has entailed, is that he has always been a lawyer at heart, arguing whatever brief he has been given, whether he is in a court of law or at the dispatch box in the House of Commons. This is to let him off the hook. His reaction to the Croatia judgement suggests, on the contrary, that even in his legal days he was no mere mercenary but a self-consciously influential figure advancing his own convictions—and if he later betrayed those convictions, that is on him.

Betray them he did. Nine years later, in January 2024, when the ICJ published its momentous interim judgement in another genocide case—that brought by South Africa against Israel—Starmer's reaction was complete silence. Far from hoping that the Court would take the opportunity to 'extend protection from genocide' to the Palestinians, in the run up to the judgement Starmer's spokesperson said it was 'not a case we would have signed on to . . . not something we would support'.[34] Despite the magnitude of the ruling and the provisional measures ordered, Starmer made no statement in response—not even a tweet.

Israel's crimes in Gaza set up a conflict between Starmer's loyalty to the British state's geopolitical allegiances and his loyalty to the laws intended to constrain what states can do. His rhetorical tactic to transcend the dilemma was to insist that 'Israel has to exercise its right to self-defence within international law'.[35] But as soon as this formulation came into contact with reality it collapsed into absurdity, as in the infamous LBC interview when he answered that Israel had the right to cut off water and electricity before adding: 'Obviously, everything should be done within international law. . . '.[36] The logic seemed to be that the crime of collective punishment was justified as long as it was committed legally.

The LBC debacle taught Starmer that, henceforth, he must refuse to give an opinion on whether any specific Israeli action was legal. 'It's unwise for politicians to stand on stages like this, or to sit in television studios, and pronounce, day-by-day, which acts may or may not be in accordance with international law', he said in the Q&A after his anti-ceasefire speech on October 31, 2023. 'It's extremely unwise and I'm not going to get involved in that kind of exercise'.[37] But he had no such reservations pronouncing on the crimes of states that were not British allies—such as Russia, of whose transgressions in Ukraine he declared: 'These are war crimes, these are absolutely appalling crimes'.[38]

Asked in June 2024 during another LBC appearance whether Israel was committing genocide in Gaza, Starmer referred back to his experience on the Croatia case, saying: 'I'm not going to sit in an LBC studio and pronounce that something is either genocide or not . . . Israel, every country has to be held properly to account in accordance with international law but the body that does that is the international court . . . and having literally argued in court for three months over the meaning of genocide, the evidence of genocide, I'm very well aware of what it is. I'm also very, very well aware that you need to have the evidence in front of you before you come to a final decision.'[39]

If it is up to the international court to decide if Israel is committing genocide, that begs the question why Starmer later gave his opinion that Israel was not. This is not just an infuriating inconsistency but a matter of grave consequence. The Genocide Convention places an obligation on states to make efforts to *prevent* genocide. Once the ICJ decided that the right of Palestinians in Gaza not to be subjected to genocide was plausibly at risk, it is difficult to imagine anything more urgent than fulfilling that obligation. Yet for all Starmer's rhetorical deference to the ICJ, when its considered judgement conflicted with Britain's geopolitical interests he simply ignored it—and continued to ignore it as prime minister. This approach led Amnesty International to conclude in January 2025 that 'the UK government's disregard for its legal obligations to prevent genocide . . . contributed to Israel's impunity and risked British complicity in serious crimes against international law.'[40]

Factional Struggle

How did the passionate lawyer crusading against genocide in 2014 become the indifferent politician unmoved by the ICJ interim judgement in 2024? There was no inkling of this trajectory when Starmer ran to be an MP in 2015. In the lead-up to that election he addressed a Camden Palestine Solidarity Campaign meeting in his future constituency of Holborn and St Pancras. It was the launch of the organisation's 'Vote Palestine' initiative and a packed audience listened to Starmer speak in front of a display of maps illustrating the progressive shrinking of Palestinian territories and a banner reading 'Kick Israeli racism out of FIFA'.[41]

There was not much inkling when he ran to be leader of the Labour Party five years later. At a hustings event organised by the Jewish Labour Movement he was the only one of four leadership candidates to say he was not a Zionist, although he qualified his position by saying 'I understand and I sympathise and I support Zionism'.[42]

But fast forward another half decade and the emphasis was very different. In December 2024, at the annual lunch of the internal party lobby group Labour Friends of Israel, Starmer made an extraordinary statement. After asserting that antisemitism had previously been 'allowed to take root and grow in our party', he declared that under his leadership Labour 'has returned to our history and heritage which is inseparable from the state of Israel and our Jewish family'.[43] Here was the complete conflation of the battle against antisemitism with the defence of Israel—and the complete identification of his party and himself with a state then engaged in a genocidal onslaught.

The controversy over Labour antisemitism is crucial to understanding how Starmer arrived at this point. Having won the leadership on a left-wing Corbynesque platform in 2020, Starmer promptly set about defining himself against his left-wing predecessor, eventually going so far as to push Jeremy Corbyn out of the Labour Party altogether. He used the issue of antisemitism to do it. But in that one sentence at the Labour Friends of Israel lunch, Starmer let slip that for him the controversy was not simply about racism against Jews, but was bound up with a historic factional struggle over Israel and Palestine.

It was not always the case that the right of the Labour Party supported Israel and the left supported Palestine. Labour Friends of Israel itself was established in 1957 by, among others, left icons Aneurin Bevan and Jennie Lee, who eulogised the early kibbutzim (Jewish collectives) as a socialist paradise.[44] Critics of Israel were a minority not only in the Labour Party but in the wider labour movement; Israel's Histadrut trade union cultivated strong ties with the British Trades Union Congress.

It was Israel's brutal invasion and occupation of Lebanon in 1982 that crystallised a left-right divide.[45] Tony Benn, then near the peak of his influence at the head of a left insurgency, resigned from Labour Friends of Israel in protest.[46] At the grassroots, anti-imperialist currents more sympathetic to the Palestinians strengthened. The right of the labour movement, horrified by the Bennite challenge and quick to crush it, redoubled its ideological commitment to Atlanticism (expressed through adherence to NATO and the nuclear deterrent) and anti-Communism. Support for Israel, an American client state in the Cold War, fitted in neatly. As we saw in the previous chapter, this position dovetailed with Tory foreign policy: Atlanticism was also pervasive within the Conservative Party as the default post-war orientation of the British establishment.

The triumph of Tony Blair in the 1990s represented the apotheosis of Labour's version of Atlanticism. In the era of the Oslo Accords, and with the left routed, the Labour right's identification with Israel came at little cost. By 2001, despite the Second Intifada raging, Jonathan Mendelsohn, an influential lobbyist and former chair of Labour Friends of Israel, could say that 'Blair has attacked the anti-Israelism that had existed in the Labour Party... The milieu has changed. Zionism is pervasive in New Labour. It is automatic that Blair will come to Labour Friends of Israel meetings'.[47] Chairing Labour Friends of Israel became 'a route to the top for ambitious young Blairites', according to former MP John Woodcock.[48] Awareness of the career opportunities to be gained by adopting a pro-Israel stance filtered down through the party to student politics, shaping future generations of Labour politicians.

In the early 2000s the Blair government enlisted in the US-led 'Global War on Terror' and took an accommodationist approach towards the right-wing Israeli government of Ariel Sharon, then engaged in the brutal suppression of the Second Intifada. Atlanticism, neoliberal economics, and support for Israel became parts of the New Labour package.[49] These issues also became linked among Blair's opponents within and beyond the Labour Party, as public opposition to the 2003 Iraq War became bound up with opposition to Israel's occupation. Throughout the New Labour period the party's grassroots had remained sympathetic to the Palestinians and Blair faced consistent pressure on this issue.[50] In Blair's own assessment, his outspoken support for Israel during the 2006 Lebanon War 'probably did me more damage than anything since Iraq'.[51]

The backlash was a long time coming but in 2015 Labour experienced a revolution with the shock election of Jeremy Corbyn as leader. Corbyn was a former chair of the Stop the War Coalition, which had been established to oppose the Bush-Blair 'War on Terror', and was a longtime patron of the Palestine Solidarity Campaign. For the first time, Labour was led by someone unequivocally committed to Palestinian rights.

The 'Labour antisemitism crisis' that unfolded under Corbyn's leadership was an unparalleled episode in British political history. The leader of the opposition came under relentless attack from not only the entire press, leading Jewish communal organisations, and even Israeli prime minister Benjamin Netanyahu (who tweeted that Corbyn deserved 'unequivocal condemnation'),[52] but also from the bulk of his own MPs as well as staff from the right of the party.[53]

We have already seen how the pro-Israel lobby exerted influence on the Conservative Party. The same was true for Labour, and it was notable that the organisations that most vociferously levelled accusations of antisemitism against the party in this period, such as the Campaign Against Antisemitism and the Board of Deputies of British Jews, also doubled as pro-Israel advocacy groups.

There is no question that some Labour Party members did express antisemitic views, usually on social media, and that the systems to deal with them were dysfunctional. There is also no question that Corbyn was right when he later said that while one antisemite was one too many, 'the scale of the problem was also dramatically overstated for political reasons by our opponents inside and outside the party, as well as by much of the media.'[54]

One of those opponents was Starmer's future chief of staff Morgan McSweeney. As Gabriel Pogrund and Patrick Maguire have disclosed in a revelatory book, McSweeney trawled pro-Corbyn Facebook groups made up of tens of thousands of people—many not even members of the Labour Party—for antisemitic comments which he then fed to *The Sunday Times*.[55] Two and a half years later McSweeney would be centrally involved in Starmer's decision to suspend Corbyn from the party for the accurate statement quoted above.[56]

The ferocity of the factional rampage against the Labour left reflected the threat Corbyn had posed to the governing elite. One of the two parties of government had, for a time, fallen out of its grasp. Corbyn's views on foreign policy, including on Israel-Palestine, had made the threat particularly potent.

It was the role of Sir Keir Starmer, an establishment neophyte, to make the Labour Party reliable again. As such, he was always bound to end up in alliance with the Atlanticist Labour right who shared the same purpose.

Starmer, a prominent member of Corbyn's shadow cabinet throughout the antisemitism controversy, publicly defended him at the time. As late as October 2019, when pro-Israel MP Louise Ellman alleged that Corbyn posed a 'danger' to the Jewish community, Starmer replied, 'I don't accept that'.[57] But in private he was already engaged as the front man for what Pogrund and Maguire have described as a 'deception without precedent'—orchestrated by McSweeney and substantially bankrolled by the pro-Israel donor Sir Trevor Chinn—to convince the Labour membership to 'abandon Corbynism without them ever realising' and make Starmer 'the Labour leader who buried the left'.[58]

From the moment he was elected Labour Party leader in April 2020 Starmer restyled himself as a crusader against antisemitism, vowing to 'tear out this poison by its roots' in his acceptance speech and insisting his 'first priority' was to tackle racism against Jews.[59] In practice this frequently meant attacking the left, often on flimsy grounds. As well as suspending Corbyn—who was later cleared and reinstated by the party but still denied the whip by Starmer, ending his thirty-seven-year spell as a Labour MP—he sacked shadow education secretary Rebecca Long-Bailey, his former leadership rival, for sharing over social media an interview with an actress that contained the claim that Israeli forces had trained American police in the tactics that killed George Floyd. Yet when worse transgressions were committed by allies of the leader, for instance when the shadow communities secretary Steve Reed referred to a Jewish businessman as a 'puppet master', no sanction was forthcoming.[60] At the grassroots level, a disproportionate number of Jewish Labour members who supported Palestinian rights or opposed Zionism found themselves in the surreal position of being suspended for antisemitism.[61]

With each turn of the wrench Starmer became more dependent on a group of advisors and allies from the right wing of the party. Support for Israel was one ingredient in the glue that helped bond together the likes of advisors McSweeney and Chris Ward; MPs Rachel Reeves, Pat McFadden, and Wes Streeting; and party fixer Luke Akehurst, who ran the advocacy group

We Believe in Israel. They were part of a nexus that encompassed Labour Friends of Israel (all the MPs named were supporters) and the Jewish Labour Movement—groups 'lionised' by McSweeney as 'the "soldiers" who had kept up the fight against Corbyn'.[62] Palestinian activism, in contrast, was disdained as 'a creature of the hard left', according to a member of Starmer's shadow cabinet.[63]

This factional conflict helps explain why Starmer went above and beyond in his public expressions of admiration for Israel, beginning well before the Hamas assault of October 7. At the annual Labour Friends of Israel lunch in 2021 Starmer repeated Harold Wilson's claim that early Israeli leaders were 'social democrats who made the desert flower', which the Palestine Solidarity Campaign condemned with some justice as a 'racist anti-Palestinian trope' (it falsely implies that Palestinians had been too backwards to cultivate the land).[64] The following year, Starmer told *The Jewish Chronicle* he did not agree with Amnesty International that Israel was an apartheid state, wrongly adding that this was 'not the Labour Party position'. In fact it was: Labour's most recent conference had voted through a motion acknowledging that 'Israel is practising the crime of apartheid as defined by the UN'.[65]

So, by the eve of October 7, Starmer was primed to back Israel to the hilt, whatever news might emanate from the Middle East. The brutality of the atrocities committed that day pushed him further. The leader had a packed schedule at Labour's annual conference that week and so it was not until October 11 that he undertook a day of media appearances in which he gave his unscripted response at length, by which time Israel's army had been unleashed. His interviews revealed a man determined not to utter a single word of caution or criticism towards Israel, nor compassion for Palestinians. Asked twice by Sky News if he had any sympathy for Palestinian civilians 'literally living under siege at the moment in Gaza' he could offer nothing, coldly replying: 'Nobody wants to see that situation, but we have to be clear where responsibility is; responsibility [is] with Hamas'.[66]

But it was Starmer's interview with LBC that proved disastrous. His assertion that 'Israel does have that right' to cut off power and water caused a storm.[67] It was not until a week later that his spokesperson first attempted to clarify the remarks, with a bogus claim that the leader had been answering 'the specific question beforehand' about 'Israel having the right to defend itself' (in fact the question beforehand had been 'What is a proportionate response?')[68] Nine days after the original comment Starmer was forced to row back his words himself, claiming on camera: 'I was not saying that Israel had the right to cut off water, food, fuel or medicines'.[69] This was not plausible—on the day of the LBC appearance he had given two other interviews in which he had answered the same question in a similar way.[70] Nor did it explain why Labour shadow ministers Emily Thornberry and David Lammy had held Starmer's line during subsequent TV appearances, where they refused to say that the Israeli blockade was a violation of international law.[71]

Starmer was accused of excusing war crimes, a morally grave charge, especially for a human rights lawyer. Yet instead of rushing to clarify, he had let the charge stand for more than a week. He either believed Israel had the right to impose a siege, or he wanted people to think he believed it—perhaps because he felt it went down well in the Westminster bubble, and even more so among his factional allies.

In the meantime, Starmer was clamping down within the party. Local Labour branches were discouraged from discussing motions on the Gaza war.[72] MPs and council leaders were advised or ordered that they must not 'under any circumstances' attend Palestine solidarity protests.[73] Some went along regardless. One of them, the former shadow minister Andy McDonald, was suspended for telling a rally: 'We won't rest until we have justice. Until all people, Israelis and Palestinians, between the river and the sea, can live in peaceful liberty'. The mere mention of the Jordan River and the Mediterranean Sea was declared 'deeply offensive' by the party in the midst of a media clamour over the protest chant 'From the river to the sea, Palestine will be free'.[74] It was not explained why McDonald's call for 'peaceful liberty' was a more serious offence than endorsing collective punishment, as the party's leader had done.

All of this had a political cost. There were signs of panic over what Labour insiders believed was a 'complete collapse in support' from Muslim communities, not helped by one 'senior Labour source' briefing that resignations of Muslim Labour councillors showed the party was 'shaking off the fleas'.[75] Starmer was dispatched to an Islamic Centre in Cardiff to mend fences but this backfired when the centre accused him of having 'gravely misrepresented' the visit on social media.[76]

The damage done to Labour by Starmer's imbalanced response to the conflict was lasting. It could be seen in the results of the July 2024 general election. While a split vote on the right between the unpopular Conservatives and the insurgent Reform opened the door to Labour's lopsided victory, the party lost five seats to pro-Palestinian independent candidates, a highly unusual phenomenon under Britain's first-past-the-post electoral system. One of those independents was Corbyn, who took on his old party and won handsomely. Labour incumbents who managed to hold on in constituencies with large Muslim populations still found their majorities slashed; the Blairite princeling Wes Streeting scraped home by just 528 votes against Palestinian independent challenger Leanne Mohamad while the anti-war campaigner Andrew Feinstein helped to cut Starmer's own vote tally in half.[77]

The significance of these shifts was obscured by Labour's huge overall majority of 174 seats. But this was achieved on the lowest share of the vote of any majority-winning party in British history at just 33.7 percent. The press dubbed it a 'loveless landslide'.[78] While Starmer's position on Gaza was not the main reason Labour failed to generate enthusiasm among the electorate as a whole, it did have an important political effect, opening an unbreachable chasm with the left, alienating substantial numbers of Muslim voters, and narrowing Labour's base—setting the stage for his astonishing descent into unpopularity in government.*

In the struggle for control of the Labour Party the issue of antisemitism had been instrumentalised and conflated with attitudes to Israel. This may explain why Starmer went too far in the aftermath of October 7. But though his rhetorical excesses can be traced to the factional landscape he inhabited, there was a more fundamental motive for his iron-clad support for Israel: he was pursuing what he perceived as the interests of the British state.

---

* Across the electorate Labour gained six percentage points in the 2024 election relative to 2019. But among voters who said they sympathised 'much more' with Palestinians than with Israelis, support for Labour fell by eighteen points. In the twenty-one constituencies where Muslims comprised over 30 percent of the population, Labour's vote share dropped by twenty-nine points. 'Starmer's Palestine Problem', *The Economist* (30 July 2025).

Starmer in Government

As prime minister Starmer displayed an entirely orthodox understanding of Britain's foreign policy priorities. First and foremost, that meant sticking to the US as closely as possible. But British policy did have some distinctive priorities of its own, and over Israel-Palestine had retained some consistent features. Whichever party was in power, Britain followed what Israeli historian Ilan Pappé has described as a 'policy of deliberate inertia'.[79] As we saw in Chapter Five, rhetorical support for Palestinians' right to self-determination was expressed without placing any pressure on Israel to realise it, Palestinian resistance of any kind was opposed, and Israel was lavished with diplomatic and practical support.[80] This is one reason, Pappé speculates, why the pro-Israel lobby had viewed the prospect of a Corbyn premiership with such alarm. The lobby was not concerned that Corbyn would change Britain's official foreign policy towards Israel. It was afraid that Corbyn might actually adhere to it.[81]

The Conservative government that preceded Starmer had pushed further in a pro-Israel direction than any other. The arrival of a new Labour government provided an opportunity to correct course. In cases where Starmer's new administration reined in policy, it was to restore continuity with traditional positions the British state believed best served its wider interests, rather than reflecting any principled concern for Palestinian rights or welfare. But where it did not, Starmer's contribution was to consolidate the significant shift in favour of Israel that he had inherited from the Tories.

The new Labour government made three course corrections: it restored funding to the UN Relief and Works Agency for Palestine Refugees in the Near East; it abandoned a legal challenge to the arrest warrants for Prime Minister Netanyahu and Israel's then defence minister Yoav Gallant issued by the International Criminal Court; and it suspended some arms export licences to Israel. It is worth examining the rationale put forward for each of these moves.

As described in Chapter One, Britain along with several other US allies suspended financial support for UNRWA, the main provider of humanitarian relief within Gaza, after Israel alleged in January 2024 that some of the agency's staff had been involved in October 7. By the time Labour came to power, only the US and the UK were still withholding funds. The fact that the British government alone had continued to follow such an extreme US policy—denying refugee aid during a humanitarian catastrophe—illustrated the extent to which the Conservatives had cleaved to the US position. But a divergence from the Biden administration over UNRWA, an issue of low strategic importance, did not threaten the Atlantic alliance.[82] Announcing the resumption of funding, the new government emphasised that the move brought the UK back into alignment with the European Union, Japan, Canada, and a host of other US allies.[83]

When it came to the ICC, Britain had long diverged from the US which had from the outset refused to join the Court. As the world's strongest military power, US opposition to a court that could constrain its primary advantage was logical. But for Britain, a much smaller power that punched above its weight by working through Western-dominated multilateral institutions, the calculation was different. It was surprising, therefore, when the outgoing Sunak government announced its intention to challenge the application for arrest warrants for Netanyahu and Gallant on the spurious grounds that the Court lacked jurisdiction. There were suggestions the move was made on behalf of the White House.[84]

Starmer's government justified dropping the challenge by claiming it felt 'very strongly about the rule of law internationally and domestically'.[85] But on the only question of consequence—whether the Israeli leaders would be arrested if they set foot on British soil—it dodged the issue. 'The vast majority [of ICC cases] never become issues for the UK legal process, law enforcement processes or for the UK government', said Yvette Cooper, the home secretary. 'If cases ever do become a matter for the UK then there is a proper legal process that has to be followed, there's a proper government process including foreign office process that has to be followed'.[86]

In the meantime, in January 2025, Starmer saw no problem offering his 'personal thanks' to Netanyahu, a man now wanted for crimes against humanity and war crimes, 'for the work done by the Israeli government to secure the release of the hostages'.[87] Britain was signalling that it would respect international law in words while doing nothing to uphold it in practice—the traditional 'policy of deliberate inertia'. The same inertia had been in evidence after a decision by the other international court, the ICJ, which concluded in July 2024 that Israel's occupation and settlement of Palestinian territories was illegal. The ICJ advised states not to provide any assistance that would maintain the unlawful situation.[88] Starmer's government said it had to consider the judgement. When asked about it seven months later, the government said it was still considering.[89]

On the issue of arms sales to Israel, Labour had previously sought to differentiate itself from the Conservatives ahead of an election in which flagging support from Muslim voters was a concern. Having called for Sunak's government to publish its legal advice, once in power Labour found that the Tories had indeed gone out on a limb to maintain arms supplies. So, in an almost comically apologetic statement, Foreign Secretary David Lammy announced in September 2024: 'It is with regret that I inform the House today, the assessment I have received leaves me unable to conclude anything other than that for certain UK arms exports to Israel there does exist a clear risk that they might be used to commit or facilitate a serious violation of international humanitarian law'.[90]

The resulting suspension of 29 out of 361 export licences earned a sharp rebuke from Netanyahu, who called the move 'shameful'.[91] But a serious rupture with the US was avoided as British components for F-35 fighter jets were 'carved out' of the deal.[92] An internal government letter from the defence secretary, John Healey, could not have been more explicit as to why: 'It would undermine US confidence in the UK and NATO at a critical juncture in our collective history and set back relations'.[93]

While the suspension of some export licenses marked a sharp and welcome contrast with the actions of the Sunak administration, British governments of the past had taken much more drastic action. Lammy himself emphasised the continuity, pointing to the arms and oil embargo imposed on Israel by Margaret Thatcher over its 1982 invasion of Lebanon and restrictions of export licences during previous Israeli attacks on Gaza in 2009 and 2014.[94] He might have added the Blair government's secret arms embargo during the Second Intifada in 2002.[95] Set in this longer history, the modest scale of the 2024 suspensions represented a step in a pro-Israel direction, especially given the importance of the F-35 to Israel's operation in Gaza.

Beyond these three course corrections the bigger picture was the consolidation of a sharp turn towards Israel made by the previous Conservative government. Upon taking over the trade negotiations inherited from the Tories, Labour declared itself 'laser-focused' on the deal.[96] As bombs rained down on Gaza, pulverising and incinerating without discrimination, Starmer described Israel as 'an important ally'.[97]

British Military Assistance to Israel

Most seriously of all, the UK may have been complicit in Israeli war crimes through hundreds of spy flights conducted by the Royal Air Force (RAF) over Gaza. The missions from the RAF Akrotiri base in Cyprus began in December 2023 under Sunak but continued under Starmer, with more than a hundred flights undertaken in the first three months of his government. Details of the missions were not divulged beyond the claim they were 'solely tasked to support hostage rescue'—a broad remit given it matched Israel's rationale for its entire military campaign.[98] Britain also allowed its airbase in Cyprus to be used as a logistics hub for US special forces flights to and from Israel, the frequency of which reportedly doubled under Starmer.[99]

This level of intelligence cooperation was unprecedentedly explicit, at a time when Israel's actions reached a new peak of brutality and destruction. Bizarrely, Starmer had no qualms alluding to it on camera during a Christmas visit to RAF Akrotiri in December 2024. 'Although we're really proud of what you're doing', he said to the base personnel, '[w]e can't necessarily tell the world what you're doing here'.[100]

In his stance towards the broader region, Starmer remained in lockstep with the Biden administration, maintaining a hard line against Iran and its allies. The UK continued direct military attacks against Yemen alongside the US as punishment for the disruption of shipping in the Red Sea by the Houthis in solidarity with Palestine. Whereas the Houthis consistently said they would stop all attacks if there was a ceasefire in Gaza, Starmer and Sunak had absurdly denied there was any connection between the two.[101] After various Israeli attacks on Iran, including the assassination of Hamas' political chief Ismail Haniyeh in Tehran, Starmer joined Biden in warning the Islamic Republic not to retaliate.[102] When Iran nevertheless launched

180 missiles at Israel in October 2024, British fighter jets 'played their part' in responding to them.[103]

Three hours after the Iranian barrage, Starmer gave a televised address from Downing Street that misinformed the British public. 'In the last few hours', he began, 'the Iranian regime has launched over 200 ballistic missiles at civilian targets in Israel'.[104] The claim was untrue: publicly available evidence already suggested Iran's missiles had been targeted at military sites rather than civilian areas, a picture later confirmed in the Israeli press.* Starmer had falsely accused Iran of a grave war crime, yet when Israel wreaked massive destruction on civilian areas in Beirut, or bombed an embassy in Damascus, or wiped the whole of Gaza off the map, his condemnations were notable only by their absence.

Despite the pro-Israel shift in British foreign policy, in cases where there was a divergence between the US and Israel, Britain unfailingly followed the White House. A joint statement from the US and UK, together with the EU and other countries, urged an immediate ceasefire on the Israel-Lebanon border in September 2024.[105] Israel went ahead and invaded Lebanon anyway. Having earlier opposed a ceasefire in Gaza, Starmer and Biden took to making half-hearted appeals for one. Israel comfortably ignored them.[106]

---

* As reported in *The Times of Israel*: 'According to foreign reports, the Nevatim Airbase in the south of Israel was one of the primary targets, with up to 32 hits identified in the base's open areas, structures, and surrounding fields. These details were revealed in satellite images and were not denied by the IDF in foreign media reports. The IDF has stressed that no fighter jets were damaged in that attack. Overseas experts noted two additional strikes near Mossad headquarters in the Glilot Junction area north of Tel Aviv and about three possible hits on structures inside the Tel Nof Airbase, near the city of Rehovot. An additional strike, on a restaurant in the "Sea and Sun" complex in northern Tel Aviv, may also have been an attempt to hit the Mossad headquarters, while a strike on a school in Gedera may have been part of the attempt to target the Tel Nof Airbase. The foreign media analysis of the strikes near the Mossad HQ and Tel Nof base is based on video footage posted on social media. Some videos show the size and depth of a crater left by a ballistic missile, while others captured from afar document the shock waves, fire, and smoke rising from the impact on the base . . . The Iranians targeted IDF bases but failed to disable Israel's forces'. Tal Schneider, 'How Effective Was Iran's Attack? The Israeli Public Doesn't Have the Full Picture', *The Times of Israel* (6 October 2024).

If there was a thread to Starmer's approach to the overall crisis, it was professed support for the international legal order while steadfastly refusing to apply the laws to Israel. With Biden in the White House espousing the same credo, Starmer could orient himself by US policy—as he had done since his anti-ceasefire speech in opposition. The return of Donald Trump to the White House in January 2025 made a nonsense of this strategy. Trump had no interest in even pretending to support a rules-based order. He was explicitly hostile to international law and placed sanctions on the ICC.[107] The US and Britain had spent decades verbally criticising yet materially enabling Israel's de facto annexation of Palestinian territory. Trump dropped the hypocrisy by effectively endorsing Israel's formal annexation of the West Bank.[108]

As successive British prime ministers before him had done, Starmer relied on deceitful claims about the hazy prospect of a two-state solution in the future to avoid having to act on Palestinian rights in the present—the ultimate instance of the 'policy of deliberate inertia'. Biden had used the same device. Neither felt a need to account for the consistent rejection of a two-state solution by Israeli governments—that was not the point.[109] But now Trump's vulgar honesty threatened to make the entire charade defunct.

Having expended so much capital to prove his dependability to the US, Starmer found the rug pulled from beneath him by an American president. The policy he had advocated had run its course. Palestinians were suffering intolerably, Gaza was destroyed, the Middle East roiled in turmoil, and international law lay shredded.

With his strategy upended, Starmer may have reflected on the things he had *not* done. As genocide raged, he had not made any meaningful attempt to stop it. He had not imposed any serious consequences on Israel. He had not put any pressure on the US. He had not committed to enforce international law. He had not condemned clear Israeli crimes and he had struggled to speak about Palestinians as if they were members of the human race.

He had not attempted these things because he did not believe they served British state interests and because they were anathema to his political allies. He had paid a political price for this posture, albeit not a considerable one and inconsequential when set against the suffering in Gaza. But Starmer's complicity will stain his reputation, and Britain's, for all time.

8

ISRAEL'S CASE AT THE HAGUE DISINTEGRATES

> Those hordes of vital statistics, those hysterical masses, those faces bereft of all humanity, those distended bodies which are like nothing on earth, that mob without beginning or end, those children who seem to belong to nobody.
>
> —*Frantz Fanon, The Wretched of the Earth*

BY OCTOBER 7, 2024, over forty-one million tonnes of rubble had been left behind by Israel's ferocious bombing campaign.[1] Much of the debris was mixed with unexploded ordnance and toxic substances that will require decades to remove.[2]

Israel had killed more than forty-one thousand Palestinians, with close to a hundred thousand injured.[3] If the same proportion of the population had been killed in Britain as in Gaza, there would have been nearly 1.4 million dead. One prominent specialist in international security affairs concluded that Israel's assault amounted to 'one of the most intense civilian punishment campaigns in history'.[4]

More than three hundred aid workers and over nine hundred health workers had been killed.[5] In September about fifty humanitarian trucks entered the Strip per day, as compared with the average of five hundred trucks that entered daily prior to the hostilities. Over 96 percent of women and infant children were not meeting their nutrient requirements. More than fifty thousand children were estimated to need treatment for acute malnutrition. Some 745,000 people faced 'emergency' levels of food insecurity; another half a million faced 'catastrophic' levels of food insecurity.

Nearly nine in ten housing units had been damaged or destroyed. Over 1.3 million people were in need of emergency shelter and essential household items. Nineteen of Gaza's thirty-six hospitals were out of service; the remainder were partially functional. 130 ambulances had been damaged.[6] Nearly 70 percent of Gaza's cropland was damaged along with more than half the agricultural wells and over 40 percent of greenhouses.[7] Some 625,000 students had no access to formal education; thirty-five of Gaza's university buildings were destroyed.[8] All told, the UN's humanitarian chief summarised, Israel had rendered Gaza 'uninhabitable'.[9]

In a statement to mark twelve months of devastation, UN experts noted: 'The serious violations of international law such as, murder, intentional targeting of civilian objects, disproportionate and indiscriminate attacks, starvation, forcible transfer, arbitrary displacement, sexual violence, persecution, and outrages against life and dignity, including disrespect for the dead, committed by Israeli Forces since the beginning of the war in Gaza in October 2023 constitute war crimes and possibly crimes against humanity'.[10]

Amidst this unprecedented death and destruction, the case for the defence set out by Israel's lawyers at The Hague had crumbled. As we saw in the introductory chapter, Israel made a series of arguments in its bid to disprove South Africa's claim that it was committing genocide in Gaza. In the pages that follow I examine them one by one.

Israel Is Committed to the Laws of War

British lawyer Malcolm Shaw KC, appearing for Israel in front of the judges at the International Court of Justice, praised 'the consistent and relentless commitment of Israeli relevant authorities to mitigate civilian harm and alleviate civilian suffering in Gaza'.[11] He added that the 'rules and principles of international humanitarian law . . . are fully respected by Israel'.[12] And he insisted that Israel is 'investing unprecedented efforts in mitigating civilian harm'.[13]

Research carried out by Airwars (published in December 2024) has found that: 'By almost every metric, the harm to civilians from the first month of the Israeli campaign in Gaza is incomparable with any 21st century air campaign. It is by far the most intense, destructive, and fatal conflict for civilians that Airwars has ever documented'.[14]

At least 5,139 civilians were killed during a period of twenty-five days in October 2023, including 1,213 women and 1,900 children. That's seven times higher than the most deadly month for children previously documented by Airwars across international conflicts.[15] Indeed, proportionally speaking, 'children make up a significantly higher number of those killed in Gaza compared to any other conflict documented by Airwars'.[16]

Airwars investigated five attacks that killed more than thirty-two children each: on October 31, for example, sixty-nine children were killed in Israeli strikes on Jabalia refugee camp.[17] Airwars also found that '82 percent of children killed died in strikes on residential infrastructure where no militant was publicly reported killed'.[18]

At least 90 percent of the 1,213 women killed died in a residential building.[19] The vast majority of civilians killed (88 percent) were killed alongside at least one family member.[20]

By May 2025, more than fifteen thousand children in Gaza had been recorded killed.[21] This exceeded the number of children killed in all the world's warzones *combined* over the three-year period 2019 to 2022.[22] On conservative assumptions regarding the number of adult male civilians killed, it is probable that the civilian proportion of fatalities in Gaza will amount to 70 or 80 percent.[23]

Thanks to remarkable reporting by Feroze Sidhwa in *The New York Times*, based on the testimonies of health workers in Gaza as well as X-rays, we now know that young children were targeted: '44 doctors, nurses and paramedics saw multiple cases of preteen children who had been shot in the head or chest in Gaza'.[24]

A surgeon said: 'One night in the emergency department . . . I saw six children between the ages of 5 and 12, all with single gunshot wounds to the skull'. Another surgeon said: 'I saw several children shot with high velocity bullet wounds, in both the head and chest'. Another surgeon said: 'Our team cared for about four or five children, ages 5 to 8 years old, that were all shot with single shots in the head ... They all died'. An anaesthesiologist said: 'It was almost a daily occurrence to have children arrive at the hospital with gunshot wounds to the head'.[25]

Israeli soldiers told *Haaretz* that the Netzarim corridor, a line drawn by Israel that stretches across Gaza to the sea, was a 'kill zone' where '[a]nyone who enters is shot'. According to an officer in Division 252, 'We're killing civilians there who are then counted as terrorists', and, 'The IDF spokesperson's announcements about casualty numbers have turned this into a competition between units. If Division 99 kills 150 [people], the next unit aims for 200'.

A reserve commander said: 'Calling ourselves the world's most moral army absolves soldiers who know exactly what we're doing'. They added: 'It means ignoring that for over a year, we've operated in a lawless space where human life holds no value'.

An officer of Division 252 explained that '[d]ivision commanders now have almost unlimited firepower authority in combat zones'. A soldier recalled receiving the order that '[a]nyone crossing the bridge into the corridor gets a bullet in the head'. When a civilian teenage boy was shot and killed in this manner, the soldier recalled their commander saying: 'Anyone crossing the line is a terrorist, no exceptions, no civilians. Everyone's a terrorist'. Of two hundred 'militants' announced killed by the IDF spokesperson, a Division 252 officer commented, 'only ten were confirmed as known Hamas operatives'.[26]

Civilian Casualties Are 'Human Shields'

Tal Becker, legal advisor to Israel's Ministry of Foreign Affairs, told the International Court of Justice at The Hague: 'Hamas has systematically and unlawfully embedded its military operations, militants and assets throughout Gaza within and beneath densely populated civilian areas'.[27]

Another of Israel's lawyers, Galit Raguan, alleged that there was '*overwhelming evidence* of Hamas' military use' of hospitals. Israel accused Hamas of a 'strategy of turning hospitals into terrorist compounds'.[28]

To justify the scale of civilian casualties, Israel and its supporters have claimed again and again that Hamas uses human shields. This rhetoric has been echoed uncritically in the West. 'Hamas is responsible for getting Palestinians killed', stated the American Israel Public Affairs Committee on October 14, 2023, citing 'human shields' as the reason.[29]

'They use Palestinian civilians as human shields. Hamas offers nothing but terror and bloodshed with no regard who pays the price', said United States President Joe Biden on October 10, 2023.[30] A week later Sir Keir Starmer, then leader of the opposition, said the same: 'They unleash terror, then hide amongst them. Women and children—used as human shields'.[31]

On October 15, 2023, British foreign secretary David Lammy attempted to parrot this extenuating claim to Victoria Derbyshire on the BBC but stumbled over his words. 'Hamas use people as as. . .', he stammered. Derbyshire finished the sentence for him—'human shields'.[32] Strip this justification away and it is laid bare that civilians were dying in such horrific numbers in Gaza not as unavoidable collateral damage but because they themselves were a target. As the UN Commission of Inquiry concluded, Israel had 'intentionally' targeted 'the civilian population' of Gaza and caused 'the near total destruction of civilian objects' as it committed the crime against humanity of 'extermination'.[33] The failure to critically scrutinise the Israeli claim of 'human shielding' is one of the factors that has made Western politicians (and media) complicit in Israeli atrocities.

'We conducted dozens of interviews with civilians and with Palestinians in areas that were designated as combat zones', reported Maha Hussaini, who works for the Euro-Med Human Rights Monitor in Gaza. 'But we have not documented one case of Palestinian armed members using civilians as human shields'.[34]

'There has to be a purpose in using a civilian as a human shield', Hussaini pointed out. 'Civilians here have been one of the main targets of the Israeli army since the beginning of the attack. So there wouldn't be a purpose in using a civilian as a human shield because the civilian himself is a target'.[35]

Bill van Esveld, the regional associate director of Human Rights Watch, confirmed: 'We don't have evidence that Palestinian armed groups are hiding right next to civilians and not allowing the civilians to leave'.[36]

In practice the allegation is based on little more than the fact that Hamas and Palestinian civilians share the same extremely small piece of territory, he said. Amnesty International UK stated in December 2024 with regards to claims that Hamas is using civilians as human shields: 'We're monitoring and investigating these claims but we don't have evidence of this during the current hostilities'.[37]

In contrast, there are numerous reports by international[38] and Israeli[39] human rights organisations, as well as by Israeli news outlets, that *Israel* uses human shields. A report in *Haaretz* newspaper in August 2024 said the practice was systematic and sanctioned by senior officers.[40]

Allegations of human shielding by Israel have been corroborated in testimonies given by Israeli soldiers to the NGO Breaking the Silence, which regards the practice as 'systematic'.[41]

An IDF soldier who served in Gaza revealed in *Haaretz* on March 30, 2025, that the practice of using Gazan civilians as human shields is authorised by senior IDF commanders and is called the 'Mosquito Protocol'. The soldier notes that each IDF platoon keeps one Palestinian captive—named a '*shawish*'—for this purpose, 'and no infantry force enters a house before a "shawish" clears it. This means there are four "shawishes" in a company, twelve in a battalion, and at least 36 in a brigade. We operate a sub-army of slaves'.[42]

As to Hamas' alleged military use of hospitals, the UN Office of the High Commissioner for Human Rights found that 'insufficient information has so far been made publicly available to substantiate these allegations, which have remained vague and broad, and in some cases appear contradicted by publicly available information'.[43]

It should be remembered that when a UN Commission of Inquiry sought to examine violations of international law in the hostilities, 'Israel obstructed the Commission's investigations and prevented its access to Israel and the Occupied Palestinian Territory'.[44] If Israel's allegations of human shielding are true, and if they suffice to explain and extenuate Israel's mass killings, why won't Israel allow the UN access to verify them?

When so few of Israel's allegations have been corroborated, when its government has a record of lying about such matters, and when it refuses to allow

UN investigators or international journalists to enter Gaza,[45] it is simply not credible to explain away the massive casualties by invoking 'human shields'.

Don't Trust the Casualty Figures

Israel argued at the International Court of Justice that the casualty figures from Gaza are 'unverified statistics provided by Hamas itself—hardly a reliable source . . . the Court is not told how many casualties are in fact militants'.[46]

Yet (as we saw in Chapter Two) reputable humanitarian agencies and researchers consider the Gaza Health Ministry to be broadly reliable and its data to be conservative.[47] Israel's claims that the civilian death toll in Gaza is exaggerated do not withstand scrutiny.[48]

It is almost certain that the Gaza death toll recorded by the health ministry is an undercount, and that the true toll will turn out to be much higher. I discuss this further in the Conclusion below.

Israel Allows Adequate Aid to Reach Gaza

Israel argued that it facilitates the passage of aid into Gaza. According to one of Israel's lawyers, 'Israel has publicly stated repeatedly that *there is no limit* on the amount of food, water, shelter or medical supplies that can be brought into Gaza'.[49]

Yet the quantity of humanitarian aid entering Gaza has repeatedly been restricted by Israel with devastating consequences (see Table 4). Human Rights Watch notes that no aid was permitted to enter Gaza between October 9, 2023, and October 21, 2023. Amnesty International reports that even as Israel subsequently loosened restrictions in response to 'immense pressure' from the outside, 'at no point' between October 2023 and early July 2024 did the Israeli authorities allow 'adequate aid and other essential life-saving supplies' to be provided. On the contrary, they 'continued to impose extreme restrictions on access into and within Gaza'.[50] Another total blockade was imposed by Israel between March 2 and May 19, 2025. The World Health Organisation said this generated 'one of the world's worst hunger crises' and reportedly caused fifty-seven children to die from malnutrition. 'This number is likely an underestimate', the WHO reported.[51]

TABLE 4. UN World Food Programme Reports on Gaza

Date	Observation	Explanation
October 2023[52]	The situation over there is catastrophic and our stocks inside Gaza are running out. Every day that passes pushed more and more people closer to starvation. . . . Only one flour mill is operating in Gaza and few bakeries are able to work so the bread supply is running short. People are lining up for hours to get bread.	The United Nations World Food Programme today renewed its call for sustained humanitarian access to Gaza.
December 2023[53]	The Northern governorates are experiencing alarming levels of hunger: almost half of the households experienced severe or very severe hunger; around 48 percent experienced moderate hunger and only four percent experienced little or no hunger. In the southern governorates, a third of the households reported high levels of severe or very severe hunger.	Since the conflict began, the Gaza Strip has remained under siege with only one border crossing open for humanitarian aid. . . . Beyond the direct disruption and destruction of food systems due to the conflict, the limited flow of humanitarian aid and the complete halt of the commercial goods have severely affected the movement and households' access to food and nutritious supplies. The shutdown of communication services and the lack of fuel have been an additional barrier to the delivery of key food commodities.
February 2024[54]	The current conditions signify the continuation of severe shortage of food, essential items, and aid.	The ongoing insecurity coupled with the complete closure of Gaza has resulted in critical shortages of essential resources, including food, water, fuel, electricity, and medical supplies. . . . Despite the influx of aid from October 21 to January 24, it is inadequate to meet the population's needs. . . . The entry of humanitarian and commercial trucks into Gaza is significantly limited to the southern governorates, mainly Rafah. Conversely, there are very few items reaching the northern governorates and other areas in the rest of the south of Gaza Strip.

(continued)

Date	Observation	Explanation
August 2024[55]	Markets across the Gaza Strip are witnessing a shortage and sharp rise in the prices of basic commodities . . . [M]ost commodities in the northern governorates are currently over 1000 percent higher than their pre-conflict levels.	The delivery of aid supplies into Gaza remains unreliable due to access restrictions and ongoing security issues. . . . Overall, the entry of humanitarian aid into Gaza has more than halved since the Rafah ground operation began and the Rafah Crossing was abruptly closed in early May, with daily truck deliveries decreasing from an average of 169 in April to 94 in May, and less than 80 in June and July.
December 2024[56]	Alarmingly, people's food consumption has been reduced to reliance on bread and pulses for the third consecutive month, with almost non-existent access to other foods items such as fresh fruit and vegetables, dairy products and meat. Dairy consumption, a critical part of the local diet, is almost nonexistent across all governorates, with intake dropping to near zero in December 2024 compared to four days per week pre-conflict. . . . In the Gaza Strip, prices of many basic food items increased by more than 1,000% compared to pre-conflict levels, with the highest increases seen in Gaza Governorate where egg prices rose by 3,114%.	WFP is striving to increase commodity flow into Gaza, but severe access restrictions, rampant insecurity and escalating violence continue to hinder humanitarian movements. In December alone, 49 out of 160 planned movements were denied access. By 16 December, barely any commercial trucks had entered Gaza, while the daily average of humanitarian trucks dropped to 87 . . . Attempts to utilize new routes remain fraught with obstacles. On 22 December, a UN convoy of 66 trucks from Philadelphi road was delayed by an airstrike on the planned route, causing a split in the convoy and resulting in 23 trucks being looted.[57]

(continued)

Date	Observation	Explanation
April 2025[58]	By early April, 80 percent of households reported difficulties accessing markets—up from 70 percent in March— highlighting a worsening trend due to the ongoing closure of crossings and renewed escalation. The lack of cash to afford essential goods, as prices remain extremely high, is the primary challenge for 95 percent of households . . . The ceasefire temporarily eased access to a wider range of food commodities—including dairy, meats, vegetables, and fruits—though supplies remained well below pre-conflict norms. However, the renewed closure in early March sharply reversed these gains.	Since the closure of the crossings on March 2, 2025, which blocked all commercial and humanitarian trucks entry into the Gaza Strip, local markets have experienced profound disruptions. The result has been a sharp surge in food prices, heightened volatility, and critical shortages of basic necessities. Numerous food and non-food items have disappeared from shelves, further straining already fragile supply chains.
June 2025[59]	Food consumption in Gaza has reached a critical low in June 2025, with food diversity collapsing to its worst level since the start of the conflict. . . . Food prices continued to rise sharply, increasing by 350 percent to as much as 4567 percent compared to pre-closure levels and by 456 percent to 7079 percent compared to pre-conflict levels.	The continued closure of crossings, intensified violence since March, soaring food prices, and extremely limited humanitarian and commercial supplies have severely restricted access to even basic food items. . . . Even though commercial and aid convoys were allowed to enter Gaza on May 19 after more than 80 days of the Israeli government's total blockade, the number of trucks that actually manages to reach their destination remains small, constant looting and dangerous roads are affecting all convoys.

Even once admitted to Gaza the aid was restricted: the Israeli military prevented much of the aid from going to the northern part of the strip.[60] As Human Rights Watch summarised the situation, 'For several months Israeli authorities repeatedly blocked aid that entered Gaza, including fuel needed to run generators for water and sanitation, from reaching areas in the north, despite reports of the severe hunger and thirst the population there was facing'.[61]

Besides restricting the entry and distribution of aid, Israel has repeatedly attacked aid workers, convoys, and premises.[62] This includes the strike on a World Central Kitchen convoy on April 1, 2024, which killed seven aid workers including three British citizens, all veterans. Predictably, such attacks led some aid organisations to pause their operations.[63]

Already in December 2023, Human Rights Watch warned that Israel was employing starvation as a method of war.[64] In February 2024, the UN special rapporteur on the right to food, Michael Fakhri, said that Israel was 'Intentionally depriving people of food . . . In my view as a UN human rights expert, this is now a situation of genocide'.[65] In March 2024, Josep Borrell, the EU's foreign policy chief, said: 'Starvation is used as a weapon of war. Israel is provoking famine'.[66] And in May 2024, among the charges brought by the prosecutor of the International Criminal Court against Netanyahu and Gallant was '[s]tarvation of civilians as a method of warfare'.[67]

Israel also argued before the ICJ that '[a]ccess to water has . . . been a priority. As with food supplies, there is no restriction on the amount of water that may enter Gaza'.[68]

Human Rights Watch, in a report entitled *Extermination and Acts of Genocide: Israel Deliberately Depriving Palestinians in Gaza of Water*, found on the contrary that 'Israeli authorities have deliberately obstructed Palestinians' access to the adequate amount of water required for survival in the Gaza Strip'.[69] Human Rights Watch further considered that 'these policies have likely contributed to thousands of deaths'[70] as lack of water leads to dehydration, poor sanitation, and disease.

In this context I quote at length a horrifying section of the Human Rights Watch report explaining how Israel prosecuted a policy of brutal siege warfare:

> Israeli authorities and forces cut off the water supply piped into Gaza from Israel and later restricted the supply, cut off the electricity supply from Israel to Gaza that was needed to operate water pumps, desalination plants, and sanitation infrastructure within Gaza, and blocked and restricted the fuel needed to run generators in the absence of electricity. They have also blocked United Nations agencies and humanitarian aid organizations from delivering critical water-related materials and other humanitarian aid from entering Gaza, damaged, and in some cases, deliberately destroyed water and sanitation infrastructure, including where Israeli forces were in control of the area, and prevented repairs by blocking imports of nearly all water-related material. Some Israeli strikes have killed water utility workers as they were trying to make repairs, while others have destroyed the main water-utility warehouse in Gaza which housed spare parts, equipment, and supplies critical to water production.[71]

It was announced in July 2024 that poliovirus was found in sewage in Gaza, leading to the first polio case in Gaza in twenty-five years.[72] Nearly a hundred American physicians and nurses who had volunteered in Gaza between October 2023 and October 2024 wrote, in a letter to the Biden administration, that 'Israel's continued, repeated displacement of the malnourished and sick population of Gaza, half of whom are children, to areas with no running water or even toilets available is absolutely shocking. It is virtually guaranteed to result in widespread death from viral and bacterial diarrheal diseases and pneumonias, particularly in children under the age of five'.[73]

This spread of disease was predictable—even desirable—in the view of some Israeli commentators. Giora Eiland, the former head of Israel's national security council, suggested that 'severe epidemics in the south of the Gaza Strip will bring victory closer ... It is precisely its civil collapse that will bring the end of the war closer'.[74]

Palestinians in Gaza did not even have the minimum quantity of litres of water per person per day necessary for drinking and washing.[75]

Human Rights Watch concluded that Israeli policy towards Gaza amounted to an act of genocide, because it inflicted conditions calculated to destroy, in whole or in part, the Palestinian group there.[76]

On March 2, 2025, Netanyahu's office announced 'that, as of this morning, all entry of goods and supplies into the Gaza Strip will cease'.[77] UNICEF confirmed on April 5, 2025: 'No aid has been allowed into the Gaza Strip since 2 March 2025—representing the longest period of aid blockage since the start of the war—leading to shortages of food, safe water, shelter, and medical supplies'.[78] UNICEF stated that Israel's policy of blocking all humanitarian aid into Gaza is 'in breach of international humanitarian law . . . with dire repercussions for children'.[79]

Israel Can Police Itself

Malcolm Shaw KC told the International Court of Justice that, 'Were it the case—which we deny—that Israeli forces have transgressed some of the rules of conflict, then the matter would be tackled at the appropriate time by Israel's robust and independent legal system'.[80] A great deal depended on this claim. If it was true that Israel possessed a 'robust and independent legal system', there would have been no need for South Africa to appeal to the ICJ. If it was false then international intervention was urgently required.

In order to discern what is likely to happen in the future, we can only look to the evidence of the past. Experience proves, to a high degree of certainty, that Israel will not hold its forces to account for violations.

We saw in our review of settler violence, and the killing of journalist Shireen Abu Akleh (Chapter Two above), that serious measures of accountability were not undertaken by Israeli authorities. We also saw (Chapter Five) that despite the commission of numerous atrocities in Operation Cast Lead, only a handful of soldiers were convicted and only one served prison time—for petty theft.

UN Human Rights Council resolutions have commented more than once on the failure of Israel to conduct adequate investigations. A 2018 resolution noted 'the systematic failure by Israel to carry out genuine investigations in an impartial, independent, prompt and effective way, as required by international law, into the violence and offences against Palestinians by the occupying forces, and to establish judicial accountability for its actions in the Occupied Palestinian Territory, including East Jerusalem.'[81]

Israeli human rights organisations have some of the richest and deepest experience with Israel's accountability mechanisms. According to Yesh Din, in the period 2017–21, complaints against Israeli soldiers concerning the harmful treatment of Palestinians had less than a 1 percent chance of leading to an indictment. The reality was that 'military law enforcement authorities systematically avoid investigating and prosecuting soldiers who harm Palestinians.' Indeed, it is hard to imagine that an occupying military force would constrain its own brutality against largely powerless victims, unless it were subjected to outside pressure. On the extraordinary occasion that a soldier is prosecuted and convicted, 'the military courts hand down extremely lenient sentences'.[82]

B'Tselem has found that Israel has merely 'a semblance of law enforcement' such that 'those responsible for harming Palestinians go unpunished, and the victims receive no compensation for the harm they suffer.' When B'Tselem demanded investigations of hundreds of incidents of misconduct that it had researched from late 2000 to 2015, it stated that complaints led to indictments in only about 3 percent of cases.

In May 2016, B'Tselem decided to cease filing complaints with Israel's military law enforcement system, which it regarded as a 'charade . . . there is no longer any point in pursuing justice and defending human rights by working with a system whose real function is measured by its ability to continue to successfully cover up unlawful acts and protect perpetrators.' As to compensation for damages, the chance of Palestinians receiving it is 'virtually nonexistent.'[83]

So much for Israel's approach to domestic accountability. Consult now the internationally mandated investigations into Israel's conduct, and an unmistakable pattern is evident: Israel refuses all cooperation. (Table 5)

TABLE 5. Israel's Commitment to Accountability

Investigation	Did Israel cooperate?	Date
UN Fact Finding Mission on the Gaza Conflict (Goldstone Report)	No[84]	2009
Independent Fact-Finding Mission on the Implications of Israeli Settlements	No[85]	2013
Independent Commission of Inquiry on Violations in the Gaza Strip	No[86]	2015
Independent Commission of Inquiry on the Gaza Protests	No[87]	2019
Ongoing Independent International Commission of Inquiry on the Occupied Palestinian Territory and Israel	No[88]	2022
Ongoing Independent International Commission of Inquiry on the Occupied Palestinian Territory and Israel	No[89]	2022
Ongoing Independent International Commission of Inquiry on the Occupied Palestinian Territory and Israel	No[90]	2023
Ongoing Independent International Commission of Inquiry on the Occupied Palestinian Territory and Israel	No[91]	2024
Ongoing Independent International Commission of Inquiry on the Occupied Palestinian Territory and Israel	No[92]	2024

This is a deplorable record for a state which claims to respect the laws of war and boasts that its army is more virtuous than any other.

Israel's supporters often claim that such international investigations are the result of a bias, even an antisemitic bias, against Israel. But there is no reason to impute antisemitism to the UN when it is plain that in every case Israel committed acts worthy of investigation: the bombing of large swathes of Gaza, the continued expansion of settlements in the West Bank, the shooting of unarmed protesters, and so forth.

The reports of the investigators, it is almost superfluous to say, evince no antisemitism whatever. But even if Israel were unfairly singled out by UN organs, it should not follow that Israel would refuse to cooperate in UN investigations. On the contrary, if Israel was indeed innocent, the necessity of cooperation would be even greater, so that the Commission would have at its disposal all the facts tending to Israel's exoneration. If the published reports failed to either incorporate or refute the Israeli arguments, Israel could then expose UN malpractice.

An innocent party always has the most to gain from an accurate and complete account of the relevant facts. Hence, if the various governments of Israel believed that they were innocent, they would have cooperated to the fullest. They would have made available every witness; they would have granted full access to their territory; they would have fulfilled every request for information. The complete absence of cooperation—no different from obstruction—over a period exceeding a decade, bespeaks a guilty conscience: a cognizance that at least some of what Israel has done is indeed indefensible and therefore must be concealed.

There is also the matter of journalists. Israel has blocked international journalists from independently accessing the Gaza Strip. The only journalists to be allowed in were those under IDF supervision. In other words, only those journalists would have access who would see and hear what Israeli commanders desired them to see and hear, and nothing else.[93] The instructive stories of British reporters who embedded with the IDF were examined in Chapter Two above.

Israel has embarked on what looks uncomfortably like a campaign of massacre against journalists who were already in the Gaza Strip. According to one study, Israel killed more journalists in Gaza after October 7, 2023, than were killed in the US Civil War, both World Wars, the Korean War, the Vietnam War (including the Cambodia and Laos theatres), the Yugoslavia wars of the 1990s, and the post-2001 Afghanistan war combined.[94] In this manner, Israel has ensured that as little information as possible would reach the world during its merciless attack on Gaza. We now know that Israel was responsible for the deaths of nearly 70 percent of all the world's journalists killed in 2024—the deadliest year for journalists since records began.[95]

Israel Has a Right to Defend Itself

Israel's lawyers contended that South Africa's application to the ICJ was an attempt 'to thwart Israel's inherent right to defend itself' and thus 'render Israel defenceless.'[96]

There is an important debate amongst lawyers and jurists about whether states have a right of self-defence against an occupied population.[97] However, even if it is granted that Israel has a right to self-defence against the territory it unlawfully occupies, it certainly does not possess the right to commit war crimes. Israel acknowledged as much in its oral argument.[98]

Israel's military offensive since October 2023 has amounted to a string of atrocities and—as the UN Commission of Inquiry found—the wilful destruction of infrastructures 'indispensable to the survival of the civilian population.'[99] Israel does not have a right to shoot children in the head, to damage or destroy nine out of every ten homes, or to displace 90 percent of the population. Given this is the case, the 'right to defend itself' formula much used by Israel's supporters in the West feels more like a distraction than an earnest argument.

Israel Has Traditionally Obeyed the Law

Israel's concluding argument referred to its 'long-standing commitment to law and morality' and asserted that 'Israel's commitment to the rule of law has remained steadfast throughout our history.'[100] The record of Israeli crimes stretches all the way back to 1948.[101] We have already reviewed the record of atrocities committed by Israel during previous attacks on Gaza. It is simply a bald falsehood to claim that Israel has been committed to international law. Instead, it has displayed the brutality typical of colonial powers throughout history.

The International Court of Justice, of all institutions, was unlikely to be persuaded that Israel had a tradition of legal probity. Two decades prior, the Court had determined in a momentous 2004 advisory opinion that Israeli settlements in the Occupied Palestinian Territory were 'established in breach of international law' and that Israel's annexation of East Jerusalem had no legal validity. The Court concluded that Israel had an 'obligation' to dismantle the separation wall it had built in the occupied West Bank and compensate Palestinians who had been harmed by it.[102]

It hardly needs saying that Israel did not abide by the Court's finding. The Israeli government boycotted the hearings, said the 'politically motivated' advisory opinion would 'find its place in the garbage can of history,'[103] continued building illegal settlements, continued construction of the illegal wall, and maintained its claim on occupied East Jerusalem as Israel's 'eternal capital'.[104]

It is perhaps worth recalling here another grave breach of international law that has been credibly imputed to Israel. As we saw in Chapter Six, several respected human rights organisations have accused Israel of apartheid—a crime against humanity under the Rome Statute of the International Criminal Court. In January 2021, the leading Israeli human rights group B'Tselem concluded that 'the entire area between the Mediterranean Sea and the Jordan River is organized under a single principle: advancing and cementing the supremacy of one group—Jews—over another—Palestinians'. This, B'Tselem said, was an 'apartheid regime'.[105] That same year, Human Rights Watch published a report finding that

> the Israeli government has demonstrated an intent to maintain the domination of Jewish Israelis over Palestinians across Israel and the OPT. In the OPT, including East Jerusalem, that intent has been coupled with systematic oppression of Palestinians and inhumane acts committed against them. When these three elements occur together, they amount to the crime of apartheid.[106]

In February 2022, Amnesty International reached the same conclusion.[107] And in July 2024, the International Court of Justice itself determined that the 'near-complete separation in the West Bank and East Jerusalem between the settler and Palestinian communities' imposed by Israel constituted a breach of the international law prohibition on 'racial segregation and apartheid'.[108]

No part of this disgraceful record is compatible with the claim made by Israel to the International Court of Justice that Israel has traditionally respected international law.

Genocidal Intent

According to Malcolm Shaw KC, the South African application failed to prove that Israel was driven in Gaza by a genocidal intent. He said that 'there is little beyond random assertions' by this or that Israeli official to prove such intent; that South Africa 'misunderstands the nature and provenance of certain comments made by some Israeli politicians'; that 'to produce random quotes that are not in conformity with government policy is . . . misleading at best'; and that '[s]ome of the comments to which South Africa refers are clearly rhetorical, made in the immediate aftermath of an event which severely traumatized Israel, but which cannot be seen as demanding genocide. They express anguish and the necessity to restore control over Israel's own territory'.[109]

The ICJ rejected this argument.[110] The Court drew attention to the dehumanising language used by the most senior Israeli officials, including Defence Minister Yoav Gallant, President Isaac Herzog, and Energy and Infrastructure Minister Israel Katz.[111] We saw in the introduction how Israeli politicians made extensive use of genocidal rhetoric after October 7.

Such statements become still more incriminating when we consider how they have been repeated by Israeli soldiers involved in operations in Gaza. A lieutenant colonel in Israel's 749 Combat Engineering Battalion wrote on Facebook on October 9, 2023: 'Now go, attack the Amalekites and totally destroy everything that belongs to them. Do not spare them; put to death men and women, children and infants, cattle and sheep, camels and donkeys'.

A master sergeant in the same battalion said on Instagram: 'House by house, street by street, neighbourhood by neighbourhood . . . Everything will be erased from you . . . until nothing remains of you'.[112] This comment was attached to a video of a home in Gaza being destroyed.

In a video posted to Instagram in October 2023, a soldier said: 'Until Gaza is wiped, no one is safe here . . . We need to destroy Gaza, end this story once and for all. To turn Gaza into beaches, soccer fields, a place that is ours'.

In a November 2023 interview, Brigadier General Yogev Bar Sheshet, who was involved in overseeing the preparedness and legality of the IDF's actions, said: 'Whoever returns here, if they return here after, will find scorched earth. No houses, no agriculture, nothing. They have no future'.

In the same November report, Colonel Erez Eshel said: 'Vengeance is a great value. There is vengeance for what they did to us. For a hundred years to come they should know that you shouldn't mess with Jews . . . This place will be a fallow land. They will not be able to live here'.

In January 2024, Lieutenant Colonel Oren said on Israeli radio: 'We need to make sure that whenever the IDF meets Gaza there is destruction. Nothing less, nothing more . . . In every place we were, there was only sand left and houses on the ground. Because in every home, unfortunately, I learned that in Gaza, there is no innocence'.[113]

Moreover, as we saw in Chapter Seven, Israeli military officials have admitted that a Telegram channel, named '72 Virgins—Uncensored', was run by members of the IDF Operations Directorate. The channel featured language such as, 'Burning their mother . . . You won't believe the video we got! You can hear their bones crunch', and, 'Exterminating the roaches . . . exterminating the Hamas rats . . . Share this beauty', as well as video of a corpse being mutilated.[114] A video showing Palestinian men and boys stripped to their underwear—in some cases tied up and blindfolded—was posted to the channel, with the following voiceover: 'Look at your heroes now Gaza. With their hands in the air. Scared in their dirty underwear'.[115]

Amnesty International notes that 'the language used by Israeli officials was frequently repeated, including by soldiers in Gaza, apparently explaining the rationale for their behaviour. The existence of a large number of these public videos and statements highlights not only systemic impunity but also the creation of an environment that emboldens, if not tacitly rewards, such behaviour'.[116]

Contrary to Shaw's claim, these genocidal statements were not random. They were a declaration of Israeli policy, with appalling consequences for the Palestinian population.*

---

* On the relation between the statements of Israeli officials and Israel's conduct in Gaza, see Yaniv Cogan, 'Targeting Civilians: Its Logic in Gaza and Israel', in Jamie Stern-Weiner ed., *Deluge: Gaza and Israel from Crisis to Cataclysm* (OR Books, 2024). 'The absolute consensus among Israeli war leaders that targeting civilians is both legitimate and necessary, together with the well-documented conduct of the IDF during the onslaught, leaves no room for doubt that Israel's assault on Gaza's civilian population has been deliberate', Cogan writes. (Ibid., p. 105) For a compendium of genocidal and otherwise incriminating statements by Israeli politicians, officials, combatants, and

Israel's Compliance with the ICJ's Provisional Measures

In its January 2024 provisional order the Court instructed Israel to take urgent measures to prevent its army committing acts which might be considered genocidal, to prevent and punish incitement to genocide, and to enable the provision of humanitarian aid. In the following paragraphs we examine whether Israel followed these instructions.

We have already seen that Israeli forces continued to kill large numbers of Palestinian civilians after January 2024. We have also seen that this killing was systematic and deliberate—not accidental—according to the testimony of medical professionals working in Gaza and according to the testimony of Israeli soldiers themselves. It is therefore fair to conclude that Israel failed to prevent genocidal acts.

Israel did not make any attempt to prevent, still less punish, incitement to genocide. Celebration of the destruction of Gaza continued in Israel after the ICJ ruling. During a February 2024 debate in the Knesset, May Golan, the minister for social equality, declared: 'I am personally proud of the ruins of Gaza, and that every baby, even 80 years from now, will tell their grandchildren what the Jews did'.[117] Nissim Vaturi, a deputy speaker of the Knesset, endorsed the suggestion that Israel should 'separate the children and women and kill the adults in Gaza'.[118]

Such rhetoric was not confined to politicians. On Israel's Channel 14, journalist Yaki Adamker said: 'The Gazans, as far as I am concerned, can starve to death. What do I care about them?'[119]

As we saw in Chapter Seven, state prosecutor Amit Aisman recommended in August 2024 that the attorney general should *not* open criminal investigations against Israeli officials who had called for the harm of Palestinian civilians.[120] In November 2024, Israel's attorney general chose not to open criminal investigations into incitement.[121] He did not give an explanation. Thus Israel did not only fail to either prevent or punish such statements, as was ordered by the Court—it failed even to investigate them.

---

public figures, see: 'Annex to the Letter Dated 27 February 2025 from the Permanent Representative of South Africa to the United Nations addressed to the President of the Security Council', S/2025/130, digitallibrary.un.org (28 February 2025).

It is therefore unsurprising that the International Commission of Jurists, a group of leading judges and lawyers, found that Israel had failed to comply with the Court's ruling.[122] Amnesty International said that Israel 'failed to take even the bare minimum steps to comply' with the Court's January order,[123] because it did not allow sufficient aid to reach Gaza. Human Rights Watch reached the same conclusion.[124]

Two months later the ICJ issued an order reaffirming the first set of provisional measures, while placing a new, urgent emphasis on the delivery of humanitarian aid. Days after this order was issued came Israel's attack on the aid convoy (April 1, 2024), killing seven aid workers. The convoy had coordinated its movements with Israel. In response, several aid organisations paused their operations. Attacks on aid operations continued. In August 2024, for example, Israeli forces opened fire on clearly marked UN World Food Programme vehicles, even though the convoy had received multiple clearances from Israel. The WFP therefore paused movement of its staff.[125]

Far from obeying the ICJ instruction to provide unhindered access to humanitarian assistance, Israel has continually blocked adequate aid from reaching the Strip while it also conducted outright attacks on aid agencies and aid workers. More than four hundred aid workers have been killed by Israel in Gaza since October 7, 2023; 2024 was the deadliest year for aid workers on record.[126]

By late March, the situation was so grave that several ICJ judges were of the opinion that the Court should have ordered the suspension of Israel's military operations. They noted that 'Israel's military operations have resulted in unprecedented levels of starvation and the absolute collapse of essential civilian infrastructure in the region.'[127]

If Israel's operations had caused unprecedented starvation and destruction to civilian infrastructure; if the very existence of Palestinians in Gaza was at risk; if all the indicators of genocide were on display[128]—then it is obvious that Israel had failed to heed the landmark provisional order of January 26.

Israel did, however, fulfil one of the provisional measures by submitting a follow-up report to the Court on April 29, 2024.[129] This report has not been made publicly available. It cannot have satisfied the Court because four weeks later the Court issued a third and even more urgent order. This reaffirmed the previous two previous sets of provisional measures and in addition instructed Israel to 'halt its military offensive, and any other action in the Rafah Governorate, which may inflict on the Palestinian group in Gaza conditions of life that could bring about its physical destruction in whole or in part'.[130]

There was some dispute about the exact import of this measure.[131] Some took the view that it meant Israel had to stop its offensive in Rafah completely; others that Israel had to stop its offensive only in so far as this threatened the existence of the Palestinian group. But whichever interpretation is selected, it is evident that Israel failed to comply.

If the measure meant that Israel had to stop its offensive completely, Israel clearly ignored the order, because the offensive continued for months afterward. If the measure meant that Israel had to stop its offensive in so far as it threatened the Palestinian group, we need only look at Israel's conduct in Rafah. Between early May and July 6, satellite imagery showed that over fifteen thousand structures had been damaged in Rafah.[132] From July to early September, a further 3,770 structures had been damaged there.[133] From September to December, again more than three thousand structures were damaged.[134]

In October 2023, the Rafah metropolitan area had been home to 275,000 people. Now the entire city was 'erased'.[135] The scale of the devastation was described by Palestinian witnesses. One resident who returned to Rafah, Amjad Abdullah, observed that it had become 'impossible to live here': 'Rafah has become a graveyard of buildings. Without water, roads, or basic infrastructure, life here is unimaginable'.[136] The mayor, Mohammed al-Sufi, said that the city had become 'uninhabitable' given the demolition of 70 percent of its infrastructure and facilities.[137] Anyone who has seen the video footage of Rafah after the assault must agree that the city was rendered uninhabitable.[138]

The Court also ordered Israel to keep the Rafah border crossing open. Israel had taken control of the Palestinian side of the Rafah crossing, which connects Gaza and Egypt, in early May 2024. Since then, the crossing remained closed, preventing the movement of people and aid and leaving two thousand trucks waiting on the Egyptian side of the border.[139] The crossing only reopened in

February 2025, after the ceasefire agreement.[140] Israel may have been in violation of the order to keep the Rafah crossing open for over eight months.[141]

To sum up, the Israeli government has persistently ignored ICJ orders to refrain from genocidal acts and genocidal incitement. I have been unable to find a single example of the British government criticising Israel for its failure to comply with ICJ instructions. Britain first trashed the South African argument that Palestinians faced a genocide. Then it did nothing when Israel failed to comply with instructions from the Court. Any assessment of Britain's complicity in what most experts already regard as a genocide may take this into account.

The same criticism applies to the British media. One need only imagine the screaming headlines if Vladimir Putin's Russia had refused to comply with urgent instruction from the world's highest court to desist from genocidal acts, incitement to genocide, and denial of humanitarian aid in Ukraine.

Yet we have been unable to find examples of UK media covering Israel's non-compliance with provisional measures ordered by the ICJ (see Table 6). This is further chilling proof that mainstream British media effectively colluded with the Israeli project to destroy Palestinian life in Gaza.

TABLE 6. Israel's Compliance with the International Court of Justice

Provisional measures indicated, January 26	Did Israel comply?
Prevent genocidal acts	No
Prevent and punish incitement to genocide	No
Enable provision of services and aid	No
Preserve evidence related to genocide	Unknown
Submit a report to the Court	Yes
Provisional measures indicated, March 28	**Did Israel comply?**
Ensure unhindered provision of aid at scale	No
Ensure military does not commit genocidal acts, including by blocking aid	No
Submit a report to the Court	Yes

(continued)

Provisional measures indicated, May 24	Did Israel comply?
Halt Rafah offensive and other actions in Rafah which may destroy Palestinian group in Gaza	No
Keep Rafah crossing open for aid and services	Unclear, likely no
Give access to UN investigators	Unknown, likely no
Submit a report to the Court	Unknown

A Growing Consensus on Genocide

The ICJ's decision to indicate provisional measures in January 2024 reflected its conclusion that Israel was engaged in a 'plausible' genocide. By early January 2025 and afterwards, a critical mass of Holocaust scholars, international law experts, UN officials, and human rights organisations had come to the conclusion that the IDF was committing genocide in Gaza. A selection are listed in Table 7.

TABLE 7. Select Authorities Affirming That Israel Is Committing Genocide

Authority	Description
Legal team of the Republic of South Africa	The legal team included renowned experts in international law such as John Dugard and Vaughan Lowe KC. South Africa's application to the International Court of Justice charged that Israel 'is committing genocide in manifest violation of the Genocide Convention.'[142]
Amnesty International	'[F]ollowing 7 October 2023, Israel committed and is committing genocide against Palestinians in Gaza.'[143]
Human Rights Watch	'Israeli authorities' and forces' actions to deprive the population of Gaza of access to water amount to acts of genocide under the Genocide Convention and the Rome Statute of the International Criminal Court.'[144]

(continued)

Authority	Description
Doctors Without Borders	'We are witnessing Israel commit genocide. . . . The UK Government is complicit in these atrocities. . . . This is not a term we use lightly. Our decision to describe what's happening in Gaza as a "genocide" is based on nearly two years of extensive, firsthand information from our teams, who are witnessing massive levels of death and destruction by Israeli forces, a campaign of ethnic cleansing and the almost total dismantling of the health care system.'[145]
B'Tselem, the Israeli information centre for human rights in the Occupied Territories	'An examination of Israel's policy in the Gaza Strip and its horrific outcomes, together with statements by senior Israeli politicians and military commanders about the goals of the attack, leads to the unequivocal conclusion that Israel is taking coordinated action to intentionally destroy Palestinian society in the Gaza Strip. In other words: Israel is committing genocide against Palestinians in the Gaza Strip'.[146]
Physicians for Human Rights–Israel	'Israel's military campaign in Gaza since October 2023 . . . constitutes genocide under the 1948 Genocide Convention'.[147]
Palestinian Human Rights Organisations Council	'The UN cannot afford to stay silent in the face of the genocide currently taking place in Gaza and must avoid repeating the mistakes of the past'.[148]
Aryeh Neier, co-founder of Human Rights Watch and president emeritus of the Open Society Foundations	'I am now persuaded that Israel is engaged in genocide against Palestinians in Gaza. What has changed my mind is its sustained policy of obstructing the movement of humanitarian assistance into the territory.'[149]

(continued)

Authority	Description
UN Special Committee to Investigate Israeli Practices Affecting the Human Rights of the Palestinian People & Other Arabs of the Occupied Territories	'The developments in this report lead the Special Committee to conclude that the policies and practices of Israel during the reporting period are consistent with the characteristics of genocide'.[150]
Francesca Albanese, UN special rapporteur on human rights in the Occupied Palestinian Territory	'[T]here are reasonable grounds to believe that the threshold indicating that Israel has committed genocide has been met'.[151]
Craig Mokhiber, former director of the New York office of the UN Office of the High Commissioner for Human Rights	'This is a text-book case of genocide'.[152]
Luis Moreno Ocampo, former chief prosecutor of the International Criminal Court	'The siege of Gaza itself . . . is a form of genocide'.[153]
Leading scholars of genocide	The Dutch newspaper *NRC* found that all eight genocide studies scholars who had published on the Gaza violence in the *Journal of Genocide Research*, the leading journal in the field, believed that Israel was committing genocide or genocidal acts there.[154]
University Network for Human Rights	'Israel's violations of the international legal prohibition of genocide amount to grave breaches of peremptory norms of international law that must cease immediately. These violations also give rise to obligations by all other States: to refrain from recognizing Israel's breaches as legal or taking any actions that may constitute complicity in these breaches; and to take positive steps to suppress, prevent, and punish the commission by Israel of further genocidal acts against the Palestinian people in Gaza'.[155]

(continued)

Authority	Description
Amos Goldberg, professor of Holocaust history at the Hebrew University of Jerusalem	'[T]here was explicit intent, a systematic pattern, and a genocidal outcome—so, I came to the conclusion that this is exactly what genocide looks like. And once you come to this conclusion, you cannot remain silent.'[156]
Omer Bartov, dean's professor of holocaust and genocide studies at Brown University	Professor Bartov concluded by May 2024 that 'it was no longer possible to deny that Israel was engaged in systematic war crimes, crimes against humanity and genocidal actions. By July 2025, he reached the 'inescapable conclusion' that 'Israel is committing genocide against the Palestinian people'.[157]
Raz Segal, endowed professor in the study of modern genocide at Stockton University	'Israel's genocidal assault on Gaza is quite explicit, open, and unashamed. Perpetrators of genocide usually do not express their intentions so clearly.'[158]
William Schabas, emeritus professor of international criminal law and human rights law at Leiden University	'The courts will make a ruling, political bodies will decide in time. But I would say: There is a very strong case for arguing that Israel's response constitutes the crime of genocide.'[159]
John Cox, director of the Center for Holocaust, Genocide & Human Rights Studies at the University of North Carolina at Charlotte	'Israel's War on Gaza is indeed genocidal . . . In the annals of genocide history, perpetrators have rarely spoken in such revealing and self-damning fashions as Israeli leaders have.'[160]
Barry Trachtenberg, the Rubin presidential chair of Jewish history at Wake Forest University	'[W]hat we're seeing now is they're embarking upon a genocidal campaign to destroy the Palestinian people in its entirety, especially those in Gaza at the moment.'[161]
Daniel Blatman, historian of the Holocaust and head of the Institute for Contemporary Jewry at the Hebrew University of Jerusalem	'a meticulous comparative examination of events over the past year leads to the painful conclusion that Israel is indeed committing genocide in Gaza.'[162]

(continued)

Authority	Description
Martin Shaw, emeritus professor of international relations and politics at the University of Sussex	'The only way we can understand what Israel is doing in an overall sense is not a series of war crimes. It is one big crime and . . . the name for that is genocide.'[163]
Avi Shlaim, emeritus professor of international relations at the University of Oxford	Israel's operation 'is an indiscriminate, murderous, and genocidal war waged by one of the strongest militaries in the world not just against Hamas but against the defenceless people of Gaza.'[164]
Lee Mordechai, historian at Hebrew University	'The enormous amount of evidence I have seen ... has been enough for me to believe that Israel is committing genocide against the Palestinian population in Gaza.'[165]
Rashid Khalidi, Edward Said professor emeritus of modern Arab studies at Columbia University	'[T]his has been the first genocide that a generation has witnessed in real time, on their devices.'[166]
Richard Falk, professor emeritus of international law at Princeton University	Israel responded to October 7 with 'the prolonged and collaborative commission of genocide.'[167]
Alfred de Zayas, professor of international law at the Geneva School of Diplomacy	'States should immediately break all commercial and diplomatic relations with Israel. Only this will signal to Israel that there is a price to pay for committing genocide.'[168]
Ilan Pappé, director of the European Centre for Palestine Studies at the University of Exeter	'What is happening now in Gaza is genocide.'[169]
Norman G. Finkelstein, author of the authoritative scholarly book on Israel's Gaza massacres	'The Israel Defense Forces, right now, is a genocidal army.'[170]
John Mearsheimer, the R. Wendell Harrison Distinguished Service professor of political science at the University of Chicago	'The basic goal here is to kill a huge number of people in the Palestinian population, and that I think easily qualifies as a genocide.'[171]

TABLE 8. Select Authorities Who Say or Imply That Israel Is Innocent of Genocide

Authority	Description
Keir Starmer	'I am well aware of the definition of genocide, and that is why I have never described this or referred to it as genocide.'[172]
David Lammy	'These are legal terms, and they must be determined by international courts. I agree with the hon. Gentleman that those terms were largely used when millions of people lost their lives in crises such as Rwanda and the Holocaust of the second world war. The way that people are now using those terms undermines their seriousness.'[173]
David Cameron	'[T]o say that that country, that leadership, that armed forces, that they have intent to commit genocide—I think that is nonsense, I think that is wrong.'[174]
Andrew Mitchell	'It is hard to overestimate the offence caused by the extraordinary rhetoric of accusing Israel of being guilty of genocide, given the antecedents and events that took place in the holocaust during the war and the fact that more Jewish people were murdered on that one day of 7 October than at any time since the end of the second world war'.[175]

9

NOBODY IS DYING OF HUNGER IN GAZA

> You can go on YouTube and see pictures of the stocked food markets in Gaza.
>
> —Times *columnist Melanie Phillips*

London, Early 2025

PARALLEL WORLDS. One belongs to ministers, their spin-doctors, officials, newspaper editors, and columnists. They are at home in Washington, Tel Aviv, Westminster, and the big media houses. For them Israel is the only democratic state in the Middle East, one of Britain's closest allies, poised on the front line between Western civilisation and Islamist barbarism. It is tacitly understood that one does not mention the International Criminal Court arrest warrant out for Israeli prime minister Benjamin Netanyahu. The ongoing genocide case at The Hague is another touchy subject. Sir Keir Starmer has banned use of the term 'genocide' at Labour Party events.[1] If pressed, Sir Keir denies a genocide is taking place, just as he denies that Israel is practicing apartheid.[2] Kemi Badenoch, leader of the Conservative Party, supports him on this. So do the British media battalions. They do not report Israeli atrocities where this can be avoided.

Approximately fifty thousand Palestinians are known to be dead. Many more lie uncounted in the rubble or on the streets. Studies assess that the real toll may be vastly higher. It is estimated that the life expectancy of Palestinians in Gaza fell by more than thirty-four years in the first twelve months of the violence.[3] The ruination of Gaza has been exhaustively documented by aid agencies, the United Nations, and human rights organisations. Israeli soldiers themselves have filmed a great deal of the destruction, providing inadvertent evidence for future war crimes tribunals by uploading their videos onto social media.[4] At great personal risk, journalists working inside Gaza have reported and filmed the atrocities. In this chapter I will attempt to explain how the officially sanctioned reality at Westminster managed to hang on for eighteen months in the face of overwhelming evidence of Israeli barbarism.

Full Stop

Part of the reason is a deep-seated reluctance to get to grips with the facts. Some Britons believe so strongly in the State of Israel that they cannot accept it would do anything immoral. This position is often understandable even if it has calamitous results. Many Jews, and not only Jews, regard Israel as the indispensable nation in light of the long history of antisemitism dating back centuries and climaxing in the Holocaust.

One example is the journalist and part-time political adviser Danny Finkelstein. Lord Finkelstein (he was ennobled by David Cameron in 2013) is an intimate friend and adviser of some of our most famous politicians. He was chief leader writer for *The Times* where he still pens a weekly column. Frequently wheeled out on prestigious current affairs shows, Finkelstein is one of the most influential people in Britain.

More significant than any of this, I suspect he would agree, is his first book. Called *Hitler, Stalin, Mum and Dad,* it tells the story of his remarkable parents. His father Ludwik Finkelstein was born in Lwow, then in Poland but now in Ukraine. His mother, Mirjam Wiener (granddaughter of Alfred Wiener, a student of antisemitism who was sounding alarm bells about the Nazis well before Hitler seized power), survived Bergen-Belsen. The book tells how his parents lived through the destruction of European civilisation. A review in *The Guardian* concluded: 'Perhaps the more people that read this brilliant book, the less likely it will be that our liberal society ever disintegrates.'[5]

In October last year, Danny Finkelstein joined a discussion on the social media platform X after the Palestinian journalist Anas al-Sharif shared a deeply upsetting video.[6] The video shows a child crying out for assistance after being injured in a drone strike. Palestinians approach to help. There is a sudden flash and the explosion of a second strike. The child's dead body is subsequently shown on the street, near the dead bodies of others around him.*

During the course of the discussion Finkelstein comes to the defence of the Israel Defence Forces, asserting that 'it's extremely unlikely'[7] the IDF would shoot a child as 'bait' and then shoot civilians coming to the child's aid. He then makes an unequivocal statement: 'An Israeli drone will not have targeted a child. Full stop.'[8] This remark suggests that he may not have watched the video or, supposing he did, managed to detach himself from the testimony of his own eyes. Either way, Finkelstein is asserting an article of faith. No matter what the evidence shows, it is a priori the case that *an Israeli drone will not have deliberately targeted a child.*

There is ample testimony that Israeli forces have targeted Palestinian children in Gaza. On November 12, 2024, Nizam Mamode, a former NHS surgeon who spent a month working in Nasser hospital in the south of the enclave, broke down in tears as he testified to the House of Commons

* On August 10, 2025, Israel killed Anas al-Sharif along with five other journalists in a targeted strike on a media tent near al-Shifa hospital. The IDF took responsibility for the slaying and alleged that al-Sharif had been a Hamas militant. Al Jazeera denied the charge, which Reporters Without Borders dismissed as having been made 'without evidence'. The Committee to Protect Journalists (CPJ) rejected what it characterised as a 'smear' and said: 'Israel is murdering the messengers . . . Deliberately targeting journalists is a war crime under international law. This massacre must end'. The UN human rights office condemned the killings as a 'grave breach of international humanitarian law'. Al-Sharif was the 184th Palestinian journalist killed by Israel since October 7, 2023. CPJ, 'Israel Kills Al Jazeera Journalists in Targeted Gaza City Airstrike', cpj.org (10 August 2025; updated 13 August 2025). Al Jazeera Staff, 'Tributes, Condemnation Pour in over Slain Al Jazeera Journalists in Gaza', aljazeera.com (11 August 2025; updated 12 August 2025). Post on X by @UNHumanRights (11 August 2025), https://x.com/unhumanrights/status/1954850777731641516. Jodie Ginsberg, 'Israel Is Wiping Out Gaza's Journalists—And It's No Longer Even Hiding It', *The Guardian* (13 August 2025).

International Development Committee that Israel would routinely bomb the tents of displaced people. He explained that Israeli quadcopter drones would then come to pick off the injured civilians, including children.* There is indeed overwhelming documentation that the IDF has targeted children as part of Israel's genocidal onslaught.[9] According to the Gaza health authority, at least 17,921 children have so far been killed.[10] Thousands of others have been permanently disabled.[11] The lives of Palestinians are dispensable in the eyes of many Israeli commanders.

I have bumped into Danny Finkelstein on and off for thirty years. We have sometimes argued but always made up our differences and (I think) been glad to see each other on the rare occasions we meet. I know from his many friends that Danny is a man of integrity, personal kindness, and decency. I am quite certain he was communicating in good faith. While writing these words I have been asking myself whether, had I come from the same family heritage as Finkelstein, I might have reached the same conclusion about the uses to which Israeli drones can be put. It's quite likely I would.

There is a further consideration that applies to others, perhaps, more than it does to Finkelstein himself. We have seen that Finkelstein's own newspaper,

---

* Nizam Mamode: What I think I found particularly disturbing was that a bomb would drop, maybe on a crowded, tented area, and then the drones would come down and—[*Nizam begins crying*]

Sarah Champion: Please take your time...

Nizam Mamode: The drones would come down and pick off civilians—children. We had description after description. This is not an occasional thing. This was day after day after day of operating on children who would say, 'I was lying on the ground after a bomb had dropped, and this quadcopter came down and hovered over me and shot me'. That is clearly a deliberate and persistent act; there was persistent targeting of civilians day after day.

UK House of Commons International Development Committee, *Oral Evidence: Humanitarian Situation in Gaza*, HC 373, committees.parliament.uk (12 November 2024), Q6. PoliticsJOE, 'Surgeon Breaks Down in Parliament Explaining How IDF Drones Target Children' (13 November 2024), https://www.youtube.com/watch?v=fgsK7noLGOM, 6m10s.

The Times, has suppressed stories that challenge the dominant Israeli narrative. Mainstream rivals, such as the *Daily Telegraph* or *Daily Mail*, are little more than Tel Aviv propaganda sheets, less likely to publish news that places the IDF in a poor light than even Israeli newspapers. BBC coverage has been constrained, likewise that of Sky and ITV. To inform himself Lord Finkelstein would have needed to step away from respectable media outlets, pay attention to Al Jazeera, and study publications such as *Declassified UK*, *Electronic Intifada*, *Drop Site News*, *Palestine Deep Dive*, *+972 Magazine*, and *Middle East Eye*. He might also have consulted the voluminous documentation published online by mainstream human rights authorities and UN agencies. It's unlikely he's done so. Like the rest of the British governing elite, he lives in a parallel world.

Nobody Is Dying of Hunger in Gaza

Melanie Phillips, a colleague of Finkelstein's at *The Times*, said it was 'completely untrue' that Israel was preventing Palestinians from accessing 'food and humanitarian supplies'. Appearing on March 14, 2024, she told a BBC *Question Time* audience: 'You can go on YouTube and see pictures of the stocked food markets in Gaza'. She also explained: 'There have been hundreds and hundreds of trucks going through Gaza, there have been hundreds of trucks stopped from going through Gaza because the food is being stolen by Hamas'.

Phillips was correct to say that YouTube videos of well-stocked shops were circulating on the internet. These videos had no time stamp on them, as *Question Time* host Fiona Bruce pointed out.[12] More to the point, the existence of food in some places is of no help to those trapped elsewhere in Gaza or those who can't afford to buy it.[13] Phillips was reinforcing a line put out by the Israeli government, whose Coordinator of Government Activities in the Territories had stated: 'there is no limit to the amount of aid that can enter Gaza'.[14]

I wrote to Melanie Phillips requesting evidence for her assertion that food and humanitarian aid was flowing smoothly into Gaza, even though human rights groups said this wasn't true. Phillips replied: 'The answers to your questions are all available from public sources. I stand by my comments'.[15]

Phillips' denial that Israel was withholding aid from people in Gaza was, as we have seen, contradicted by a consensus of UN agencies and international human rights groups. They were clear that by restricting the entry of aid, obstructing aid distribution, and attacking aid recipients Israel was deliberately causing hunger in Gaza. In January 2024, approximately two months before Phillips' comments, aid agencies had called for dramatically increased humanitarian access to northern Gaza. Israel instead 'repeatedly impeded' humanitarian access and hindered the delivery of 'essential supplies'.[16] The observed result was a 'surge of people with malnutrition, dehydration and related illnesses' as '[s]evere hunger' forced some to survive on 'wild plants and animal fodder'.[17]

Just ten days before Phillips' *Question Time* appearance the director-general of the World Health Organisation had reported that children were 'dying of starvation'.[18] He specified that 'lack of food resulted in the deaths of 10 children' in Kamal Adwan, the only paediatrics hospital in northern Gaza. Four days after Phillips spoke, the Integrated Food Security Phase Classification (IPC) warned that 'famine' in northern Gaza was 'imminent' unless 'full access' was granted for food, water, and medicines.[19]

This worst-case scenario was averted the following month when Israel eased aid restrictions in response to overwhelming international pressure—no thanks to Phillips. But Israel tightened restrictions again when international attention moved on. The same pattern obtained when Israel imposed near-total blockades in November 2024 and March 2025. The Crisis Group observes that we have been 'witnessing an experiment: an attempt to indefinitely maintain Gaza's population below the famine threshold while turning food into a weapon of war'.[20]

In December 2024, Amnesty International concluded that Israel's deliberate blocking, impeding, and limiting of humanitarian aid was evidence that Israel had committed genocide in Gaza.[21]

Phillips gave no evidence for her claim that aid was being stolen by Hamas. The World Food Programme later said it had no reason 'at all' to conclude that Hamas was looting aid.[22] As the Conclusion will discuss, evidence would soon emerge that lifesaving aid was being stolen in Gaza by criminal gangs backed by Israel.

Israel apologists have persisted with their claim that reports of hunger in Gaza were false. On December 19, 2024, David Collier posted on X that 'Nobody is dying of thirst in Gaza. Nobody is dying of hunger. Israel is defending itself against terrorists. Human Rights Watch & Amnesty are trying to redefine (belittle) words in the English language (like genocide) to demonise and ostracise Israel. They are spreading lies.'[23]

Two days *before* Collier's X pronouncement that 'nobody is dying of hunger' the charity ActionAid warned that people were being forced to choose between risking death or injury 'while queuing for food' or else 'starving to death', and that 'up to 75,000 people have been almost entirely cut off from supplies of food for more than 60 days' in the northern part of the enclave.[24]

A few days later Oxfam confirmed that 'humanitarian organisations operating in Gaza were receiving calls from vulnerable people trapped in homes and shelters that had completely run out of food and water' earlier that month, that some people had been reduced to eating leaves, and that some families had 'no food or shelter'.[25]

Local health officials reported that children in Gaza were already dying of malnutrition-related causes in December 2023.[26] UNICEF reported that a baby boy died as a result of starvation in Gaza just ten days before Collier's tweet—though only made this public the day after Collier's intervention. UNICEF's Rosalia Bollen described the circumstances:

> The stories I heard over the past months will torment me forever. Let me share one: this summer we met with a baby boy, also named Saad, he was seven months old. His mother's miracle after years of trying to conceive. He weighed just 2.7 kilograms at 7 months—a fraction of what a baby his age should. Eleven days ago, his fragile body gave out after not getting enough nutritious food. He was born in war and left this world without being given a chance to live in peace. I cannot even start to imagine the depth of suffering of his parents. The suffering is not merely physical. It is also psychological.[27]

In light of all the above we wrote to David Collier asking him to explain his statement that '[n]obody is dying of hunger' in Gaza, given what these humanitarian organisations were documenting and reporting at the time. He replied: 'The Action Aid warning is built from a statement made by Amjad Al-Shawa, director of the Palestinian NGOs Network (PNGO)'. He added that the Oxfam statement 'does not divulge the source of its logistical information (so probably Hamas)'. He also suggested that UNICEF's account of the death of Saad was 'hearsay evidence'.*

Collier, who styles himself an 'Investigative Journalist',[28] would go on to launch the campaign that led the BBC to remove its film *Gaza: How to Survive a War Zone* from iPlayer on the grounds that one of protagonists was the thirteen-year-old son of a Hamas government official.[29] The film had set out to show the Gaza tragedy through the eyes of children.

Jake Wallis Simons writes in *The Spectator* and *Daily Telegraph*, and has appeared on BBC *Question Time*. During much of the Gaza conflict he was editor of *The Jewish Chronicle*. In June 2024 his *Telegraph* column carried the headline 'Israel Is Not Committing Genocide in Gaza'. To give substance to his argument Wallis Simons wrote: 'Every aspect has been either disproven or cast into irretrievable doubt', stating that 'the 37,000 casualty figure is not reliable—the combatant-to-civilian casualty ratio now likely stands at about 1:1'.[30]

The previous month the Israeli press attributed the claim of a 1:1 ratio between civilian and combatant casualties to Israeli prime minister Benjamin Netanyahu. He had told the writer Dan Senor: 'Fourteen thousand have been killed, combatants, and, probably around sixteen thousand civilians have been killed'.[31] Government spokesman Avi Hyman doubled down on Netanyahu's numbers, adding, 'Israel is setting the new gold standard for

---

* David Collier answered via an open letter published on his website. I asked ActionAid for a response. It said: 'The information we share is informed by trusted local sources, including doctors, humanitarian workers, and civil society organisations, and is cross-verified through credible bodies such as UN OCHA, other UN agencies, local hospitals, and technical groups such as the Integrated Food Security Phase Classification (IPC), which assesses famine conditions'. Oxfam told us: 'Our story used data from the United Nations Office for the Coordination of Humanitarian Affairs (OCHA), who provided Oxfam with the details of food and water deliveries to Northern Gaza from 6 October to 16 December'. When we approached UNICEF, the agency confirmed that 'Saad very sadly died in the Autumn of last year'.

urban warfare with what appears to be the lowest civilian-to-combatant casualty ratio in history'.[32] Wallis Simons was repeating a Netanyahu talking point for which no serious evidence had been provided beyond the word of the Israeli prime minister and his spokesperson and with which the expert consensus disagreed.

For the record, Israeli casualty figures for Gaza should be taken with boulders of salt. 'It's astonishing to hear the reports after every operation, regarding how many terrorists were killed', one Israeli soldier told *Haaretz*. 'You don't need to be a genius to realise that you don't have hundreds or dozens of armed men running through the streets of Khan Yunis or Jabaliya, fighting the IDF'.[33] 'There's no real count, the IDF doesn't collect bodies of terrorists it kills, there's a huge amount of people who were killed in the Strip and there's no trace of them, they were evaporated by massive Air Force bombardments', prominent Israeli military reporter Alon Ben David said in August 2024. 'No one has an accurate measure, they rely on burial statistics in Gaza'.[34]

This was not the first time that Wallis Simons was careless in his treatment of evidence. While he was editor, *The Jewish Chronicle* published articles by an Israeli contributor named Elon Perry. It later emerged that Perry's CV was questionable, and his articles were accused of fabrication. His work was subsequently removed from the *Chronicle*'s website.[35] The scandal prompted four of the paper's best-known columnists to resign.[36]

In January 2025 the *Spectator* editor and former Tory cabinet minister Michael Gove floated in *The Jewish Chronicle* the idea that the 'men and women of the IDF' should be nominated for the Nobel Peace Prize.[37] The Nobel Peace Prize was intended by its founder to be given to 'those who, during the preceding year, shall have conferred the greatest benefit to humankind'.[38] Gove's suggestion that it should be handed to the Israeli army opens him up to the charge of atrocity denial.

Either Gove was unaware that the IDF was committing atrocities or, even more alarming, he considered that the IDF should be celebrated despite them. According to a recent study of the Ethiopian civil war, atrocity denial 'is often anchored in instrumental calculations, as it facilitates implicated parties escaping legal and political accountability'. The authors also note that it is a 'defense mechanism, designed to blunt distressing emotions, and its effect on violence is permissive—neutralizing the uncomfortable emotive sentiments that might otherwise constrain conflict in the future'.[39]

Gove's suggestion that the IDF might be given the Nobel Peace Prize is symptomatic of the way the British political and media class nullifies the experience of Palestinians. He blanks them out. For him they have no humanity. It is as if they do not exist. Gove is the editor of Britain's most acclaimed political magazine and an iconic member of our political establishment.

Think about it. Think about the consequences if you are Palestinian. We in Britain should also consider what that means for us, and what sort of nation we have become.*

Howard Jacobson

A year after the Hamas atrocities on October 7 the Booker Prize-winning novelist and public intellectual Howard Jacobson wrote an article in *The Observer* newspaper that linked reporting of Israel's Gaza offensive to the medieval blood libel that Jews murder gentile children for their blood. Jacobson's contribution articulated a concern, which was doubtless not confined to him, that there was a link between reporting of brutalities in Gaza and a revival of the ancient curse of antisemitism. He is a fine writer and I quote his argument at length:

> It is hateful to be accused of what you haven't done, but more hateful still to be accused of what you would never dream of doing and what you cannot bear to see done.

---

* I wrote to Michael Gove giving him a chance to reply to my comment that he had laid himself open to the charge of atrocity denial in his *Jewish Chronicle* article. He replied: 'I hope I made explicit my analysis that the IDF had helped advance peace by weakening Hizbollah, contributing to Bashar Assad's fall and damaging Hamas's capacity to inflict terror on both Israel and the people of Gaza. I explicitly criticised Anthony Blinken [*sic*] and Joe Biden for a strategy of inconstant support for Israel which was "inflicting more misery on both the Israeli and the Palestinian peoples". While Peter and I differ fundamentally on the causes of and solution to conflict in the Middle East I believe we both care about the suffering of innocents'.

> Hence the hurt, the anger and the fear that Jewish people have been experiencing in the year since Hamas's barbaric massacre of Israelis on 7 October and the no less barbaric denials, not to mention celebrations of it, as night after night our televisions have told the story of the war in Gaza through the death of Palestinian children. Night after night, a recital of the numbers dead. Night after night, the unbearable footage of their parents' agony. The savagery of war. The savagery of the Israeli onslaught. But for many, writing or marching against Israeli action, the savagery of the Jews as told for hundreds of years in literature and art and church sermons.
>
> Here we were again, the same merciless infanticides inscribed in the imaginations of medieval Christians. Only this time, instead of operating on the midnight streets of Lincoln and Norwich, they target Palestinian schools, the paediatric wards of hospitals, the tiny fragile bodies of children themselves.[40]

Jacobson comes close to accusing British journalists of fabricating Israeli atrocities:

> Even when there are other explanations for the devastation, no one really believes them. Reporters whose reports are proved wrong see no reason to apologise. No amendment of their calumnies. What is there to apologise for? It *could* have been true.
>
> Ask how Israel is able to target innocent children with such deadly accuracy and no one can tell you. Ask why they would *want* to target innocent children and make themselves despised among the nations of the Earth and no one can tell you that either. Hate on this scale seeks no rational explanation. Hate feeds off the superstitions that fed it last time round.[41]

Jacobson provides no evidence to support his suggestion that reporters invent or fabricate Israeli atrocities. In reality the footage shown on mainstream channels is constantly regulated to protect the sensibilities of a domestic TV audience. Every morning for the last eighteen months the *Middle East Eye* bureau chief in Jerusalem, my colleague Lubna Masarwa, has sifted through the overnight videos and photographs coming in from our correspondents in Gaza. When I visit her she sometimes shows them to me. The little smashed bodies horribly twisted out of shape. Tiny skulls with brains blown out. The rows of dead babies set out as if they were dolls in a playroom. Burnt and charred bodies. Once seen they live with you forever. These images as a rule don't make it onto mainstream outlets in Britain, nor should they.

How she manages to view all this daily I don't know. We worry for her. She uses meditation techniques and is a teacher of Sufi Islam. All British TV channels will have access to this sort of material and almost never use it. Many Arabic channels do show it and that is one reason why countries like the United States and Britain, which supply arms and intelligence support to the Israeli army, are held in ever greater contempt crossing into hatred across the globe.

The mainstream British media has tended to play down stories of atrocities against Palestinian children. One example concerns six-year-old Hind Rajab, who set out with her family to escape Gaza's Tel al-Hawa neighbourhood. The IDF fired on the car, killing five family members and leaving just Hind and her fifteen-year-old cousin Layan alive.[42] Layan was in touch with the Palestine Red Crescent Society. In the recording of her telephone call she can be heard saying that a tank is firing on the car, then screams as she too is shot dead.[43]

At this point Hind remains alive, surrounded by her six dead relatives. The Red Crescent phones her, arranges safe passage with Israel, then sends two paramedics in an ambulance.[44] The Israelis kill them, along with Hind.[45] The corpses were only discovered two weeks later, once the IDF had pulled out of Gaza City.[46] The BBC headlined the story as 'Hind Rajab, 6, Found Dead in Gaza after Phone Calls for Help.'[47]

The fate of Hind Rajab illustrated the daily horror facing Palestinians in Gaza. It is not difficult to imagine the wall-to-wall coverage it would have attracted had Hind been Israeli and had Palestinians killed her and her family in similar circumstances.

Howard Jacobson has excuses for his ignorance. Like every other consumer of conventional media, much of the truth has been studiously kept from him by politicians and editors.

There is a paradox here. Jacobson would have had a better chance of knowing the answer to the anguished questions he raised about child casualties in his *Observer* article had he been a regular consumer of Israeli investigative reporting, which has been readier to expose IDF atrocities than have British newspapers and broadcasters.* In April 2024, a +972 *Magazine* investigation showed how the Israeli military employed artificial intelligence to track down Palestinians as targets for assassination.[48] Journalists at +972 also identified the existence of an automated system called 'Where's Daddy?' This tracked targeted individuals but waited to carry out bombings until they got home.[49]

The result, the +972 investigation stated, 'is that thousands of Palestinians—most of them women and children or people who were not involved in the fighting—were wiped out by Israeli airstrikes, especially during the first weeks of the war, because of the AI program's decisions'.[50] One military intelligence officer told +972 that '[w]e were not interested in killing [Hamas] operatives only when they were in a military building or engaged in a military activity. On the contrary, the IDF bombed them in homes without hesitation, as a first option. It's much easier to bomb a family's home. The system is built to look for them in these situations'.[51]

British media have been equally coy about telling the public of the Israeli military's longstanding 'Dahiya doctrine',[52] which calls for using massive, disproportionate force and the deliberate targeting of civilian infrastructure (set out in Chapter Four above). This provides part of the answer to Jacobson's question about how Israel is 'able to target innocent children with such deadly accuracy': The Israeli military has indiscriminately attacked the entire population and infrastructure of Gaza—men, women, and children alike. Within this campaign of 'widespread, systematic destruction',[53] it is

* For example, *Haaretz* collected testimonies from Israeli soldiers and medical professionals who worked at the Sde Teiman detention centre, revealing systematic torture there, and exposed that the IDF Operations Directorate was running a racist Telegram channel that advertised Israeli soldiers inflicting widespread destruction in Gaza, mutilating corpses, and abusing detainees. Yaniv Kubovich, 'Graphic Videos and Incitement: How the IDF Is Misleading Israelis on Telegram', *Haaretz* (12 December 2023). Shay Fogelman, 'We Served on Israel's Sde Teiman Base. Here's What We Did to Gazans Detained There', *Haaretz* (16 August 2024).

(as discussed above) well documented that Israeli forces have in addition specifically targeted children for death. If Jacobson is in any doubt that Israel has the technological capacity to accomplish this, he should ask the IDF. As Israeli snipers shot hundreds of civilians, including children, protesting in the Great March of Return, the IDF stated that 'we know where every bullet landed'.[54]

In September 2024, the Gaza Ministry of Health published a list containing the names of 34,344 Palestinians who at that point were known to have been killed during Israel's annihilation of Gaza. The list, which contained the names of more than eleven thousand children, sorted the dead by age.[55] Fourteen pages dealt only with the names of babies under the age of one—707 in all.[56]

The bigger problem with Jacobson's analysis is not his ignorance of the facts. It is the conceptual error embodied in his statement that 'it is hateful to be accused of what you haven't done'. Yet nobody is reflexively accusing Howard Jacobson or all other British Jews of responsibility for the slaughter of Palestinian children. It would be disgraceful were they to do so. The military arm of the state of Israel is to blame, as well as the politicians who direct it, and to a lesser extent the Israeli public that backs the slaughter as well as everyone who enables it from afar. Jacobson is muddling up Israel with the Jewish people. The evidence suggests that a large number of Jews around the world feel horrified by what Israel has done in Gaza.* Many of them are British. Some are national treasures, such as Miriam Margolyes, Michael Rosen, and Alexei Sayle. Daniel Levy, a former peace negotiator and current president of the US/Middle East Project, is another. He recently spoke at the United Nations Security Council of the need for 'an acknowledgement of the power asymmetry between an occupying, colonizing state and

---

* In November 2024, a survey by Israel's Ministry for Diaspora Affairs and Combatting Antisemitism found that 41.3 percent of American-Jewish teenagers aged 14–18 agreed with the statement that Israel is 'committing genocide' in Gaza while 66 percent of American-Jewish teenagers aged 14–18 said that they sympathise with the Palestinian people as a whole. MEE Staff, 'One-Third of Jewish-American Teens Say They "Sympathise" with Hamas, Israeli Government Poll Shows', *Middle East Eye* (22 November 2024). See also: Zainab Iqbal, 'Why So Many Young Jewish Americans Are Anti-Zionist', *Middle East Eye* (8 February 2024).

an occupied, colonized, stateless people'.[57] Avi Shlaim, emeritus professor of International Relations at Oxford University, is yet another. As we saw in Chapter Two, Shlaim's voice is excluded from mainstream discourse even though he is among the most distinguished historians of modern Israel. As far as I can tell he is ignored because he is a critic of the Israeli state.

The mainstream media view that only pro-Israel Jews possess legitimate voices dates back to well before the latest events in Gaza and has produced serious distortions in British public discourse. One of the most striking has been the treatment of left-wing Jews inside Sir Keir Starmer's Labour Party, particularly those supportive of former leader Jeremy Corbyn. A report by Jewish Voice for Labour (JVL), which was founded as a left wing, pro-Palestinian Labour Party pressure group, estimates that Jewish members of the Labour Party, as a population share, have faced almost *five times* more investigations on complaints of antisemitism than have non-Jewish Labour members.[58]

The problem, says JVL, is its support for Palestinian rights. JVL defines itself as being part of the 'universalist Jewish tradition for freedom', declaring itself 'committed to the struggle against all racism, including antisemitism, and for freedom and justice for all, including the Palestinian people'.[59]

In a submission made four years ago to the Equality and Human Rights Commission, JVL argued that, before Starmer, Labour leaders had 'sought to hear from diverse Jewish perspectives. But the party now limits its engagement with British Jews to groups who claim to represent "the Jewish community" but who in fact represent only one position within it'. JVL claimed that the party 'is, in effect, collaborating with these groups to delegitimise Jewish dissent'.[60]

Jewish Voice for Labour contended that the Labour Party was 'pursuing disciplinary cases against members who have been critical of Israel or expressed support for Palestinian rights', rather than antisemites. It added: 'The assumption of disciplinary investigations is that all Jews are Zionists and/or that anti-Zionists are not proper Jews and indeed are antisemitic, delegitimising an entire swathe of Jewish opinion and tradition'.[61]

I interviewed JVL's co-chair, the retired civil servant Jenny Manson, in her Golders Green home. She told me: 'For the first time in my life as a Jew living in the UK I feel persecuted, hated, and shunned by the apparatus of the Labour Party and the loud voices of some sections of the Jewish community. The weapon used too often is to call us JVL activists antisemitic. Bizarre and wicked.'[62]

Jewish Voice for Labour is not just persecuted within the Labour Party. It's hardly allowed any space in mainstream media—the same media that has tended to ignore or downplay the Jewish bloc on the pro-Palestinian marches. It's easy to see why: the presence of Jews renders the official story that the protestors are pro-Hamas and antisemitic incomprehensible.

The Weaponisation of Anti-Semitism

The assumption that Israel embodies the values and interests of British Jews means that those standing up for Palestinian rights can be represented as antisemites, even if they are themselves Jewish. This makes it an easy matter to drive Palestinians from the public domain and delegitimise those who support their case as bigots.

This logic has been exploited by Israeli prime minister Benjamin Netanyahu and his allies to discredit any individual or institution that criticises Israel. On January 26, 2024, after the International Court of Justice ruled that the Palestinians faced a plausible risk of genocide in Gaza, the Israeli president Isaac Herzog (who was quoted in the ruling) said that the holding of the hearing was a 'blood libel that undermines the very values on which this court was established.'[63] Israel's national security minister Itamar Ben-Gvir alleged: 'This court does not seek justice but rather the persecution of the Jewish people.'[64]

The following day the *Daily Telegraph* ran an article by Jake Wallis Simons that bore the headline: 'The ICJ Has Been Captured by Anti-Semitic Propaganda'. His article included this sneering and inaccurate denunciation: 'The Jews must take all measures to avoid committing genocide, the judges snorted.'[65]

Here Simons was treating the Israeli government as synonymous with '[t]he Jews'. When Palestinians make the same conflation, they are denounced as antisemites.[66] As for South Africa's exhaustively argued case, prepared and propounded by a team of eminent jurists from multiple continents, Simons had this to say: 'South Africa's case was self-evidently absurd, pernicious and dripping with the oldest hatred'.[67]

Ten months later the International Criminal Court issued warrants for the arrest of Netanyahu and Gallant for war crimes and crimes against humanity. Netanyahu responded by declaring that these warrants were issued 'by biased judges motivated by antisemitic sentiments against the one and only Jewish state'.[68] He added: 'The antisemitic decision of the international court in The Hague is a modern Dreyfus trial, and it will end the same way'.[69] Once again the British media stretched out a helping hand, with the *Telegraph* giving space to a column trashing the ruling as 'simple, outrageous anti-Semitism'.[70] The newspaper provided no evidence to support the claim.

On March 23, 2024, Israel's then foreign minister Israel Katz announced that the United Nations had become an 'antisemitic and anti-Israeli body that shelters and emboldens terror'.[71] The UN secretary general António Guterrez had the temerity to criticise Israel for blocking humanitarian aid. Six months later Katz declared the seventy-five-year-old former Portuguese prime minister 'persona non grata in Israel'.[72] Three weeks after that the *Daily Telegraph* stated: 'António Guterres needs to be replaced if the UN is to retain any shred of credibility'.[73]

Josep Borrell, high representative of the European Union for foreign affairs and security policy, became another Katz target after he condemned an Israeli airstrike on a school-turned-shelter in Nuseirat refugee camp.[74] Rescuers said it killed eighteen people including six UN workers. Israel Katz stated that Borrell 'is an antisemite and Israel-hater' who was behaving in a way 'reminiscent of history's worst anti-semites'.[75]

Pretty well any high-profile figure is liable to find themselves at the receiving end of smears from supporters of Israel.* One such was Pope Francis. Right to his death in April this year, every evening at 7:00 p.m. sharp, he called Father Gabriel Romanelli, priest of the only Roman Catholic church in

* One exception to this category: actual antisemites, provided they are considered supportive of Israel. The well-documented antisemitism of Donald Trump and Elon Musk, for example, was typically overlooked in the mainstream.

Gaza.* In December 2023, Pope Francis condemned the IDF's sniping of a Palestinian Christian mother and daughter—Nahida and Samar Anton—while they were sheltering in church premises.[76] Pope Francis stated:

> I continue to receive very serious and sad news about Gaza. Unarmed civilians are targets for bombs and shootings. And this happened even within the parish complex of the Holy Family, where there are no terrorists, but families, children, people who are sick and have disabilities, sisters. A mother and her daughter . . . were killed, and other people wounded by snipers as they were going to the bathroom . . . Some say: 'this is terrorism and war'. Yes, it is war, it is terrorism.[77]

In August 2024, footage of the Pope making these remarks was reshared on X. The British pro-Israel blogger David Collier reposted the video, adding: 'For almost 2000 years the church persecuted the Jews. He is just following a long history of anti-Jewish activity'.[78]

Melanie Phillips joined forces with Collier. On November 21, 2024, the *Times* columnist wrote an article for the Jewish News Syndicate that attacked Pope Francis over his contribution to a new book published for the Catholic Church's jubilee year. The Pope had written: 'According to some experts, what is happening in Gaza has the characteristics of a genocide. We should investigate carefully to determine whether it fits into the technical definition formulated by jurists and international bodies'.[79] The Pope also wrote: 'Defense must always be proportionate to the attack. When there is something disproportionate, one shows a tendency to dominate which goes beyond what is moral'.

Responding to these remarks, Phillips said that the suggestion that Israel was committing genocide was 'cynical linguistic inversion and moral

* Father Romanelli was lightly injured while three others were killed after an Israeli attack on the Church of the Holy Family on July 17, 2025. See: Vatican News, 'Israeli Forces Strike Catholic Parish in Gaza', *Vatican News* (17 July 2025). On Pope Francis and Father Romanelli see: Salvatore Cernuzio, 'Pope in Video Call with Gaza Parish: "I Pray for You"', *Vatican News* (22 January 2025).

bankruptcy of the highest order'. According to Phillips, the Pope had used 'language that makes Jews shudder. When he suggests that the Jews may be guilty of genocide, it's hard not to hear echoes of his predecessors' accusation that the Jews were guilty of deicide—the claim that lay behind centuries of Jewish slaughter'.

She also accused the Pope of regurgitating 'the ancient Christian theological hatred of the Jews and the desire to obliterate them'. Her conclusion: 'Pope Francis has made himself an accomplice of evil'.[80]

Undeterred, in December 2024 the Pope condemned Israeli airstrikes in Gaza, stating: 'This is cruelty. This is not war'.[81] In response the Israeli foreign ministry condemned the Pope for 'double standards and the singling out of the Jewish state and its people'.[82] Given that 'double standards' featured as an example in Israel's preferred definition of antisemitism, this was a thinly veiled allegation of anti-Jewish bigotry.

None of the above justifications of Israeli conduct were based on logic or fact. Supporters of Israel demanded to be judged by a special standard. They collapsed the long-accepted distinction between truth versus *falsehood* and distinguished instead between truth and *heresy*. Netanyahu and his supporters felt strongly that they had been granted access to a unique *moral* truth. This state of grace produced two marvellous consequences. Whatever Israel did, however barbarous or illegal, was in some profounder sense virtuous. All criticism from opponents, however well-documented and grounded in law, was morally delinquent. Israel was granting itself total freedom to do what it liked, and to shape the world as it wished. Too many British politicians and journalists nodded along.

Easier to Criticise the British Army Than the IDF

Muazzaz Abayat recoiled with confusion and terror as I approached his bed in a Bethlehem hospital. He assumed I was coming to beat him up. Muazzaz had emerged from Israel's Negev prison a few days earlier. He was still mentally in his prison cell. He'd been beaten or tortured repeatedly during his nearly nine-month term in Israeli captivity, during which time his bodyweight had more than halved. His suffering was sculpted in his face.

Looking terrified as he spoke, he expressed disbelief that 'peaceful people with no power can be starved, tortured and killed' in the twenty-first century, with no protection, legal representation or international outrage. He recalled that one prisoner, Abu Asab, had died in a cell near his. 'They beat him to death and left him to die'.[83]

Like other inmates Abayat compared the Negev prison where he had been held to the notorious US facility at Abu Ghraib. By profession a Bethlehem butcher, he was never charged with any crime.[84]

Weeks later the Israeli human rights group B'Tselem issued a study of prisoner abuse.* B'Tselem titled its report 'Welcome to Hell'. It was published two days after reports in Israeli media that nine soldiers were accused of raping a Palestinian prisoner at the Sde Teiman detention centre. According to a report in *Haaretz*, injuries included 'a ruptured bowel, a severe injury to his anus, lung damage and broken ribs'.[85] Earlier the UN found that at least fifty-three Palestinian detainees had died in Israeli custody since

---

* B'Tselem's harrowing report collected testimonies from Palestinians who had been detained in Gaza, the West Bank, and Israel itself: 'Their testimonies uncover a systemic, institutional policy focused on the continual abuse and torture of all Palestinian prisoners. This includes frequent acts of severe, arbitrary violence; sexual assault; humiliation and degradation; deliberate starvation; forced unhygienic conditions; sleep deprivation; prohibition on, and punitive measures for, religious worship; confiscation of all communal and personal belongings; and denial of adequate medical treatment. These descriptions appear time and again in the testimonies, in horrifying detail and with chilling similarities. The prisoners' testimonies lay bare the outcomes of a rushed process in which more than a dozen Israeli prison facilities, both military and civilian, were converted into a network of camps dedicated to the abuse of inmates. Such spaces, in which every inmate is intentionally condemned to severe, relentless pain and suffering, operate in fact as torture camps'. The report documents a Palestinian male detainee being sodomised with a vegetable while being recorded by Israeli prison officers, as well as 'blows to the genitals and other body parts of naked prisoners; the use of metal tools and batons to cause genital pain; the photographing of naked prisoners; penises being grabbed; and strip-searches for the sake of humiliation and degradation'. It confirms that a Gazan detainee held at Sde Teiman detention centre had to have his leg amputated as a result of torture by Israeli forces and inadequate medical treatment. B'Tselem, *Welcome to Hell: The Israeli Prison System as a Network of Torture Camps* (August 2024), pp. 5, 58–61, 70–71.

October 7.[86] By February 2025 this figure had reached sixty, rising again to seventy-three by July.[87]

The details of the UN and B'Tselem reports are scarcely believable. They bring tears to the eyes. I can find no reaction, let alone the outcry one might have expected, from Keir Starmer, Rishi Sunak or Simon Walters, the British ambassador to Israel. Yet these were systematic war crimes committed on a horrifying scale by a country already on trial at the International Court of Justice for potential genocide.[88]

Inside Israel there was no condemnation from Prime Minister Netanyahu or President Herzog. Nor from opposition politicians Benny Gantz or Yair Lapid. As for Israel's national security minister Ben-Gvir, his spokesperson said that the minister was 'proud' of his prison policy, adding that it was in line with international law.[89] He defended the reservists facing potential charges of rape.[90] Israeli media reaction was more than relaxed. During one televised show a panellist suggested it should be legal to use rape as a form of torture.[91] These were unmistakable signs of a society in a state of advanced moral decay.

In 2021, Britain's then defence secretary Ben Wallace made a statement to parliament condemning British abuse of Iraqi detainees. He cited 'offences of assault and inhuman treatment' and made it plain that 'we deplore and condemn all such incidents'.[92] Compare that to David Lammy's belated statement to parliament in September 2024 concerning Israel's abuse of detainees in the Occupied Palestinian Territory. Lammy said the government was 'deeply concerned by credible claims of mistreatment of detainees', adding that these concerns had been 'forcefully' raised with the Israeli government.[93]

Compare the language here: Lammy said the British government was 'deeply concerned' about Israeli abuses whereas Wallace was clear that the British government's position was to 'deplore and condemn' the British Army's crimes.

Lammy referred to Israel's abuse of detainees simply as 'mistreatment' whereas Wallace characterised the British military's abuse of detainees as 'shocking and shameful incidents'.[94] The allegations made against British forces in Iraq are deadly serious but do not approach the scale of the inhuman conditions reportedly inflicted by Israel on Palestinian prisoners.

The same comparison can be made in media coverage. BBC *Panorama* and *The Sunday Times* carried out a joint investigation in 2019 into war crimes committed by the British Army in both Iraq and Afghanistan. They uncovered evidence of British soldiers torturing Iraqi civilians to death and murdering Afghan civilians, including children.[95] It is telling that there have been no investigations by BBC *Panorama* or *The Sunday Times* dedicated to Israeli war crimes. British mainstream politicians and media have a tendency to deal with Israeli atrocities in the muted tone of a bank manager drawing apologetic attention to a bounced check from a specially favoured client.

10

I SOLD MY FOOTAGE TO REUTERS

If you just stick to the facts and hold firm, truth is simply truth.

—*Annet de Graaf*

IN THIS CHAPTER I concentrate on a grotesque case of misreporting. The British media screened footage of Israeli football hooligans attacking Dutch citizens. But they suggested to viewers they were witnessing the opposite: Dutch thugs attacking Jews. This was a story which, as so often in British reporting of Gaza, conveniently fitted the Israeli narrative—and was duly amplified by British and Israeli politicians.

On November 8, 2024, the world awoke to the horrific news that a pogrom had been carried out in Amsterdam—the home of Anne Frank—against fans of the Israeli soccer team, Maccabi Tel Aviv, who were visiting the city for a Europa League fixture against Ajax.

'Youths on scooters . . . criss-crossed the Dutch capital in "hit-and-run" attacks on Maccabi Tel Aviv supporters', reported the BBC. The violence, it said, 'was especially shocking coming on the eve of commemorations marking *Kristallnacht*, the 1938 Nazi pogroms against German Jews'.[1]

'[A]ntisemitic rioters attacked Jews, Israeli citizens, just because they were Jews', said Israeli prime minister Benjamin Netanyahu.[2]

President Joe Biden condemned what he called 'despicable' attacks that 'echo dark moments in history when Jews were persecuted'.[3] And UK Foreign Secretary David Lammy said he was 'horrified' by what he called the 'antisemitic attacks on Israeli citizens'.[4]

Netanyahu declared he was dispatching 'two rescue planes' to Holland to bring Israelis home.[5]

But there was no pogrom in Amsterdam. The events of November 7 and 8 in the city were a case study in media manipulation, lazy journalism, and straightforwardly misleading reporting that served to perpetuate a narrative of Israelis as victims and Palestinians and their supporters as aggressors.

This is what happened.

A section of Maccabi's fan base have a well-deserved reputation for racism and violence. They have been filmed attacking anti-Netanyahu supporters at rallies. And when the club signed an Arab player he was booed and abused by his own fans.[6]

In March 2024 they were filmed beating an Arab man unconscious in the streets of Athens.[7]

The arrival of foreign football fans in a city is often an intimidating event, replete with its own rituals. Young male supporters derive a sense of power from physically taking over the streets.

In Amsterdam on the evening of November 6, the night before the Ajax-Maccabi game, Israeli supporters gathered in large numbers in the town centre chanting, in English, 'fuck you, fuck you Palestine'.

On two occasions they tore down Palestinian flags. Crucially a taxi was attacked.[8]

Taxi drivers throughout the world operate networks to provide assistance to each other when there is danger. Amsterdam is no exception and taxis quickly converged on the site of the attack.

Some 12 percent of Amsterdam's population is Muslim,[9] many hailing from Morocco. Large numbers of Muslims work as taxi drivers. As in Muslim communities throughout the world, feelings ran high over Gaza.

Just after 1:00 a.m. a message came through on a WhatsApp group chat that there was a big gathering of Maccabi fans in the Holland Casino in the town centre. The taxis now moved there and a number of Israeli fans found themselves subject to abuse and harassment as they left for their hotels.

Police say that in one of the WhatsApp groups they were monitoring, a member posted: 'TOMORROW AFTER THE MATCH AT NIGHT - PART 2 - JEW HUNT'.[10]

The following afternoon hundreds of Maccabi fans gather in Amsterdam's Dam Square, lighting flares and chanting. Individual pro-Palestinian demonstrators are roughed up.[11]

Elsewhere Ajax fans attempt to attack a small pro-Palestinian demo.[12] Ajax has a tradition of being a 'Jewish club', rather like Tottenham Hotspur in England: none of the violence in Amsterdam would be between Maccabi and Ajax fans.

Where Tottenham fans refer to themselves as 'yids', Ajax fans call themselves 'Super Jews'. In both cases abuse from rival fans often takes an antisemitic form. Ajax fans are called 'cancer Jews'[13] and some of the pro-Palestinian demonstrators echo this, shouting 'cancer Zionist, cancer Jews' at their assailants.

Maccabi fans also gather to taunt the pro-Palestine demo. One group of six allegedly make throat-slitting gestures, prompting two demonstrators to attack one of them. Dutch media later report that the man attacked was an Israeli police officer involved in work on national security issues.[14]

As they made their way to Amsterdam's Central Station for the journey to the stadium, Maccabi fans were filmed singing 'Death to the Arabs' and 'Let the Israeli army win and fuck the Arabs'.[15] At the start of the game some of them sang and chanted through a minute's silence for the victims of the flooding in Spain.[16] Spain is perceived as being sympathetic to the Palestinians.

The game ended at around 11:00 p.m.— Maccabi losing 5-0—and Maccabi fans took trains back to the centre of town.

There a local freelance photographer and video journalist called Annet de Graaf was waiting for them. She specialises in photographing and filming Amsterdam's police but had been surprised to find very few present.

Around 11:45 p.m. a group of about thirty Maccabi fans ran past her. She says they were already in an 'aggressive' mood. They began letting off fireworks and were soon joined by other fans outside the Central Station.

At 12:06 a.m. she filmed a fifty-one second clip that showed a mob of Maccabi fans chasing three local men down the street. One was caught and beaten.[17] A longer video shot immediately afterwards by a teenage journalist called Ome Bender shows Maccabi fans picking up pieces of wood and rampaging through the streets. They also threaten him and tell him to stop filming.[18]

Annet would stay in the area until around 2:00 a.m. She says she did not witness any actual attacks on Maccabi supporters, although she heard fireworks and a lot of shouting.

Videos posted online show that a number of attacks did occur during this period, mainly in side streets where groups of local youths were able to isolate and corner either individuals or small groups.[19]

'Where you from?' they demand. A flurry of kicks and punches follow for those they believe to be Israelis. The word Gaza is frequently heard. 'This is for the children', shouts one assailant in English as he assaults a cowering figure.

'Now you know how it feels', shouts another, again in English, throwing a firework at a figure attempting to flee.

In one video a man holding a child's hand is slapped around the head. Some fans are made to shout 'Free Palestine'.

Police quickly arrive and surround the main group of Maccabi supporters and shepherd them to their hotels. By 1:45 a.m. the city is quiet.

By the standards of European football hooliganism, the violence has been limited. As the authorities take stock at 3:00 a.m. they find there have been just seventeen emergency calls.

Six Maccabi supporters have received hospital treatment, one of them with a broken leg.[20]

What converts an ugly fracas into an international incident is the reaction of the Israeli government, which comes extraordinarily quickly.[21]

The Israeli ambassador to Holland, Modi Ephraim, texts the mayor of Amsterdam, Femke Halsema, just before 1:00 a.m. saying he is 'receiving calls about incidents'. She assures him the police are on top of it.[22]

Shortly afterwards Ephraim contacts the Israeli Foreign Ministry's 'Operations Room'. Benjamin Netanyahu, who notoriously slept through the night of October 6/7,[23] is woken at 3:00 a.m. Israeli time, 2:00 a.m. in Amsterdam—just two hours after the violence began.[24]

An hour later Israel's ambassador to the UN, Danny Danon, posts on X:

> We are receiving very disturbing reports of extreme violence against Israelis and Jews on the streets of Holland. There is a pogrom currently taking place in Europe in 2024. These are the true faces of the supporters of the radical terrorism we are fighting. The western world needs to wake up now!! This is the time when the UN should immediately and clearly condemn the violence of the Palestinians and their supporters.[25]

By now Ambassador Ephraim has told Mayor Halsema his government plans to send rescue planes. This is formally announced at 4:00 a.m.[26]

At 5:00 a.m. Ephraim texts the far-right Dutch politician Geert Wilders.[27] Within minutes Wilders posts on X in English: 'Looks like a Jew hunt in the streets of Amsterdam. Arrest and deport the multicultural scum that attacked Maccabi Tel Aviv supporters in our streets'.[28]

Under intense international pressure the Dutch feel they have little option but to accept the Israeli framing of events.

Mayor Halsema gives a press conference the next morning. 'We look back on a pitch-black night, and it is still dark today', she says. '[T]his brings back memories of pogroms . . . I am furious. I am ashamed'.[29]

Halsema would later say she regretted the use of the word pogrom:

> We were completely caught off guard by Israel. At 3 am, Prime Minister Netanyahu was already giving a lecture about what happened in Amsterdam, while we were still gathering the facts . . . the word pogrom became very political and actually became propaganda . . . used to discriminate against Moroccan Amsterdammers, Muslims.[30]

At a later trial of one of those accused of attacks on Maccabi fans, Holland's Public Prosecutor said his 'violence was not motivated by antisemitic sentiment' but had been 'influenced by the situation in Gaza and the equating of Maccabi supporters with the Israeli army'.[31] Some Maccabi supporters were army reservists.[32]

By then it was too late. The mayor's initial rhetoric was echoed by leaders around the world. The result was the unprecedented spectacle of the entire global media/political establishment rallying to the defence of racist football hooligans.[33]

Most remarkable of all, major international news outlets led their reports with footage or photographs from the fifty-one second video Annet de Graaf had shot at 12:06 a.m. showing a mob of Maccabi fans attacking individual Dutch citizens. It was almost universally reported as showing the precise opposite.[34]

That this should have happened is an indictment of the quality of journalism in newsrooms around the world.

Annet posted the video on X at 12:18 a.m. Dutch time, writing, in Dutch: 'Brawl in front of Amsterdam Central Station'. In a post twenty-three minutes earlier she'd made it clear, in English, that the group she was following were Maccabi fans.[35]

She made this clear again, in Dutch, in posts at 12:39 a.m.[36] and 12:43 a.m.[37]

Any close examination of the 12:06 a.m. clip would have shown that a number of the attackers were wearing the signature blue and yellow of Maccabi.

Annet quickly became aware her footage was being misrepresented. At 2:35 a.m. Dutch time pro-Israel blogger Eyal Yakoby posted it with the words: 'Breaking: Middle Eastern migrants continue to hunt down Jews in the streets of Amsterdam'.[38]

Annet responded, in English, just twenty minutes later: '[Y]ou are spreading fake news, this is a group of Maccabi supporters starting a fight and beating one Dutch man'.[39]

At 4:01 a.m. Dutch time Annet corrected a now deleted post by *Israel National News,* writing in English; 'You are misleading people with my created footage. What you see at the video is a group of Maccabi supporters beating a Dutch man.'[40]

By this time Annet was talking to the Reuters news agency. They offered her a hundred euros for the rights to the footage, eventually agreeing to pay two hundred. Annet made it crystal clear to them that the footage showed Maccabi supporters.[41]

'I sold my footage to Reuters to protect my footage and to make sure it was delivered to the world quickly and with accurate information', Annet says. It proved a misplaced hope.

Reuters provides footage to hundreds of news outlets worldwide. Clips are accompanied by a 'dope sheet', which gives information about what they show.

The dope sheet for Annet's footage told clients: 'Clashes broke out outside Amsterdam Central station in the early hours of Friday [November 8] in what Israeli authorities said was an attack targeting Israeli citizens . . . Eyewitness video showed a group of men running down a pavement and across a road as they chased some men and hit them.'[42]

Nowhere did it reflect Annet's clear statement that the 'group of men' were Maccabi supporters.

The dope sheet was updated at 7:14 a.m. Dutch time on November 8 to include the line: 'An eyewitness at the scene claims these people are fans of Maccabi Tel Aviv, however Reuters can not [*sic*] independently verify this claim.'[43]

This dope sheet was shared with Annet by a journalist on November 9. The following afternoon she wrote angrily to Reuters. 'I am not an eyewitness. I am the originator of the material. And I know for certain who these men were because I had been following them for 15 minutes.'[44]

By this time the teenager Ome Bender had posted his footage from the same location, also clearly identifying the people shown as Maccabi fans.[45]

On November 11 Reuters responded: 'We were not able to prove beyond doubt who was attacking who, due to their distance from the camera, the darkness of the video and the general disarray'. However, at this point, the dope sheet was updated to reflect the fact that Annet had been following the group for fifteen minutes.[46]

By now it was more than three days after Annet had posted the video and the story had dropped out of the headlines.

Even more remarkable was the behaviour of Sky News.

On the evening of November 8 Annet de Graaf was interviewed on Sky. Sky has subsequently been unable to provide Annet with a copy of this interview. But she says she gave a clear description of what her footage showed.[47]

On the morning of November 9 Sky News broadcast a piece by journalist Alice Porter that stood out from others in that it accurately reflected the events of November 7/8, putting the violence that followed the match in the context of the behaviour of Israeli fans over the previous two days.

It featured Annet de Graaf's 12:06 a.m. video accompanied by the script-line: 'Maccabi fans were seen attacking locals as a police car can be seen driving by'.[48]

Within hours it was taken down and replaced by a re-edited version of the report. The new video was accompanied by an editor's note stating: 'This is a re-edit of a previous video which didn't meet Sky News' standards for balance and impartiality'.[49]

In the new version, events in Amsterdam were reframed as 'antisemitic'.[50] Crucially, the line over Annet's footage was rewritten to say: 'A video posted on social media shows a large group of hooded men dressed in black, running down the street, and striking people at random'.[51]

Sky News was now suggesting it didn't know who they were.

The executive editor of Sky had instructed Porter, a junior reporter, to revoice the piece. He told me that he believed 'the original video didn't meet editorial standards because it didn't properly reflect overnight statements by Dutch politicians and the Dutch King who believed that the violence had been motivated by antisemitism'.[52]

Annet wrote to complain to Porter; to Barbara Serra, who had interviewed her on the evening of November 8; and to the Sky employee who had booked her for the interview. Porter and Serra did not respond. The interview booker told her he would look into it but never got back.[53]

Annet is now looking into the possibility of legal action against both Sky and Reuters.

Outlets such as *The Guardian*[54] and *The Washington Post*[55] did eventually produce more detailed, balanced analyses of the events in Amsterdam. The BBC belatedly acknowledged that its use of Annet's footage 'could have given' a misleading impression. The statement was published on its little read 'Corrections and Clarifications' page just before Christmas.[56]

Few other news outlets made any attempt to correct their inaccurate descriptions of Annet's material.

'Fifty-one seconds of footage has changed my life', Annet says. 'I didn't realise it would turn into such a political, evil mess. Sky and Reuters deceived me. What I've learned from this whole experience is that truth is incontrovertible. If you just stick to the facts and hold firm, truth is simply truth. Reuters and Sky thought they were dealing with a simpleton. But I wasn't prepared to be messed around'.*

* Reuters sent this statement: 'Reuters always works to independently verify UGC content [User Generated Content] before stating the provider's description of it as fact. Our original reporting about this incident and the video included initial claims from Israel, accurately attributed to their embassy in the US, that the attack was on Israelis. In the first release of the video, the participants were described as a "group of men" chasing and hitting "some men". We initially omitted the creator's account of events due to an oversight in the production chain inside Reuters. As Reuters continued to report, the news agency sought to address these issues and acknowledged that the omission gave rise to a possible misimpression about what the video depicted. The script and shot list that accompany each video edit was updated and corrected to include the creator's description of the video, that Maccabi Tel Aviv fans, Ajax supporters and locals were involved in altercations and noted that Reuters could not independently verify the nationalities and identities of participants in the footage. Reuters is committed to reporting news fairly, accurately and independently in keeping with the Thomson Reuters Trust Principles'. Sky said: 'Sky News is committed to accurate, impartial, and fair reporting that adheres to the Ofcom Broadcasting Code and our own rigorous editorial guidelines. We cover thousands of stories across thousands of hours each year and remain one of the most trusted news brands in the UK, according to Ofcom data'. I am grateful to Sky for speaking with me on an agreed off-the-record basis which enabled me to better understand their version of events.

The world's media had been astonishingly quick to leap on and amplify the narrative presented by the Israelis in the immediate aftermath of the Amsterdam violence.

Annet's determination to set the record straight so far as her own footage was concerned confronted news outlets with a dilemma. It was clear that a core piece of evidence revealed the precise opposite to the narrative they were reporting. In response they dragged their feet, obfuscated, and, in many instances, simply ignored the facts.

The contrast is painfully revealing of the mindset in the upper echelons of newsrooms around the world.

There are two sides to the story of what happened in Amsterdam. Certainly some Dutch Muslims attacked Maccabi supporters after the match, with no question that the violence was connected to Israel's assault on Gaza. The WhatsApp post calling for a 'JEW HUNT' was very ugly as were some of the chants. But some Maccabi fans had themselves perpetrated or provoked violence by attacking people and chanting racist slogans like 'Death to Arabs'—this at a moment when Israel's popular conscript army, in which some of the fans will have served, was committing well-documented atrocities against Palestinians. The media did not report these events in an even-handed way. Stirred up by Israeli politicians they reported on an anti-Jewish pogrom that didn't happen.

Evidence that contradicted this story was distorted to fit the narrative. Respected outlets including Reuters, Sky News, and the BBC presented footage of Maccabi supporters attacking Dutch people as if it showed attacks by Dutch racists against Jews. This was another example where media incompetence and deference to Israel led to factual errors which presented pro-Palestinians as the aggressors and Israeli football thugs as victims.

Arriving back at Ben Gurion Airport in Tel Aviv on November 8, Maccabi supporters danced and sang: 'Let the Israeli army win and fuck the Arabs'. They also sang: 'Why is school out in Gaza? There are no children left there'—a mocking reference to the fact that more than thirteen thousand Palestinian children had been killed by the Israeli military since October 7.[57]

Western news editors chose not to dwell on these images.

11

BEACHFRONT PROPERTY IN GAZA

I am in blood
Stepp'd in so far that, should I wade no more,
Returning were as tedious as go o'er.
—*Macbeth, Act Three, Scene Four*

October 2024

WE HEAR word of a conference on Israeli resettlement of Gaza. We drive from Jerusalem to the Gaza border to join it. We pass by the areas devastated on October 7, including some of the bomb shelters into which, in scenes of unbridled horror, Hamas gunmen threw grenades and slaughtered civilians with automatic gunfire. People have come to honour or to mourn the dead, leaving messages and pictures. These have become places of pilgrimage. More than a year after the Hamas atrocities, grief hangs heavy in the air. In the distance smoke billows from the Jabalia refugee camp, under attack by Israeli tank assault and air strikes. People have parked their cars to watch.

The conference is held in a closed military zone. Given that settling Gaza is not, as of yet, official Israeli government policy, this army support feels meaningful. The event is held in the open air, with singing and dancing creating the atmosphere of a revivalist meeting.

The regular thud of outgoing artillery fire interrupts speeches and is greeted with cries of 'God bless our brave soldiers'.[1] Many of the men present carry machine guns or pistols. 'In the event of a terrorist infiltration', booms the PA announcer, 'we ask you please not to fire your weapon. Let the security handle it. This is for everyone's safety'.

Supporters have come from across the world. A great grandmother from Melbourne is one of many who wear stickers supporting Meir Kahane, the late American-born rabbi and convicted terrorist. Kahane preached, according to the journalist and scholar Joshua Leifer, 'a shocking mixture of violent, exterminationist ethnonationalism and apocalyptic religious fundamentalism' while claiming that 'violence was a Jewish value and revenge a divine commandment'.[2]

We meet a businessman from Tel Aviv. He explains that Gaza would be 'a good solution for the real estate problem. We are a small country and there's big land here we can use'.[3]

We ask him how much seafront property might be worth. He replies, 'it will be a bargain. Properties in Tel Aviv next to the sea cost 20–50 million shekels. Here we can sell cheap'.[4] He is on the parliamentary candidates list for Otzma Yehudit (translation: Jewish Power) and predicts that its leader, Itamar Ben-Gvir, will be the next prime minister. We saw above that Ben-Gvir, the national security minister, carries the Kahanist flame in Israeli politics. He is due to arrive at the settler conference later in the afternoon.

The message that Gaza is up for grabs is led by organiser Daniella Weiss, from the settler group Nachala. She announces that families are ready to move to the edge of the enclave, claiming that 'millions of dollars' have been allocated for temporary housing units. Already six settler groups and more than seven hundred families are, she says, interested. Palestinians must leave Gaza. She tells us that they should go 'to England, to Africa, to Turkey'.[5]

Born under the British mandate at the end of World War Two, seventy-nine-year-old Weiss is queen of the settlers. According to the Nachala website she was 'raised in the ideology of the Lehi Underground Movement'—also known as the Stern Gang—which formed 'the background to all her communal undertakings'.[6] As I described in Chapter Two, Lehi was one of the Zionist terror groups that carried out the massacre of Palestinian Arabs at Deir Yassin in April 1948.*

Israel generally grants settlers the same impunity given to the Stern Gang eighty years ago. Nobody was ever charged in connection with the Deir Yassin massacre. Daniella Weiss has been a presence within the settler movement ever since Israel's occupation began.[7] Like most settlers she believes that Jews have a right to the land of biblical Israel ('Judea and Samaria'). In June 2024 Canada became the first country to sanction Weiss for 'facilitating, supporting or financially contributing to acts of violence by Israeli extremist settlers against Palestinian civilians and their property'.[8] Many dismiss Weiss' plans for the settlement of Gaza as fantasy. Prime Minister Benjamin Netanyahu has called the idea 'unrealistic'.[9] Weiss points out that many said the same about her ambitions in the West Bank. Today it's overrun by settlers: 'We have the political support, the public support and the experience of 55 years of settling Judea [and] Samaria and the Golan Heights. More than 330 settlements. We have accumulated a lot of experience to do this politically'.[10]

'Clearing Out' Gaza

The first foreign leader to visit Donald Trump at the White House is Benjamin Netanyahu. Trump unveils his plan: Palestinians will leave Gaza and 'are not going to want to go back'.[11] A Kahanist dream. The forcible deportation of a population is defined as a crime against humanity by the

---

* On April 9, 1948, members of the Irgun and Stern Gang attacked the Palestinian village of Deir Yassin, killing at least 107 Palestinians, many of them children, women, and the elderly. A 1948 report filed by the British delegation to the United Nations noted that the killing of 'some 250 Arabs, men, women and children . . . took place in circumstances of great savagery', continuing: 'Women and children were stripped, lined up, photographed, and then slaughtered by automatic firing and survivors have told of even more incredible bestialities. Those who were taken prisoner were treated with degrading brutality'. Al Jazeera, 'The Deir Yassin Massacre: Why It Still Matters 75 Years Later', aljazeera.com (9 April 2023).

International Criminal Court.[12] Trump is advocating ethnic cleansing, a term popularised in connection with the Yugoslav Wars in the 1990s.*

Back in London the next day's *Times* headline reads as follows: 'Trump Says US Will Take over Gaza Strip and Make It "Riviera of Middle East"'. The *Times* report neglects to inform readers that the mass displacement of Palestinians is a war crime.[13] *The Telegraph* produces a near identical headline.[14] Inside the paper an analysis piece makes the case that 'Trump's plan to make Gaza great again could really work'.[15] A BBC headline omits the expulsion plan entirely: 'Trump Suggests the US Could "Take over" and Redevelop Gaza as He Hosts Netanyahu'.[16] By contrast, Reuters avoids weasel words and plainly states: 'Trump Suggests Permanently Displacing Palestinians from Gaza'.[17]

Media reports make little of a throwaway line from Donald Trump, possibly informed by intelligence briefing, that Gaza's population has shrunk to around 1.7 to 1.8 million from 2.3 million before Israel's onslaught.[18] Media outlets do not ask where half a million Palestinians have gone. Trump describes Gaza as 'a demolition site. Virtually every building is down'.[19] He is by implication stating that Israel has committed grave international crimes. If Gaza is a demolition site, and virtually every building has been knocked down, one can only conclude that Israel has conducted one of the most brutal and indiscriminate bombing campaigns in the twenty-first century, a scale of destruction that is consistent with genocide.**

The failure of the British media to make anything of this commentary from the most pro-Israel of all US presidents is another reminder of its

---

* The *Cambridge Dictionary* defines ethnic cleansing as 'the organized, often violent attempt by a particular cultural or racial group to completely remove from a country or area all members of a different group'. Trump's scheme to remove Palestinians from Gaza, as part of an organised plan, fell within this definition.

** In his meeting with King Abdullah of Jordan a few days later, Trump used even more denunciatory language—again apparently without understanding the indictment he was issuing against the State of Israel. 'I've watched it so long, all the death and destruction of Gaza. A civilization has been wiped out in Gaza', he said. Intentionally wiping out a civilization is the definition of genocide. The American Presidency Project, 'Remarks Prior to a Meeting with King Abdullah II of Jordan and an Exchange with Reporters', presidency.ucsb.edu (11 February 2025).

indifference to Palestinian life. I could find no examples of journalists noting, much less correcting, the by this point long-debunked claim promoted by Netanyahu at the press conference that Hamas 'burned babies alive' on October 7.[20] There is no mention that an international warrant is already out for Netanyahu's arrest on suspicion of crimes against humanity, surely relevant in the context of this White House event. These indefensible omissions in the British press and broadcast coverage are consistent with patterns of reporting on Israel's destruction of Gaza since October 7.

Background to the Trump Plan

The Trump scheme had a lengthy gestation. As we have seen, versions of it were floated in two British outlets, *Fathom* and *The Spectator*, in the aftermath of October 7, by retired major general Giora Eiland and Douglas Murray respectively. Eiland wrote: 'The people should be told that they have two choices; to stay and to starve, or to leave. If Egypt and other countries prefer that these people will perish in Gaza, this is their choice. I prefer something that is more reasonable'.[21] Murray, an ally of Donald Trump, had entertained the proposition that Israel might 'clear all the Palestinians from that benighted strip', adding that '[i]t could be a good time to do it'.[22]

Within days of October 7, Israel's Intelligence Ministry drew up a plan for expelling Palestinians from Gaza into the Egyptian Sinai desert. It argued that ethnic cleansing 'will yield positive, long-term strategic outcomes for Israel, and is an executable option. It requires determination from the political echelon in the face of international pressure, with an emphasis on harnessing the support of the United States and additional pro-Israeli countries for the endeavor'.[23] Eiland agreed, saying that civilians from Gaza 'should cross the border to Egypt, temporarily or permanently'.[24]

When Egypt rejected the idea, Israeli finance minister Bezalel Smotrich promoted 'voluntary migration of the Arabs of Gaza to the countries of the world'.[25] Not to be outshone, Ben-Gvir insisted: 'We must promote a solution to encourage the emigration of the residents of Gaza'.[26] Netanyahu himself reportedly instructed an advisor to prepare a plan to reduce Gaza's population to the 'minimum possible' and said he was looking for countries to absorb Gazan refugees.[27] September 2024 saw the publication of what became known as the Generals' Plan, a proposal to expel the entire civilian population from northern Gaza to the south, then impose a starvation siege on the north.[28] The Generals' Plan was presented and promoted by Eiland. The BBC's Jeremy Bowen reported the following month that the plan appeared to be 'at the very least a strong influence on the tactics being used against the population' in Gaza.[29]

All these calls anticipated Donald Trump's proposal for 'a beautiful area to resettle people, permanently, in nice homes.'[30] Having gotten an American green light for ethnic cleansing, Netanyahu explicitly embraced it as an Israeli objective: 'We are demolishing more and more houses, they have nowhere to go back to,' he told the Knesset's Foreign Affairs and Defence Committee in May 2025. 'The only obvious outcome will be Gazans wishing to emigrate out of the Strip. Our main problem is finding receptive countries.'[31] He later added that Israel 'will take over Gaza and maintain security control forever . . . A decision has been made to go all the way.'[32]

Starmer and Trump

For Sir Keir Starmer, the return of Donald Trump as US president at the start of 2025 presented a particular challenge. Starmer had until then outsourced his position on Israel's wars to the Biden administration. That was not so easy to do with Trump, whose 'Gaza Plan' envisaged the US 'owning' Gaza, forcibly ejecting its population, and developing the ruins into prime 'real estate.'[33] Since the cornerstone of the plan was the explicit ethnic cleansing of Palestinians, it attracted no open support from other countries—except Israel, whose prime minister made its implementation a condition of ending the military onslaught.[34]

With Trump shifting the US position to one the UK could not formally support, a rhetorical gap opened between the two countries. In March 2025 an emboldened Israel ended a brief ceasefire to resume its onslaught on Gaza with even greater ferocity while preventing all food and aid from entering the Strip. In May, Israel 'intensified' its offensive still further with the avowed aim of 'conquering' and holding Gaza.[35] While US support stayed steadfast, the UK could not officially endorse actions so diametrically opposed to its longstanding positions.

In mid-May, Starmer issued a joint statement with Emmanuel Macron and Mark Carney, the leaders of France and Canada, declaring their strong opposition to 'the expansion of Israel's military operations in Gaza', which they described as 'disproportionate' and 'egregious'.

'If Israel does not cease the renewed military offensive and lift its restrictions on humanitarian aid', the statement read, 'we will take further concrete actions in response'.[36] Finance Minister Smotrich branded the statement antisemitic, charging that Starmer, Macron, and Carney had 'morally aligned themselves with a terrorist organisation'.[37]

Thereafter British government ministers began to refer to Israel's continuing operation in Gaza as 'intolerable'.[38] In the House of Commons, Starmer said a ceasefire was 'the only way to free the hostages'. He had previously opposed a ceasefire on the grounds it would leave the hostages 'still held'.[39]

Taking its cue from the government, the British media changed gear. Suddenly Israeli atrocities against Palestinians, such as the killing of nine children from the same family near Khan Younis in May 2025, were reported prominently and graphically.[40] The BBC ran a long though belated piece by its Middle East editor Jeremy Bowen asking whether Israel was breaking international law—and even committing genocide.[41]

This rhetorical shift from the government was not supported by substantial measures, despite a threat of 'further action' if Israel did not change course. Initially all that materialised was the suspension of the UK's trade talks with Israel and the sanctioning of three Israeli settler activists, two settler outposts, and two settler organisations. Among those sanctioned was Daniella Weiss, who had featured in a consciousness-changing BBC documentary about the West Bank by Louis Theroux.[42] Later, two Israeli ministers, Ben-Gvir and Smotrich, were also sanctioned '[i]n their personal capacity' for their 'repeated incitements of violence against Palestinian communities'.[43]

There remains a mystery about these sanctions. The Starmer government went out of its way to make clear that the measures were directed at incitement to settler violence in the West Bank.[44] The situation there was indeed horrifying, as the Israeli state routinely colluded in settler pogroms. Yet no comparable punishment was directed at Israel's criminal conduct in Gaza where the situation was far more deadly, Israeli atrocities far more widespread, and the humanitarian situation unspeakable.

Why did Starmer hold off applying sanctions in connection with Gaza? There are two plausible answers. The first is that the British government would have implicitly acknowledged its own complicity had it sanctioned Netanyahu and other Israelis in connection with incitement to violence and crimes against humanity committed by Israel in Gaza.

The second is that he failed to sanction the bloodstained Israeli prime minister because Britain preferred to carry on doing business as normal with Israel. On May 13, an unpublicised gathering was held at the British Museum to celebrate seventy-seven years since Israel's declaration of independence. The event, which was organised by the Israeli embassy, was attended by Kemi Badenoch, Nigel Farage, the comedian Jimmy Carr and—importantly—the minister for defence procurement and industry Maria Eagle. In remarks to the attendees Eagle celebrated the Britain-Israel alliance, recounting how '[t]he UK stood with Israel, with the RAF conducting surveillance flights over the Eastern Mediterranean in support of hostage rescue efforts.'[45]

The independent MP Shockat Adam later asked David Lammy in parliament: 'If the Foreign Secretary does indeed believe that the behaviour of the Israeli Government is abominable, may I ask why a Minister partied with the Israelis just last week, while 370 Gazans were massacred and the world was mourning for them? Does that not undermine trust in the UK's role in this conflict?'[46]

Lammy answered: 'it is important that we make a distinction between the Israeli people and the current direction of the Israeli Government, and I insist that we be precise in our language on that point.'[47]

This was either pedantry, dishonesty or culpable ignorance on Lammy's part. The party referred to by Adam was organised by the Israeli embassy and attended by the Israeli ambassador, Tzipi Hotovely: this was not, as Lammy seemed to imply, a non-governmental or unpolitical Israeli event.

A week after trade talks were suspended, Britain's trade envoy to Israel, Lord Austin, popped up in Haifa to 'drum up business.'[48] He need not have bothered—export data showed British arms sales to Israel were actually ballooning. Britain exported more pounds worth of military equipment in the final three months of 2024—after the suspension of twenty-nine export licences by the Labour government—than it had done in the years 2020–23 combined.[49]

Britain continued to supply components to the 'global pool' of spare parts for the F-35 fighter jet—so crucial to Israel's operation in Gaza and responsible for untold carnage on the ground. The carve-out of F-35 parts from the arms export licence suspensions in September 2024 was the subject of a legal challenge by the Palestinian human rights organisation Al-Haq. In court, the cynicism of the government's position was laid bare. It argued it had no evidence that international humanitarian law was breached in Gaza because it did not know what Israel had intended to target in each attack. As one of Al-Haq's lawyers in the case, Dearbhla Minogue, explained, 'It's absolutely absurd to say: "Oh well we don't know what Israel's side of the story is for each individual incident, so we can't come to a conclusion on any of them"'.

Using this logic, the government's lawyers also claimed there was no genocide in Gaza because they had seen no evidence of breaches of international humanitarian law.[50] This contradicted what had become the government's official holding position—that it could not determine whether genocide was occurring before the International Court of Justice had ruled.

Britain went on shielding Israel from charges of genocide and supplying arms as well as F-35 components even as it described Israel's actions as 'intolerable'. For all its professed outrage over Israel's starvation blockade on Gaza, Britain did not even attempt to airlift aid to the territory itself, despite having previously done so.[51] Britain still refused to recognise Palestine as a state or commit itself to the prosecution of Israeli war criminals, including British nationals who may have served in the IDF. Crucially, British surveillance flights continued unabated from RAF Akrotiri in Cyprus.[52]

Lammy denied that information from the flights was being given to the Israeli military to help with the Israeli campaign, telling the BBC's *Today* programme in July 2025: 'We are not assisting, and it would be quite wrong for the British government to assist, in the prosecution of this war in Gaza. We are not doing that and would never do that'.[53] But just a few weeks later, *The Times* received confirmation from government sources that '[i]ntelligence gathered by undisclosed RAF aircraft... is being handed over to the Israeli military so it has real-time information on the movement of captured Israelis'. The admission came after an American spy plane hired by the UK to undertake the RAF mission accidentally left its transponder on while overflying the live battle zone of Khan Younis. *The Times* quoted former British Army major general Charlie Herbert saying: 'in reality that intelligence is just as likely to be used as targeting for Hamas and others'.[54]

The picture of an essentially unchanged strategic position, with Starmer continuing to genuflect before an out-of-control US president, was confirmed when Israel launched its air assault on Iran in June 2025. International law forbids resort to force except in self-defence against an armed attack or else an imminent and overwhelming military threat. The Israeli attack on Iran—later joined by the US—was an aggression, defined at Nuremberg as the supreme international crime.

When it became clear that Israel's action was coordinated with the US, the British prime minister—despite having been 'cut out of the loop'—absurdly characterised Israel's unprovoked aggression as an act of 'self-defence'.[55] Among the first casualties of the new war was the government's shift towards tougher rhetoric on Gaza—a G7 statement signed by Britain on June 17 represented a retreat even from the UK's previous position, with a ceasefire in Gaza now made contingent on 'the resolution of the Iranian crisis'.[56]

Faced with unambiguous cases of unlawful military action, involving assassinations and the targeting of Iranian civilian infrastructure with the goal of regime change, Starmer painfully avoided answering whether Israel's attack on Iran was legal.[57] Yet again, faced with a choice between clinging to the US or standing up for international law, he had chosen the former.

Starmer and the Protestors

The most consistent voice speaking for international law remained the Palestine solidarity marchers. For them the arrival of the Starmer administration had coincided with a shift in tone. The inflammatory rhetoric deployed by the Sunak government against pro-Palestinian demonstrations was abandoned for a more measured approach in public communications.

Despite this softer rhetoric the policing of protests became more authoritarian. Though the Conservative government had put pressure on the police, the policing of the marches had largely adhered to established protocols. Under the stewardship of a new home secretary, Yvette Cooper, this changed.

The new dispensation became evident in the run-up to the Gaza ceasefire march on January 18. It was led by high-profile figures including Jeremy Corbyn MP and his one-time shadow chancellor John McDonnell MP. The delegation planned to walk towards the BBC building carrying bunches of flowers symbolising their respect and sadness for the children killed in Gaza.

The organisers acknowledged they would likely be stopped by police before reaching their destination. If stopped, they intended to peacefully lay the flowers at the feet of the police as a symbolic gesture of their obstruction.[58]

The delegation moved from Whitehall towards Portland Place, where the BBC is located. Among them was Stephen Kapos, an eighty-seven-year-old survivor of the Holocaust, who was interviewed for this book after the event.[59] He said that a thin line of police officers linking arms formed before the protesters reached Trafalgar Square.

When the delegation approached this line the police 'melted away', according to Kapos. Footage from the day appears to back this up. He says there may have been some 'minimal contact' between protesters and police at that line but nothing that would justify mass arrests.

Kapos believes this police line was strategically placed to 'trap' protesters into committing a technical misdemeanour. Further along, protesters encountered another police line. This time, according to Kapos, the police 'actually let us virtually go through'. Again, Kapos suggests this was a deliberate tactic to catch protesters in a technical violation of the police-demanded route.

Yet more police and police vans were waiting near the National Gallery. Chief steward Chris Nineham attempted to negotiate with police to go further. Suddenly, 'as if they were shot out of a cannon', a group of policemen grabbed Nineham, Kapos says. They pushed him to the ground in what he describes as 'predetermined violence'. Following the incident, Palestine Solidarity Campaign Director Ben Jamal instructed protesters to turn around. The group headed back towards Trafalgar Square, where police reportedly told protesters they had 'no right' to be.

Stephen Kapos received a letter from police inviting him to a formal interview. He was cited for two contraventions of Sections 12 and 14 of the Public Order Act 1986. First, he was accused of taking part in a group that marched from the assembly point towards a prohibited area against police orders. Second, he was cited for breaching a police line in the process. Jeremy Corbyn and John McDonnell were interviewed under caution, again a ramping up of political pressure by the police.

The police arrested seventy-seven marchers, alleging 'a coordinated effort to breach Public Order Act conditions and cause serious disruption to Londoners'.[60] The high number of arrests contrasted starkly with minimal tallies on previous Gaza demonstrations. Something had changed. Labour was keen to echo the police's narrative. Following the arrests, Home Secretary Yvette Cooper wrote on X: 'Everyone should be able to worship in peace. [The Met Police] have my support in ensuring that synagogues were not disrupted'.[61]

Cooper was here referring to objections from the pro-Israel Board of Deputies of British Jews that the march would cause disruption at the Central Synagogue on Great Portland Street, about two hundred yards from the BBC's Broadcasting House.*

* See Post by @BoardofDeputies on X (14 January 2024). The rally organisers insisted that 'there has not been a single documented case of threat or incident at a synagogue in relation to the national Palestine marches that have taken place' as of January 2025, adding that 'we count a large, self-organised Jewish bloc as some of our most indefatigable supporters'. They were supported by a letter signed eventually by more than a thousand members of the British Jewish community. The statement, signed by senior lawyers Sir Geoffrey Bindman KC and Sir Stephen Sedley KC, author Gillian Slovo, film director Mike Leigh, actress Miriam Margolyes, and singer/songwriter Leon Rosselson, criticised the Met's BBC protest ban as bowing to 'partisan campaigning aimed at preventing peaceful and lawful assembly'. We approached the Community Security Trust (CST), a charity that 'advises and represents the UK's Jewish community on matters of antisemitism, terrorism, policing, and security', to respond to the march organisers' assertion that there has not been a documented threat or incident at a synagogue related to the national Palestine marches. They would not give an on-the-record response.

But the home secretary's logic did not appear to make sense. The organisers had agreed to change the route of the march so that it would start in Whitehall and end rather than begin at the BBC. That way there could be no danger of disturbing worshippers emerging from Shul on Saturday morning—not least because the demonstration would end up at the BBC several hours after Shul had ended. This plan had, however, been rejected by the police, who seemed determined to prevent any protest against the national broadcaster.[62]

Green Party Deputy Leader Zack Polanski, a Jewish member of the London Assembly who spoke at the demonstration, wrote to the home secretary to express frustration over statements by her and the police. In particular he rejected Cooper's claim that mass arrests had prevented disruption at the synagogue: 'Many Jewish participants, including myself, find this accusation offensive. The goal was to protest the BBC's failure to report the genocide accurately, and this was planned [for] . . . way after [Shul] services had ended'.[63]

He added: 'Public trust in our institutions is already fragile. Politicising the police and smearing innocent people only worsens this. I urge you to review the evidence including footage from body worn cameras from the event, retract your comments and clarify the situation with the Metropolitan Police'.[64]

Polanski also noted Metropolitan Police tweets alleging that people were 'forcing through' police lines. 'Such language feeds false and often racist

---

The CST's 2023 and 2024 *Antisemitic Incident Reports* do attribute incidents of antisemitism to London Palestine solidarity events. In 2023, the CST recorded 'at least 44' incidents that 'took place at, or on the way to or from, anti-Israel protests or vigils for the hostages', while the charity recorded twenty-eight such incidents in 2024 (a figure which may have been higher but for a technical hitch). As the CST does not provide incident specifics, it is not possible to determine whether any of these recorded incidents occurred at a synagogue or to verify an individual incident's connection to a national Palestine march. We asked the Board of Deputies and the Central Synagogue the same question but received no response from either. 'UPDATED: 1000+ Jews Reject Met Police Ban on BBC Palestine Protest', jewishvoiceforlabour.org.uk (17 January 2025). Palestine Solidarity Campaign, 'The March for Palestine Is STILL ON—Despite the Met Police's Attempt to Disrupt It', thecanary.co (17 January 2025).

narratives about the Palestine Solidarity Campaign's protests that have been peaceful', Polanski said.[65]

In an interview for this book,[66] Polanski said the police had 'lied' by claiming marchers actively broke through police lines. Polanski and the organisers say they were allowed through by officers.

Holocaust Survivors and Descendants Against the Genocide

By chance I had interviewed Stephen Kapos two years earlier, several months before October 7. He'd told me how he remembered, as a small boy in Hungary in 1944, his mother and aunts cutting out yellow stars and sewing them onto his clothes. He also remembered hiding from the Arrow Cross fascist movement, which rounded up Jews, shot them, and dumped them into the Danube.

He spoke of the clandestine shuffle between safe houses in Buda, when Jewish boys were spirited from one place to another to avoid detection from the local SS officers as the Russian army approached and fighting engulfed them. He remembered the panic of his aunt, who was in charge of a group of boys pretending to be war orphans, when she was invited to sit for a mournful Christmas meal with Wehrmacht officers. It was a scene worthy of Quentin Tarantino's *Inglourious Basterds*: 'I remember the long white table, set beautifully with the Christmas Tree at one end, and the huge swastika flag at the other. We were seated between these old German soldiers. My aunt was in a panic, because if any boy had wanted to go to the loo, the cover would have been blown'.[67]

When interviewed again in the aftermath of the march Kapos explained he had been a regular attender: 'I am in a small group entitled "Holocaust Survivors and Descendants Against the Genocide". Quite a lengthy title. We have placards that we hang from our necks and stand on the sides of marches, mainly to show the demonstrators that we're really identified as Jews, to show that there is no uniformity of support for the Israeli actions during the genocide'.

He compared his experience of being on the run in Hungary towards the end of World War Two with the plight of Palestinians in Gaza:

> We were hiding in children's homes with false papers and names. But because of the fighting, we had to relocate several times, which was extremely hard to do because we were also in hiding. So we had this combination of fearful situations—we did not have safe destinations, just temporary ones, and then we'd move again and so on.
>
> This was quite similar to some of these very spontaneous, short-term orders to move out for the Palestinians and then go to a supposedly safe location. What it means for a family to uproot on such drastic, short notice is an experience that is difficult to understand from the outside, but we were well within it. It means that sometimes you have to make a decision about what to do with a family member who cannot move. I can imagine how awful that is.
>
> Also, having to follow or not follow orders and information from your enemy, and yet make life-defining decisions based on that kind of information. Again, this resonates with certain experiences within my family.

Kapos described the protest marches as 'extremely friendly sorts of places where people very often attend as family travellers with children and all kinds.'[68] As a Holocaust survivor, Kapos is incensed by characterisations of the protests as 'hate marches' or antisemitic gatherings. He is not the only one.

Thirteen Holocaust survivors and survivor descendants wrote to *The Guardian* opposing the ban on the national demonstration outside the BBC on January 18, stating: 'Along with thousands of other openly Jewish protesters, we have attended numerous Palestine demos in London and have received nothing but support and warmth from our fellow demonstrators. To suggest that the 18 January march is a threat to Jews, or is in any way antisemitic, is simply a fabrication in order to restrict everyone's right to protest.'[69]

And forty Holocaust survivors and their descendants wrote an open letter following the news of Kapos' police interview, saying: 'Any repression of the right to protest is bad enough—but to persecute a Jewish 87 year old whose Holocaust experiences compel him to speak out against the Gaza genocide, is quite appalling.

'This very concerning development makes it even more important for Jews to speak out against the genocide'.[70]

There is a paradox here. Politicians and media portray the marchers as anti-British. In truth they profoundly represent British values as these have traditionally been understood: belief in fairness, tolerance, the rule of law. Standing up for the underdog. Compassion, kindness, a sense of civic responsibility and what George Orwell called decency. A belief in community, solidarity, and human rights, and a conviction that we owe a duty not just to ourselves and our own communities but to all human beings.

British journalists and politicians, acting in a de facto alliance with the far right, have painted the marchers as supporters of terrorism and enemies of civilisation—for having the audacity to march against the livestreamed slaughter of Palestinians in Gaza. These accusations carry no weight. The peace marchers have been supporting a global moral order that is under attack.

The Atlantic Charter and the United Nations

In support of Israel, British politicians, backed by mainstream media, have given the green light to mass murder, assassination, torture, law-breaking, and chaos. In the process they have repudiated the international legal order that Britain herself helped establish to prevent a repetition of the horrors of World War Two.

In August 1941, Winston Churchill and Franklin D. Roosevelt met at sea off the coast of Newfoundland. By this time, Hitler's Germany had conquered much of Europe and the threat of Nazi tyranny had grown to enormous proportions.

After days of meetings, Churchill and Roosevelt agreed the text of what has come to be known as the Atlantic Charter. Their document listed the 'common principles' that would shape American and British policy and provide the basis 'for a better future of the world'.

Churchill and Roosevelt hoped for 'a peace which will afford to all nations the means of dwelling in safety within their own boundaries, and which will afford assurance that all the men in all the lands may live out their lives in freedom from fear and want'.

They declared their belief 'that all of the nations of the world, for realistic as well as spiritual reasons, must come to the abandonment of the use of force'.[71]

These principles would go on to be enshrined in the UN Charter, whose preamble states that 'the peoples of the United Nations', being determined 'to save succeeding generations from the scourge of war, which twice in our lifetime has brought untold sorrow to mankind, and to reaffirm faith in fundamental human rights, in the dignity and worth of the human person, in the equal rights of men and women and of nations large and small, and to establish conditions under which justice and respect for the obligations arising from treaties and other sources of international law can be maintained, and to promote social progress and better standards of life in larger freedom' will work to practice tolerance, maintain international peace and security, ensure that armed force will not be used 'save in the common interest', and promote economic and social development for all.[72]

At the San Francisco Conference of 1945, where the UN Charter was agreed and signed, Britain played a crucial role: 'it cannot be denied', reflected the diplomat Gladwyn Jebb, 'that in the production of the great plan now brought to fruition at San Francisco, HMG in the UK played a very great, perhaps even a preponderating part'.[73] Jebb himself was appointed the first acting secretary general of the new body.

The UN was thus in large part a British invention. The very first meeting of the UN General Assembly was held in London, January 1946, at Methodist Central Hall, while the Security Council first met at Church House, Westminster.[74] 'Foreign Office officials', says Foreign, Commonwealth, and Development Office historian Richard Smith, 'played a key role in planning and establishing the UN'.[75]

The values underpinning the UN were reasserted as recently as the 2021 G7 summit in Cornwall, when Prime Minister Boris Johnson and US President Joe Biden signed a 'revitalised' New Atlantic Charter. The two leaders resolved to 'strengthen the institutions, laws, and norms that sustain international co-operation to adapt them to meet the new challenges of the 21st century, and guard against those that would undermine them'. They also pledged to 'remain united behind the principles of sovereignty, territorial integrity, and the peaceful resolution of disputes'.[76]

This magnificent vision has always been more aspirational than descriptive. But with the brazen destruction of Gaza it has entirely collapsed.

The United Nations has come under brutal attack—literally so. With the support of the United States and Britain, Israel has killed well over three hundred workers from the United Nations Relief and Works Agency,[77] the largest supplier of humanitarian aid to Palestinians.

The US, again supported by Britain, was dismissive of the United Nations' judicial arm, the International Court of Justice, after its provisional order on genocide in January 2024. More recently Britain and the United States did nothing to support the ICJ's advisory opinion, issued on July 19, 2024, that the Israeli occupation of the West Bank and Gaza is illegal and that Israel's settlement policy is in breach of the Fourth Geneva Convention.[78] Britain didn't lift a finger in support of Gladwyn Jebb's successor, the UN secretary general António Guterres, even as he came under persistent personal attack.

We have refused to allow the United Nations to play the peace-making role envisaged more than eighty years ago. In a bleak irony that could never have been predicted when the United Nations Charter was agreed, the United States and Britain have undermined to the point of wrecking the institutions set up after the Second World War to ensure a fair and peaceful world. In an even bleaker irony those who stood up for Churchill and Roosevelt's vision have been reviled and stigmatised as enemies of civilisation itself.

By the darkest and most terrible irony of all, the motive for this epochal wrecking has been to abet Israel, state of the Jews, the people whose monumental suffering provided the moral impetus for bringing the post-war order into being.

Enter David Cameron

The United Nations is not the only global institution assailed by the United States and Britain. The same applies to the International Criminal Court. We have already seen how the Sunak government dismissed the ICC decision to issue arrest warrants against Israeli prime minister Netanyahu and his then defence minister Yoav Gallant. They stood accused of responsibility for '[s]tarvation of civilians as a method of warfare', '[e]xtermination and/or murder . . . as a crime against humanity', and '[p]ersecution as a crime against humanity'.[79]

In June 2025 *Middle East Eye* reported that Britain had threatened the ICC chief prosecutor Karim Khan ahead of that decision.

MEE said that David Cameron, then British foreign secretary, phoned Khan while the prosecutor was on an official visit to Venezuela on April 23, 2024. It also reported Cameron as having said that if the ICC issued warrants for the arrest of Israeli leaders, Britain would 'defund the court and withdraw from the Rome Statute'.[80]

To his enormous credit, Khan, a British citizen, seemingly stood up to Lord Cameron. Six months later, in November 2024, the ICC went ahead and issued arrest warrants for Benjamin Netanyahu and his former defence minister Yoav Gallant. *Middle East Eye* reported that Lord Cameron took an 'aggressive tone' and shouted over Khan.

If *Middle East Eye* is correct that Cameron resorted to menaces in order to protect the reputation of Netanyahu, a suspected war criminal, this would place Britain among a group of gangster nations and rogue states for whom might is right. Other members of this group include Netanyahu's Israel, Trump's United States, and Putin's Russia (which issued an arrest order for Khan in 2023 in response to ICC warrants issued against Russian president Vladimir Putin and his commissioner for children's rights).

True to form, no mainstream British media publication followed up the *Middle East Eye* story, though it has been followed by foreign media and alternative outlets. According to *MEE*, Cameron told Khan he was 'on the brink of making a huge mistake. You sometimes need to take a step back and consider things'.

MEE reported that Khan would not give ground, telling the foreign secretary there was a 'serious risk' that many in the world would view the rules-based order as 'not being applied equally'. This confrontation between a principled adherence to the rule of law and the thuggish intimidation of raw power repeats itself again and again through history. In British relations with the ICC, I know of nothing comparable to Cameron's conversation with the ICC chief prosecutor.*

Lord Cameron, Karim Khan, and the British Foreign Office declined to comment. Friends of Lord Cameron have told me that there was a 'robust call', but insisted that he did not threaten to defund the ICC and renounce the Rome Statute. They have also told me that Lord Cameron 'simply pointed out that there would be strong voices in the Conservative Party that would adopt that approach'.

---

* There is ample precedent elsewhere. In 2002, Bush administration official and prominent neoconservative John Bolton reportedly travelled to the Hague offices of José Bustani, then head of the Organization for the Prohibition of Chemical Weapons. 'Cheney wants you out', Bustani remembers Bolton saying, referring to the then US vice president. 'You have 24 hours to leave the organization . . . We know where your kids live. You have two sons in New York'. In 2024, Khan's predecessor as ICC chief prosecutor Fatou Bensouda claimed she had faced 'thug-style tactics' including 'direct threats to my person and family' while working on sensitive cases. A *Guardian* investigation reported that Yossi Cohen, then head of Israel's Mossad intelligence agency, had met secretly with Bensouda and exerted pressure on her not to proceed with an investigation into Israel. Cohen was allegedly acting as Netanyahu's 'unofficial messenger' and is alleged to have told Bensouda: 'You don't want to be getting into things that could compromise your security or that of your family'. According to *The Guardian*, this was part of a wider Israeli 'war' against the Court that began in 2015 and involved surveillance, hacking, interceptions, and a diplomatic 'smear campaign'. See: Mehdi Hasan, '"We Know Where Your Kids Live": How John Bolton Once Threatened an International Official', theintercept.com (29 March 2018) (Bolton). Harry Davies, 'Revealed: Israeli Spy Chief 'Threatened' ICC Prosecutor over War Crimes Inquiry', *The Guardian* (28 May 2024) ('war'). Harry Davies et al., 'Spying, Hacking and Intimidation: Israel's Nine-Year "War" on the ICC Exposed', *The Guardian* (28 May 2024). Harry Davies, 'Former ICC Chief Prosecutor Says She Faced Threats and "Thug-Style Tactics"', *The Guardian* (27 November 2024) (Cohen). A spokesperson for Israel's Prime Minister's Office accused *The Guardian* of 'false and unfounded allegations'.

As this book went to press, in August 2025, Khan's position had become desperate. In February 2025 Donald Trump sanctioned the ICC chief prosecutor because of the arrest warrants issued for Netanyahu and Gallant. *MEE* reports: 'He has had his US visa revoked and his wife and children have been banned from travelling to the US. His bank accounts have been frozen in the UK'. Friends have told me that he cannot go shopping or pay his utility bills as a result.

Back to *MEE*, reporting in June 2025: 'Khan is currently on leave after attempts to suspend him failed, and pending a UN investigation into allegations of sexual misconduct towards a colleague. He denies the allegations, which have not been referred to Dutch police.'[81]

We should note here that the Rome Statute that established the ICC does not just outlaw the commission of war crimes. It also criminalises those who seek to prevent war crimes from being prosecuted.

The relevant passage of the Rome Statute, Article 70(1)(d), awards the Court jurisdiction over those responsible for '[i]mpeding, intimidating or corruptly influencing an official of the Court for the purpose of forcing or persuading the official not to perform, or to perform improperly, his or her duties'.

A threat to 'defund the court and withdraw from the Rome Statute' falls squarely within ICC jurisdiction. It may also constitute an offence under British common law.[82]

CONCLUSION: GAZA, JULY 2025

The horror! The horror!
—*Joseph Conrad, Heart of Darkness*

GAZA HAS LONG been one of the world's most densely populated places. Now the surviving population is squeezed into less than 20 percent of the enclave, with most of the territory under Israeli military control or displacement orders. One toilet for two hundred people. Mice, rats, and parasitic worms proliferate. The stink. The shame. Little or no privacy, a special problem for women. Some try not to drink water to avoid going to the toilet.[1] A rise in premature births, low birth weights, and deformities. Toxic weapons used by the IDF, including white phosphorus, are the probable cause of the latter.[2]

Renewed warnings of famine,[3] the most extreme form of food crisis, when food vanishes and communities collapse amidst mass death. As recalled in Chapter Nine, famine warnings in March and November 2024 prompted international pressure that forced Israel to relax its blockade. But only for a while. In March 2025 another Israeli closure led to renewed alarm.[4] Amnesty International, which months earlier concluded that Israel was perpetrating genocide, calls the situation a 'manmade catastrophe'.[5]

No level of international condemnation seems able to induce Israel to let the population breathe. With the iron-clad support of the United States, abetted by British military and diplomatic complicity, no change is forthcoming: the ruin of Gaza continues without the least abatement.

The Gaza Humanitarian Foundation

Israel partly opened the borders in late May 2025 to allow in small amounts of aid.[6] This time it used its own aid distribution vehicle: the so-called Gaza Humanitarian Foundation (GHF). This is an Israeli-American-backed project tasked with taking over aid delivery in Gaza at the expense of the traditional agencies, including those of the UN. It is there to serve Israeli objectives.

First it is a propaganda tool, to polish the image of the Israeli campaign.

Second, it gives Israel more direct control over aid distribution, which in turn enables it to manipulate the population of Gaza and smooth the process of taking over the Strip. By distributing aid primarily in the south, Israel can force the population to move there—as a prelude to its deportation.

Third, Israeli aid distribution centres become a lure to entrap desperate Palestinians and kill them.

The GHF was registered in Delaware, USA, in February 2025. In Gaza it bypassed the UN and employed armed American private security contractors; little was known about who funded it or where it originated.

Jake Wood, an American veteran experienced in humanitarian operations, resigned as head of the GHF in May: he confessed that 'it is not possible to implement this plan while also strictly adhering to the humanitarian principles of humanity, neutrality, impartiality, and independence, which I will not abandon'.[7]

Johnnie Moore, a Christian evangelical preacher and public relations executive, is executive chairman: 'Moore . . . was among President Trump's evangelical "advisory board" of faith leaders who laid hands on the president and prayed for him in the Oval Office'.*

The secretary general of the Norwegian Refugee Council, Jan Egeland, explained that the GHF was 'militarised, privatised, politicised' and 'not in

* I have drawn heavily on the investigative reporting of BBC State Department correspondent Tom Bateman: 'Searching for Answers about US-Backed Aid Agency in Gaza', bbc.co.uk (15 June 2025). See also: Tom Bennett, 'Head of Controversial Israel-Backed Gaza Aid Group Resigns', bbc.co.uk (26 May 2025). Mahmoud Mushtaha, 'How Israel Is Engineering Gaza's Social Collapse', 972mag.com (12 June 2025).

conformity with neutrality'.[8] Tom Fletcher, emergency relief coordinator at the UN, called the Israeli aid distribution model a 'fig leaf for further violence and displacement', which 'makes starvation a bargaining chip'.[9]

Israeli aid distribution centres became the sites of a succession of massacres, for the most part unreported in the Western media—note that Israel has continued to keep international journalists out of Gaza.

This was predictable and predicted. Jeremy Konyndyk, the head of Refugees International, warned after the first day of GHF distribution that the risk of another flour massacre* was 'baked into the GHF model'.[10] Konyndyk concluded that '[t]he Israeli government is weaponizing aid and all involved with the GHF are abetting war crimes'.[11]

It is still not known who exactly is behind this mysterious so-called aid agency. *The New York Times* reported that the plan originated in Israel.[12]

What is clear is that the GHF had nothing to do with humanitarianism: scores of innocent, despairing Palestinians were slaughtered because the proper organisations were not being allowed to do their work. It is hard to avoid the conclusion that Israel wanted a licence to kill and expel.

This became especially obvious after an investigation by the Israeli newspaper *Haaretz*. IDF officers and soldiers told *Haaretz* they were ordered to fire at unarmed crowds near food distribution sites in Gaza, even when no threat was present.

One soldier testified: 'We open fire early in the morning if someone tries to get in line from a few hundred meters away, and sometimes we just charge at them from close range. But there's no danger to the forces. I'm not aware of a single instance of return fire. There's no enemy, no weapons'.[13]

Both Prime Minister Benjamin Netanyahu and Defence Minister Israel Katz rejected these claims as 'blood libels'. In a joint statement they added:

---

* The 'flour massacre' took place on February 29, 2024, when an aid convoy made its way to Gaza City. Desperate Palestinians pulling boxes of flour and canned food surrounded it. Israeli troops opened fire. More than a hundred people were killed, many by Israeli gunfire. BBC analysis framed the episode as an authorless tragedy: 'Aid Convoy Tragedy Shows Fear of Starvation Haunts Gaza'.

'These are vicious lies designed to discredit the IDF—the most moral army in the world'.[14]

Israel has exploited connections with criminal elements in Gaza. Yasser Abu Shabab, a Palestinian man who had served time for drug trafficking, became an Israeli contractor. His gang, the 'Popular Forces' of armed men in Rafah, was reportedly provided with Kalashnikov rifles by the Israelis.[15] The group looted UN humanitarian aid, sold it on the black market, and acted as an Israeli proxy in depopulated areas.[16]

Videos show the men operating with Israeli soldiers in southern Gaza. Abu Shabab's own family published a statement disowning him and confirming his links to Israeli forces. Prime Minister Netanyahu was unabashed.[17] 'On the advice of security officials', he said, 'we activated clans in Gaza that oppose Hamas. What's wrong with that?' For months Israeli officials had blamed aid scarcity on Gaza on alleged looting by Hamas; claims for which they provided no evidence and which international relief officials could not corroborate. Now it was revealed that Israel's own collaborators in Gaza were behind the looting.

The head of the United Nations Office for the Coordination of Humanitarian Affairs in the Occupied Palestinian Territory, Jonathan Whittall, said in June 2025: 'The real theft of aid since the beginning of the war has been carried out by criminal gangs, under the watch of Israeli forces'.[18]

Israel's +972 *Magazine* described Israel's strategy as 'not mere military conquest but engineered disintegration' whereby 'Israel actively cultivates Gaza's collapse by empowering criminal militias, fragmenting authority, and dismantling every pillar of Palestinian social infrastructure'.[19]

Not that there is much left to dismantle. Twenty months of Israeli assault has destroyed or damaged 92 percent of Gaza's housing along with 89 percent of water, sanitation, and hygiene infrastructure. Less than 5 percent of cropland remains available for cultivation.[20]

The Death Toll

In late June 2025 the Gaza Health Authority updated its list of those killed in the war. The first ten pages of the 1,227-page document covered babies under six months old: 486 in all. The document listed 17,121 children killed under eighteen years old. In all it presented details of 55,202 people killed, 9,126 of them women.[21]

Israel apologists have devoted considerable efforts to discrediting the work of the heath authority on the purported basis that it is contradictory, biased, and exaggerates the number of deaths.[22] Most respected authorities think the ministry's efforts heroic and its findings conservative.

University of London researchers led by Professor Michael Spagat, an authority on deaths in conflict, made public their own analysis around the same time as the Gaza Health Ministry.

Spagat worked with the Palestinian political scientist Dr. Khalil Shikaki on a survey of a representative sample of two thousand Gaza households.* They estimate that from October 7, 2023, to January 5, 2025, Israel's offensive caused 75,200 violent deaths and 8,540 excess nonviolent deaths, for a total of 83,740 Palestinian deaths.

This estimate of 75,200 violent deaths dwarfs the figure of 49,090 violent deaths from the Gaza Health Ministry for the same period. This indicates that the Health Ministry data is a reliable *minimum* and all but certain to be a significant underestimate. Bear in mind that all of this data stems from before the imposition of Israel's complete siege in March 2025 and the resumption of its onslaught. The number of violent deaths, and very probably nonviolent excess deaths, has risen sharply since then.

Another study in *The Lancet* has estimated that there were sixty-four thousand traumatic injury deaths from October 7, 2023, to June 30, 2024, which implies '41% under-reporting in the MoH estimate over the same period'.[23] This estimate does not include those killed after June 2024. If excess deaths are counted, i.e. not merely violent deaths but also deaths caused by lack of

* The survey 'collected information on the vital status of 9,729 household members and their newborns, including whether they are alive or dead'. The summary of the survey read: 'The essence of the questionnaire is to first build a roster of the respondent's household members as of October 6, 2023, and then to account for each member's post-October-7 fate, including whether they are alive, dead, or missing'. See Michael Spagat et al., 'Violent and Nonviolent Death Tolls for the Gaza War: New Primary Evidence', medrxiv.org (23 June 2025), https://doi.org/10.1101/2025.06.19.25329797.

food, disruption to services, and so on, the toll will be even greater.[24] On the basis of *The Lancet* study, *The Economist* estimated that between 4 and 5 percent of Gaza's pre-war population may have been killed.[25] In Britain, this would translate to around *three million fatalities.*

In August 2024 the Israeli newspaper *Haaretz* reported that 'a cold examination of the numbers killed in the Gaza Strip reveals this is one of the bloodiest wars since the beginning of the century.'[26]

The Role of Britain

We bear a heavy responsibility for the deaths in Gaza, third in line only behind Israel and its primary patron and collaborator the United States. We helped enable the daily slaughter, destruction, disease, starvation, and human misery. We could have stopped arms sales. We could have sanctioned Israel. We could have ended military support.

We could have come to the aid of the Palestinians. We could have supported a special war crimes tribunal, as we did in former Yugoslavia and Rwanda. We could have submitted evidence at The Hague, as we did after the Bosnian Genocide. We could have deployed sanctions, as we did against Putin, and held Israel's leaders personally accountable for their atrocities. We could have sent British navy ships to Gaza to relieve the blockade. We could even have made the moral case for a no-fly zone over Gaza to protect its inhabitants, as we did to protect Kurds against Saddam Hussein.[27]

Damn you Keir Starmer. Damn you Rishi Sunak. Damn you Lammy, Cameron, Cleverly. A second damn for Lammy for shaking Benjamin Netanyahu's bloodstained hand.

Damn you Mitchell and Falconer, the bag carriers.

Damn you Lindsay Hoyle, Commons Speaker who wrecked a ceasefire motion and got Starmer off the hook.

Damn the Foreign Office officials who put their pensions before Palestinian lives.

Shame on the British military which trained, advised, and supported the genocidal Israeli army. Damn you Admiral Sir Tony Radakin. As chief of the defence staff you had the power to stop this. You have brought Britain's armed forces into disrepute.

Damn the arms manufacturers who have profited from supplying the Israeli military. Damn you BAE Systems, profiteers from death.

Damn the special relationship. It's led Britain into a cesspit.

Damn the politicians and journalists who never reported on or cared about the deaths of Palestinian journalists targeted and killed by Israel.

Damn the blood-soaked British newspaper industry. Damn you Murdoch. Damn you Rebekah Brooks. Damn you Victoria Newton, editor of *The Sun*. Damn you Tony Gallagher. You are *The Times* editor who awarded space to Yoav Gallant, wanted by the ICC for alleged war crimes including the use of starvation as a weapon of war and crimes against humanity. Damn you Professor Niall Ferguson for co-writing that article.[28]

Damn you Chris Evans, editor of the *Daily Telegraph*, for turning your newspaper into one of Israel's propaganda tools. Damn you Zanny Minton Beddoes of *The Economist*. You allowed your renowned journal to denounce the International Court of Justice genocide judgment as a 'show trial'.[29] You knew that Israel was turning Gaza into a 'hellscape' yet still demanded: 'fight on'.[30]

Damn you *Daily Mail* editor Ted Verity and your offshore proprietor Lord Rothermere. Damn you Michael Gove. Damn *The Spectator*.

Damn the ignorant, lavishly paid, cruel, canting newspaper columnists and studio hosts. Damn the know-nothing reporters who peddled lies and twisted the facts. Damn the reporters who were too afraid to search out the truth.

Damn those who passed by on the other side. Damn the Archbishop of Canterbury, who refused to meet a Bethlehem pastor.*

---

* On the grounds that he had shared a platform with Jeremy Corbyn MP. The archbishop, to his credit, later apologised to Pastor Munther Isaac. Patrick Wintour, 'Pastor Says Welby Would Not Meet Him If He Spoke at Palestine Rally with Corbyn', *The Guardian* (21 February 2024).

Damn the moral cowards at the top of the BBC: Samir Shah, Robbie Gibb, Tim Davie, Richard Burgess. Damn you for failing to understand the meaning of the great institution you have disgraced, or why it mattered so much.

Damn the atrocity deniers. Damn those who treated Palestinians as less than human. Damn those who viewed Palestinians as statistics. Damn the ideologists. Damn the 'clash of civilisation' barbarians. Damn the Great Replacement conspiracists. Damn the neoconservatives—never embarrassed, humbled, or sated.

Damn the extreme right for your bigotry and racism. Damn you Nigel Farage. Damn you Tommy Robinson. Damn you Douglas Murray.

Damn you Priti Patel. Damn you Kemi Badenoch.

Damn the self-appointed guardians of public discourse who smeared those who marched for peace as terror supporters. Damn Suella Braverman. Damn Yvette Cooper.

Damn the supporters of Israel who turned the charge of antisemitism, one of the great evils of human history, into a cheap propaganda weapon to cover for Israeli crimes.

Damn the lobbyists. Damn you Conservative Friends of Israel. Damn you Labour Friends of Israel—with a second damn for your disreputable jolly to Tel Aviv at the height of the slaughter.*

Damn those who didn't care. Damn those who did care but were afraid to act. Damn those who intimidated them into inertia. Damn the cowards and the careerists.

Damn those who put power before morality. Damn the pragmatists. Damn those who had their doubts but didn't voice them.

Damn those who didn't know. Damn those who didn't want to know. Damn those who didn't understand. Damn those who didn't want to understand.

---

* 'LFI Delegation Visits Israel and Palestine as Conflict Reaches 600 Days', lfi.org.uk (30 May 2025). See also: Hamish Morrison, 'Labour Politicians Fail to Declare All-Expenses-Paid Trip to Israel', *The National* (14 July 2025).

Damn all who were complicit in this brazen, public, and protracted crime against humanity.

I expect you all think you will get away with it. You have in the past. But the world may be starting to change.

The Search for Justice

Britain is a signatory to the Rome Statute of the International Criminal Court. The ICC has jurisdiction with respect to the crime of genocide, crimes against humanity, war crimes, and the crime of aggression.

Article 25(3) of the Statute provides that a person shall be criminally responsible and liable for punishment for a crime within the jurisdiction of the Court if that person:

> (a) Commits such a crime, whether as an individual, jointly with another or through another person, regardless of whether that other person is criminally responsible;
> (b) Orders, solicits or induces the commission of such a crime which in fact occurs or is attempted;
> (c) For the purpose of facilitating the commission of such a crime, aids, abets or otherwise assists in its commission or its attempted commission, including providing the means for its commission.

We see then that Article 25(3)(c) expressly stipulates that those who facilitate genocide, crimes against humanity, and war crimes are criminally responsible for their actions and liable to punishment by the Court.

It is evident that British ministers have left themselves open to accusations of facilitating genocide, crimes against humanity, and war crimes, in view of their policy in relation to Israel's devastating onslaught in Gaza.

As we saw in the introduction, the facilitation of the above crimes is integrated as an offence under Britain's own laws, in particular under the International Criminal Court Act 2001, section 52, which prohibits conduct ancillary to genocide, crimes against humanity, and war crimes. The section applies to conduct committed outside the United Kingdom as well as inside England and Wales.

There is, however, a problem. Section 53(3) of the Act may vitiate the prospect of the successful prosecution of British ministers, for it provides that '[p]roceedings for an offence shall not be instituted except by or with the consent of the Attorney General'.

The Attorney General is appointed, and can be dismissed, by the prime minister. The Attorney General is therefore a creature of the government who would be unlikely to prosecute misconduct by their colleagues and party—even if that misconduct reaches the pitch of the facilitation of genocide.[31]

It seems unlikely that British ministers will be punished given the state of British law. It is therefore hard to avoid the conclusion that the British politicians who have provided arms, intelligence, diplomatic cover, and moral support for Israel's destruction of Gaza will not soon be brought to justice. The improbability of any prosecution *tomorrow* notwithstanding, there can be little doubt about their guilt.

Change of Consciousness

This conclusion may have given comfort to British leaders and their advisers that there will be no price to pay for facilitating Israel's genocidal campaign in Gaza. But this reliance on the politicisation and pliancy of the British legal system may no longer be enough. This is because it fails to take account of the change of consciousness that has swept the world since October 7. The heroism and self-sacrifice of journalists inside Gaza have enabled billions to witness the carnage Israel has inflicted. Many have understood that the United States has been at the heart of the Israeli military machine, and in consequence that Britain is complicit in both US and Israeli barbarism.

They have watched Britain and the United States torch the 'rules-based order' to protect Israel as it incinerated homes and people in Gaza. They have watched as Britain and the United States trashed the decisions of the International Court of Justice, defied the UN, defunded its agencies, and sought to thwart the work of the International Criminal Court. In the aftermath of World War Two we helped establish a network of global institutions to avoid a repeat of the horrors of World War Two, of which the most terrible was the Holocaust. We have undermined those institutions to accommodate Israel's genocide in Gaza.

Any illusions that may have been harboured about Western commitment to moral or legal norms have been dispelled. Those seeking justice now know for sure that the West is not on their side: they need to look elsewhere. There are signs of a new approach. In March 2025, the International Centre for Justice for Palestinians announced the launch of Global 195, a cross-border initiative to pursue suspected war criminals involved in the assault on Gaza. The goal is to create a global net to catch those responsible for international law violations.

Legal teams in different states will submit criminal complaints to national police forces and will open private prosecutions against war crimes suspects. These suspects will include soldiers who have served in the IDF; Israeli personnel across the chain of command, including the political leadership; and others suspected of involvement in war crimes, including British politicians. The legal coalition intends to expand to 'all countries across the globe'.[32]

The evidence already collected by the ICJP includes 135 eyewitness testimonies from people in Gaza as well as open-source intelligence.[33] This evidence meets the required criminal standard for British and international courts.

In effect, these lawyers are attempting to fill the gap left by traditional law enforcement agencies. They will initiate prosecutions where the existing authorities have failed to do so.

This means complaints about potential war crimes perpetrated by British ministers, for example, will not be confined to a single jurisdiction: they will be made in other states too. If a lawyer in another country succeeds in persuading a court to issue an arrest warrant against British ministers, then an Interpol red notice for arrest could be issued against them. This strategy would increase the pressure on British authorities, and authorities in other jurisdictions, to take action against the suspected war criminals.

The ICJP also intends to continue requesting arrest warrants for suspected British citizens inside Britain. Here there is another international mechanism in play. The Rome Statute, to which Britain is a party, states that 'it is the duty of every State to exercise its criminal jurisdiction over those responsible for international crimes'.[34] Britain therefore has an obligation to investigate such crimes. If it fails to do so, it is possible for the International Criminal Court to become involved, i.e., to launch its own investigation and to issue warrants for the arrest of suspects.

In this fresh effort to pursue justice, the role of civil society and collective action at the international level will be paramount. Even if one country fails—even if the ICC fails—195 states will not all fail. There is already a seed of this new vision in The Hague Group, a body of states from the Global South devoted to upholding the rule of law in relation to Palestine.[35] Indeed, if the ICC ends up shirking its duties, it is not out of the question that a new institution might be established by states more earnest about and respectful of international law.[36]

The historic ICJ ruling of July 19, 2024, has further devastating legal repercussions for states that continue to support Israel. The Court found that Israel's prolonged occupation of Gaza and the West Bank is illegal and that Israel must end its presence in the occupied territories as rapidly as possible. It condemned Israel's 'sustained abuse . . . of its position as an occupying Power, through annexation and an assertion of permanent control over the Occupied Palestinian Territory and continued frustration of the right of the Palestinian people to self-determination', as a violation of 'fundamental principles of international law'.[37]

The Court devoted a section of the ruling to consequences for other states—that includes Britain. '[A]ll states', said the Court, are 'under an obligation not to render aid or assistance in maintaining the situation created by Israel's illegal presence in the Occupied Palestinian Territory'.[38] States also have a duty 'to take steps to prevent trade or investment relations that assist in the maintenance of the illegal situation created by Israel in the Occupied Palestinian Territory'.[39]

This ruling of the world's highest tribunal will no doubt be significant when British courts, and other courts around the world, are called upon to judge the conduct of our politicians.

All this could and should mark an epochal change. The 'civilised' West has always postured as the guardian of the international rule of law. But we may soon find that Justice has new guardians—better guardians—who will consider that the lives of non-Western people also have worth.

The British public was against this horror from the start. Even as both major parties opposed a truce, with the media demonising Palestine solidarity protestors as bigots and thugs, a majority of citizens continued to support a Gaza ceasefire.

Hundreds of thousands of ordinary people turned out week after week for months on end to demonstrate, occupy, and take action against British complicity. These heroic efforts vindicated the basic decency of the British public. But government policy barely changed.

Foreign policy in Britain is conducted in a closed world. It is made by a small elite on behalf of opaque interests. Gaza has shown that where state security is invoked, the media defers and parties converge.

The insulation of ruling bodies from public opinion left British citizens powerless to rescue the people of Gaza. Preventing future outrages by our leaders calls for more than legal accountability. It requires bringing democracy to Britain's state and society, whose governing institutions are now indelibly disgraced.

NOTES

Introduction

1. See, e.g., UN General Assembly Resolution 3151 G (XXVIII) of 14 December 1973.
2. Chris McGreal, 'Worlds Apart', *The Guardian* (6 February 2006).
3. Desmond Tutu, 'Apartheid in the Holy Land', *The Guardian* (29 April 2002).
4. 'Address by President Nelson Mandela at International Day of Solidarity with Palestinian People, Pretoria', mandela.gov.za (4 December 1997).
5. John Dugard ed., *The South West Africa/Namibia Dispute: Documents and Scholarly Writings on the Controversy Between South Africa and the United Nations* (University of California Press, 1973), p. xi.
6. International Court of Justice (ICJ), *South West Africa Cases (Ethiopia v. South Africa; Liberia v. South Africa)*, Second Phase, Judgment (18 July 1966). For discussion see Ryan M. Irwin, 'Apartheid on Trial: South West Africa and the International Court of Justice, 1960–66', *The International History Review* 32.4 (2010), pp. 636–37. John Dugard, *Confronting Apartheid: A Personal History of South Africa, Namibia and Palestine* (Jacana, 2018), pp. 25–28.
7. ICJ, *Application of the Convention on the Prevention and Punishment of the Crime of Genocide in the Gaza Strip (South Africa v. Israel)*, Public Sitting—Verbatim Record (11 January 2024) pp. 23, 59–60.
8. Ibid., p. 22.
9. Ibid., p. 33.

10. Ibid., p. 34.
11. Ibid., pp. 34–35.
12. Ibid., p. 35.
13. Ibid.
14. Ibid., p. 36.
15. Ibid., pp. 36–37, 39. Israeli soldiers were recorded in December dancing and singing, 'We know our motto: there are no uninvolved', and that they obey one command, 'to wipe off the seed of Amalek'. In November, Israeli soldiers were filmed chanting and singing: 'May their village burn; may Gaza be erased'. Ibid., p. 36.
16. Ibid., pp. 83–84.
17. *South Africa v. Israel*, Verbatim Record (12 January 2024), p. 12.
18. Ibid.
19. Ibid., pp. 12–13.
20. Ibid., p. 14.
21. Ibid.
22. Ibid.
23. Ibid., p. 32.
24. Ibid., p. 33.
25. Ibid., p. 34.
26. Ibid.
27. Ibid., pp. 74–75
28. *South Africa v. Israel*, Court Order (26 January 2024), p. 22.
29. Ibid., p. 23.
30. See 'UK Judges' and Lawyers' Open Letter Concerning Gaza', lawyersletter.uk (3 April 2024). For a thorough analysis of the Court's reasoning on this point, see: Norman G. Finkelstein, *Gaza's Gravediggers: An Inquiry into Corruption in High Places* (OR Books, 2025), chap. 4.
31. *South Africa v. Israel*, Court Order (26 January 2024), pp. 30–32.
32. Barak voted with the majority instructing Israel to prevent and punish incitement to genocide and ensure the provision of humanitarian aid. Ibid., p. 31.
33. Sam Sokol, 'Failure to Throw Out Genocide Claims a "Mark of Disgrace" on ICJ, Netanyahu Declares', *The Times of Israel* (26 January 2024).

34. TOI Staff, '"A Blood Libel": Herzog Says ICJ "Twisted My Words" to Support "Unfounded" Contention', *The Times of Israel* (29 January 2024).
35. Raffi Berg and Anna Holligan, 'ICJ Says Israel Must Prevent Genocide in Gaza', bbc.co.uk (26 January 2024).
36. Bethan McKernan, 'Israeli Officials Accuse International Court of Justice of Antisemitic Bias', *The Guardian* (26 January 2024).
37. 'World Reacts to ICJ Interim Ruling in Gaza Genocide Case Against Israel', aljazeera.com (26 January 2024).
38. Jacob Magid, '210 US Lawmakers Blast South Africa's "Defamatory" Genocide Charge Against Israel', *The Times of Israel* (24 January 2024).
39. Daily Mail Comment, 'Hamas Is Bent on Genocide, Not Israel', *Daily Mail* (26 January 2024).
40. Leader, 'Show Trial', *The Economist* (20 January 2024).
41. James Shotter, 'Top UN Court Orders Israel to Comply with International Law on Genocide', *Financial Times* (26 January 2024). Mehul Srivastava and James Shotter, 'ICJ's Israel Judgment Seeks to Restore Rule of Law to a Brutal Conflict', *Financial Times* (27 January 2024).
42. Jennifer Scott, '"Nonsense" for South Africa to Accuse Israel of Genocide, Says Foreign Secretary', news.sky.com (15 January 2024).
43. UK Foreign, Commonwealth, and Development Office (FCDO), 'International Court of Justice Interim Ruling on South Africa vs Israel: FCDO Statement', gov.uk (27 January 2024).

Chapter One

1. Andrew Mitchell, 'Israel and the Occupied Palestinian Territories', andrew-mitchell-mp.co.uk (14 November 2023).
2. TOI Staff and Agencies, 'Israel Revises Death Toll from Oct. 7 Hamas Assault, Dropping It from 1,400 to 1,200', *The Times of Israel* (11 November 2023).
3. Airwars, *Analysis: Gaza, October 2023* (December 2024), p. 5.
4. Ibid.
5. Ibid. Airwars, an independent research organisation, identified at least 5,139 civilian fatalities in Gaza that occurred in October 2023 as a result of Israeli bombing. The Gaza Health Ministry documented over eight

thousand fatalities by the end of the month. Airwars has confirmed that there is a high correlation between data collected by the Gaza Health Ministry and open-source reports with regards to fatalities. UN OCHA, 'Hostilities in the Gaza Strip and Israel | Flash Update #25', ochaopt.org (31 October 2023) (eight thousand). Rowena De Silva et al., 'One Name, Two Lists', https://gaza-civilians.airwars.org/ (24 July 2024).

6. UK Prime Minister's Office, 'PM Words One Week On from the Start of Hamas Terrorist Attacks', gov.uk (14 October 2023).
7. UK Prime Minister's Office, 'Prime Minister Deploys UK Military to Eastern Mediterranean to Support Israel', gov.uk (13 October 2023).
8. UK House of Commons, 'Israel and Gaza', hansard.parliament.uk (16 October 2023).
9. 'Annex to the Letter Dated 27 February 2025 from the Permanent Representative of South Africa to the United Nations addressed to the President of the Security Council', S/2025/130 (28 February 2025), p. 48, para. 94.
10. Asher McShane, 'Israel "Has the Right" to Withhold Power and Water from Gaza, Says Sir Keir Starmer', lbc.co.uk (11 October 2023). The video is available online.
11. Video clip posted by @BBCNewsnight on X (12 October 2023), https://x.com/BBCNewsnight/status/1712401412120879271.
12. BBC Politics Liveblog, 'Israel Must Act Within International Law, Says Labour's Lammy', bbc.co.uk (15 October 2023 at 9:36 a.m.). Video clip posted by @BBCPolitics on X (15 October 2023), https://x.com/BBCPolitics/status/1713497893544308749.
13. Video clip posted by @ITVNewsPolitics on X (20 October 2023), https://x.com/ITVNewsPolitics/status/1715309817110110433.
14. UK House of Commons, 'Israel and Gaza', hansard.parliament.uk (23 October 2023). Sir Keir avoided expressly mentioning that Israel was the perpetrator of the devastating siege.
15. Aletha Adu and Kiran Stacey, 'Dozens of Labour MPs Defy Keir Starmer to Vote for Ceasefire in Gaza', *The Guardian* (15 November 2023).
16. Sam Francis and Henry Zeffman, 'Labour Calls for Immediate Humanitarian Ceasefire in Gaza for First Time', bbc.co.uk (21 February 2024).

17. MEE Staff, 'Israel-Palestine War: UK Home Secretary Says Waving Palestinian Flag Could Be an Offence', *Middle East Eye* (10 October 2023).
18. 'David Cameron Describes Blockaded Gaza as a "Prison"', bbc.co.uk (27 July 2010).
19. 'Security Council Fails to Adopt Resolution Demanding Immediate Humanitarian Ceasefire in Gaza on Account of Veto by United States', press.un.org (8 December 2023). Thirteen out of fifteen Security Council members supported the resolution but the US deployed its veto.
20. *Sunday Morning with Trevor Phillips*, Sky News (14 January 2024), https://www.youtube.com/watch?v=3VJ5JaiHvgc.
21. Prior to the latest hostilities, UNRWA ran 284 schools in Gaza, 22 primary health facilities, and provided emergency food and cash assistance to 1.2 million people there. 'UNRWA in Action', unrwa.org (24 February 2023).
22. In October 2024, the Israeli Knesset passed two bills: one banned UNRWA from operating inside Israel and the other prohibited Israeli authorities from contact with UNRWA. 'Potentially "Deadly" Consequences Could Arise from Israel's UNRWA Ban: UNICEF', news.un.org (31 October 2024).
23. As of January 9, 2025, 266 UNRWA team members had been killed in Gaza during the latest hostilities. 'UNRWA 'Situation Report #155 on the Humanitarian Crisis in the Gaza Strip and the West Bank, including East Jerusalem', unrwa.org (16 January 2025).
24. UNRWA, 'UNRWA Claims versus Facts—Press Release', un.org (February 2024).
25. Lindsey Hilsum, 'Israel's Evidence of UNRWA Hamas Allegations Examined', channel4.com (5 February 2024). According to the *Financial Times*, 'The intelligence assessment, which has been seen by the FT, provides no evidence for the claims.' Mehul Srivastava and Andrew England, 'Head of UN Agency for Palestinians Defies Israeli Calls to Quit', *Financial Times* (3 February 2024). See also Julian Borger, 'Israel Has Yet to Provide Evidence of UNRWA Staff Terrorist Links, Colonna Report Says', *The Guardian* (22 April 2024).
26. Jonathan Cook, 'Israel-Palestine War: Israel Is Caught Lying Time and Again. And Yet We Never Learn', *Middle East Eye* (23 October 2023).
27. Lindsey Hilsum, 'Israel's Evidence of UNRWA Hamas allegations Examined', channel4.com (5 February 2024).

28. It is difficult to tell whether UNRWA suffered financially from the Cameron decision. Britain was already paid up to the May year-end when funding was paused. Between late May 2024 and July 2024, it would *seem* that the government was not sending UNRWA any new money. But Labour reversed the decision shortly after coming to office at the July 2024 election. Nevertheless the British decision to pause funding was damaging to UNRWA because it gave credibility to Israeli claims.
29. Phelan Chatterjee, 'UNRWA: Restart Aid to Palestinian UN Agency, EU Urges', bbc.co.uk (24 April 2024). The EU called on donor states to resume funding in April.
30. CAAT, 'UK Export Licences Approved for Military Goods to Israel Since April 2015', caat.org.uk (2024).
31. Louisa Brooke-Holland, *UK Arms Exports to Israel,* House of Commons Research Briefing (8 January 2025), p. 10.
32. CAAT, *Arming Genocide: UK Arms Sales to Israel, the Partial Export License Suspension, and the F-35 Exemption* (6 December 2024), p. 6. CAAT points out that in most cases it is difficult to identify which aircraft has been used.
33. Ibid., p. 2.
34. UK Secretary of State for International Trade Anne-Marie Trevelyan, 'Statement UINHCWS449', questions-statements.parliament.uk (8 December 2021).
35. Brooke-Holland, *Exports,* pp. 5–6.
36. My analysis of Andrew Mitchell's Commons performance relies on Mark Curtis, 'Andrew Mitchell: Apologist for Genocide', *Declassified UK* (18 March 2024).
37. Ibid.
38. Ibid.
39. Ibid.
40. Ibid.
41. Ibid.
42. Hagai El-Ad, 'Why B'Tselem Stopped Cooperating with Israeli Military Investigations', *Haaretz* (17 January 2018).
43. Mark Curtis, 'Andrew Mitchell: Apologist for Genocide', *Declassified UK* (18 March 2024).

44. Ibid.
45. Ibid.
46. Marcus White, 'Gaza Surgeon Describes Drones Targeting Children', bbc.co.uk (13 November 2024).
47. Human Rights Watch, *Precisely Wrong: Gaza Civilians Killed by Israeli Drone-Launched Missiles* (2009).
48. Mark Curtis, 'Battle-Tested in Gaza: Britain's Next Drones?' *Declassified UK* (20 June 2024).
49. 'Statement of ICC Prosecutor Karim A.A. Khan KC: Applications for Arrest Warrants in the Situation in the State of Palestine', icc-cpi.int (20 May 2024).
50. UK House of Commons, 'Israel and Gaza', hansard.parliament.uk (20 May 2024).
51. UK House of Commons Foreign Affairs Committee, 'Oral Evidence: Work of the Foreign, Commonwealth and Development Office', HC 325 (9 January 2024), Q636–641.
52. The Independent, 'Watch Again: David Cameron Questioned by Foreign Affairs Committee' (9 January 2024), https://www.youtube.com/watch?v=okgfM_JnS_0.
53. Foreign Affairs Committee, 'Oral Evidence', Q651.
54. Ibid., Q624.
55. Ibid., Q601–603. Cameron eventually said that Gaza was 'de facto' occupied. (Ibid., Q604)
56. Asked whether he had received legal advice that Israel was in breach of international law, Lord Cameron replied: 'The short answer to that is no'—before qualifying and going on to say 'it is not really a yes or no answer'. (Ibid., Q654)
57. Patrick Wintour, 'Cameron Urged to publish Foreign Office Legal Advice on Israel's War in Gaza', *The Guardian* (22 March 2024).
58. Lammy did not raise the issue of Cameron's embarrassing performance before the Foreign Affairs Select Committee in debates with Andrew Mitchell in January 2024. See UK House of Commons, 'Israel and the Occupied Palestinian Territories', hansard.parliament.uk (29 January 2024); 'Palestinian State: Recognition', hansard.parliament.uk (30 January 2024).

59. David Hearst, 'Israel-Palestine War: Starmer's Gaza Betrayal Shows He Is Failing as a Leader', *Middle East Eye* (23 October 2023).
60. Private information.
61. Post by @Nigel_Farage on X (19 October 2023). Farage had temporarily stepped back as Reform leader in favour of Richard Tice, returning to the top job in June 2024.
62. 'Interview: Bret Baier of Fox News Interviews Donald Trump Parts 1 and 2 - February 9, 2025', rollcall.com (n.d.) (Trump). Avraham Bloch, 'After Not Liking Netanyahu's Words: Limor Son Har Melech Stunned the Knesset Committee', *Ma'ariv* (11 May 2025) [Hebrew] (Netanyahu).
63. See, e.g., Camilla Tominey, 'Admitting Gazan Refugees Would Be Proof That Britain Has a Death Wish', *The Telegraph* (18 May 2024).
64. Post by @Nigel_Farage on X (17 December 2023).
65. Airwars, *Patterns*, p. 2. 'This is nearly seven times higher than even the most deadly month for children previously recorded by Airwars'. Ibid.
66. Posts by @TiceRichard on X (4 May 2024, 6 May 2024).
67. Posts by @TiceRichard on X (2 March 2024).
68. Posts by @TiceRichard on X (21 November 2024, 23 November 2024).
69. Post by @TiceRichard on X (5 April 2024).
70. Post by @TRobinsonNewEra on X (7 October 2024).
71. Post by @TRobinsonNewEra on X (1 October 2024).
72. Post by @TRobinsonNewEra on X (2 July 2024).

Chapter Two

1. Video clip posted by @SkyNews on X (25 October 2023), https://x.com/SkyNews/status/1717279204130037806. When I challenged Austin on this interview he replied: 'My understanding in the moment of that interview was that Gillerman was talking specifically about the Hamas perpetrators of the atrocities when talking about "human animals"'.
2. Anshel Pfeffer, 'Tzipi Hotovely Is the Ugly, Extremist Face of Israel. British Jews Should Welcome Her', *Haaretz* (19 June 2020).
3. Centre for Media Monitoring (CfMM), *Media Bias Gaza 2023–24* (March 2024), p. 56.
4. Ibid., pp. 56–58.

5. 'Israel-Hamas War: "Time for Hamas to Pay the Price"—Israel's Ambassador to the UK', news.sky.com (16 October 2023).
6. Tzipi Hotovely—Swords of Iron, 'ציפי חוטובלי Tzipi Hotovely - ראיון ל-BBC - תאריך: 29/10/2023' (30 October 2023), https://www.youtube.com/watch?v=W9bUFxO9P-c.
7. Staff Writer, 'Israel's Oldest Fighter, 95, Says "Don't Give Up" in Mission to Boost Troop Morale', *Daily Express* (10 October 2023).
8. IDF Editorial Team, 'I Fought in the Lehi', idf.il (29 November 2021). See also CfMM, *Media Bias*, pp. 54–55.
9. Tzvi Fishman, 'Lehi Fighter Recalls 1948 Battle at Deir Yassin', *Jewish Press* (21 May 2020).
10. John Phillips, 'Sapper Ernest Charles William Summers, 14480437, 199 Rly. Workshops, Royal Engineers', cwgc.org (20 November 2023).
11. Ibid. See also Calder Walton, 'Coat Bomb and Explosive Prosthesis: British Intel Files Reveal How the Zionist Stern Gang Terrorized London', *Haaretz* (2 December 2017).
12. Ofer Aderet, 'Zionist Militia's Efforts to Recruit Nazis in Fight Against the British Are Revealed', *Haaretz* (21 June 2023).
13. Des Freedman, 'For Western Media, Israel's Bombing of Gaza Is Not "Deadly"', *Declassified UK* (30 January 2024).
14. Nataliya Vasilyeva, 'Israel Vows to Fight On After 24 Killed in IDF's Single Deadliest Day in Gaza', *The Telegraph* (23 January 2024).
15. Katie Davis, '24 Israeli Soldiers Killed in "Deadliest Battle of Gaza War" as Two Buildings Explode & Leave Them Buried Beneath Rubble', *The Sun* (23 January 2024).
16. Jason Burke, 'Twenty-Four Soldiers Killed in Deadliest Day for Israeli Forces of Gaza War', *The Guardian* (23 January 2024).
17. Michael Howie and Matt Watts, 'Israel Says 24 Soldiers Killed in Deadliest Day for Its Forces in Gaza Since War Began', *The Standard* (23 January 2024).
18. Neri Zilber and Mai Khaled, 'Israel Says 24 Soldiers Killed in One Day as Benjamin Netanyahu Resists Ceasefire Calls', *Financial Times* (23 January 2024).
19. Shweta Sharma and Chris Stevenson, 'Deadliest Day for Israeli Army Since Start of Gaza War as 24 soldiers Killed', *The Independent* (23 January 2024).

20. A partial exception came on October 25, when the BBC referenced 'Palestinians *reporting* the deadliest day in Gaza' (emphasis added).
21. Posts by @DPJHodges on X (8 February 2025).
22. Though the tweet has been deleted a screenshot was published in CfMM, *Media Bias*, p. 25.
23. Tominey, 'Admitting'.
24. Richard Ferrer, 'Regime-Change Invasion Is Surely Only Hours Away and With It the End of Hamas - Comment', *Daily Express* (10 October 2023). The archived version is available here: https://web.archive.org/web/20231008184849/https://www.express.co.uk/comment/expresscomment/1821380/Israel-and-hamas-at-war-israel-music-festival-palestine-surprise-attack.
25. Jewish Voice for Labour, '"The Mohammedans Are Taking Over"', jewishvoiceforlabour.org.uk (27 February 2024).
26. Giora Eiland, '"A New Turning Point in the History of the State of Israel. Most People Don't Understand That"', fathomjournal.org (October 2023).
27. Nadav Rapaport, 'What Is Israel's "Generals' Plan" and What Does It Mean for the War on Gaza?' *Middle East Eye* (15 October 2024).
28. Knesset News, 'Foreign Affairs and Defense Committee Discusses "Generals' Plan" for Gaza; Maj.-Gen. (Res.) Eiland: "It Can Change the Reality"', main.knesset.gov.il (18 September 2024). Jeremy Bowen, 'Israeli Attack on Northern Gaza Hints at Retired General's "Surrender or Starve" Plan for War', bbc.co.uk (12 October 2024).
29. Alan Johnson and Jack Omer-Jackaman, 'For the Total Defeat of Hamas, Against the "Total Siege" of Gaza', fathomjournal.org (October 2023).
30. *South Africa v. Israel*, Application Institution Proceedings and Request for the Indication of Provisional Measures (29 December 2023), para. 101.
31. Douglas Murray, 'Britain Must Stand Up Against Those Who Support Hamas', *The Spectator* (14 October 2023).
32. International Committee of the Red Cross, 'Deportation', casebook.icrc.org (n.d.).
33. Audio clip posted by @jrc1921 on X (9 October 2023), https://x.com/jrc1921/status/1711283441944113237. See also CfMM, *Media Bias*, pp. 38 (Ingram), 39 (Reeves). Alicia Kearns MP, chair of the House of Commons Foreign Affairs Committee, later reminded the foreign secretary

David Cameron that 'British law currently does consider Gaza to be an occupied power'. UK House of Commons Foreign Affairs Committee, *Oral Evidence: Work of the Foreign Commonwealth and Development Office*, HC 325, committees.parliament.uk (9 January 2024). Q602. See also ibid., Q603–4.

34. Avi Shlaim, *Three Worlds: Memoirs of an Arab-Jew* (London: Oneworld, 2023).
35. Byline Times Reporter, 'Sangita Myska: More Media Figures Sign Open Letter to LBC Expressing "Deep Concern" About Her Departure', *Byline Times* (14 May 2024).
36. Sam Kiley, 'War of Words', *Evening Standard* (5 September 2001).
37. Interview with the author, March 2025.
38. Peter Oborne and James Jones, 'The Pro-Israel Lobby in Britain: Full Text', *openDemocracy* (13 November 2009). The following section draws on this article.
39. Private conversation at the time of my 2009 documentary on Britain's pro-Israel lobby or Channel 4. John Lyons, who spent six years in Jerusalem as Middle East correspondent for *The Australian*, has written an eye-opening book on the difficulties of reporting from Israel and the occupied territories. John Lyons, *Dateline Jerusalem: Journalism's Toughest Assignment* (Monash University Publishing, 2021).
40. For *The Guardian*'s response to this claim see: Leader, 'Seaman Lets It Slip', *The Guardian* (17 October 2002).
41. Jason Burke, 'Israeli Envoy Lashes Out at British Left', *The Guardian* (4 April 2004).
42. Jonathan Dimbleby, 'Dimbleby: Fearful BBC Risks Losing Its Way', *Index on Censorship* (13 May 2009).
43. 'EMBARGOED UNTIL 11:00 ON THURSDAY 16 APRIL', zionistfederation.blogspot.com (19 April 2009).
44. CAMERA, 'Press Release on Key BBC Ruling Against Mideast Editor Jeremy Bowen', camera.org (15 April 2009).
45. Oborne and Jones, 'Pro-Israel Lobby'.
46. Dimbleby, 'Fearful'.
47. Greg Philo and Mike Berry, *More Bad News from Israel* (Pluto Press, 2011), pp. 336–68, 394–98 (quote at 394). The general bias towards the Israeli

perspective notwithstanding, some reports did feature critical language on the consequences of Israel's 2008–9 offensive for civilians in Gaza. Ibid., pp. 362–68.

48. Centre for Media Monitoring, *BBC on Gaza-Israel 2023–24: One Story, Double Standards* (June 2025). All facts and figures in the section below are drawn from the CfMM report.
49. The Nakba was mentioned as providing context for October 7 in one out of nearly four thousand online articles and thirty-three times out of more than twenty-one thousand broadcast clips.
50. Jeremy Bowen, 'Israel Is Accused of the Gravest War Crimes—How Governments Respond Could Haunt Them for Years to Come', bbc.co.uk (8 June 2025).
51. Post by @martinshawx on X (18 June 2025).
52. Jonathan Cook, 'Why BBC Editors Must One Day Stand Trial for Colluding in Israel's Genocide', jonathancook.substack.com (20 June 2025).
53. Mark Curtis, '"National Scandal": The BBC's Gaza Cover-Up', *Declassified UK* (15 January 2025).
54. Bron Maher, 'As Many People Think BBC Is Pro-Israel as Think It Is Pro-Palestine, Poll Finds', *Press Gazette* (4 December 2023.
55. *Panorama—October 7th: One Year On* (BBC One, 7 October 2024).
56 Mallory Moench, 'Nearly 70% of Gaza War Dead Verified by UN Are Women and Children', bbc.co.uk (8 November 2024).
57. Haaretz, 'Israel's Dead: The Names of Those Killed in Hamas Attacks, Massacres and the Israel-Hamas War', *Haaretz*, (19 October 2023).
58. Thirty-six Israeli children were killed on October 7. By October 9, 2024, it was reported by the UN Office for the Coordination of Humanitarian Affairs (OCHA) that more than 11,350 children had been identified killed in Gaza. (UN OCHA, 'Reported Impact Snapshot | Gaza Strip (9 October 2024)', ochaopt.org (9 October 2024).
59. Gabrielle Tétrault-Farber, 'Despite Biden's Doubts, Humanitarian Agencies Consider Gaza Toll Reliable', reuters.com (27 October 2023). See also Matthew Ghobrial Cockerill, 'Civilian Casualties in Gaza: Israel's Claims Don't Add Up', aoav.org.uk (28 October 2024). Adam Gaffney, 'Don't Believe the Conspiracies About the Gaza Death Toll', *The Nation*

(30 May 2024). Mike Spagat, 'Netanyahu Got It Wrong Before the US Congress: IDF's Clean Performance in Gaza Is a Lie', aoav.org.uk (2 August 2024).

60. Assma Maad, 'Why the Gaza Health Ministry's Death Count Is Considered Reliable', *Le Monde* (13 October 2024).

61. Mitchell Prothero, 'Israeli Intelligence Has Deemed Hamas-Run Health Ministry's Death Toll Figures Generally Accurate', *VICE News* (25 January 2024).

62. Zeina Jamaluddine et al., 'Traumatic Injury Mortality in the Gaza Strip from Oct 7, 2023, to June 30, 2024: A Capture-Recapture Analysis', *The Lancet* 405.10477 (8 February 2025), pp. 469–77. This finding was corroborated by a June 2025 preprint study. Michael Spagat et al., 'Violent and Nonviolent Death Tolls for the Gaza War: New Primary Evidence', medrxiv.org (23 June 2025).

63. Israeli Prime Minister's Office, 'Statement from PM Naftali Bennett Following the Sad Death of Al-Jazeera Journalist Shireen Abu-Aqla', gov.il (11 May 2022).

64. Zein Assaf, *Hegemonic Frames in Mainstream Coverage on Palestine: A Case Study of Shireen Abu Akleh's Killing*, Georgetown University in Qatar (Digital Georgetown, 2023), p. 12. See also pp. 2, 5, 13.

65. Raja Abdulrahim and Ben Hubbard, 'Trailblazing Palestinian Journalist Killed in West Bank', *The New York Times* (11 May 2022). The archived version is available here: https://web.archive.org/web/20220511145346/https://www.nytimes.com/2022/05/11/world/middleeast/shireen-abu-akleh-al-jazeera-dead.html.

66. Assaf, Hegemonic *Frames*, pp. 11–12.

67. Norman G. Finkelstein, *Image and Reality of the Israel-Palestine Conflict* (Verso Books, 2001; first edition 1995), pp. 56–60.

68. UN Security Council Official Records, S/PV.1348 (6 June 1967), para. 155. For discussion see Finkelstein, *Image and Reality*, pp. 140–41.

69. Robert Mackey, 'Israel Attempts to Smear Razan al-Najjar, Palestinian Medic It Killed, Calling her "No Angel"', *The Intercept* (8 June 2018). On Israel's broader misrepresentations of the Gaza protests see Muhammad Shehada and Jamie Stern-Weiner, 'Debunking Myths About the Palestinian Protests', *VICE* (12 June 2018).

70. Sufian Taha, 'Israeli Police Attack Funeral Procession for Shot Journalist Shireen Abu Aqleh', *The Guardian* (13 May 2022).
71. Post by @BBCWorld on X, https://x.com/BBCWorld/status/1525107671430471684 (13 May 2022).
72. Tom Bateman, 'Shireen Abu Aqla: Israel Says "High Probability" Soldier Killed Reporter', bbc.co.uk (5 September 2022).
73. Al Jazeera, 'Israeli Forces Killed Abu Akleh "Without Justification", UN Inquiry Says', aljazeera.com (16 October 2023).
74. Don Macintyre, a veteran political journalist who served as Jerusalem correspondent for *The Independent*, was among the congregation. Peter Oborne, 'Shireen Abu Akleh Killing: Why All Journalists Must Push for Justice', *Middle East Eye* (1 July 2022).
75. Reporters Without Borders (RSF), '"At the Rate Journalists Are Being Killed in Gaza, There Will Soon Be No One Left to Keep You Informed"', rsf.org (26 September 2024).
76. Committee to Protect Journalists, 'Journalist Casualties in the Israel-Gaza War', cpj.org (4 February 2025).
77. RSF, 'At the Rate'.
78. ActionAid, 'Gaza Is World's Deadliest Place for Journalists', actionaid.org.uk (2 May 2024).
79. By April 2025, according to UNRWA, 408 aid workers including more than 280 UNRWA staff had been killed in Gaza since October 7, 2023. In June 2025, UN secretary-general António Guterres said that '[m]ore than one in every 50 UNRWA staff has been killed in this atrocious conflict. This is the highest staff death toll in United Nations history'. 'Gaza Aid Worker Killings: One Humanitarian Still Missing in Mass Grave', news.un.org (1 April 2025). 'Number of Aid Workers Killed in Gaza Conflict, Highest in UN History: Guterres', news.un.org (5 June 2025).
80. RSF, 'Ismail al-Ghoul's Killing: Targeted and Discredited, Palestinian Journalists Suffer Double Punishment in Gaza', rsf.org (30 August 2024).
81. Ibid.
82. Al Jazeera Staff, 'Al Jazeera Refutes "Baseless" Israeli Allegations Against Ismail al-Ghoul', aljazeera.com (1 August 2024).

83. 'Al Jazeera Reports Its Journalist Killed in Israeli Strike on Gaza', *The Straits Times* (16 December 2024).
84. Thaslima Begum, '"Fadi Is Fighting for His Life": Israel Blocks Evacuation of Cameraman Shot in Gaza', *The Guardian* (14 January 2025).
85. Al Jazeera Staff, 'To Kill a Family: The Loss of Wael Dahdouh's Family to an Israeli Bomb', aljazeera.com (1 November 2023). See also Nesrine Malik, '"I Couldn't Cry over My Children Like Everyone Else": The Tragedy of Palestinian Journalist Wael al-Dahdouh', *The Guardian* (31 October 2024).
86. Jack Jeffery and Jon Gambrell, 'Israel Accuses 6 Al Jazeera Journalists in Gaza of Being Palestinian Militants', apnews.com (24 October 2024). See also Reporters Without Borders, 'Gaza: RSF Is Alarmed by the Israeli Army's Serious Accusations Against Six Al-Jazeera Journalists and Calls for Their Protection', rsf.org (25 October 2024).
87. Transcripts of interviews with Youmna ElSayed and Maha Hussaini for Al Jazeera Investigative Unit film, *GAZA*, shared with the author.
88. I am drawing here on Council for Arab-British Understanding (CAABU) Director Chris Doyle's thoughtful statement: 'Palestinian Journalists Deserve International Protection', *Arab News* (2 December 2024).
89. Post by @AbubakerAbedW on X (9 January 2025), https://x.com/AbubakerAbedW/status/1877305118414033001.
90. UK House of Commons Foreign Affairs Committee, *Oral Evidence: Work of the Foreign, Commonwealth and Development Office*, HC 385 (27 November 2024), Q114. Video is available at DawnNews English, 'UK's Lammy Says, "There Are No Journalists In Gaza"' (30 November 2024), https://www.youtube.com/watch?v=NpbK2pAiejk, 1:50.
91. Doyle, 'Palestinian Journalists'.
92. Douglas Murray, 'I've Seen Hamas' Brutality First Hand—Communities Are Decimated, Streets Are Littered with Bodies & Homes Are Rubble', *The Sun* (15 November 2023).
93. For a debunking of Israeli claims about al-Shifa hospital, see Louisa Loveluck et al., 'The Case of al-Shifa: Investigating the Assault on Gaza's Largest Hospital', *The Washington Post* (21 December 2023).
94. AFP, 'Two Premature Babies Die at Al Shifa Hospital in Gaza Due to Power Cuts', *Al Arabiya* (11 November 2023).

95. Ibid.
96. Murray watched people moving south down Salahadin St. at approximately the same moment described by Al Jazeera English correspondent Youmna ElSayed and freelancer Mohammed ElHelou in the *GAZA* film. Al Jazeera English, 'Investigating War Crimes in Gaza' (3 October 2024), https://www.youtube.com/watch?v=kPE6vbKix6A, 20m30s–-23m57s. See also Youmna ElSayed's evidence that there were no Hamas troops at the al-Shifa hospital; ibid., 56m56s.
97. Peter Robinson and Douglas Murray, 'A Dangerous Moment, with Douglas Murray', hoover.org (4 June 2024). Murray also repeated the unevidenced Israeli line that there was a fatality ratio of 'roughly one terrorist killed to one civilian' though he had the grace to acknowledge that this was 'a horrible calculus'.
98. Jared Malsin, 'How the Israeli-Palestinian Conflict Affected Journalists', *Columbia Journalism Review* (30 October 2014).
99. Ibid.
100. BBC News, 'BBC Goes Inside Al-Shifa Hospital with the Israeli Army -BBC News' (16 November 2023), https://www.youtube.com/watch?v=qNzWbP64Nmw.
101. UN OHCHR, *Thematic Report: Attacks on Hospitals during the Escalation of Hostilities in Gaza (7 October 2023 - 30 June 2024)*, ohchr.org (31 December 2024), para. 16.
102. Post by @MouinRabbani on X (11 August 2024), https://x.com/MouinRabbani/status/1822499670070804542.
103. '[T]he IDF has not released sufficient evidence to enable independent verification of these claims, and in some cases, statements from the IDF have not been supported by information it subsequently released'. UN OHCHR, *Thematic Report*, para. 16.
104. Loveluck et al., 'The Case of al-Shifa'.
105. Ibid.
106. *Report of the Independent International Commission of Inquiry on the Occupied Palestinian Territory, including East Jerusalem, and Israel*, A/79/232 (11 September 2024), para. 92. The Commission was able to verify information 'indicating that members of armed groups had entered Shifa' hospital with Israeli security forces vehicles that were stolen on 7 October'.

107. Ibid.
108. Ibid., para. 91.
109. Ibid., para. 2.
110. Iona Cleave et al., 'Israeli Troops Bring Baby Incubators & Supplies to Gaza's al-Shifa Hospital after "Targeted Operation" to Hunt Hamas', *The Sun* (15 November 2023). The body of the article mentioned human rights concerns but the effect of the overall framing is to portray Israeli forces heroically.
111. Richard Kemp, 'Too Many Want to Believe Hamas's Hospital Lies', *The Telegraph* (20 November 2023).
112. Limor Simhony Philpott, 'What's the Truth about Gaza's al-Shifa Hospital?' *The Spectator* (21 November 2023).
113. Ibid.
114. Physicians for Human Rights–Israel, *Destruction of Conditions of Life: A Health Analysis of the Gaza Genocide* (July 2025), pp. 5, 47, 49.
115. Clarissa Ward, 'Watch Clarissa Ward Report from Inside Gaza for the First Time Since War Began', *CNN* (14 December 2023).
116. Julia Frankel, 'Israel's Military Campaign in Gaza Seen as Among the Most Destructive in Recent History, Experts Say', *The Independent* (21 December 2023).

Chapter Three

1. Amnesty International, *Israel/OPT: Amnesty International's Research into Hamas-Led Attacks of 7 October 2023 and Treatment of Hostages* (2 December 2024), p. 1.
2. 'October 7: How Hamas Attacked Israel Minute-by-Minute', *Haaretz* (18 April 2024).
3. Human Rights Watch, *"I Can't Erase All the Blood from My Mind": Palestinian Armed Groups' October 7 Assault on Israel* (17 July 2024).
4. Video clip posted by @i24NEWS_EN on X (10 October 2023), https://x.com/i24NEWS_EN/status/1711697093151056355.
5. Roland Oliphant et al., 'Hamas Massacres Babies and Children', *Daily Telegraph* (10 October 2023).

6. Bel Trew, '"They Decapitated Women and Children. We Saw Dead Babies", an Israeli Major Claims. The Bodies Are Hidden So It's Impossible to Verify. But This Village Smells of Death', *The Independent* (11 October 2023).
7. Anshel Pfeffer, 'Hamas "Cut the Throats of Babies" in Massacre', *The Times* (11 October 2023).
8. Giles Sheldrick, 'Horror at "Pure Evil Beheading of Babies"', *Daily Express* (11 October 2023).
9. United Hatzalah, 'Eli Beer, President of United Hatzalah Testimonials from October 7th, 2023, at the RJC' (5 November 2023), https://www.youtube.com/watch?v=B0AkHJse8d4, 5m37s.
10. Video clip posted by @SaulStaniforth on X (16 October 2023), https://x.com/SaulStaniforth/status/1713813662052372519.
11. Video clip posted @atruper on X (16 November 2023), https://x.com/atrupar/status/1724965009359261858.
12. Keir Starmer, 'PM Statement on One-Year Anniversary of the October 7th Attacks', gov.uk (6 October 2024).
13. Nir Hasson and Liza Rozovsky, 'Hamas Committed Documented Atrocities. But a Few False Stories Feed the Deniers', *Haaretz* (4 December 2023).
14. Al Jazeera English, *October 7 | Al Jazeera Investigations* (20 March 2024), https://www.youtube.com/watch?v=_0atzea-mPY, 40m42s.
15. Daniel Estrin, 'The Israeli Village Grieving the Biggest Loss from Oct. 7, One Year Later', *NPR* (7 October 2024).
16. Daily Mail World, 'Israel Frontline: "I Saw a Beheaded Baby" - Inside Kibbutz Where Hamas Killed 108 People' (16 October 2023), https://www.youtube.com/watch?v=Wsbd_dV8Xf8, 4m10s.
17. The Sun, 'Israeli Commander Tells of Horror at Discovering Baby Beheaded by Hamas Savages' (15 October 2023), https://www.youtube.com/watch?v=ZD2JHiY3y6s, 1m49s.
18. Al Jazeera Investigations, *October 7*, 36m35s.
19. Josh Breiner et al., '"Please Come Save Us": Recordings of Kibbutz Hostage Standoff Reveal Scope of Israel's Oct. 7 Failure', *Haaretz* (10 October 2024).

See also Liza Rozovsky, 'Four Members of One Israeli Family Killed in October 7 Hamas Attack Laid to Rest in Kibbutz Be'eri', *Haaretz* (4 September 2024).

20. Al Jazeera Investigations, *October 7*, 37m41s.
21. AFP, 'Israel Social Security Data Reveals True Picture of Oct 7 Deaths', *France24* (15 December 2023).
22. Al Jazeera Investigations, *October 7*, 43m25s.
23. Al Jazeera Investigations, *October 7*, 31m10s.
24. Middle East Eye, 'Survivor Speaks: Israeli Forces Shot Their Own Civilians' (16 October 2023), https://www.youtube.com/watch?v=rTQcjyhPOIk, 0m38s.
25. Emanuel Fabian, 'Failure and Slaughter: IDF's Be'eri Probe Shows Army's Colossal Errors, Residents' Bravery', *The Times of Israel* (11 July 2024).
26. Yaniv Kubovich, 'IDF Ordered Hannibal Directive on October 7 to Prevent Hamas Taking Soldiers Captive', *Haaretz* (7 July 2024).
27. Huthifa Fayyad, 'Names of 710 Palestinian Newborns Killed by Israeli Forces in Gaza Published', *Middle East Eye* (16 September 2024).
28. Madjid Zerrouky, 'Gaza's Health Ministry Reveals Names of Several Thousand Dead, over 11,355 of Them Are Minors', *Le Monde* (21 September 2024).

Chapter Four

1. Council for Arab-British Understanding, 'Overview of Party Stances on Palestine', caabu.org (n.d.).
2. Camilla Tominey, 'For the First Time in My Life I'm Beginning to Fear for the Future of Britain', *Daily Telegraph* (3 November 2023).
3. John Anderson and Douglas Murray, 'Conversations: Douglas Murray, Journalist and Author', johnanderson.net.au (8 November 2023), from 58m50s.
4. Post by @DouglasKMurray on X (2 November 2023), https://x.com/DouglasKMurray/status/1720158403308204206.
5. Thomas Mackintosh and Emily Atkinson, 'London Protests: Met Condemns "Extreme Violence" of Far-Right', bbc.co.uk (12 November 2023).

6. For a round-up of the following day's newspaper headlines see 'Newspaper Round Up: 12th of November 2023', tomorrowspapers.co.uk (n.d.).
7. UK House of Commons Home Affairs Committee, *Policing of Protests: Third Report of Session 2023–24*, committees.parliament.uk (21 February 2024), pp. 23–24.
8. Ibid., p. 14.
9. Ibid., pp. 14, 33.
10. Labour MPs Jeremy Corbyn and John McDonnell were 'interviewed under caution' on January 19, 2025. Amy Walker, 'Corbyn and McDonnell Face Police Interview after Pro-Palestinian Rally', bbc.co.uk (19 January 2025).
11. Professor Gus John and Professor Gargi Bhattacharyya.
12. As *The Guardian* revealed, government lawyers warned Braverman that inflammatory immigration rhetoric risked inspiring a far-right terror attack. Mark Townsend, 'Suella Braverman Was Warned "Hate Speech" Could Inspire Far Right', *The Guardian* (6 November 2022).
13. Channel 4 News, 'Braverman: Pro-Palestinian Protests Are "Hate Marches"' (30 October 2023), https://www.youtube.com/watch?v=8YSuJUmdXHU.
14. Nandini Naira Archer, 'Arrest Rate at "Openly Criminal" Palestine Protests Is Lower Than Glastonbury', opendemocracy.net (7 February 2024).
15. Ben Reiff, 'A "No-Go" for Jews? The Making of a Moral Panic in London', 972mag.com (13 March 2024). For the Glastonbury comparison see Archer, 'Arrest Rate'.
16. Suella Braverman, 'Suella Braverman's Article: Police Must Be Even Handed With Protestors', *The Times* (8 November 2023).
17. Sam Francis, 'Rishi Sunak Sacks Suella Braverman as Home Secretary', bbc.co.uk (13 November 2023).
18. Wafaa Shurafa and Samy Magdy, 'More Than 29,000 Palestinians Have Been Killed in Gaza Since War's Start, Health Ministry Says', pbs.org (19 February 2024).
19. International Criminal Court, 'Information for Victims: State of Palestine', ICC-01/18, icc-cpi.int (21 November 2024; accessed on 14 February 2025).
20. John McEvoy, 'Did Israel Bomb British Doctors with UK-Supplied Weaponry?' *Declassified UK* (7 February 2024). Matt Kennard, 'UK Admits Nine Israeli Military Planes Have Visited Britain Since Gaza Bombing

Began', *Declassified UK* (8 February 2024). Mark Curtis, 'U.K. Is Training Israeli Military in Britain', *Declassified UK* (12 February 2024).

21. UK House of Commons, 'UK-Israel Free Trade Agreement: Fourth Round Negotiations', HCWS325, hansard.parliament.uk (11 March 2024).
22. Robert Peston, 'Labour's Gaza Ceasefire Motion in Lockstep with SNP - What Happens Next?' itv.com (20 February 2024). Labour MP Harriet Harman later said that it was not possible for Labour to overlook its differences with the SNP motion, in particular its 'condemning the Israelis for what they describe as collective punishment'. Judith Duffy, 'Labour MP Harriet Harman Rejected Gaza Motion as It "Condemned Israelis" for Collective Punishment', *The National* (28 February 2024).
23. 'Satellite Images Show 30% of Gaza Destroyed, UN Centre Says', reuters.com (2 February 2024).
24. Kiran Stacey, 'Commons Speaker Apologises after Gaza Ceasefire Debate Descends into Chaos', *The Guardian* (21 February 2024).
25. This was confirmed by the clerk of the House, the main constitutional advisor to Parliament. On an opposition day, there is conventionally one opposition motion and a government amendment. UK Parliament Deposited Papers, 'Letter Dated 21/02/2024 from Clerk of the House Tom Goldsmith to Speaker Lindsay Hoyle. . .', DEP2024-0193 depositedpapers.parliament.uk (21 February 2024).
26. Kiran Stacey, 'How Kier Starmer Averted Gaza Ceasefire Vote Crisis', *The Guardian* (21 February 2024).
27. Stacey, 'Commons Speaker Apologises'. Ben Quinn, 'Why Is the Commons Speaker Facing Calls to Quit and What Happens Next?' *The Guardian* (22 February 2024).
28. UK House of Commons, 'Speaker's Statement', hansard.parliament.uk (21 February 2024).
29. UK House of Commons, 'Ceasefire in Gaza', hansard.parliament.uk (21 February 2024).
30. Noa Hoffman, 'Respect the Ref: Michael Gove Backs Lindsay Hoyle and Says the "Real Issue" Is Extremist Thugs after Commons Ceasefire Chaos', *The Sun* (22 February 2024).
31. I am grateful to Andrew Feinberg, White House correspondent of *The Independent*, for supplying me with the tape of Farage's speech.

32. Andrew Feinberg, 'Nigel Farage Tells Right-Wing US Event That "Religious Sectarianism" Is New Threat in UK', *The Independent* (22 February 2024).
33. Post by @DouglasKMurray on X (22 February 2024), https://x.com/DouglasKMurray/status/1760656066742833547.
34. Daniel Martin, 'Lindsay Hoyle: The Speaker from a Very Political – and Very Labour – Family', *The Telegraph* (21 February 2024).
35. David Wilcock and James Tapsfield, 'Rishi Sunak Accuses Lindsay Hoyle of Allowing Pro-Palestinian "Extremists" to "Intimidate" Him. . .', *MailOnline* (22 February 2024).
36. Peter Oborne, *Fate of Abraham: Why the West Is Wrong About Islam* (Simon & Schuster, 2022).
37. Melanie Phillips, 'Islamophobia and Antisemitism Are Not the Same', *The Sunday Times* (26 February 2024).
38. Suella Braverman, 'Islamists Are Bullying Britain into Submission', *The Telegraph* (22 February 2024).
39. Robert Jenrick, 'Why Does the Left Consider It Islamophobic to Want to Expel the Cancer of Extremism from Britian?' *Mail on Sunday* (2 March 2024).
40. Video clip posted by @GBNEWS on X (26 February 2024), https://x.com/GBNEWS/status/1762215171500446015.
41. Post by @IsabelOakeshott on X (26 February 2024), https://x.com/IsabelOakeshott/status/1762112249575956650.
42. Post by @RupertLowe10 on X (23 February 2024), https://x.com/RupertLowe10/status/1760939030496116930.
43. Post by @TRobinsonNewEra (Tommy Robinson) on X (26 February 2024), https://x.com/TRobinsonNewEra/status/1762137423054504233.
44. Post by @RishiSunak on X (25 February 2024), https://x.com/RishiSunak/status/1761717752891338880.
45. Matt Strudwick, '"From the River to the Sea" Is Projected onto Big Ben. . .', *MailOnline* (22 February 2024).
46. UK House of Commons, 'Business of the House', hansard.parliament.uk (22 February 2024).
47. David Woode and Steven Swinford, 'MPs Condemn "From the River to the Sea" Projection on Parliament', *The Times* (23 February 2024).

48. Yaacov Shavit, 'Ideology, World View, and National Policy: The Case of the Likud Government 1977–1984', *The Jerusalem Journal of International Relations* 9.2 (1987), pp. 107–8.
49. 'Netanyahu Brandishes Map of Israel That Includes West Bank and Gaza at UN Speech', *The Times of Israel* (22 September 2023).
50. UnHerd, 'Israeli Ambassador Debates "From the River to the Sea"', unherd.com (27 October 2023).
51. B'Tselem, *A Regime of Jewish Supremacy from the Jordan River to the Mediterranean Sea: This Is Apartheid*, btselem.org (12 January 2021).
52. 'Jo Cox: Man Jailed for "Terrorist" Murder of MP', bbc.co.uk (23 November 2016).
53. 'Sir David Amess: Man Found Guilty of Murdering MP', bbc.co.uk (11 April 2022).
54. Alpa Patel and Rebecca Cafe, 'London Hate Crime: Worry over "Significant Fracture" in Communities', bbc.co.uk (23 November 2023). The Community Security Trust and Tell MAMA are frequently cited sources of statistics on antisemitism and Islamophobia, respectively, in the UK. For information on their methodologies, including the CST's inclusion of anti-Israel sentiment in its accounting of antisemitism, see: CST, *Antisemitic Incidents 2024* (2025), pp. 14, 32–33. Tell MAMA, *The New Norm of Anti-Muslim Hate: Tell MAMA Report* (2025).
55. Crown Prosecution Service, 'Chorley Man Sentenced after Sending Threatening Social Media Message to Sir Lindsay Hoyle MP', cps.gov.uk (16 July 2024).
56. Julia Atherley, '"Malicious" Messages: Commons Speaker Lindsay Hoyle "Threatened..."', *The Sun* (3 July 2024).
57. Caroline Gall, 'Man Jailed for "Burn in Hell" Emails to MP', bbc.co.uk (10 September 2024).
58. Shannon Mahanty, 'Speaking Truth to Power: MP Zarah Sultana on Westminster's Toxic Politics', *Elle* (9 May 2024).
59. Ibid.
60. Video clip posted by @TalkTV on X (22 February 2024), https://x.com/TalkTV/status/1760614085824000062.
61. Post by @HugoGye on X (22 February 2024), https://x.com/HugoGye/status/1760616524987924690.

62. Email to my colleague Josiah Mortimer from the Met press office (January 23, 2025): 'We never had any record of any arrests on 21 Feb'.
63. Political TV, 'Politics Live | 26th February 2024' (26 February 2024), https://www.youtube.com/watch?v=CRmjpolqxvc, 14m02s. See also #994, political-lies.co.uk (26 February 2024), https://political-lies.co.uk/last-week-we-saw-protests-outside-our-own-house-of-commons-extremely-aggressive-violent-protests-from-islamist-extremists-and-we-should-be-able-to-say-we-are-concerned-about-what-we-are-see.
64. I contacted Rachel Maclean to give her the opportunity to provide evidence for her dramatic claims about violent and aggressive protests by 'Islamist extremists'. She replied: 'I stand by what I said and it is easy to find examples of the types of protests I referred to back then'. She cited 'projection of an anti-semitic and violent statement [i.e., 'From the river to the sea / Palestine will be free'] on to the Houses of Parliament' on February 21, 2024, and a protest on Westminster Bridge a month *earlier* on January 6, 2024. (In respect of the latter, she provided a link to a *Times of Israel* article that referred to 'several small scuffles'.) She also cited a pro-Palestinian demonstration that took place more than three months *later* on May 28, 2024. She told us that '[l]eaving and entering the Parliamentary estate has felt threatening and intimidating due to the presence of these groups and many of us find them intimidating. I have to walk over Westminster Bridge on a daily basis running the gamut of these individuals'.
65. James Walker, 'Police Respond to Claim That Labour Glasgow Office Was "Stormed"', *The National* (21 February 2024).
66. Eleni Courea and Josh Halliday, 'British MPs Fearful of Violent Attacks as tensions over Gaza War Increase Threats', *The Guardian* (23 February 2024).
67. UK House of Commons, 'Ceasefire in Gaza', hansard.parliament.uk (21 February 2024).
68. UK House of Commons, 'Speaker's Statement', hansard.parliament.uk (21 February 2024).
69. Stephen Flynn, 'Westminster Stitch-Up Blocks SNP Ceasefire Vote', snp.org (21 February 2024).
70. Patrick Maguire and Gabriel Pogrund, *Get In: The Inside Story of Labour under Starmer* (Bodley Head, 2025), p. 366.

71. Posts by @nicholaswatt on X (21 February 2024), https://x.com/nicholaswatt/status/1760315363542122769.
72. Caroline Wheeler et al., 'After a Week of Chaos, Sir Lindsay Hoyle Is Running Out of Options', *The Times* (25 February 2024).
73. The Labour motion was passed by 'acclamation' and it is difficult to say for certain whether it really commanded a majority; no individual votes were recorded.
74. YouGov, 'From What You've Read and Heard, Do You Think There Should or Should Not Be an Immediate Ceasefire in Israel and Palestine?' yougov.co.uk (19 October 2023).
75. A.J.P. Taylor, *The Trouble Makers* (Panther, 1969), p. 17. Based on Taylor's Ford Lectures at Oxford, Hilary term, 1956. Also Taylor: 'Today's realism will appear tomorrow as short-sighted blundering. Today's idealism is the realism of the future'.

Chapter Five

1. Matthew Hughes, 'From Law and Order to Pacification: Britain's Suppression of the Arab Revolt in Palestine, 1936–39', *Journal of Palestine Studies* 39.2 (2010), pp. 6–22. Tom Bateman, 'UK Apology Sought for British War Crimes in Palestine', bbc.co.uk (7 October 2022).
2. I am relying here on Ilan Pappé, *Lobbying for Zionism on Both Sides of the Atlantic* (Oneworld, 2024), pp. 189–96.
3. Rosemary Hollis, 'Palestine and the Palestinians in British Political Elite Discourse: From "The Palestine Problem" to "the Two-State Solution"', *International Relations* 30.1 (2016), p. 16.
4. Colter Louwerse, *The Struggle for Palestinian Rights: The Palestinian Campaign for Self-Determination and Statehood at the United Nations, 1967–1989*, PhD thesis (University of Exeter, 2022), chaps. 3 and 6. Colter Louwerse, '"Tyranny of the Veto": PLO Diplomacy and the January 1976 United Nations Security Council Resolution', *Diplomacy & Statecraft* 33.2 (2022), pp. 303–29.
5. Hollis, 'Palestine', p. 20.
6. The British Consulate in Jerusalem has issued a continuous stream of statements condemning demolitions, evictions, and illegal settlements in the West Bank for years. The statements keep coming because Israel simply ignores the objections of Britain and other countries. At the same time,

British officials lost all serious interest in Palestinian rights, as illustrated by the '2030 Roadmap' signed by Britain and Israel and discussed in Chapter Six below.

7. UN Office for the Coordination of Humanitarian Affairs (UN OHA), 'Increase in Settler Violence: Remarks Provided to the Press', ochaopt.org (5 August 2023).
8. B'Tselem, 'Settler Violence = State Violence', btselem.org (25 November 2021).
9. Yolande Knell and David Gritten, 'Netanyahu's Hard-Line New Government Takes Office in Israel', bbc.co.uk (29 December 2022).
10. B'Tselem, 'The Pogrom in Huwarah and Other Palestinian Communities in the Northern West Bank: The Jewish Supremacy Regime in Action', btselem.org (12 March 2023).
11. 'Palestine's Huwara Should Be Wiped Out: Top Israeli Minister', aljazeera.com (1 March 2023).
12. Ibid. Smotrich attempted to backtrack later, saying: 'I did not mean wipe out the village of Huwara, rather act in a targeted manner against the terrorists and supporters of terrorism living there and to exact a heavy price from them in order to restore security to the [Jewish] residents of the area'. See Jacob Magid, 'Smotrich's DC Visit Still on amid Uproar, but US Officials Not Planning to Meet Him', *The Times of Israel* (3 March 2023).
13. Post by @UKinJerusalem on X (3 March 2023).
14. Yaniv Kubovich, 'Israeli Army Chief Says Hawara Riots Were Mismanaged, No Disciplinary Measures to Be Taken', *Haaretz* (9 March 2023). 'Huwwara Assaults: Probe Concludes No Disciplinary Action against Israel Army Officials', *Middle East Eye* (10 March 2023).
15. Amira Hass, 'Settler Violence in the West Bank Isn't an Oversight, It's a Longstanding Policy', *Haaretz* (1 July 2023).
16. Lubna Masarwa and Peter Oborne, 'Israel Blocked UK Foreign Secretary from Visiting Palestinian Village Terrorised by Settlers', *Middle East Eye* (3 October 2023).
17. Channel 4 News (11 October 2023). See also David Gilmour, 'Israeli Foreign Minister Stops Interview to Dismiss Gaza Question, Highlight Israeli Pain', mediaite.com (12 October 2023).

18. For a guide to Israel's obligations see Amnesty International, *Destination: Occupation—Digital Tourism and Israel's Illegal Settlements in the Occupied Palestinian Territories* (2019), chap. 3.
19. ICJ, *Legal Consequences Arising from the Policies and Practices of Israel in the Occupied Palestinian Territory, including East Jerusalem*, Advisory Opinion (19 July 2024), para. 285.
20. Human Rights Watch, *Why They Died: Civilian Casualties in Lebanon during the 2006 War* (September 2007), pp. 4, 40.
21. Ibid. In the villages of Srifa, Siddiquine, Aita al-Sha'ab, and Bint Jbeil hundreds of homes were completely destroyed.
22. Yaniv Cogan, 'Targeting Civilians: Its Logic in Gaza and Israel', in Jamie Stern-Weiner ed., *Deluge: Gaza and Israel from Crisis to Cataclysm* (OR Books, 2024), p. 100.
23. Eitan Shamir, 'Gadi Eisenkot's Challenges and Opportunities', *besacenter.org* (8 December 2014). The article is positive about Eisenkot's record.
24. Zeev Maoz, *Defending the Holy Land: A Critical Analysis of Israel's Security & Foreign Policy* (University of Michigan Press, 2006), p. 626.
25. Colter Louwerse, 'Is Hamas to Blame for the Failure to Resolve the Israel-Palestine Conflict?' in Jamie Stern-Weiner ed., *Deluge: Gaza and Israel from Crisis to Cataclysm* (OR Books, 2025), pp. 70–77.
26. Paul Scham and Osama Abu-Irshaid, *Hamas: Ideological Rigidity and Political Flexibility* (United States Institute of Peace, June 2009).
27. Alvaro de Soto, UN Special Coordinator for the Middle East Peace Process, *End of Mission Report* (May 2007), para. 124.
28. House of Commons Foreign Affairs Committee, *Global Security: The Middle East*, Eighth Report of Session 2006–7, HC 363 (The Stationery Office Limited, 13 August 2007), para. 60.
29. Alastair Crooke, 'Our Second Biggest Mistake', *London Review of Books* 29.13 (5 July 2007) (Britain). David Rose, 'The Gaza Bombshell', *Vanity Fair* (3 March 2008) (US). Gregg Carlstrom, 'MI6 Offered to Detain Hamas Figures', aljazeera.com (25 January 2011) (Britain).
30. De Soto, *End*, para 56.
31. Jonathan Steele, 'Middle East: Palestinians "Routinely Torture" Rival Detainees', *The Guardian* (29 July 2008). Raf Sanchez, 'Palestinian Security

Forces Accused of Using Torture "to Crush Dissent" in Gaza and Occupied West Bank', *The Telegraph* (23 October 2018).

32. Amnesty International et al., *The Gaza Strip: A Humanitarian Implosion* (6 March 2008).
33. 'Gaza Unemployment Levels "Among Worst in World"', bbc.co.uk (14 June 2011).
34. Dov Weissglas quoted in Aluf Benn, 'U.S. Backs Israel on Aid for Humanitarian Groups, Not Hamas', *Haaretz* (16 February 2006).
35. 'Gaza Residents "Terribly Trapped"', bbc.co.uk (4 November 2008).
36. 'ICRC Says Israel's Gaza Blockade Breaks Law', bbc.co.uk (14 June 2010).
37. House of Commons International Development Committee, *The Humanitarian and Development Situation in the Occupied Palestinian Territories*, Eleventh Report of Session 2007–8, vol. 1, HC 522-I (The Stationery Office Limited, 17 July 2008), para. 29.
38. Human Rights Watch, 'Memorandum Submitted to the House of Commons Select Committee on Foreign Affairs', publications.parliament.uk (April 2008).
39. Amnesty International et al., *Failing Gaza: No Rebuilding, No Recovery, No More Excuses—A Report One Year After Operation Cast Lead* (22 December 2009), p. 15.
40. *Report of the United Nations Fact-Finding Mission on the Gaza Conflict* (25 September 2009), para. 1893.
41. Amnesty International, *Operation 'Cast Lead': 22 Days of Death and Destruction* (2009), pp. 27–28.
42. Human Rights Watch, *Beyond Burning: The Ripple Effects of Incendiary Weapons and Increasing Calls for International Action* (7 November 2024).
43. Amnesty International, *22 Days*, pp. 76–77.
44. Amnesty International, 'Operation "Cast Lead" – 22 Days of Death and Destruction. Facts and Figures', amnesty.org (2 July 2009).
45. Norman G. Finkelstein, *Gaza: An Inquest into Its Martyrdom* (University of California Press, 2018), p. 54.
46. Amnesty International, *22 Days*, p. 55.
47. Finkelstein, *Gaza*, p. 54.
48. Ibid., pp. 53–54.

49. Ibid., pp. 60–61.
50. Breaking the Silence, *Soldiers' Testimonies from Operation Cast Lead, Gaza 2009* (February 2011), p. 85.
51. Cogan, 'Targeting Civilians', p. 102.
52. Finkelstein, *Gaza*, p. 81.
53. UK House of Commons, 'Gaza', hansard.parliament.uk (12 January 2009).
54. UN General Assembly, 'Follow-Up to the Report of the United Nations Fact-Finding Mission on the Gaza Conflict', A/RES/64/10 (1 December 2009).
55. UK Foreign Secretary David Miliband, 'Letter to Vivian Wineman and Mick Davis of the Jewish Leadership Council' (5 November 2009). Reproduced in Jessica Elgot, 'Miliband Rejects Pleas over Goldstone UN Vote', *Jewish Chronicle* (6 November 2009).
56. Finkelstein, *Gaza*, p. 66.
57. Ian Black and Ian Cobain, 'British Court Issued Gaza Arrest Warrant for Former Israeli Minister Tzipi Livni', *The Guardian* (14 December 2009).
58. Herb Keinon, 'Miliband "Shocked" at Livni's Warrant', *The Jerusalem Post* (15 December 2009). Ian Black, 'Gordon Brown Reassures Israel over Tzipi Livni Arrest Warrant', *The Guardian* (16 December 2009).
59. James Blitz, 'Miliband Attacks Warrant on Israeli', *Financial Times* (16 December 2009).
60. John McEvoy, 'Israel Lobbied Britain to Change Law on War Crimes Arrests', *Declassified UK* (19 September 2024).
61. Taken from Finkelstein, *Gaza*, pp. 240, 311.
62. Includes one Thai civilian.
63. Finkelstein, *Gaza*, p. 240.
64. UK House of Commons, 'Ukraine (Flight MH17) and Gaza', hansard.parliament.uk (21 July 2014).
65. Ibid.
66. UK Foreign, Commonwealth, and Development Office (FCDO), 'Foreign Secretary: Gaza Human Rights Resolution Will Not Aid Peace Process', gov.uk (23 July 2014).
67. UK House of Commons, 'Ukraine (Flight MH17) and Gaza'.
68. FCDO, 'Foreign Secretary Comments on the Situation in Gaza, gov.uk (5 August 2014).

69. UN Human Rights Council, *Ensuring Respect for International Law in the Occupied Palestinian Territory, including East Jerusalem*, A/HRC/RES/S-21/1 (23 July 2014).

70. FCDO, 'Gaza Human Rights Resolution'.

71. Campaign Against the Arms Trade (CAAT), 'UK Must Stop Arming Israel', caat.org.uk (27 August 2014). Cahal Milmo, 'Israel-Gaza Conflict: Revealed—Britain's "Role" in Arming Israel', *The Independent* (2 August 2014).

72. Department for Business, Innovation & Skills (BIS), 'Government Announces Findings of Review of Licensed Exports to Israel', go.uk (12 August 2014).

73. BIS, 'Review of Export Licensing Procedures for Israel', gov.uk (14 July 2015).

74. UK House of Commons, 'Gaza', hansard.parliament.uk (14 July 2014).

75. Finkelstein, *Gaza*, p. 214.

76. UK House of Commons, 'Ukraine (Flight MH17) and Gaza'.

77. UK House of Commons, 'Gaza'.

78. 'Foreign Secretary Philip Hammond Addresses 500 Delegates at CFI Party Conference Reception', cfoi.co.uk (7 October 2015). See also David Cronin, *Balfour's Shadow: A Century of British Support for Zionism and Israel* (Pluto Press, 2017), p. 170. Cronin shows that ministers were aware of the humanitarian catastrophe in Gaza.

79. Patrick Wintour and Rowena Mason, 'Lady Warsi Resigns over UK's "Morally Indefensible" Stance on Gaza', *The Guardian* (5 August 2014).

80. Matthew Holehouse, 'George Osborne: Baroness Warsi Resignation over Gaza "Disappointing and Unnecessary"', *The Telegraph* (5 August 2014).

81. R. J., 'Rule Number One of Nonviolent Resistance: It Can't Work If It's Misrepresented as Violent', in Jamie Stern-Weiner ed., *Deluge: Gaza and Israel from Crisis to Cataclysm* (OR Books, 2024).

82. *Report of the Detailed Findings of the Independent International Commission of Inquiry on the Protests in the Occupied Palestinian Territory* (18 March 2019), p. 104.

83. UN OCHA estimated that 23,313 Palestinians were injured during the demonstrations, including by tear-gas inhalation. Ibid., para. 402.

84. Ibid., para. 692. See also ibid., paras. 519, 526, 536, 537.
85. Ibid., p. 2.
86. Ibid., paras. 30–33.
87. Amnesty International, 'Israel: Arms Embargo Needed as Military Unlawfully Kills and Maims Gaza Protesters', amnesty.org (27 April 2018).
88. UK House of Commons, 'Gaza Border Violence', hansard.parliament.uk (15 May 2018).
89. Ibid.
90. Ibid.
91. This comparison is made in R. J., 'Rule Number One', p. 92.
92. Yousef Munayyer, 'Palestinian Non-Violence Relies on Global Non-Silence', *The Guardian* (21 May 2010).

Chapter Six

1. David Rose, '"I'll Always Stand by Israel' Sunak Tells CFI Event', *The Jewish Chronicle* (22 January 2024). The only national outlet to report the lunch was *MailOnline*.
2. Al Jazeera, 'Gaza Death Toll Surpasses 25,000 as Israel Escalates Assault', aljazeera.com (21 January 2024).
3. Oxfam, 'Daily Death Rate in Gaza Higher Than Any Other Major 21st Century Conflict - Oxfam', oxfam.org.uk (11 January 2024).
4. CFI YouTube, 'Prime Minister Rishi Sunak Addresses CFI Annual Business Lunch' (23 January 2024),
5. CFI YouTube, 'President Herzog Address at CFI Annual Business Lunch 2024' (24 January 2024), https://www.youtube.com/watch?v=mCc8i9o_-fY.
6. Azriel Bermant, *Margaret Thatcher and the Middle East* (Cambridge University Press, 2016), pp. 10–11.
7. UN General Assembly Resolution 43/176 (15 December 1988).
8. David Cronin, 'Sunak Takes British Support for Israel to New Extreme', *Declassified UK* (16 October 2023).
9. Monty Modlyn and Margaret Thatcher, 'Interview for *Jewish Chronicle*', margaretthatcher.org (12 June 1981; first published 19 June 1981).
10. Human Rights Watch, *The Israeli Army and the Intifada Policies that Contribute to the Killings* (August 1990), p. 144.

11. B'Tselem, *The Interrogation of Palestinians During the Intifada: Ill-Treatment, "Moderate Physical Pressure" or Torture?* (March 1991).
12. Sources and discussion in Jamie Stern-Weiner, 'The Power of Mass Nonviolent Resistance in Palestine—Part 1', jamiesternweiner.wordpress.com (16 April 2018).
13. Modlyn and Thatcher, 'Interview'.
14. 'Ex-President Rivlin: Queen Elizabeth "Believed That Every Israeli Was Either a Terrorist or a Son of a Terrorist"—Report', *The Times of Israel* (9 December 2024).
15. One of Faiza Shaheen's offences was to 'like' a tweet featuring a sketch by the American Jewish comedian Jon Stewart, about how he gets called a 'self-hating Jew' when he criticises Israel; the tweet referenced the 'Israel lobby'. When Stewart was told that his sketch had been the cause of Shaheen's downfall, he responded: 'what the actual f**k. . .'. Joe Sommerlad, 'Jon Stewart Calls Rejection of UK Candidate for Liking One of His Sketches "Dumbest Thing since Boris Johnson"', *The Independent* (30 May 2024). See also MEE Staff, 'Faiza Shaheen to Stand as Independent after Being Blocked by Labour over Israel Posts', *Middle East Eye* (5 June 2024).
16. Rachel Cunliffe, 'How the Faiza Shaheen Row Helps Keir Starmer', *New Statesman* (30 May 2024).
17. For example, Mehdi Hasan, 'Britain's Israel Lobby', *New Statesman* (16 November 2009); John Mearsheimer, 'John Mearsheimer: "The Israel Lobby Is as Powerful as Ever"', newstatesman.com (10 February 2024).
18. Mark Curtis, '"National Scandal': The BBC's Gaza Cover-Up', *Declassified UK* (15 January 2025).
19. Matt Kennard and Phil Miller, 'How the Israel Lobby Got Hezbollah Banned in Britain', *Declassified UK* (26 September 2024).
20. Peter Oborne, 'Why Ilan Pappé's New Book on the Israel Lobby Is a Must-Read', *Middle East Eye* (24 June 2024).
21. Hil Aked, *Friends of Israel: The Backlash Against Palestine Solidarity* (Verso Books, 2023), p. 3.
22. Quoted in Aked, pp. 2–3.
23. Peter Oborne and James Jones, 'The Pro-Israel Lobby in Britain: Full Text', *openDemocracy* (13 November 2009).

24. For a discussion of the collapse of the Tory Arabists see Peter Oborne, 'How Britain's Conservatives Became Unconditional Supporters of Israel', *Middle East Eye* (1 June 2021).
25. Yara Hawari, 'The Tories Can Never Be True Friends of Palestine', aljazeera.com (2 June 2023).
26. Peter Oborne, "It's Time to Put Conservatives' Links with Israel under the Spotlight', *The Independent* (3 April 2024). See also Peter Oborne, 'False Friends', *The Spectator* (19 May 2018).
27. Richard Evans, 'The Wrong Side of History', *New Statesman* (2 March 2024).
28. MEE Staff, ''Tory Peer Accuses UK Government of "Effectively Boycotting" Israeli Minister', *Middle East Eye* (9 March 2023).
29. 'Theresa May Announces Government's Formal Adoption of IHRA Anti-Semitism Definition at CFI Annual Business Lunch', cfoi.co.uk (13 December 2016).
30. 'The Platform of Otzma Yehudit', jewishvirtuallibrary.org (n.d.).
31. Human Rights Watch, 'Gaza: Latest Israeli Plan Inches Closer to Extermination', hrw.org (15 May 2025).
32. Jeremy Sharon, 'Ben Gvir Calls to "Encourage Emigration", Resettle Gaza at Ultra-Nationalist Rally', *The Times of Israel* (14 May 2024).
33. B'Tselem, *Welcome to Hell: The Israeli Prison System as a Network of Torture Camps* (August 2024).
34. UK Foreign, Commonwealth, and Development Office (FCDO), 'Foreign Ministers' Joint Statement on Measures Targeting Itamar Ben-Gvir and Bezalel Smotrich', gov.uk (10 June 2025).
35. Zeev Sternhell, 'Why Benjamin Netanyahu Loves the European Far-Right', *Foreign Policy* (24 February 2019). Suzanne Schneider, 'How Israel's Illiberal Democracy Became a Model for the Right', *Dissent* (Spring 2024). Associated Press, 'Israel's Antisemitism Conference Draws Europe's Far-Right Leaders to Jerusalem', nbcnews.com (28 March 2025).
36. The film can be viewed online at mikenagoya, 'Dispatches: Inside Britain's Israel Lobby 2009' (1 September 2013), https://www.youtube.com/watch?v=lby-BP5xVRI.
37. Oborne and Jones, 'The Pro-Israel Lobby'.
38. Aked, *Friends*, p. 90.

39. Will Woodward, 'Hague's Criticism of Israel Enrages Leading Tory Donor', *The Guardian* (3 August 2006). Hague confined himself to saying that 'elements' of Israel's response were disproportionate.
40. Lord Stanley Kalms, 'Letters to the Editor', *The Spectator* (5 August 2006).
41. See my 2009 *Dispatches* documentary on the Israel lobby. See also Oborne and Jones, 'The Pro-Israel Lobby'.
42. Norman G. Finkelstein, *Gaza: An Inquest into Its Martyrdom* (University of California Press, 2018), pp. 240, 311.
43. Conservative Friends of India also hosted a hustings in 2022.
44. David Rose, 'Liz Truss Pledges to Review Moving UK Embassy to Jerusalem If Elected PM', *The Jewish Chronicle* (5 August 2022).
45. Norman G. Finkelstein, *Gaza's Gravediggers: An Inquiry into Corruption in High Places* (OR Books, 2025), Appendix.
46. Rob Merrick, 'Boris Johnson Condemns International Criminal Court Palestine Investigation as "Attack on Israel"', *The Independent* (14 April 2021). For the letter itself, see post by @CFoI on X (13 April 2021), https://x.com/CFoI/status/1382057470810587141.
47. Matt Kennard, 'Former British Minister: "The Israelis Think They Control the Foreign Office. And They Do!"', *Declassified UK* (4 June 2021).
48. Ibid. For an account of Stuart Polak's directorship of CFI, see Phil Miller and Simon Hooper, 'Israel Lobbyist in House of Lords Claims Thousands of Pounds in Public Money', *Declassified UK* (19 July 2024).
49. Kennard, 'Former British Minister'.
50. Chris Mullin, "Alan Duncan's Diaries: An Insider's Account of Boris Johnson, Brexit and Britain's Middle East Secrets', *Middle East Eye* (3 May 2021).
51. See the documentary series by the Al Jazeera Investigative Unit: *The Lobby* (2017).
52. Ian Cobain and Ewen MacAskill, 'Israeli Diplomat Caught on Camera Plotting on "Take Down" UK MPs', *The Guardian* (7 January 2017).
53. Kennard, 'Former British Minister'.
54. Peter Oborne, 'Boris Johnson Says Matter of Israel Embassy Plot Is "Closed". He's Wrong—It's a Scandal', *Middle East Eye* (9 January 2017).
55. Al Jazeera Investigative Unit, 'UK: Israel Funding Spin Trips as It Smears Critics', aljazeera.com (12 January 2017).

56. Ibid. This is a paraphrase by Al Jazeera rather than a direct quote from LFI.
57. Ibid.
58. Oborne, 'Boris Johnson Says'.
59. Nina Lloyd, 'Boris Johnson Claims Bugging Device Found in His Bathroom after Netanyahu Visit', *The Independent* (4 October 2024).
60. Antony Lerman, *Whatever Happened to Antisemitism? Redefinition and the Myth of the 'Collective Jew'* (Pluto Press, 2022).
61. Jamie Stern-Weiner, *The 'New Antisemitism': A Historically Informed Case Study Analysis*, PhD thesis (University of Oxford, 2024), chap. 3. See also Jamie Stern-Weiner, *The Politics of a Definition: How the IHRA Working Definition Is Being Misrepresented* (Free Speech on Israel, April 2021).
62. 'Working Definition of Antisemitism', holocaustremembrance.com (n.d.). IHRA adopted the definition on May 26, 2016.
63. Stern-Weiner, *New Antisemitism*.
64. 'Challenging the IHRA Definition of Antisemitism', lawfare.fmep.org (15 July 2025; regularly updated).
65. Jamie Stern-Weiner, 'The IHRA Working Definition of Antisemitism: Delegitimizing Criticism of Israel', palquest.org (n.d.).
66. 'CFI Parliamentary Chairman Sir Eric Pickles: Theresa May a "Good Friend of Jewish Community"', cfoi.co.uk (15 July 2016).
67. UK Prime Minister's Office, 'Government Leads the Way in Tackling Anti-Semitism', gov.uk (12 December 2016). See also 'Theresa May Announces Government's Formal Adoption of IHRA Anti-Semitism Definition at CFI Annual Business Lunch', cfoi.co.uk (13 December 2016).
68. 'Theresa May Announces Government's Formal Adoption of IHRA Anti-Semitism Definition at CFI Annual Business Lunch', cfoi.co.uk (13 December 2016).
69. 'Intellectuals Respond to IHRA Definition of Antisemitism', palestine-studies.org (30 November 2020).
70. UK Prime Minister's Office, 'Government Leads the Way'.
71. Greg Heffer, 'Labour Warned against Introducing a "Blasphemy Law" by Adopting an Official Definition of Islamophobia after Far-Right Riots', *Daily Mail* (10 August 2024).
72. Areeb Ullah, 'Boycott Bill: Pro-Palestine Groups Not Invited to Give Evidence to MPs', *Middle East Eye* (6 September 2023).

73. Peter Oborne, 'Boycott Bill: Britain's Political Gift to Netanyahu', *Middle East Eye* (11 September 2023).
74. The letter was disclosed by BBC reporters Ione Wells and Tom Bateman: Ione Wells and Tom Bateman, 'No 10 Warned Israel Boycotts Bill Enables Russia', bbc.co.uk (11 July 2023).
75. Oborne, 'Boycott Bill'.
76. Lee Harpin, 'Cleverly and Cohen Sign UK-Israel Bilateral Trade Roadmap Agreement', *Jewish News* (23 March 2023).
77. Post by @TzipiHotovely on X (21 March 2023), https://x.com/TzipiHotovely/status/1638299908389101568.
78. 'Written Evidence Submitted by Labour Friends of Israel (MENA0005)', committees,parliament.uk (October 2023), para. 46; available at https://committees.parliament.uk/writtenevidence/125240/pdf/.
79. FCDO, '2030 Roadmap for UK-Israel Bilateral Relations', gov.uk (21 March 2023).
80. Ibid.
81. The UN Human Rights Council resolved to 'urgently establish an ongoing, independent, international commission of inquiry to investigate, in the Occupied Palestinian Territory, including East Jerusalem, and in Israel, all alleged violations of international humanitarian law and abuses of international human rights law'. UN Office of the High Commissioner for Human Rights, 'The Independent International Commission of Inquiry on the Occupied Palestinian Territory, including East Jerusalem, and Israel', ohchr.org (n.d). The British government voted against.
82. Mark Curtis, *Unpeople: Britain's Secret Human Rights Abuses* (Vintage, 2004), pp. 41–42, 129.
83. Frank Barat, 'The Crime of Apartheid', aljazeera.com (7 September 2011).
84. B'Tselem, *A Regime of Jewish Supremacy from the Jordan River to the Mediterranean Sea: This Is Apartheid* (January 2021). Human Rights Watch, *A Threshold Crossed: Israeli Authorities and the Crimes of Apartheid and Persecution* (April 2021). Amnesty International, *Israel's Apartheid against Palestinians: Cruel System of Domination and a Crime against Humanity* (February 2022). The executive director of Amnesty International Israel, Molly Malekar, disagreed with Amnesty's finding of

apartheid, although she rejected claims that Amnesty is biased against Israel and that Amnesty is anti-Semitic. Tani Goldstein, 'Amnesty's Israel Chief Criticizes Group's Report Accusing Israel of Apartheid', *The Times of Israel* (21 February 2022).

85. Ilan Baruch and Alon Liel, 'It's Apartheid, Say Israeli Ambassadors to South Africa', groundup.org.za (8 June 2021).
86. '2030 Roadmap'.
87. Ibid.
88. Jonathan Guyer, 'Israel's New Right-Wing Government Is Even More Extreme Than Protests Would Have You Think', *Vox* (20 January 2023).

Chapter Seven

1. 'Airwars Assessment', airwars.org (19 March 2025).
2. David Gritten, 'Jabalia: Israel Air Strike Reportedly Kills Dozens at Gaza Refugee Camp', bbc.co.uk (31 October 2023).
3. 'UN Rights Office Says Israeli Attacks on Jabalia Could Be "War Crime"', aljazeera.com (2 November 2023).
4. Kareem Khadder et al., 'Catastrophic Damage after Second Israeli Airstrike Hits Gaza Refugee Camp', edition.cnn.com (1 November 2023).
5. UN Office for the Coordination of Humanitarian Affairs, '*Hostilities in the Gaza Strip and Israel | Flash Update #25*', ochaopt.org (31 October 2023).
6. David Gritten, 'Israel's Military Says It Fully Controls Communities on Gaza Border', bbc.co.uk (9 October 2023).
7. Rory Carroll, 'UN's António Guterres Calls for Immediate Ceasefire to End "Epic Suffering" in Gaza', *The Guardian* (25 October 2023). UN General Assembly Resolution, 'Protection of Civilians and Upholding Legal and Humanitarian Obligations', A/RES/ES-10/21 (27 October 2023). Jacob Magid, 'UN Resolution Calling for Immediate Gaza Ceasefire Passes with Overwhelming Majority', *The Times of Israel* (27 October 2023).
8. Lewis Denison and Harry Horton, 'Starmer Backs "Humanitarian Pause" in Gaza amid Backlash but Resists Calling for Ceasefire', itv.com (25 October 2023). Muslim Census Team, 'Labour and Conservatives Losing the Muslim Vote', muslimcensus.co.uk (26 October 2023).

9. Kate Whannel, 'Labour Divisions Deepen over Gaza Ceasefire Stance', bbc.co.uk (27 October 2023).
10. YouGov, 'From What You've Read and Heard, Do You Think There Should or Should Not Be an Immediate Ceasefire in Israel and Palestine?' yougov.co.uk (19 October 2023).
11. 'Keir Starmer's Speech on the International Situation in the Middle East', labour.org.uk (31 October 2023).
12. UK House of Commons, 'Engagements', hansard.parliament.uk (13 November 2024). 'British Premier Tells UK Parliament There Is No Genocide in Gaza', *Middle East Monitor* (13 November 2024).
13. Starmer also stated this explicitly in an LBC radio call-in show on June 18, 2024: 'Having literally argued in court for three months over the meaning of genocide, the evidence of genocide, I'm very well aware of what it is.' 'UK Labour Party Leader Refuses to Accept Genocide Is Happening in Gaza', *Middle East Monitor* (21 June 2024).
14. ICJ, *Application of the Convention on the Prevention and Punishment of the Crimes of Genocide (Croatia v. Serbia)*, Public Sitting—Verbatim Record (7 March 2014), pp. 19–20.
15. Israel Prime Minister's Office, 'Statement by PM Netanyahu', gov.il (19 July 2024).
16. Dana Karni et al., 'Israel Vows to Escalate War with New Plan to "Conquer" Gaza', edition.cnn.com (6 May 2025).
17. 'Annex to the Letter Dated 27 February 2025 from the Permanent Representative of South Africa to the United Nations addressed to the President of the Security Council', S/2025/130 (28 February 2025), Annex I, paras. 10 ('Amalek'), 40 ('terrorists'), 44 ('maternity ward'), 52 ('brought it upon'); Annex II, paras. 5 ('animals'), 6 ('evil', 'sons of Satan'). Ahmad Tibi, 'Israel, Stop Killing Children in Gaza', *Haaretz* (2 June 2025) ('children should be killed'). Nir Hasson, 'Knesset Debate Reveals Not Everyone Thinks Starving Gazan Children Is a Bad Thing', *Haaretz* (10 May 2025) ('sickest doctor').
18. Chen Maanit, 'State Prosecutor Advises against Probing Israeli Ministers, MKs Who Called to Harm Gazans', *Haaretz* (19 August 2024).
19. International Commission of Inquiry, *Detailed Findings*, A/HRC/56/CRP.4 (10 June 2024), paras. 420–22, 427, 434, 437–38, 450, 451, 458,

464, 468. Passages quoted in Jamie Stern-Weiner and Avi Shlaim, 'Israel's Road to Genocide', in Avi Shlaim, *Genocide in Gaza: Israel's Long War on Palestine* (The Irish Pages Press, 2024), pp. 305–6.

20. Younis Tirawi and Eran Maoz, 'EXCLUSIVE: Inside Israel's Insta-Genocide', zeteo.com (10 June 2024).
21. Amnesty International, *'You Feel Like You Are Subhuman': Israel's Genocide Against Palestinians in Gaza* (December 2024), p. 264.
22. Stern-Weiner and Shlaim, 'Israel's Road', p. 289.
23. UK House of Commons, 'Middle East', hansard.parliament.uk (28 October 2024). Imran Mulla, 'Arab Public Figures Demand David Lammy Apologise for Genocide Comments', *Middle East Eye* (31 October 2024).
24. ICJ, *Croatia v. Serbia*, Public Sitting—Verbatim Record (7 March 2014), p. 13.
25. ICJ, *Croatia v. Serbia*, Public Sitting—Verbatim Record (5 March 2014), p. 33.
26. Ibid., p. 29 (Vukovar). Peter Beaumont et al., '"Everything Is Gone": How Israeli Forces Destroyed Jabaliya Refugee Camp', *The Guardian* (18 December 2024) (Jabalia).
27. Asher McShane, 'Israel "Has the Right" to Withhold Power and Water from Gaza, Says Sir Keir Starmer', lbc.co.uk (11 October 2023).
28. ICJ, *Croatia v. Serbia*, Public Sitting—Verbatim Record (5 March 2014), p. 39.
29. UN Office of the High Commissioner for Human Rights, *Thematic Report: Attacks on Hospitals During the Escalation of Hostilties in Gaza (7 October 2023 – 30 June 2024)*, ohchr.org (31 December 2024), p. 3.
30. ICJ, *Croatia v. Serbia*, Public Sitting—Verbatim Record (5 March 2014), p. 33.
31. Ibid., p. 34.
32. ICJ, *Croatia v. Serbia*, Summary of Judgment (3 February 2015), pp. 16–18.
33. Post by @Keir_Starmer on X (3 February 2015), https://x.com/Keir_Starmer/status/562515743645114369: 'Judgment today in ICJ where I argued for Croatia – will the Court develop the law to extend protection from genocide?'
34. Post by @lmharpin on X (10 January 2024), https://x.com/lmharpin/status/1745076094347153706.

35. 'UK Labour Party Leader Refuses', *Middle East Monitor*.
36. McShane, 'Israel "Has the Right"'.
37. 'Keir Starmer Speech', chathamhouse.org (31 October 2023).
38. '"People of Ukraine Need Justice": Starmer Calls for Investigation of War Crimes during Kyiv Visit', itv.com (16 February 2023).
39. 'UK Labour Party Leader Refuses', *Middle East Monitor*.
40. Amnesty International UK, 'Israel/OPT: Genocide "Matter of Law and Evidence, Not Opinion" and UK Government Must Ensure Accountability', amnesty.org.uk (26 January 2025).
41. 'General Election Candidates Urged to Support Sanctions against Israel', hamhigh.co.uk (4 April 2015). Brendan Carlin, 'Red Faces for Labour as Sir Keir Starmer's Antisemitism Purge Takes a Hit after He Appeared at a Meeting which Included a Call to Punish "Israeli Racism"', *Mail on Sunday* (26 September 2021).
42. Lee Harpin, 'Sir Keir Starmer Tells Packed JLM Labour Leadership Hustings He "Would Not Describe" Himself as a Zionist', *The Jewish Chronicle* (14 February 2020).
43. 'Prime Minister Keir Starmer's Speech to LFI's 2024 Annual Lunch', lfi.org.uk (2 December 2024).
44. Ilan Pappé, *Lobbying for Zionism on Both Sides of the Atlantic* (Oneworld, 2024), p. 171.
45. Paul Kelemen, *The British Left and Zionism: History of a Divorce* (Manchester University Press, 2012), pp. 167, 169, 171–77.
46. Imogen Resnick, 'Irreconcilable Difference? The 1982 Lebanon War, British Jews, and the Political Left', *The Oxford Middle East Review* 3.1 (2019), pp. 76–77.
47. Pappé, *Lobbying*, p. 435.
48. John Woodcock, 'Blair, Labour and Palestine', *Progress Online* (3 October 2013; link has expired as Progress no longer exists).
49. Toby Greene, *Blair, Labour and Palestine: Conflict Views on Middle East Peace After 9/11* (Bloomsbury, 2013), pp. 44–50.
50. Greene, *Blair*, pp. 50–53, 95–96, 126–27, and passim.
51. Quoted in Greene, *Blair*, p. 193. See also Rosemary Hollis, *Britain and the Middle East in the 9/11 Era* (The Royal Institute for International Affairs, 2010), pp. 152–53.

52. Post by @netanyahu on X (13 August 2018), https://x.com/netanyahu/status/1029046307481153542.
53. For critical scrutiny of this episode see Greg Philo et al., *Bad News for Labour: Antisemitism, the Party and Public Belief* (Pluto Press, 2019). Jamie Stern-Weiner ed., *Antisemitism and the Labour Party* (Verso Books, 2019). Ben Gidley et al., 'Labour and Antisemitism: A Crisis Misunderstood', *The Political Quarterly* 91.2 (2020), pp. 413–21.
54. Sienna Rodgers, 'Corbyn Claims Labour Antisemitism Was "Dramatically Overstated"', labourlist.org (29 October 2020).
55. Patrick Maguire and Gabriel Pogrund, *Get In: The Inside Story of Labour Under Starmer* (Bodley Head, 2025), p. 37.
56. This episode is discussed in Paul Holden, *The Fraud: Keir Starmer, Labour Together, and the Crisis of British Democracy* (OR Books, 2025).
57. BBC, *Andrew Marr Show* (20 October 2019), http://news.bbc.co.uk/1/shared/bsp/hi/pdfs/20101902.pdf, p. 9.
58. Maguire and Pogrund, *Get In*, pp. 14–15.
59. Kevin Schofield, 'READ IN FULL: Sir Keir Starmer's Victory Speech after Being named New Labour Leader', politicshome.com (4 April 2020). 'Starmer: Rebuilding Trust with Jewish Community "Number One Priority"', bbc.co.uk (25 June 2020).
60. Patrick Maguire, '"Antisemitic" Tweet from Starmer Ally', *The Times* (7 July 2020).
61. Iain Watson, 'Jewish Group Steps Up Pressure on Keir Starmer', bbc.co.uk (16 September 2023).
62. Maguire and Pogrund, *Get In*, p. 324.
63. Ibid., p. 348.
64. 'Keir Starmer's Speech to LFI's Annual Lunch 2021', lfi.org.uk (16 November 2021). Alex MacDonald, 'Labour Leader Keir Starmer Slammed for "Colonial" Speech on Israel and BDS', *Middle East Eye* (17 November 2021).
65. Elliot Chappell, 'Labour Conference Passes Young Labour Israel and Palestine Motion', *LabourList* (27 September 2021). 'Labour Conference Policy 2018, 2019 & 2021', labourandpalestine.org.uk (n.d.). Post by @JewishChron on X (7 April 2022), https://x.com/JewishChron/status/1512015624335155209.

66. Post by @alexnunns on X (12 October 2023), https://x.com/alexnunns/status/1712445127522767047.
67. McShane, 'Israel "Has the Right"'. Katie Neame and Tom Belger, 'Labour Denies Starmer Justified Israel's Water and Electricity Blockade of Gaza', *LabourList* (18 October 2023).
68. "I Was Not Saying That Israel Had the Right to Cut Off Water, Food, Fuel or Medicines"', political-lies.co.uk (20 October 2023).
69. Post by @ITVNewsPolitics on X (20 October 2023), https://x.com/ITVNewsPolitics/status/1715309817110110433.
70. '"I Was Not Saying"', political-lies.co.uk. Post by @OfSymbols on X (25 April 2024), https://x.com/OfSymbols/status/1783490671157948704.
71. '"I Was Not Saying"', political-lies.co.uk. Post by @BBCNewsnight on X (12 October 2023), https://x.com/BBCNewsnight/status/1712401412120879271 (Thornberry). Post by @implausibleblog on X (15 October 2023), https://x.com/implausibleblog/status/1713492418958401564 (Lammy).
72. Tom Belger, 'Israel-Palestine: Have Labour CLPs Been "Gagged" from Debate or Motions?' *LabourList* (25 October 2023).
73. Shehab Khan, 'Exclusive: Labour Leaders Tell MPs and Council Leaders Not to Attend Palestine Protests', itv.com (14 October 2023).
74. Tim Baker, 'Andy McDonald: Senior Labour MP Suspended over "Deeply Offensive" Comments at Pro-Palestine Rally', news.sky.com (30 October 2023).
75. Denison and Horton, 'Starmer Backs "Humanitarian Pause"'. 'Labour Oxford Councillors Quite over Starmer Comments on Israel Gaza War', bbc.co.uk (14 October 2023). Kiran Stacey et al., 'Labour Deeply Divided over Starmer's Line on Israel-Hamas War', *The Guardian* (20 October 2023).
76. Nadeem Badshah, 'Starmer "Gravely Misrepresented" Meeting, Say Muslim Leaders in Wales', *The Guardian* (24 October 2023).
77. Parveen Akhtar, 'Changing Pattern amongst Muslim Voters: The Labour Party, Gaza and Voter Volatility', electionanalysis.uk (n.d.).
78. Sam Coates, 'General Election: Uneasy Voters Hand Labour a "Loveless Landslide" Shattering Traditional Voting Patterns', news.sky.com (5 July 2024).

79. Pappé, *Lobbying*, p. 209.
80. Within these boundaries, what British policy makers mean by Palestinians' right to self-determination has evolved. For a summary of the changes, see Rosemary Hollis, 'Palestine and the Palestinians in British Political Elite Discourse: From "The Palestine Problem" to "the Two-State Solution,"' *International Relations* 30.1 (2016), pp. 3–28.
81. Pappé, *Lobbying*, p. 471.
82. UK Foreign, Commonwealth, and Development Office (FCDO), 'UK to Restart Funding to UNRWA', gov.uk (19 July 2024).
83. Ibid.
84. Geoffrey Robertson, 'Labour Faces Its First Moral Test in Power. Will It Protect Netanyahu from Being Prosecuted by the ICC?' *The Guardian* (10 July 2024).
85. Kiran Stacey, 'Britain Drops Its Challenge to ICC Arrest Warrants for Israeli Leaders', *The Guardian* (26 July 2024).
86. Post by @LBC on X (22 November 2024), https://x.com/LBC/status/1859890644002439357.
87. UK Prime Minister's Office, 'PM Call with Prime Minister Netanyahu of Israel: 21 January 2025', gov.uk (21 January 2025).
88. Raffi Berg, 'UN Top Court Says Israeli Occupation of Palestinian Territories Is Illegal', bbc.co.uk (19 July 2024).
89. UK House of Commons, 'Israel and the Occupied Palestinian Territories', hansard.parliament.uk (6 February 2025).
90. FCDO, 'UK Policy on Arms Export Licenses to Israel: Foreign Secretary's Statement', gov.uk (2 September 2024).
91. Imran Mulla, 'In Search of a Coherent Labour Policy on Gaza', *Middle East Eye* (3 January 2025).
92. Phil Miller, 'Labour Avoided Full Arms Embargo on Israel to Protect Special Relationship', *Declassified UK* (18 November 2024).
93. Patrick Wintour, 'Judicial Review Must be Heard on How UK Can Sell F-35 Parts to Israel, Judge Rules', *The Guardian* (31 January 2025). Forced to defend the decision against a legal challenge from campaigners, Sir James Eadie—senior barrister representing the government—later admitted: 'The F-35 carve out accepts that there is clear risk that F-35 components might be used to commit or facilitate a serious violation of [international

humanitarian law] but determines that in the exceptional circumstances outlined by the defence secretary, these exports should nonetheless continue'. Miller, 'Labour Avoided'.

94. FCDO, 'UK Policy Arms Export'.
95. Imran Mulla, 'The Six British Prime Ministers Who Have Restricted Arms Sales to Israel', *Middle East Eye* (2 September 2024) (Heath). John Hooper and Richard Norton-Taylor, 'Secret UK Ban on Weapons for Israel', *The Guardian* (13 April 2002) (Blair).
96. Mark Curtis, 'Labour "Laser-Focused" on Israel Trade Deal Amid Ongoing Genocide', *Declassified UK* (29 August 2024).
97. Emma Soteriou, 'UK Has Not Undermined Israel over Suspension of Arms Sales, Says PM as He Calls for De-escalation in Middle East', lbc.co.uk (25 September 2024).
98. Matt Kennard, 'Keir Starmer's 100 Spy Flights over Gaza in Support of Israel', *Declassified UK* (3 October 2024). British intelligence teams were on the ground in Israel throughout the war, 'assisting Israeli intelligence in collecting and analysing information related to the hostages', according to *The New York Times*. Julian E. Barnes et al., 'U.S. Intelligence Helped Israel Rescue Four Hostages in Gaza', *The New York Times* (8 June 2024).
99. Action on Armed Violence, 'Cyprus, Israel, and the Covert War: Is Britain Complicit in Gaza's Bloodshed?' aoav.org.uk (10 October 2024).
100. UK Prime Minister's Office, 'PM's Address to British Troops in RAF Akrotiri, Cyprus: 10 December 2024', gov.uk (10 December 2024).
101. UK House of Commons, 'Action against Houthi Maritime Attacks', hansard.parliament.uk (23 January 2024). For the motivations of the Houthis see Helen Lackner and Daniel Denvir, 'What Yemen's Houthis Want', *Jacobin* (2 March 2024).
102. Kathryn Armstrong, 'UK's Starmer Urges Iran to Refrain from Israel Attack', bbc.co.uk (12 August 2024).
103. As they had during an earlier missile strike in April. Alex Barton, 'British Fighter Jets "Played Part" in Defending Israel from Iranian Attack', *The Telegraph* (2 October 2024).
104. 10 Downing Street, 'Prime Minister Keir Starmer on Iran Missile Attack on Israel' (1 October 2024), https://www.youtube.com/watch?v=WWIdS1WddGI.

105. FCDO, 'Situation between Lebanon and Israel: Joint Statement, 26 September 2024', gov.uk (26 September 2024).
106. The US had shifted to calling for a ceasefire in March 2024.
107. This was in retaliation for the Netanyahu and Gallant arrest warrants.
108. Harry Davies et al., 'Dozens of Countries Speak Out against Trump Sanctions on ICC', *The Guardian* (7 February 2025). Andrew Roth and Bethan McKernan, 'Israel Will Resume War in Gaza Unless More Hostages Freed This Week, Says Netanyahu', *The Guardian* (11 February 2025).
109. TOI Staff, 'Netanyahu Boasts of Thwarting the Establishment of a Palestinian State "For Decades"', *The Times of Israel* (20 February 2024). Abeer Salman et al., 'Netanyahu Against Rejects Palestinian Sovereignty amid Fresh US Push for Two-State Solution', edition.cnn.com (21 January 2024).

Chapter Eight

1. UNITAR, 'Gaza: Debris Generated by the Current Conflict Is 14 Times More Than the Combined Sum of All Debris Generated by Other Conflicts Since 2008', unitar.org (1 August 2024).
2. UN General Assembly, *Report of the Special Committee to Investigate Israeli Practices Affecting the Human Rights of the Palestinian People and Other Arabs of the Occupied Territories*, A/79/363 (20 September 2024), para. 34.
3. UN Office for the Coordination of Humanitarian Affairs (UN OCHA), 'Humanitarian Situation Update #227 | Gaza Strip', ochaopt.org (8 October 2024).
4. Professor Robert Pape quoted in Julia Frankel, 'Israel's Military Campaign in Gaza Seen as Among the Most Destructive in Recent History, Experts Say', apnews.com (11 January 2024).
5. UN OCHA, 'Reported Impact Snapshot | Gaza Strip', ochaopt.org (9 October 2024).
6. Ibid.
7. Ibid.
8. Ibid.
9. AP at the United Nations, 'UN Warns Gaza Is Now "Uninhabitable" as War Continues', *The Guardian* (5 January 2024).

10. UN Office of the High Commissioner for Human Rights (OHCHR), '7 October: UN Experts Call for End of Violence and Accountability after Year of Human Loss and Suffering and Blatant Disregard for International Law', ohchr.org (7 October 2024).
11. ICJ, *Application of the Convention on the Prevention and Punishment of the Crime of Genocide in the Gaza Strip (South Africa v. Israel)*, Public Sitting—Verbatim Record (12 January 2024), p. 34.
12. Ibid., pp. 23–24.
13. Ibid., p. 39.
14. Airwars, *Patterns of Harm Analysis: Gaza, October 2023* (December 2024), p. 2.
15. Ibid., pp. 2, 15.
16. Ibid., p. 12.
17. Ibid., p. 14. The report notes that, 'prior to the war in Gaza, the highest death toll among children in a single event documented by Airwars was 32'.
18. Ibid.
19. Ibid., p. 15.
20. Ibid., p. 16.
21. UN OCHA, 'Reported Impact Snapshot | Gaza Strip', ochaopt.org (7 May 2025).
22. Save the Children, 'GAZA: 3,195 Children Killed in Three Weeks Surpasses Annual Number of Children Killed in Conflict Zones Since 2019', savethechildren.org.uk (29 October 2023). The number of children killed in all war zones during the period 2019–22 was 12,193, according to UN figures.
23. Mike Spagat, 'Netanyahu Got It Wrong Before the US Congress: IDF's Clean Performance in Gaza Is a Lie', aoav.org.uk (2 August 2024). Matthew Ghobrial Cockerill, 'Civilian Casualties in Gaza: Israel's Claims Don't Add Up', aoav.org.uk (28 October 2024). Fatalities among civilian men tend to outnumber those of civilian women, as civilian men are more likely to take risks in war situations.
24. Feroze Sidhwa, '65 Doctors, Nurses and Paramedics: What We Saw in Gaza', *The New York Times* (9 October 2024).
25. Ibid.

26. Yaniv Kubovich, '"No Civilians. Everyone's a Terrorist": IDF Soldiers Expose Arbitrary Killings and Rampant Lawlessness in Gaza's Netzarim Corridor', *Haaretz* (18 December 2024).
27. ICJ, *South Africa v. Israel*, Public Sitting—Verbatim Record (12 January 2024), p. 18.
28. Ibid., pp. 43–44. Italics in original.
29. Cited in Peter Beinart, *Being Jewish after the Destruction of Gaza: A Reckoning* (Atlantic Books, 2025), p. 61.
30. Jonathan Feldstein, 'Thank You President Biden, Now Let's Get Down to Business', *Israel365News* (18 October 2023).
31. Keir Starmer, 'Keir Starmer's Statement to the Commons on Israel & Gaza', *labour.org.uk* (16 October 2023).
32. Given the absence of an evidential base for these claims about human shields, it is remarkable how little pushback there has been from Western media organisations. Political TV, 'Sunday with Laura Kuenssberg | 15th October 2023 | Israel-Hamas Conflict' (15 October 2023), https://www.youtube.com/watch?v=1ZxJUOG6Bks. Victoria Derbyshire (who was standing in for Kuenssberg) is as good a journalist as the BBC has.
33. International Commission of Inquiry, *Detailed Findings*, A/HRC/56/CRP.4 (10 June 2024), paras. 420, 422, 468.
34. Al Jazeera Investigations, 'War Crimes in Gaza', aljazeera.com (7 October 2024).
35. Ibid.
36. Ibid.
37. Amnesty International UK, 'Q&A on Gaza', *amnesty.org.uk* (6 December 2024).
38. Amnesty International, *Amnesty International Report 2010: The State of the World's Human Rights* (2010), p. 183. See also Al Jazeera English, *Investigating War Crimes in Gaza | Al Jazeera Investigations* (3 October 2024), https://www.youtube.com/watch?v=kPE6vbKix6A, 58m02s.
39. B'Tselem, 'Human Shields', btselem.org (11 November 2017).
40. Editorial, 'Israel's Use of Human Shields on the Battle Field Is a War Crime', *Haaretz* (14 August 2024). Yaniv Kubovich and Michael Hauser Tov, 'Haaretz Investigation: Israeli Army Uses Palestinian Civilians to Inspect Potentially Booby-trapped Tunnels in Gaza', *Haaretz* (13 August 2024).

41. Bel Trew, 'Stripped and Held at Gunpoint, the Gaza Schoolboys "Forced to be Israel's Human Shields"', *The Independent* (31 August 2024).
42. Anonymous, 'In Gaza, Almost Every IDF Platoon Keeps a Human Shield, a Sub-Army of Palestinian Slaves', *Haaretz* (30 March 2025).
43. UN OHCHR, *Thematic Report: Attacks on Hospitals during the Escalation of Hostilities in Gaza (7 October 2023 – 30 June 2024)*, ohchr.org (31 December 2024), para. 15.
44. UN Press Release, 'Israeli Authorities, Palestinian Armed Groups Are Responsible for War Crimes, Other Grave Violations of International Law, UN Inquiry Finds', ohchr.org (12 June 2024).
45. Reporters Without Borders (RSF), 'One Year in Gaza: How Israel Orchestrated a Media Blackout on a Region at War', rsf.org (3 October 2024).
46. ICJ, *South Africa v. Israel*, Public Sitting—Verbatim Record (12 January 2024), p. 19.
47. Gabrielle Tetrault-Farber, 'Despite Biden's Doubts, Humanitarian Agencies Consider Gaza Toll Reliable', reuters.com (27 October 2023). Chris McGreal, 'Can We Trust Casualty Figures from the Hamas-run Gaza Health Ministry?' *The Guardian* (27 October 2023). Michael Spagat and Daniel Silverman, 'Is the Hamas-run Ministry of Health Data on Fatalities in Gaza to Be Trusted?' aoav.org.uk (1 November 2023). Benjamin Q. Huynh et al., 'No Evidence of Inflated Mortality Reporting from the Gaza Ministry of Health', *The Lancet* 403.10421 (6 January 2024), pp. 23–24. Rowena De Silva et al., 'One Name, Two Lists: Matching Open Source Evidence with Official Gaza Death Tolls', https://gaza-civilians.airwars.org (24 July 2024).
48. Spagat, 'Netanyahu Got It Wrong'. Cockerill, 'Civilian Casualties'. Adam Gaffney, 'Don't Believe the Conspiracies About the Gaza Death Toll', *The Nation* (30 May 2024).
49. ICJ, *South Africa v. Israel*, Public Sitting—Verbatim Record (12 January 2024), p. 47. Italics in original.
50. Human Rights Watch, 'Israel: Starvation Used as Weapon of War in Gaza', hrw.org (18 December 2023). Amnesty International, *Subhuman*, p. 146.
51. World Health Organization, 'People in Gaza Starving, Sick and Dying As Aid Blockade Continues', who.int (12 May 2025).

52. World Food Programme (WFP), 'World Food Programme Appeals for Sustained Access to Gaza to Provide Food Lifeline', reliefweb.int (17 October 2023).
53. WFP, 'Gaza - Food Security Assessment - December 2023', reliefweb.int (6 December 2023).
54. WFP, 'Gaza Market Monitoring Flash Update #6', docs.wfp.org (2 February 2024).
55. WFP, 'WFP Palestine – Market Monitor – Gaza, August 2024', reliefweb.int (26 August 2024).
56. WFP, 'Market Monitor – Gaza', docs.wfp.org (December 2024).
57. WFP, 'WFP Palestine Emergency Response External Situation Report #42', reliefweb.int (26 December 2024).
58. WFP, 'Market Monitor – Gaza', fscluster.org (April 2025).
59. WFP, 'Market Monitor – Gaza', docs.wfp.org (June 2025).
60. Human Rights Watch (HRW), *Extermination and Acts of Genocide: Israel Deliberately Depriving Palestinians in Gaza of Water* (19 December 2024), p. 11.
61. Ibid., p. 12.
62. Ibid., pp. 13–14.
63. Save the Children et al., 'Joint Letter to White House on Attack on Humanitarian Workers in Gaza', savethechildren.org (4 April 2024).
64. HRW, 'Israel: Starvation Used as Weapon of War in Gaza', hrw.org (18 December 2023). See also Oxfam, 'Starvation as Weapon of War Being Used against Gaza Civilians', oxfam.org.uk (25 October 2023).
65. Nina Lakhani, 'Israel Is Deliberately Starving Palestinians, UN Rights Expert Says', *The Guardian* (27 February 2024).
66. 'EU's Borrell Says Israel Is Provoking Famine in Gaza', reuters.com (18 March 2024).
67. International Criminal Court, 'Statement of ICC Prosecutor Karim A.A. Khan KC: Applications for Arrest Warrants in the Situation in the State of Palestine', icc-cpi.int (20 May 2024).
68. ICJ, *South Africa v. Israel*, Public Sitting—Verbatim Record (12 January 2024), p. 51.
69. HRW, *Extermination*, p. 1.
70. Ibid., p. 4.

71. Ibid., p. 5. These acts bear a striking resemblance to the suggestion of Giora Eiland, in the British-based journal *Fathom*, that after expelling the population of Gaza to Egypt, 'we can also bomb the water facilities in Gaza so there will be no water'. Eiland was reportedly an advisor to Israeli defence minister Yoav Gallant. See: Giora Eiland, '"A New Turning Point in the History of the State of Israel. Most People Don't Understand That"', fathomjournal.org (October 2023).
72. HRW, *Extermination*, p. 18.
73. Quoted in ibid., p. 23.
74. ICJ, *South Africa v. Israel*, Application (9 December 2023), para. 102.
75. HRW, *Extermination*, pp. 1–3.
76. HRW, *Extermination*, pp. 28–29.
77. Jaroslav Lukiv and Paul Adams, 'Israel Blocks Entry of All Humanitarian Aid into Gaza', bbc.co.uk (2 March 2025).
78. UNICEF, 'More Than a Million Children in the Gaza Strip Deprived of Lifesaving Aid for over One Month', unicef.org (5 April 2025).
79. Ibid.
80. ICJ, *South Africa v. Israel*, Public Sitting—Verbatim Record (12 January 2024), p. 31.
81. UN Human Rights Council, *Violations of International Law in the Context of Large-Scale Civilian Protests in the Occupied Palestinian Territory, Including East Jerusalem*, A/HRC/RES/S-28/1 (18 May 2018).
82. Yesh Din, 'Data Sheet: Law Enforcement against Israeli Soldiers Suspected of Harming Palestinians and Their Property—Yesh Din Figures for 2017–2021', yesh-din.org (21 December 2022), p. 1.
83. B'Tselem, 'No Accountability', btselem.org (11 November 2017).
84. *Report of the United Nations Fact-Finding Mission on the Gaza Conflict*, A/HRC/12/48 (25 September 2009), para. 20. See also paras. 144, 162, 1179, 1376, 1595, 1694, 1763.
85. *Report of the Independent International Fact-Finding Mission to Investigate the Implications of the Israeli Settlements on the Civil, Political, Economic, Social and Cultural Rights of the Palestinian People Throughout the Occupied Palestinian Territory, Including East Jerusalem*, A/HRC/22/63 (7 February 2013), para. 7.

86. *Report of the Detailed Findings of the Independent Commission of Inquiry Established Pursuant to Human Rights Council Resolution S-21/1*, A/HRC/29/CRP.4 (24 June 2015), para. 3.
87. *Report of the Detailed Findings of the Independent International Commission of Inquiry on the Protests in the Occupied Palestinian Territory*, A/HRC/40/CRP.2 (18 March 2019), p. 2. See also paras. 30–33.
88. *Report of the Independent International Commission of Inquiry on the Occupied Palestinian Territory, including East Jerusalem, and Israel*, A/HRC/50/21 (9 May 2022), para. 5.
89. *Report of the Independent International Commission of Inquiry on the Occupied Palestinian Territory, including East Jerusalem, and Israel*, A/77/328 (14 September 2022), para. 5.
90. *Report of the Independent International Commission of Inquiry on the Occupied Palestinian Territory, including East Jerusalem, and Israel*, A/78/198 (5 September 2023), para. 45.
91. *Report of the Independent International Commission of Inquiry on the Occupied Palestinian Territory, including East Jerusalem, and Israel*, A/HRC/56/26 (14 June 2024), para. 5.
92. *Report of the Independent International Commission of Inquiry on the Occupied Palestinian Territory, including East Jerusalem, and Israel*, A/79/232 (11 September 2024), para. 2.
93. 'Israeli authorities continue to close access into Gaza for foreign journalists. The few reporters who have been permitted to enter Gaza from the outside were only able to do so under the strict surveillance of the Israeli army'. RSF, 'One Year in Gaza: How Israel Orchestrated a Media Blackout on a Region at War', rsf.org (3 October 2024). A rare exception was CNN's Clarissa Ward, who was able to report from Rafah in southern Gaza without an IDF escort (as discussed in Chapter Two).
94. Nick Turse, *News Graveyards: How Dangers to War Reporters Endanger the World* (Watson Institute for International & Public Affairs, 1 April 2025), p. 2. The figure for the number of journalists killed in World War Two has been contested. See: Alex Farber, 'John Simpson Criticised over "Debunked" Data on Gaza Journalist Deaths', *The Times* (14 August 2025).
95. Committee to Protect Journalists, 'Deadliest Year on Record for Journalists; 70% Killed by Israel', cpj.org (12 February 2025). The UN

special rapporteur on freedom of expression, Irene Khan, listed the means by which Israel has made reporting from Gaza exceptionally difficult, including killings, destroying press facilities, intimidation, and refusing to allow foreign journalists access to the Strip. See UN General Assembly, 'Global Threats to Freedom of Expression Arising from the Conflict in Gaza', A/79/319 (23 August 2024), paras. 17–25.

96. ICJ, *South Africa v. Israel*, Public Sitting—Verbatim Record (12 January 2024), p. 17.

97. See, for example, Norman G. Finkelstein, *Gaza: An Inquest into Its Martyrdom* (University of California Press, 2018), pp. 234–37. Noura Erakat, 'No, Israel Does Not Have the Right to Self-Defense in International Law against Occupied Palestinian Territory', *Jadaliyya* (11 July 2014). Norman G. Finkelstein and Jamie Stern-Weiner, 'Israel Has No Right of Self-Defense Against Gaza', *Jacobin* (27 July 2018).

98. 'Of course, Israel does not have any right to violate the law, still less to commit genocide'. ICJ, *South Africa v. Israel*, Public Sitting—Verbatim Record (12 January 2024), p. 39.

99. Independent International Commission of Inquiry on the Occupied Palestinian Territory, including East Jerusalem, and Israel, *Detailed Findings on the Military Operations and Attacks Carried Out in the Occupied Palestinian Territory from 7 October to 31 December 2023*, A/HRC/56/CRP.4 (10 June 2024), para. 450.

100. ICJ, *South Africa v. Israel*, Public Sitting—Verbatim Record (12 January 2024), pp. 71–72.

101. The reader might study the Deir Yassin massacre, the Tantura massacre, the expulsion of Palestinians from Lydda and Ramle, and many other instances.

102. ICJ, *Legal Consequences of the Construction of a Wall in the Occupied Palestinian Territory*, Advisory Opinion (9 July 2004), paras. 75–78 (East Jerusalem), 120 (settlements), 151–52 ('obligation', compensation).

103. 'UN Rules against Israeli Barrier', news.bbc.co.uk (9 July 2004; 'garbage can'—Raanan Gissin, senior aide to Prime Minister Ariel Sharon). Xinhua, 'Sharon Orders Continuation of Barrier Building in W. Bank', reliefweb.int (11 July 2004; 'politically motivated'—Prime Minister Sharon).

104. Israel's defiance was subsequently registered by the Court. See ICJ, *Legal Consequences Arising from the Policies and Practices of Israel in the Occupied*

Palestinian Territory, Including East Jerusalem, Advisory Opinion (19 July 2024), para. 67.

105. B'Tselem, *A Regime of Jewish Supremacy from the Jordan River to the Mediterranean Sea: This Is Apartheid* (January 2021).
106. Human Rights Watch, *A Threshold Crossed: Israeli Authorities and the Crimes of Apartheid and Persecution* (April 2021), p. 10.
107. Amnesty International, *Israel's Apartheid Against Palestinians: Cruel System of Domination and Crime Against Humanity* (February 2022), p. 266.
108. ICJ, *Legal Consequences Arising from the Policies and Practices of Israel in the Occupied Palestinian Territory, Including East Jerusalem*, Advisory Opinion (19 July 2024), paras. 225, 229.
109. ICJ, *South Africa v. Israel*, Public Sitting—Verbatim Record (12 January 2024), pp. 31–32, 34.
110. ICJ, *South Africa v. Israel*, Order (26 January 2024), paras. 30, 50–54.
111. Ibid., para. 52.
112. Younis Tirawi and Sami Vanderlip, '"Our Job Is to Flatten Gaza. No One Will Stop Us"', *Drop Site* (22 October 2024).
113. Amnesty International, *Subhuman*, pp. 264–65.
114. Yaniv Kubovich, 'Israeli Army Admits Running Unauthorized Graphic Gaza Influence Op', *Haaretz* (4 February 2024).
115. Video clip posted and translated by @ireallyhateyou on X (21 December 2023), https://x.com/ireallyhateyou/status/1737949238754218067.
116. Amnesty International, *Subhuman*, p. 280.
117. 'Israeli Minister Says "Proud" of Gaza Destruction', *Anadolu Agency* (22 February 2024). See also: Post by @GolanMay on X (19 February 2024), https://x.com/GolanMay/status/1759675501424042329.
118. Mera Aladam, 'Senior Israeli Official Says All Palestinian Adults in Gaza "Should be Eliminated"', *Middle East Eye* (24 February 2025).
119. Natalie Merzougi and Maria Rashed, 'Has Israel Taken Enough Action to Prevent Alleged Incitement to Genocide?' bbc.co.uk (27 August 2024).
120. Chen Maanit, 'State Prosecutor Advises against Probing Israeli Ministers, MKs Who Called to Harm Gazans', *Haaretz* (19 August 2024).
121. Jeremy Sharon, 'AG Decides Not to Open Criminal Probes into Senior Officials for Gaza Incitement', *The Times of Israel* (25 November 2024).

122. 'The International Commission of Jurists (ICJ) condemns the continued failure by Israel and other States to comply with, and give full effect to, the provisional measures (PMs) indicated by the International Court of Justice (the Court) in its Order of 26 January 2024'. International Commission of Jurists, 'Gaza: One Month On, Israel Fails to Comply with the Order of the International Court of Justice', icj.org (26 February 2024).
123. Amnesty International, 'Israel Defying ICJ Ruling to Prevent Genocide by Failing to Allow Adequate Humanitarian Aid to Reach Gaza', amnesty.org (6 February 2024).
124. 'The Israeli government has failed to comply with at least one measure in the legally binding order from the International Court of Justice . . . Israel continues to obstruct the provision of basic services and the entry and distribution within Gaza of fuel and lifesaving aid'. Human Rights Watch, 'Israel Not Complying with World Court Order in Genocide Case', hrw.org (26 February 2024).
125. David Gritten and Yaroslav Lukov, 'World Food Programme Halts Gaza Staff Movements'', bbc.co.uk (28 August 2024).
126. '2024 Deadliest Year Ever for Aid Workers, UN Humanitarian Office Reports', news.un.org (22 November 2024). International Rescue Committee, 'The IRC Calls for the Immediate Protection of Aid Workers in Gaza, Following the Killing of Partner Health Workers', rescue.org (9 April 2025).
127. ICJ, *South Africa v. Israel*, Joint Declaration of Judges Xue, Brant, Gómez Robledo, and Tladi (28 March 2024), para. 3.
128. 'All the indicators of genocidal activities are flashing red in Gaza'. ICJ, *South Africa v. Israel*, Declaration of Judge Yusuf (28 March 2024), para. 12.
129. ICJ, *South Africa v. Israel*, Order (24 May 2024), para. 12.
130. Ibid., para. 57.
131. Adil Ahmad Haque, 'Halt: The International Court of Justice and the Rafah Offensive', justsecurity.org (24 May 2024).
132. UNOSAT, 'UNOSAT Gaza Strip 8th Comprehensive Damage Assessment', unosat.org (31 July 2024).
133. UNOSAT, 'UNOSAT Gaza Strip Comprehensive Damage Assessment', unosat.org (29 September 2024).

134. UNOSAT, 'UNOSAT Gaza Strip Comprehensive Damage Assessment', unosat.org (13 December 2024).
135. Nir Hasson et al., 'Rafah Is Gone. Razed to the Ground. And It's Not the Only City Wiped Out by the Israeli Army', *Haaretz* (12 June 2025).
136. Mohamed Solaimane, 'Palestinians Hoping to Return to Gaza's Rafah Find City in Ruins", aljazeera.com (20 January 2025).
137. Ibid.
138. 'Drone Footage Shows the Scale of Destruction in Gaza's Rafah – Video', *The Guardian* (21 January 2025).
139. Dan Johnson, 'Two Thousand Aid Trucks Stuck at Rafah Border, Aid Group Warns', bbc.co.uk (23 May 2024).
140. 'Rafah Crossing Opened After Nearly Nine Months of Closure', gisha.org (4 February 2025).
141 Israeli authorities blamed Egypt for failing to cooperate to open the crossing. Egypt rejected this allegation. It should be noted that prior to the Israeli takeover in May, the UN OCHA estimated that over eleven thousand truckloads of supplies had been delivered to Gaza via the Rafah crossing. This, along with the crossing's reopening after the January 2025 ceasefire, would imply that Israel bore primary responsibility for the full closure of the crossing. UN OCHA, 'Gaza Crossings: Movement of People and Goods', ochaopt.org (n.d.).
142. ICJ, *South Africa v. Israel*, Application (29 December 2023), para. 1.
143. Amnesty International, *Subhuman*, p. 35.
144. HRW, *Extermination*, p. 176.
145. Doctors Without Borders (MSF), 'Gaza Genocide', msf.org.uk (updated 10 July 2025). The organisation had earlier lent force to allegations of genocide but refrained from drawing independent conclusions about Israel's intent. MSF, *Gaza: Life in a Death Trap* (December 2024), p. 5.
146. B'Tselem, *Our Genocide* (July 2025), p. 4.
147. Physicians for Human Rights–Israel, *Destruction of Conditions of Life: A Health Analysis of the Gaza Genocide* (July 2025), p. 5.
148. Al-Haq et al., 'Letter: Palestinian Organizations Express Disappointment and Call for an Inquiry Regarding the Special Adviser on the Prevention of Genocide's Failure to Fulfil Her Mandate in Addressing Israel's Ongoing Genocide in Gaza', alhaq.org (7 February 2024), p. 5.

149. Aryeh Neier, 'Is Israel Committing Genocide?' *New York Review of Books* (6 June 2024).
150. *Report of the Special Committee to Investigate Israeli Practices Affecting the Human Rights of the Palestinian People and Other Arabs of the Occupied Territories*, A/79/363 (20 September 2024), para. 69.
151. *Anatomy of a Genocide: Report of the Special Rapporteur on the Situation of Human Rights in the Palestinian Territories Occupied Since 1967, Francesca Albanese*, A/HRC/55/73 (1 July 2024), p. 1. At least six other UN special rapporteurs reached the same conclusion.
152. Craig Mokhiber, 'Resignation Letter' (28 October 2023), https://www.documentcloud.org/documents/24103463-craig-mokhiber-resignation-letter.
153. Anisha Patel and Hassan Ben Imran, 'The ICC Can No Longer Ignore the Genocide in Gaza', aljazeera.com (21 April 2024).
154. Kasper van Laarhoven et al., 'Zeven Gerenommeerde Wetenschappers Vrijwel Eensgezind: Israël Pleegt in Gaza Genocide', *NRC* (14 May 2025) [Dutch].
155. International Human Rights Clinic—Boston University School of Law et al., *Genocide in Gaza: Analysis of International Law and Its Application to Israel's Military Actions Since October 7, 2023* (15 May 2024), p. 4.
156. Elias Feroz and Amos Goldberg, 'Israeli Historian: This Is Exactly What Genocide Looks Like', *Jacobin* (11 July 2024).
157. Omer Bartov, 'As a Former IDF Soldier and Historian of Genocide, I Was Deeply Disturbed by My Recent Visit to Israel', *The Guardian* (13 August 2024). Omer Bartov, 'I'm a Genocide Scholar. I Know It When I See It', *The New York Times* (15 July 2025).
158. Raz Segal, 'A Textbook Case of Genocide', *Jewish Currents* (13 October 2023).
159. Julia Prosinger and William Schabas, 'Human Rights Expert: "A Strong Case that Israel's Response Constitutes the Crime of Genocide"', *Der Spiegel* (29 November 2024). Schabas has also made powerful criticisms of David Lammy and Keir Starmer for their hypocritical policy in relation to accusations of genocide. See Sondos Asem, 'Top Genocide Scholar Calls Starmer and Lammy "Hypocrites" over Gaza Stance', *Middle East Eye* (18 November 2024).

160. John Michael Cox, 'It Is Every Individual's Obligation to Confront the Current Siege in Gaza', iccforum.com (22 February 2024).
161. Islam Dogru, 'American Jewish Scholar Says Israel Has Launched "Genocidal Campaign of Extermination" in Gaza', *Anadolu Agency* (22 February 2024).
162. Daniel Blatman and Amos Goldberg, 'There's No Auschwitz in Gaza. But It's Still Genocide', *Haaretz* (30 January 2025).
163. Post by @martinshawx on X (5 August 2024), https://x.com/martinshawx/status/1820389008880361676. Shaw is the author of *What Is Genocide?* second ed. (Polity, 2015).
164. Avi Shlaim, *Genocide in Gaza: Israel's Long War on Palestine* (The Irish Pages Press, 2024), p. 142.
165. Lee Mordechai, *Bearing Witness – Gaza*, version 6.7.0, witnessing-the-gaza-war.com (5 July 2025), pp. 5, 7.
166. Rashid Khalidi, 'The Neck and The Sword', *New Left Review* (May/June 2024).
167. Richard Falk, 'The Gaza Genocide Exposes Tragic Flaws in World Order during the Ceasefire Moment', *richardfalk.org* (n.d.).
168. Post by @Alfreddezayas on X (4 December 2024), https://x.com/Alfreddezayas/status/1864207640349302810.
169. Melissa Chemam, 'For Ilan Pappé, Gaza Genocide Brings More Urgency to Studying the History and Crimes of Zionism', *The New Arab* (24 July 2024).
170. Norman Finkelstein, 'Norman Finkelstein: Build a Majority for Palestine', *Jacobin* (8 May 2024).
171. Glenn Greenwald and John Mearsheimer, *Prof. John Mearsheimer on Israel's Destruction of Gaza . . . SYSTEM UPDATE #434*, rumble.com (4 April 2025)- 19:50.
172. UK House of Commons Debate, 'Engagements', hansard.parliament.uk (13 November 2024).
173. UK House of Commons, 'Middle East', hansard.parliament.uk (28 October 2024). Lammy was responding to a question from Nick Timothy MP, asking him 'to say that there is not a genocide occurring in the Middle East'.
174. Jennifer Scott, '"Nonsense" for South Africa to Accuse Israel of Genocide, Says Foreign Secretary', news.sky.com (15 January 2024).
175. UK House of Commons, 'Israel and Gaza', hansard.parliament.uk (27 February 2024).

Chapter Nine

1. Imran Mulla, 'UK: Labour Party Bans Words 'Genocide' and 'Apartheid' from Conference', *Middle East Eye* (22 September 2024).
2. Xander Elliards, 'UK Prime Minister Keir Starmer Dismisses Idea of Genocide in Gaza', *The National* (13 November 2024). Jake Wallis Simons, 'Israel Is Not an Apartheid State, Says Keir Starmer as He Apologises for the Corbyn Years', *The Jewish Chronicle* (7 April 2022).
3. Michel Guillot et al., 'Life Expectancy Losses in the Gaza Strip during the Period October, 2023, to September, 2024', *The Lancet*, 405.10477 (8 February 2025), pp. 478–85. Pre-war life expectancy in Gaza was 75.5 years.
4. Al Jazeera English, 'Investigating War Crimes in Gaza | Al Jazeera Investigations' (3 October 2024), https://www.youtube.com/watch?v=kPE6vbKix6A.
5. Rohan Silva, 'Hitler, Stalin, Mum and Dad by Daniel Finkelstein Review – A Family in Peril', *The Guardian* (4 June 2023).
6. Video clip posted by @AnasAlSharif0 on X (18 October 2024), https://x.com/AnasAlSharif0/status/1847352625974399346.
7. Post by @Dannythefink (Daniel Finkelstein) on X (20 October 2024), https://x.com/Dannythefink/status/1847952125436780889.
8. Post by @Dannythefink (Daniel Finkelstein) on X (20 October 2024), https://x.com/Dannythefink/status/1847962557446803851.
9. Chris McGreal, '"Not a Normal War": Doctors Say Children Have Been Targeted by Israeli Snipers in Gaza', *The Guardian* (2 April 2024).
10. UN Office for the Coordination of Humanitarian Affairs (OCHA), 'Reported Impact Snapshot | Gaza Strip (23 July 2025)', ochaopt.org (23 July 2025).
11. Human Rights Watch, *"They Destroyed What Was Inside Us": Children with Disabilities Amid Israel's Attacks on Gaza* (September 2024).
12. Political TV, *Question Time | 14th March 2024* (14 March 2024), https://www.youtube.com/watch?v=Y5Qp1S1616M, 33m42s–35m50s.
13. Amnesty International, *'You Feel Like You Are Subhuman': Israel's Genocide against Palestinians in Gaza* (December 2024), pp. 176–77.
14. Einav Halabi, 'COGAT: "There Is No Limit to the Amount of Aid That Can Enter Gaza"', *Ynet* (24 February 2024).
15. Both the letter and response dated July 7, 2025. I also asked Phillips for evidence of stocked food shops and food being stolen by Hamas.

16. Amnesty International, *Subhuman*, pp. 178–79.
17. Amnesty International, *Subhuman*, p. 188.
18. Post by @DrTedros (Tedros Adhanom Ghebreyesus) on X (4 March 2024), https://x.com/DrTedros/status/1764652624492515832.
19. Integrated Food Security Phase Classification, *Famine Review Committee: Gaza Strip, March 2024—Conclusions and Recommendations* (18 March 2024), p. 2.
20. International Crisis Group, 'The Gaza Starvation Experiment', crisisgroup.org (6 June 2025).
21. Amnesty International, *Subhuman*, pp. 200–1.
22. 'UN Food Chief Rebuts Israeli Claims: No Sign Hamas Is Stealing Gaza Aid', *Middle East Eye* (25 May 2025).
23. Post by @mishtal (David Collier) on X (19 December 2024), https://x.com/mishtal/status/1869719613078204496.
24. ActionAid, 'Food Shortages in Gaza Leave Families Starving', actionaid.org.uk (17 December 2024).
25. Oxfam, 'Just Twelve Trucks Distribute Food and Water in North Gaza Governorate in 2.5 Months', oxfam.org.uk (23 December 2024).
26. Lena Masri et al., 'As Gaza Suffers, Hunger Watchdog Refrains from Using the F Word: Famine', reuters.com (30 December 2024).
27. Rosalia Bollen, '"Cold, Sick and Traumatized" - The Ongoing Nightmare for Children in Gaza', unicef.org (20 December 2024).
28. Profile of @mishtal (David Collier) on X (accessed 7 March 2025), https://x.com/mishtal.
29. Bart Schut, 'UK Journalist Who Blew Whistle on BBC Gaza Documentary: "I Caught Them in Bed with Hamas"', *The Times of Israel* (7 March 2025). Collier declared 'VICTORY!' when the 'BBC Hamas propaganda video' was pulled. Post by @mishtal (David Collier) on X (21 February 2025), https://x.com/mishtal/status/1892890139224953102.
30. Jake Wallis Simons, 'Israel Is Not Committing Genocide in Gaza', *The Telegraph* (22 June 2024). Simons did not cite any source for the alleged 1:1 combatant-to-civilian casualty ratio. I wrote to Wallis Simons giving him a chance to defend his reporting but he did not respond.

31. Lazar Berman, 'Netanyahu: Ratio of Hamas Combatants to Gazan Civilians Killed in Ongoing War Is about 1:1', *The Times of Israel* (13 May 2024).
32. 'Israel Releases New Gaza Death Toll, Claims Historically Low Civilian Deaths', jns.org (16 May 2024).
33. Yaniv Kubovich, 'Israel Created "Kill Zones" in Gaza. Anyone Who Crosses into Them Is Shot', *Haaretz* (31 March 2024). I am grateful to Yaniv Cogan for alerting me to this quote. In unpublished research Cogan shows that Israeli casualty reports have been implausible.
34. Post by @IShvartztuch on X (4 August 2024), https://x.com/IShvartztuch/status/1820168108885037462 [Hebrew]. I am grateful to Yaniv Cogan for finding and translating this quote.
35. Ben Reiff, 'Why Did a British Jewish Newspaper Publish Fake Israeli Intelligence?' 972mag.com (11 September 2024). Peter Beaumont, 'Crisis at Jewish Chronicle as Stories Based on "Wild Fabrications" Are Withdrawn', *The Guardian* (14 September 2024). Peter Beaumont et al., 'How the Elon Perry Fabrication Scandal Shook the Jewish Chronicle', *The Guardian* (20 September 2024).
36. Matthew Weaver, 'Columnists Quit Jewish Chronicle over Gaza Stories Based on "Fabrications"', *The Guardian* (15 September 2024).
37. Michael Gove, 'The IDF Should Be Nominated for the Nobel Peace Prize', *The Jewish Chronicle* (8 January 2025).
38. Alfred Nobel, 'The Nobel Prize', nobelprize.org (n.d.).
39. Michael Woldemariam and Yilma Woldgabreal, 'Atrocity Denial and Emotions in the Ethiopian Civil War', *Aggression and Violent Behavior* 73 (2023).
40. Howard Jacobson, 'Tales of Infanticide Have Stoked Hatred of Jews for Centuries. They Echo Still Today', *The Observer* (6 October 2024).
41. Ibid.
42. Owen Jones, 'Hind Rajab's Death Has Already Been Forgotten. That's Exactly What Israel Wants', *The Guardian* (18 August 2024).
43. Forensic Architecture, *The Killing of Hind Rajab*, forensic-architecture.org (n.d.).
44. Meg Kelly et al., 'Palestinian Paramedics Said Israel Gave Them Safe Passage to Save a 6-Year-Old Girl in Gaza. They Were All Killed', *The Washington Post* (16 April 2024). See also Jones, 'Hind'.

45. Des Freedman, '"Found Dead in Gaza"? No, Murdered by Israel', *Declassified UK* (10 May 2024).
46. Forensic Architecture, *Hind Rajab*.
47. Lucy Williamson, 'Hind Rajab, 6, Found Dead in Gaza Days after Phone Calls for Help', bbc.co.uk (10 February 2024). Sky News did better: Stuart Ramsay, '"I'm So Scared, Please Come": Heartbreaking Final Moments of Girl, 5, Killed in Gaza', news.sky.com (8 October 2024).
48. Yuval Abraham, '"Lavender": The AI Machine Directing Israel's Bombing Spree in Gaza', 972mag.com (3 April 2024).
49. Ibid.
50. Ibid.
51. Ibid.
52. One exception could be found in *The Guardian*: Paul Rodgers, 'Israel's Use of Disproportionate Force Is a Long-Established Tactic – With a Clear Aim', *The Guardian* (5 December 2023).
53. B'Tselem, *Our Genocide* (July 2025), p. 17.
54. Hazem Balousha and Oliver Holmes, 'The Gaza Strip Mourns Its Dead after Protest Is Met with Bullets', *The Guardian* (31 March 2018).
55. UN OCHA, 'Humanitarian Situation Update #218 | Gaza Strip', ochaopt.org (16 September 2024).
56. Eric Tlozek et al., 'How the Death Toll in Gaza Is Recorded and Why Experts Say It Is Likely an Undercount', abc.net.au (18 October 2024).
57. Daniel Levy, *Meeting of the United Nations Security Council, Tuesday February 25, 2025— "The Situation in the Middle East Including the Palestinian Question"*, usmep.us (25 February 2025), p. 1.
58. Jewish Voice for Labour, 'How Labour's Claim of Countering Antisemitism Has Resulted in a Purge of Jews', jewishvoiceforlabour.org.uk (5 August 2021).
59. David Hearst and Peter Oborne, 'UK's Labour Accused of "Purging Jews" from Party over Antisemitism Claims', *Middle East Eye* (12 August 2021).
60. JVL, 'Purge'.
61. Hearst and Oborne, 'UK's Labour Accused'.
62. Ibid.
63. Israel Ministry of Foreign Affairs, 'President Herzog Addresses ICJ Ruling', gov.il (28 January 2024).

64. Bethan McKernan, 'Israeli Officials Accuse International Court of Justice of Antisemitic Bias', *The Guardian* (26 January 2024).
65. Jake Wallis Simons, 'The ICJ Has Been Captured by Anti-Semitic Propaganda', *The Telegraph* (27 January 2024).
66. Brendan O'Neill, 'The BBC's Gaza Farce Takes Another Sinister Turn', *The Spectator* (26 February 2025).
67. Simons, 'The ICJ Has Been Captured'.
68. Israeli Prime Minister's Office, 'Statement by PM Netanyahu', gov.il (21 November 2024).
69. Ibid.
70. Zoe Strimpel, 'Europe Can't Stay Silent in the Face of the ICC's Offensive Israel Warrants', *The Telegraph* (24 November 2024).
71. Post by @Israel_katz on X (23 March 2024), https://x.com/Israel_katz/status/1771534978364383484.
72. Post by @Israel_katz on X (2 October 2024), https://x.com/Israel_katz/status/1841422324890812763.
73. Telegraph View, 'UN Double Standards Leave a Bad Taste', *The Telegraph* (24 October 2024).
74. TOI Staff and AFP, 'Katz Again Accuses Borrell of Antisemitism, Trades Jibes with Senior EU Diplomat', *The Times of Israel* (15 September 2024). Israel claimed that the strike targeted a Hamas command and control centre 'but did not provide evidence or details'. Emma Graham-Harrison, 'Six UN Aid Workers Among 18 Killed in Israeli Strike on Gaza School', *The Guardian* (12 September 2024).
75. TOI Staff and AFP, 'Katz Again Accuses'.
76. See: Maija Ehlinger et al., 'Pope Speaks Out after IDF Sniper Kills Two Women Inside Gaza Church, Per Catholic Authorities', edition.cnn.com (18 December 2023). AFP, 'Mother, Daughter Killed by Israel Army in Gaza Church Grounds: Patriarchate', *France24* (16 December 2023).
77. Pope Francis, 'Angelus', vatican.va (17 December 2023).
78. Post by @mishtal (David Collier) on X (16 August 2024), https://x.com/mishtal/status/1824439349015961950.
79. Melanie Phillips, 'The Pope's Embrace of Evil Discourse', jns.org (21 November 2024).
80. Ibid.

81. Pope Francis, 'Christmas Greetings of the Holy Father to the Roman Curia for the Exchange of Christmas Greetings', vatican.va (21 December 2024). The Pope also pointed out that the Patriarch of Jerusalem 'was not allowed into Gaza, as had been promised'.
82. AFP and TOI Staff, 'Israel Accuses Pope of Ignoring Hamas Cruelty after He Criticizes Gaza Airstrikes', *The Times of Israel* (22 December 2024).
83. See Palestine Liberation Organization, 'The Israeli Occupation Authorities Assassinate the Detainee Thaer Abu Asab from Qalqilia in Negev Prison', plo.ps (19 November 2023).
84. Lubna Masarwa and Peter Oborne, '"I Have the Prison Inside Me": The Emaciated Palestinian Bodybuilder Broken by Israel', *Middle East Eye* (12 July 2024). After this story was published, an Israeli Prison Service spokesperson told us: 'We are not aware of the claims you described, and as far as we know, no such events have occurred. As documented in his file, the prisoner was examined and treated medically by IPS [Israel Prison Service] finest doctors throughout his incarceration in accordance with his medical complaints, his prior medical condition, and medical protocols'.
85. Hagar Shezaf et al., 'Sde Teiman Doctor Who Saw Abused Gazan Detainee: "I Couldn't Believe an Israeli Prison Guard Could Do Such a Thing"', *Haaretz* (30 July 2024).
86. UN Office of the High Commissioner for Human Rights (OCHR), 'UN Report: Palestinian Detainees Held Arbitrarily and Secretly, Subjected to Torture and Mistreatment', ohchr.org (31 July 2024). UN OHCHR, *Thematic Report: Detention in the Context of the Escalation of Hostilities in Gaza (October 2023-June 2024)*, ohchr.org (31 July 2024).
87. Amnesty International, 'Release of Civilian Hostages Held in Gaza and Arbitrarily Detained Palestinians Must Be Immediate and Not Hinge on Ceasefire Negotiations', amnesty.org (28 February 2025). B'Tselem, *Our Genocide* (July 2025), p. 61.
88. Rome Statute of the International Criminal Court, Article 7(1)(f) and Article 8(2)(a)(ii).
89. Graham-Harrison et al., 'Torture'. Lubna Masarwa and Peter Oborne, 'War on Gaza: Israel Has Created Its Own Abu Ghraib—And the World Is Silent', *Middle East Eye* (9 August 2024).

90. Jotam Confino, 'Watch: Hard-Right Israeli MPs Storm Controversial Detention Camp', *The Telegraph* (29 July 2024).
91. Yasmin Levy, 'Sitting with Raskin Yehuda Schlesinger Who Supports Sex Crimes against Detainees, and Everything Is Fine', *Haaretz* (7 August 2024) [Hebrew]. Schlesinger later retracted his statements. See: TOI Staff, 'Israeli Journalist Retracts Call for "Policy" of Sodomizing Palestinian Terror Suspects', *Times of Israel* (8 August 2024).
92. UK House of Commons, 'Closure of Service Police Legacy Investigations', hansard.parliament.uk (18 October 2021).
93. UK House of Commons, 'Middle East Update', hansard.parliament.uk (2 September 2024).
94. UK House of Commons, 'Closure'.
95. Insight, 'War Crimes Scandal: Army "Covered Up Torture and Child Murder" in the Middle East', *The Times* (17 November 2019).

Chapter Ten

1. Paul Kirby, 'We Must Not Turn Blind Eye to Antisemitism, Says Dutch King after Attacks on Israeli Football Fans', bbc.co.uk (8 November 2024).
2. Benjamin Weinthal, 'Netanyahu Condemns Antisemitic Pogrom in Amsterdam, Warns World Leaders Attacks Will Spread If Don't Act', foxnews.com (10 November 2024).
3. Post by @POTUS46Archive on X (8 November 2024), https://x.com/POTUS46Archive/status/1854953886328799588.
4. AFP, 'UK Foreign Minister Says "Horrified" at Amsterdam Attacks', *The Times of Israel* (8 November 2024).
5. Shiryn Ghermezian, 'Netanyahu Dispatches Planes to Rescue Israeli Soccer Fans Following Violent "Pogrom" in Amsterdam', *Algemeiner* (8 November 2024).
6. Felix Tamsut, 'When Far-Right Football Fans Take to the Streets in Israel', *DW* (8 July 2020).
7. Video clip posted by @trtworld on X, https://x.com/trtworld/status/1766058782876995789.

8. Bas Blokker and Mark Lievisse Adriaanse, 'How Amsterdam Briefly Became a Battleground in the Gaza War', *NRC* (28 December 2024) [Dutch].
9. Mamnun Khan, 'Salams from Amsterdam', beingbritishmuslims.com (15 October 2024).
10. Blokker and Adriaanse, 'How Amsterdam'.
11. Post by @YounessOuaali on X, https://x.com/YounessOuaali/status/1854543274402336798 (accessed 27 February 2025; account now suspended). Post by @Radlab72 on X (18 November 2024), https://x.com/Radlab72/status/1858605544879091966.
12. Blokker and Adriaanse, 'How Amsterdam'.
13. Jasmin Seijbel et al., 'Expressing Rivalry Online: Antisemitic Rhetoric among Dutch Football Supporters on Twitter', *Soccer & Society* 23.8 (2022), pp. 834–48, especially p. 841.
14. 'Mohammed Achtervolgde Maccabi-Fans met Een Riem in Amsterdam', *NOS* (10 December 2024) [Dutch].
15. Middle East Eye, 'Maccabi Tel Aviv Hooligans Chant Racist, Anti-Arabs Slogans Ahead of Match in Amsterdam' (8 November 2024), https://www.youtube.com/shorts/_HRUV86bVa0.
16. Blokker and Adriaanse, 'How Amsterdam'.
17. Post by @_WMedia_ (Annet de Graaf) on X (7 November 2024), https://x.com/_WMedia_/status/1854664685469028610.
18. BENDER, 'ISRAËLISCHE HOOLIGANS ZETTEN AMSTERDAM OP ZIJN KOP (ENG SUB)' (8 November 2024), https://www.youtube.com/watch?v=ySHIOYyJ95A.
19. Video footage showing such attacks was posted by @YounessOuaali on X. The links no longer work as this account was suspended. See also video clips posted by @nexta_tv on X (8 November 2024), https://x.com/nexta_tv/status/1854788417134956739.
20. Blokker and Adriaanse, 'How Amsterdam'.
21. Ibid.
22. Ibid.
23. Yossi Verter, 'Netanyahu's Lies Laid Bare: How Israel Ignored the Roadmap to the October 7 Disaster', *Haaretz* (31 August 2024).
24. Blokker and Adriaanse, 'How Amsterdam'.

25. Post by @dannydanon on X (8 November 2024), https://x.com/dannydanon/status/1854705141338776050.
26. Blokker and Adriaanse, 'How Amsterdam'.
27. Ibid.
28. Post by @geertwilderspvv on X (8 November 2024), https://x.com/geertwilderspvv/status/1854740777143849265.
29. Arjen Schreuder, 'Mayor Femke Halsema Looks Back on Pitch-Black Night: "Unbearable and Indigestible. This Outburst of Anti-Semitism Is Un-Amsterdam"', *NRC* (8 November 2024) [Dutch].
30. Abby Chitty, 'Amsterdam Mayor Says She Regrets Use of Word "Pogrom" to Describe Attacks on Israelis', *Euronews* (19 November 2024).
31. News Wires, 'Prosecutors Call for Two-Year Sentence for Suspect in Amsterdam Football Violence', *France24* (11 December 2024). NL Times, 'Amsterdam Riot Suspects on Trial Say Anti-Semitic Slurs Were Not Meant for All Jews', *NL Times* (11 December 2024).
32. Photos posted by @trackingisrael on X (8 November 2024), https://x.com/trackingisrael/status/1854918862724383044.
33. Richard Sanders for Double Down News, *What REALLY Happened in Amsterdam* (14 November 2024), https://www.youtube.com/watch?v=DvTyg1kJGzM.
34. Ibid., 0m00s–5m55s.
35. Video clip posted by @_WMedia_ on X (7 November 2024), https://x.com/_WMedia_/status/1854658996872896929.
36. Video clip posted by @_WMedia_ on X (7 November 2024), https://x.com/_WMedia_/status/1854669943213576239.
37. Video clip posted by @_WMedia_ on X (7 November 2024), https://x.com/_WMedia_/status/1854670939356905551.
38. Video clip posted by @EYakoby on X (8 November 2024), https://x.com/EYakoby/status/1854699233409925428.
39. Post by @_WMedia_ on X (8 November 2024), https://x.com/_WMedia_/status/1854704169560531426.
40. Post by @_WMedia_ on X (8 November 2024), https://x.com/_WMedia_/status/1854720976434466893. Although the original message has been deleted Annet de Graaf shared it at 4:03 a.m. in a WhatsApp conversation with Reuters.

41. WhatsApp conversation shared with the author.
42. Photocopy of dope sheet shared with Annet de Graaf by a journalist and provided to the author.
43. Electronic copy of dope sheet shared with Annet de Graaf by a German and provided to the author.
44. WhatsApp conversation shared with the author.
45. Video clip posted by @OmeBender on X (8 November 2024), https://x.com/OmeBender/status/1854894829697712570.
46. Email to Annet de Graaf from Reuters, shared with the author.
47. Information provided by Annet de Graaf.
48. The Dreamer, 'Alice Porter @SkyNews Explaining What Really Happened in Amsterdam before Removing the Video' (10 November 2024), https://www.youtube.com/watch?v=Ghbry1QaarI, 0m55s.
49. Post by @SkyNews on X (9 November 2024), https://x.com/SkyNews/status/1855320057750208979. The tweet has apparently been deleted; the editor's note may still be read at: 'What We Know About Violence Involving Football Fans in Amsterdam', news.sky.com (9 November 2024).
50. @SkyNews, 'Violence in Amsterdam: What We Know So Far' (9 November 2024), https://www.youtube.com/shorts/a8p79_5RvCs.
51. Ibid., 1m30s.
52. Kirby, 'We Must'.
53. Information from Annet de Graaf.
54. Guardian News, 'How the Football Fan Violence Unfolded in Amsterdam' (15 November 2024), https://www.youtube.com/watch?v=0ece-22koko.
55. Loveday Morris et al., 'How Antisemitism, Israeli Nationalism and Anger over Gaza Clashed in Amsterdam', *The Washington Post* (18 December 2024).
56. BBC, 'Corrections and Clarifications - Archive 2024: Newsnight/BBC News Channel, 8 November 2024', bbc.co.uk (23 December 2024).
57. @MiddleEastEye, 'Maccabi Tel Aviv Hooligans Chanting Anti-Arab Chants at Tel Aviv Airport' (9 November 2024), https://www.youtube.com/shorts/kbFiWwY6dYw. *The New York Times* reported that the Maccabi fans also chanted this in Amsterdam: 'Videos from Thursday showed Israeli fans shouting anti-Arab chants on their way to the match as the police escorted them near Amsterdam's central train station to ensure their safety amid anger over the Gaza war. One of their chants said: "Why

is there no school in Gaza? There are no children left there'". Jim Tankersley et al., 'Amsterdam Bars Protests after Antisemitic Attacks on Soccer Fans', *The New York Times* (9 November 2024).

Chapter Eleven

1. This section is partly based on Peter Oborne and Lubna Masarwa, 'As Gaza Burns, Israeli Settlers Make "Real Estate" Plans', *Middle East Eye* (22 October 2024).
2. Joshua Leifer, 'Kahane's Ghost: How a Long-Dead Extremist Rabbi Continues to Haunt Israel's Politics', *The Guardian* (20 March 2025).
3. Oborne and Masarwa, 'As Gaza Burns'.
4. Ibid.
5. Ibid.
6. 'Meet the Team', nachalaisrael.org (n.d.).
7. The International Court of Justice determined in July 2024 that Israel's occupation has become unlawful. For an argument that it was unlawful from the outset, see Norman G. Finkelstein, *Gaza's Gravediggers: An Inquiry into Corruption in High Places* (OR Books, 2025), chap. 3.
8. Global Affairs Canada, 'Canada Imposes Second Round of Sanctions on Perpetrators of Extremist Settler Violence against Civilians in West Bank', canada.ca (27 June 2024).
9. Oborne and Masarwa, 'As Gaza Burns'.
10. Ibid.
11. Jeff Mason and Kanishka Singh, 'Trump Suggests Permanently Displacing Palestinians from Gaza', reuters.com (4 February 2025).
12. Rome Statute of the International Criminal Court, Article 7(1)(d).
13. David Charter and Will Pavia, 'Trump Says US Will Take over Gaza Strip and Make It "Riviera of Middle East"', *The Times* (5 February 2025).
14. The *Telegraph* headline read: 'Trump Offers to Turn Gaza into "Riviera of Middle East"'. The headline has since been altered; a screenshot of the original version is available at Owen Jones, 'Trump Proposes the US Taking over Gaza Genocide. Our Media Normalises It', *Owen Jones BattleLines* (5 February 2025).

15. Jake Wallis Simons, 'Trump's Plan to Make Gaza Great Again Could Really Work', *The Telegraph* (5 February 2025).
16. The headline has since been altered; a screenshot of the original version is available at Jones, 'Trump Proposes'.
17. Mason and Singh, 'Trump Suggests'.
18. The BBC and *The Telegraph* cite Trump's remark that Gaza's population is now 1.8 million but they don't expand on this to explain the implication. *The Telegraph* reported: 'Mr Trump said that the 1.8 million Palestinians in Gaza should relocate to neighbouring countries that he described as having "humanitarian hearts" and "great wealth"'. See Angus Cochrane, 'Swinney Attacks Trump's Gaza "Take over" Plans', bbc.co.uk (5 February 2025). Akhtar Makoii, 'Can Trump Actually Take over Gaza?' *The Telegraph* (5 February 2025). For full context see Jones, 'Trump Proposes'.
19. MEE Staff, 'Full Text of Trump and Netanyahu's Explosive News Conference', *Middle East Eye* (5 February 2025).
20. Ibid.
21. Giora Eiland, '"A New Turning Point in the History of the State of Israel. Most People Don't Understand That"', fathomjournal.org (October 2023).
22. Douglas Murray, 'Britain Must Stand Up against Those Who Support Hamas', *The Spectator* (14 October 2023).
23. Israel Intelligence Ministry Policy Department, 'Policy Paper: Options for a Policy Regarding Gaza's Civilian Population' (13 October 2023), https://www.scribd.com/document/681086738/Israeli-Intelligence-Ministry-Policy-Paper-on-Gaza-s-Civilian-Population-October-2023.
24. Paul Adams, 'Israel Has No Plan for Gaza after War Ends, Experts Warn', bbc.co.uk (28 October 2023).
25. Post by Bezalel Smotrich on Facebook (14 November 2023), https://www.facebook.com/Bezazelsmotrich/posts/pfbid022zGgfWXWV2zTohVPc9oAKonUkBzSRRR7DvhbVx2DV2tsAcQF1SeqAzwLgei7bHRml.
26. Mick Krever et al., 'Israel's Far-Right Wants to Move Palestinians Out of Gaza. Its Ideas Are Gaining Attention', edition.cnn.com (17 January 2024).
27. Quoted in Jamie Stern-Weiner and Avi Shlaim, 'Israel's Road to Genocide' in Avi Shlaim, *Genocide in Gaza: Israel's Long War on Palestine* (The Irish Pages Press, 2024), p. 292.

28. 'The Generals' Plan—An Initiative of Maj. Gen. (res.) Giora Eiland – Summary' (n.d.), https://hamefakdim-bemiluim.org/%D7%AA%D7%95%D7%9B%D7%A0%D7%99%D7%AA-%D7%94%D7%90%D7%9C%D7%95%D7%A4%D7%99%D7%9D.
29. Jeremy Bowen, 'Israeli Attack on Northern Gaza Hints at Retired General's "Surrender or Starve" Plan for War', bbc.co.uk (12 October 2024).
30. 'Trump Suggests Displaced Palestinians in Gaza Be "Permanently" Resettled Somewhere Else – Video', *The Guardian* (5 February 2025).
31. Post and translation by @ireallyhateyou on X (11 May 2025), https://x.com/ireallyhateyou/status/1921613021769580987.
32. Post and translation by @ireallyhateyou on X (13 May 2025), https://x.com/ireallyhateyou/status/1922098876120481802.
33. Betsy Klein and Irene Nasser, 'Trump Describes Gaza as a "Big Real Estate Site" as He Doubles Down on Plans to Redevelop the Enclave', edition.cnn.com (9 February 2025).
34. Lazar Berman and Nava Freiberg, 'Netanyahu Sets Implementation of Trump's Gaza Relocation Plan as New Condition for Ending War', *The Times of Israel* (22 May 2025).
35. Jason Burke, 'Netanyahu Says New Offensive in Gaza Focused on Consolidating Seizure of Territory', *The Guardian* (5 May 2025).
36. UK Prime Minister's Office, 'Joint Statement from the Leaders of the United Kingdom, France and Canada on the Situation in Gaza and the West Bank', gov.uk (19 May 2025).
37. 'Israel's Smotrich Slams UK, Canada, France for Calling for End of War in Gaza', *Middle East Eye* (20 May 2025).
38. Kiran Stacey and Patrick Butler, 'Keir Starmer Calls Israel's Recent Actions in Gaza "Appalling and Intolerable"', *The Guardian* (4 June 2025).
39. UK House of Commons, 'UK-EU Summit', hansard.parliament.uk (20 May 2025). Labour Party Press Release, 'Keir Starmer's Speech on the International Situation in the Middle East', labour.org.uk (31 October 2023).
40. Gabrielle Weiniger et al., 'Israeli Airstrike Kills Nine of Doctor's Ten Children', *The Times* (24 May 2025).
41. Jeremy Bowen, 'Israel Is Accused of the Gravest War Crimes – How Governments Respond Could Haunt Them for Years to Come', bbc.co.uk

(8 June 2025). The Board of Deputies of British Jews complained that Bowen's story was 'campaigning journalism'. Board of Deputies of British Jews, 'Board of Deputies President Writes to BBC Executives over Bowen Piece', bod.org.uk (8 June 2025).

42. Tom Bennett, 'UK Sanctions "Godmother" of Israel's Settler Movement Daniella Weiss', bbc.co.uk (20 May 2025).
43. UK Foreign, Commonwealth, and Development Office, 'UK and Partners Unite to Sanction Ministers Inciting West Bank Violence', gov.uk (10 June 2025).
44. Ibid.
45. Imran Mulla, 'Kemi Badenoch, Nigel Farage and Jimmy Carr Attend Secret Israeli Party at British Museum', *Middle East Eye* (15 May 2025).
46. UK House of Commons, 'Israel and the Occupied Palestinian Territories', hansard.parliament.uk (20 May 2025).
47. Ibid.
48. Patrick Wintour, 'UK Accused of "Garbled Messaging" as Trade Envoy Visits Israel to Boost Links', *The Guardian* (28 May 2025).
49. Campaign Against the Arms Trade, 'New Figures Reveal Massive Increase in UK Arms Exports to Israel as Government Defends F-35 Exemption in Court', caat.org.uk (15 May 2025).
50. Owen Jones, 'UK LIES About Israel Arms Sales EXPOSED – w/. Dearbhla Minogue' (29 May 2025), https://www.youtube.com/watch?v=PL2eUOIDDCM.
51. Craig Langford, 'UK Confirms RAF Gaza Flights Focus Only Hostage Search', ukdefencejournal.org.uk (22 May 2025).
52. Imran Mulla, 'Corbyn Presents Inquiry Bill as UK Spy Planes Continue Flights over Gaza', *Middle East Eye* (21 May 2025).
53. David Lammy interviewed on BBC *Today* (21 July 2025). See audio clip posted by @Hamza_a96 on X (22 July 2025), https://x.com/Hamza_a96/status/1947601993826242715.
54. Larisa Brown, 'RAF Still Carrying Out Surveillance Flights over Gaza for Israel', *The Times* (5 August 2025). Larisa Brown, 'Blunder Reveals UK Hired Foreign Contractors for Gaza Spy Mission', *The Times* (6 August 2025).

55. Larisa Brown and Steven Swinford, '"Unreliable" UK Not Told in Advance about Israel's Attack on Iran', *The Sunday Times* (13 June 2025). 'Starmer: UK Pushing for Israel-Iran "De-Escalation"', bloomberg.com (13 June 2025).
56. 'G7 Leaders' Statement on Recent Developments between Israel and Iran', g7.canada.ca (17 June 2025).
57. Gary Gibbon, 'Is Starmer in the Dark about Trump's Plan for Middle East?' channel4.com (17 June 2025).
58. Palestine Solidarity Campaign, 'Statement on the Events of Saturday 18 January at Whitehall and Trafalgar Square', palestinecampaign.org (19 January 2025).
59. Interview carried out for me by Josiah Mortimer, chief reporter of *Byline Times*.
60. 'More Than 70 Arrested at Palestine Solidarity Campaign Protest', news.met.police.uk (18 January 2025). This page appears to have since been removed. An archived version is available at: https://archive.ph/taAPi#selection-225.0-236.0.
61. Post by @YvetteCooperMP on X (18 January 2025), https://x.com/YvetteCooperMP/status/1880726807659639064.
62. Palestine Solidarity Campaign, 'The Attempt to Block Our Protest at the BBC Is Discriminatory and Anti-Democratic', palestinecampaign.org (14 January 2025).
63. 'Letter from Zack Polanski AM to Home Secretary: Palestine Marches', london.gov.uk (20 January 2025).
64. Ibid.
65. Ibid.
66. Interview carried out for me by Josiah Mortimer, chief reporter for *Byline Times*.
67. David Hearst and Peter Oborne, 'The Holocaust Survivor Who Can No Longer Call Labour Home', *Middle East Eye* (17 May 2023).
68. Interview carried out for me by Josiah Mortimer, chief reporter for *Byline Times*.
69. 'Holocaust Survivors and Descendants Sign Open Letter Opposing Ban on BBC Protest', *palestinecampaign.org*, 12 January 2025.
70. Jewish Voice for Labour, 'Defend Stephen Kapos – Free Speech on Palestine', jewishvoiceforlabour.org.uk (20 March 2025).

71. The Atlantic Charter (14 August 1941), https://www.nato.int/cps/en/natohq/official_texts_16912.htm.
72. United Nations Charter (26 June 1945), https://www.un.org/en/about-us/un-charter/full-text.
73. Gill Bennett and Richard Smith eds., *Britain & the Making of the Post-War World: The Potsdam Conference & Beyond* (2020), p. 41.
74. Richard Smith, 'The Foreign Office and the Creation of the UN' (23 October 2020), https://blogs.fcdo.gov.uk/drrichardsmith/2020/10/23/the-foreign-office-and-the-creation-of-the-un.
75. Ibid.
76. The New Atlantic Charter (10 June 2021), https://www.gov.uk/government/publications/new-atlantic-charter-and-joint-statement-agreed-by-the-pm-and-president-biden/the-new-atlantic-charter-2021.
77. UN OCHA, 'Reported Impact Snapshot | Gaza Strip (18 June 2025)', ochaopt.org (18 June 2025).
78. ICJ, *Legal Consequences Arising from the Policies and Practices of Israel in the Occupied Palestinian Territory, including East Jerusalem*, Advisory Opinion (19 July 2024).
79. International Criminal Court, 'Statement of ICC Prosecutor Karim A.A. Khan KC: Applications for Arrest Warrants in the Situation in the State of Palestine', icc-cpi.int (20 May 2024).
80. David Hearst and Imran Mulla, 'Exclusive: David Cameron Threatened to Withdraw UK From ICC over Israel War Crimes Probe', *Middle East Eye* (9 June 2025). There was no comment from Lord Cameron, and the British Foreign Office and Karim Khan declined to comment.
81. Ibid.
82. Sondos Asem and Imran Mulla, 'Could David Cameron Be Prosecuted for Threatening the ICC?' *Middle East Eye* (11 June 2025).

Conclusion

1. Nir Hasson, 'As Living Space in Gaza Shrinks, Remaining Pockets Endure Hellish Conditions', *Haaretz* (20 June 2025).
2. Cordelia Freeman and Hala Shoman, 'No Justice in a Genocide: Sexual and Reproductive Health and Rights in Gaza', *Sexual and Reproductive Health*

Matters (23 June 2025), pp. 1–10. See also: Yolande Knell and Callum Tulley, '"I Begged for Help, but Only God Answered": Growing Dangers of Pregnancy and Childbirth in Gaza', bbc.co.uk (3 June 2025).

3. World Food Programme (WFP), 'FAO and WFP Early Warning Report Reveals Worsening Hunger in 13 Hotspots: Five with Immediate Risk of Starvation', wfp.org (16 June 2025).
4. Mads Gilbert et al., 'Israel Is Starving Gaza to Death, and Still the World Does Nothing', *Middle East Eye* (1 May 2025).
5. Amnesty International, 'USA: Veto of UN Resolution on Lifting Gaza Aid Restrictions and Release of Hostages Is Shameful and Inhumane amid Israel's Ongoing Genocide', amnesty.org (4 June 2025).
6. Ahmed Ahmed and Ibtisam Mahdi, '"The Hunger Games": Inside Israel's Aid Death Traps for Starving Gazans', 972mag.com (20 June 2025).
7. Tom Bennett, 'Head of Controversial Israel-Backed Gaza Aid Group Resigns', bbc.co.uk (26 May 2025).
8. Ibid.
9. UN Under-Secretary-General for Humanitarian Affairs and Emergency Relief Coordinator Tom Fletcher, 'UN Relief Chief Calls on Security Council to Act Decisively to Prevent Genocide in Gaza', un.org (13 May 2025).
10. Post by @JeremyKonyndyk on X (2 June 2025), https://x.com/JeremyKonyndyk/status/1929360435339280751.
11. Post by @JeremyKonyndyk on X (2 June 2025), https://x.com/JeremyKonyndyk/status/1929360454138077327.
12. Patrick Kingsley et al., 'New Gaza Aid Plan, Bypassing U.N. and Billed as Neutral, Originated in Israel', *The New York Times* (24 May 2025).
13. Nir Hasson et al., '"It's a Killing Field": Soldiers Ordered to Shoot Deliberately at Unarmed Gazans Waiting for Humanitarian Aid'. *Haaretz* (27 June 2025).
14. 'PM, Katz Accuse Haaretz of "Libel" after Report Reveals Troops Ordered to Open Fire on Aid-Seeking Gazans', *The Times of Israel* (27 June 2025).
15. Lorenzo Tondo and Jamal Risheq, 'From Gaza Prisoner to "the Israeli Agent": How Rise of Abu Shabab Could Ignite New Phase of War', *The Guardian* (10 June 2025).

16. Rayhin Uddin, '"Popular Forces": Who Are the Gaza Gangsters Being Armed by Israel?' *Middle East Eye* (12 June 2025).
17. Lorenzo Tondo, 'Netanyahu Defends Arming Palestinians Clans Accused of Ties with Jihadist Groups', *The Guardian* (6 June 2025).
18. Ibid.
19. Mahmoud Mushtaha, 'How Israel Is Engineering Gaza's Social Collapse', 972mag.com (12 June 2025).
20. UN Office for the Coordination of Humanitarian Affairs (OCHA), 'Reported Impact Snapshot | Gaza Strip (18 June 2025)', ochaopt.org (18 June 2025).
21. I have relied on the devastating Haaretz analysis: Nir Hasson, '100,000 Dead: What We Know About Gaza's True Death Toll', *Haaretz* (26 June 2025). For the University of London preprint study, already cited, see Michael Spagat et al., 'Violent and Nonviolent Death Tolls for the Gaza War: New Primary Evidence', medrxiv.org (23 June 2025).
22. See, for example, Andrew Fox's report for the Henry Jackson Society, *Questionable Counting: Analysing the Death Toll from the Hamas-Run Ministry of Health in Gaza* (December 2024). This paper was ably refuted by Michael Spagat and Gabriel Epstein. 'Flawed Critique: How Andrew Fox's Report on Gaza Death Toll for the Henry Jackson Society Lacks Evidence for Key Claims', aoav.org.uk (22 December 2024).
23. Zeina Jamaluddine et al, 'Traumatic Injury Mortality in the Gaza Strip from Oct 7, 2023, to June 30, 2024: A Capture–Recapture Analysis', *The Lancet* 405.10477 (8 February 2025), pp. 469–77.
24. Ibid.
25. 'How Many People Have Died in Gaza?' *The Economist* (8 May 2025).
26. Nir Hasson, 'The Numbers Show: Gaza War Is One of the Bloodiest in the 21st Century', *Haaretz* (14 August 2024). The article employed the database of the Uppsala Conflict Data Program.
27. This idea was one of a number of eye-catching proposals suggested in July 2025 by former British diplomat Alexandra Hall Hall: 'Ten Things the UK Could Do If It Truly Cared About Palestinians', *Middle East Eye* (5 July 2025).
28. Niall Ferguson and Yoav Gallant, 'Israel Has Done Most of the Job—Now Trump Can Finish It', *The Times* (20 June 2025).

29. Editorial, 'Charging Israel with Genocide Makes a Mockery of the ICJ', *The Economist* (18 January 2024).
30. Editorial, 'Why Israel Must Fight On', *The Economist* (2 November 2023).
31. This is understood. It was observed by Brendan O'Hara, an MP of the Scottish National Party, that 'under current law, proceedings for international crimes cannot be brought without the consent of the Attorney General. Ultimately that means that *decisions to prosecute these crimes will be a political decision*. Consequently, the UK cannot possibly play as meaningful a part in ensuring justice and accountability as it should'. UK House of Commons, 'Universal Jurisdiction (Extension)', hansard.parliament.uk (25 April 2023). Emphasis added.
32. 'Global 195: International Legal Coalition Launched to Pursue Israeli War Crimes Suspects across the World', icjpalestine.com (18 March 2025).
33. Ibid.
34. Rome Statute of the International Criminal Court, Preamble.
35. The Hague Group was founded on January 31, 2025, and so far includes eight states: Bolivia, Honduras, Senegal, Colombia, Malaysia, South Africa, Cuba, and Namibia. Its inaugural joint statement expresses the conviction that 'collective action through coordinated legal and diplomatic measures at both national and international levels is an urgent imperative to uphold the principles of justice and accountability that form the foundation of the UN Charter'. The Hague Group, 'Inaugural Joint Statement', thehaguegroup.org (31 January 2025).
36. The ICC was founded by an international treaty. A new body might emerge the same way.
37. ICJ, *Legal Consequences Arising from the Policies and Practices of Israel in the Occupied Palestinian Territory, including East Jerusalem*, Advisory Opinion (19 July 2024), para. 261.
38. Ibid., para. 279.
39. Ibid., para. 278.

Peter Oborne is associate editor of *Middle East Eye* and columnist for *Byline Times* and *Declassified UK*. He has worked as political editor of *The Spectator* and political columnist for the *Daily Mail* and *Daily Telegraph*, and is the author of numerous books including *Sunday Times* bestseller *The Assault on Truth* and *The Fate of Abraham: Why the West Is Wrong about Islam.*

www.ingramcontent.com/pod-product-compliance
Lightning Source LLC
Jackson TN
JSHW031739250626
104373JS00001B/1
* 9 7 8 1 6 8 2 1 9 4 2 6 3 *